D1477775

Linear Factor Models in Finance

Elsevier Finance

aims and objectives

- books based on the work of financial market practitioners, and academics
- presenting cutting edge research to the professional/practitioner market
- combining intellectual rigour and practical application
- covering the interaction between mathematical theory and financial practice
- to improve portfolio performance, risk management and trading book performance
- covering quantitative techniques

market

Brokers/Traders; Actuaries; Consultants; Asset Managers; Fund Managers; Regulators; Central Bankers; Treasury Officials; Technical Analysts; and Academics for Masters in Finance and MBA market.

series titles

Return Distributions in Finance
Derivative Instruments: theory, valuation, analysis
Managing Downside Risk in Financial Markets: theory, practice & implementation
Economics for Financial Markets
Performance Measurement in Finance: firms, funds and managers
Real R&D Options
Forecasting Volatility in the Financial Markets
Advanced Trading Rules
Advances in Portfolio Construction and Implementation
Computational Finance
Linear Factor Models in Finance

series editor
Dr Stephen Satchell

Dr Satchell is the Reader in Financial Econometrics at Trinity College, Cambridge; Visiting Professor at Birkbeck College, City University Business School and University of Technology, Sydney. He also works in a consultative capacity to many firms, and edits the journal *Derivatives: use, trading and regulations* and the *Journal of Asset Management*.

Linear Factor Models
in Finance

John Knight and Stephen Satchell

ELSEVIER
BUTTERWORTH
HEINEMANN

AMSTERDAM • BOSTON • HEIDELBERG • LONDON • NEW YORK • OXFORD
PARIS • SAN DIEGO • SAN FRANCISCO • SINGAPORE • SYDNEY • TOKYO

Elsevier Butterworth-Heinemann
Linacre House, Jordan Hill, Oxford OX2 8DP
30 Corporate Drive, Burlington, MA 01803

First published 2005

British Library Cataloguing in Publication Data
A catalogue record for this book is available from the British Library

Library of Congress Cataloguing in Publication Data
A catalogue record for this book is available from the Library of Congress

ISBN 0 7506 6006 6

For information on all Elsevier Butterworth-Heinemann
finance publications visit our website at
www.books.elsevier.com/finance

Typeset by Newgen Imaging Systems (P) Ltd, Chennai, India

Working together to grow
libraries in developing countries

www.elsevier.com | www.bookaid.org | www.sabre.org

ELSEVIER   BOOK AID
             International   Sabre Foundation

Transferred to Digital Printing in 2008

Contents

12 Making covariance-based portfolio risk models sensitive to the rate at which markets reflect new information   249
Dan diBartolomeo and Sandy Warrick, CFA

13 Decomposing factor exposure for equity portfolios   262
David Tien, Paul Pfleiderer, Robert Maxim and Terry Marsh

Contributors

Chris Adcock is Professor of Financial Econometrics in the University of Sheffield. His career includes several years working in quantitative investment management in the City and, prior to that, a decade in management science consultancy. His research interests are in the development of robust and non-standard methods for modelling expected returns, portfolio selection methods and the properties of optimized portfolios. He has acted as an advisor to a number of asset management firms. He is the founding editor of the *European Journal of Finance*.

George A. Christodoulakis is an academic with experience from the University of Exeter, the Cass Business School of City University in London, the Technical University of Crete as well as the Bank of Greece. He has followed undergraduate and postgraduate studies at the AUEB Athens and further postgraduate and doctoral studies at the University of London, Birkbeck College. His expertise concerns econometric and mathematical finance aspects of risk, especially market and credit risk. He publishes research work in international refereed journals and books and is a frequent speaker in international conferences.

Theofanis Darsinos is an Associate at Deutsche Bank's Fixed Income and Relative Value Research Group. He has a Ph.D. in Financial Economics from the University of Cambridge and a BSc in Mathematics from the University of London. During 2002–2003 he was an honorary research associate at the Department of Applied Economics, University of Cambridge.

Dan diBartolomeo is President and founder of Northfield Information Services, Inc. He serves on the boards of the Chicago Quantitative Alliance, Woodbury College, and the American Computer Foundation, and the Boston Committee on Foreign Relations. He is an active member of the Financial Management Association, QWAFAFEW, the Society of Quantitative Analysts, the Southern Finance Association and the Eastern Finance Association. Dan teaches a continuing education course sponsored by the Boston Security Analyst Society. He has published numerous articles and papers in a variety of journals, and has contributed chapters to several finance textbooks.

Greg N. Gregoriou is assistant professor of finance and faculty research coordinator in the School of Business and Economics at the State University of New York (SUNY, Plattsburgh). He is also hedge fund editor of the peer-reviewed journal *Derivatives Use, Trading and Regulation*. He has authored 25 articles on hedge funds, managed futures and CTAs in various US and UK peer-reviewed publications. He was awarded best paper prize with Fabrice Rouah and Robert Auger at the Administrative Sciences

Association of Canada (ASAC) Conference in London, Ontario, in May 2001. He also has over 20 professional publications in brokerage and pension fund magazines.

Ka-Man Lo received her Ph.D. (Economics) from the University of Western Ontario and is presently a senior lecturer of finance at the University of Waikato. Her research interests are concentrated on asset pricing and market microstructure.

Terry Marsh received his MBA and Ph.D. degrees from the University of Chicago and is now Associate Professor of Finance at the UC Berkeley and a former chairman of the Finance Group. Prior to joining UCB he was an Associate Professor of Finance at MIT. He has been awarded Batterymarch and Hoover Institution Fellowships and is a Fellow, CPA, Australian Society of Accountants. He has consulted for the New York Stock Exchange, the Options Clearing Corporation, the Industrial Bank of Japan, New Japan Securities and Banamex, and was a member of the Presidential Task Force on Market Mechanisms investigating the 1987 stock market crash. He is a co-founder and principal of Quantal International, Inc. and Quantal Asset Management, and a member of the board of directors of MetaMatrix. He was a Yamaichi Fellow and Visiting Professor of Economics at the University of Tokyo in 1993.

Robert Maxim has a BS degree in economics from UC Irvine and a Masters in Financial Engineering from UC Berkeley. He was an Operations Research Analyst for the US Navy, and is an Associate at Quantal International.

Paul Pfleiderer has MA and Ph.D. degrees from Yale University. He is the William F. Sharpe Professor of Finance at the Graduate School of Business, Stanford University, and has been head of the finance group since 1995. He was awarded a Batterymarch Fellowship in 1987. He teaches in Stanford's Executive Education seminars, has consulted for Bankers Trust and Banamex, and is a principal and co-founder of Quantal International, Inc. and Quantal Asset Management.

Mario Pitsillis was born and completed his secondary education in Cyprus. He attained a BSc (Economics) degree at the LSE graduating with a First Class Honours in 1996. He continued with an M.Phil. Finance degree at Cambridge University in 1997 and completed a Ph.D. degree in Economics also at Cambridge University in 2003 under the supervision of Dr Stephen Satchell. Mario has worked at the Department of Economics of the University of Cyprus and is currently with the Laiki Group, a Cypriot bank in Nicosia, Cyprus.

Fabrice Rouah is Institut de Finance Mathématique de Montréal (IFM2) Scholar, and Ph.D. Candidate in Finance, McGill University, Montreal, Quebec. Fabrice is a former Faculty Lecturer and Consulting Statistician in the Department of Mathematics and Statistics at McGill University. He specializes on the statistical and stochastic modelling of hedge funds, managed futures, and CTAs, and is a regular contributor in peer-reviewed academic publications on alternative investments.

James Sefton began his career with a PhD in mathematical system theory before taking a position at the Department of Applied Economics, Cambridge University. He then moved to National Institute of Economic of Social Research to work on the NI Global Economic Model. Since then he has worked on a variety of projects including one to compile the first set of UK Generational Accounts (which now forms the basis of HM Treasury's annual Long-term Fiscal Sustainability Report). In 2001 he was appointed to a Chair of Economics at Imperial College. In addition, over the last five years, he has worked as senior quantitative analyst for Union Bank of Switzerland (UBS).

Professor Stephen Satchell is the Academic Advisor to many financial institutions, a Fellow of Trinity College, Cambridge, the Reader in Financial Econometrics at Cambridge University, and a visiting Professor at Birkbeck College and CASS Business School. He specializes in Econometrics and Finance and has published over 80 articles in refereed journals. He has Ph.D.s from Cambridge University and the LSE. He is editor of *Journal of Asset Management* and *Derivatives, Use, Trading, and Regulation*.

Alan Scowcroft is a Managing Director and the Global Head of Equities Quantitative and Derivatives Research at UBS Investment Research. Since joining UBS Phillips & Drew as an econometrician in 1984, he has worked on every aspect of quantitative modelling from stock valuation to asset allocation. He has been closely associated with the pioneering work on equity style and portfolio analysis developed by UBS. Educated at Ruskin College, Oxford, and Wolfson College, Cambridge, where he was awarded the Jennings prize for academic achievement, Alan's current research interests include optimization and practical applications of Bayesian econometrics in finance.

Alvin Stroyny is Chairman of EM Applications and has worked in Factor Analysis algorithms since 1980. He has developed robust methods of maximum likelihood factor analysis and applied such techniques to large data sets of stock returns. These factor models are currently in use by several investment firms in the US, Europe and Asia. Dr Stroyny has a Ph.D. from the University of Wisconsin on 'Heteroskedasticity and Estimation of Systematic Risk', and has taught finance at Marquette University and the University of Wisconsin. He has also worked at Yamaichi, Fortis, and the Bank of New York.

David Tien is Assistant Professor of Finance at Santa Clara University and Research Associate at Quantal International. His research focuses on equity risk modelling and the relationship between trading activity and exchange rate dynamics. He completed his doctorate in finance at UC Berkeley with a specialization in international finance. Prior to that he earned a master's degree in financial mathematics at the University of Chicago and a bachelor's degree from the School of Foreign Service at Georgetown University.

Sandy Warrick is an engineering graduate of MIT, and worked for a number of years in the defence industry, during which time he received master's degrees in Management and Computer Science. In order to pursue a career in Investment Analysis, he joined one of the first graduating classes in the Carnegie Mellon Computational Finance Program. He has been with Northfield Information Services full time since 2001.

Dr Tim Wilding is the Head of R&D at EM Applications, where he has specialized in factor modelling and optimization techniques. He holds a Ph.D. from the Department of Physics at Cambridge University. Dr Wilding has ten years of experience in building models of equity returns and volatility in several different markets. At EM Applications, Dr Wilding has developed new optimization techniques and robust estimation routines to fit several types of factor model.

Introduction

This book on linear factor models starts with an introductory chapter allowing readers to familiarize themselves with the academic arguments about such models. Chapters 2 to 7 constitute academic contributions while Chapters 8 to 13 are contributions from a number of leading quantitative practitioners.

Both of us are delighted with the range of chapters especially from practitioners for whom the cost of contributing is rather high. The order of the chapters implies no ranking or favouritism and the contents of the chapters reflect the importance and central position that linear factor models hold in portfolio formation and risk management.

John Knight and Stephen Satchell

1 Review of literature on multifactor asset pricing models

Mario Pitsillis

Abstract

The purpose of asset pricing theory is to understand the prices or values or returns of claims to uncertain payments, for example stocks, bonds and options. The most important factor in the valuation is the risk of payments of the asset under examination. This chapter reviews the literature on the foundations of asset pricing theory. More specifically, in section 1.1 multifactor models are discussed as particular specifications of the stochastic discount factor. Theoretical arguments and empirical evidence of the operation of multiple risk factors in asset markets are surveyed in sections 1.1 and 1.2 in order to provide the justification for the choice of the particular risk factors in this thesis. A survey of the basic empirical methods and issues inherent in the estimation of multifactor models is also carried out in section 1.3. The chapter concludes with a brief outline of the research questions that the thesis aspires to address.

1.1 Theoretical reasons for existence of multiple factors

Asset pricing can be absolute or relative. In relative asset pricing assets are valued on the basis of the prices of some other assets, without asking where the prices of these other assets come from. One particular example is the Black-Scholes option pricing formula. However, it is absolute asset pricing that is the central problem in finance, namely, understanding the prices of assets by reference to their exposure to fundamental sources of macroeconomic risk. Empirical work beginning with Chen et al. (1986) has already documented links between macroeconomics and finance and yet no satisfactory theory explains these relationships. Thus, understanding the fundamental macroeconomic sources of risk in the economy remains the best hope for identifying pricing factors that are robust across different markets and samples. Empirically determined risk factors may not be stable.

The cornerstone of modern asset pricing theory is that *price equals expected discounted payoff*. This central idea can be formulated in terms of the stochastic discount factor approach[1], a universal paradigm for asset pricing. Using mathematical notation, this statement can be summarized in the following two equations:

$$p_t = E_t(m_{t+1}x_{t+1}) \tag{1.1}$$

$$m_{t+1} = f(data, parameters), \tag{1.2}$$

---

[1] Rubinstein (1976), Shiller (1982), Hansen and Jagannathan (1991), Cochrane (2001).

where p_t is the asset's price at time t, x_{t+1} is the asset payoff at time $t + 1$, E_t denotes the expectation operator taken at time t, f denotes some function, and m_{t+1} is the stochastic discount factor. The stochastic discount factor is a random variable that can be used to compute market prices today by discounting, state by state, the corresponding payoffs at a future date. Under uncertainty, each asset must be discounted by a specific discount factor. The power of the stochastic discount factor approach lies in the fact that, as shown by equation (1.1), correlation of a *single* discount factor with each asset-specific payoff generates asset-specific risk corrections.

The advantages of the stochastic discount factor approach to asset pricing are its universality, unification of more specific theories and simplicity. For example, stock, bond and option pricing, which have developed as quite distinct theories, can now be seen as special cases of the same pricing theory. Moreover, different models of asset pricing, such as the well-known Capital Asset Pricing Model (CAPM) by Sharpe (1964) and Lintner (1965b) and the Arbitrage Pricing Theory (APT) by Ross (1976), can now be derived as different specifications of the stochastic discount factor. In practice, this simply amounts to different choices of the f function in equation (1.2) which constitutes the economic content of the model. At the empirical level, the unified framework of the stochastic discount factor approach facilitates a deeper understanding of the econometric issues involved in estimation.

In the most general case of a preference-free environment, the stochastic discount factor or state-price density is associated with the prices of Arrow-Debreu securities and the probabilities of realization of particular states. The conditions prevailing in this environment define restrictions on the stochastic discount factor. The law of one price, the no arbitrage condition and the completeness of markets are sufficient conditions for the existence of a stochastic discount factor, a positive stochastic discount factor, and a unique stochastic discount factor, respectively.

In a preference-dependent environment, where we need to value at time t a payoff at time $t + 1$, the stochastic discount factor is related to the marginal utility of consumption. The pricing equation is derived from the first order conditions for the investor's decision of how much to save and consume in order to maximize his utility, assuming he can freely buy or sell as much of the payoff as he or she wants.

A typical investor's utility function is:

$$U(c_t, c_{t+1}) = u(c_t) + \beta E_t[u(c_{t+1})],$$

where c_t is consumption at time t and c_{t+1} is consumption at time $t + 1$, a random variable. It is reasonable to assume that investors prefer a consumption stream that is steady over time and across states of nature. The utility function $u(.)$ is increasing and concave to reflect desire for more consumption and the declining marginal value of additional consumption. Investors' impatience to the time dimension is captured by the discount factor β. Investors' aversion to risk is captured by the curvature of the function $u(.)$.

Under these conditions, the basic pricing equation is:

$$p_t = E_t \left[\beta \frac{u'(c_{t+1})}{u'(c_t)} x_{t+1} \right] \tag{1.3}$$

where $\beta \frac{u'(c_{t+1})}{u'(c_t)} \equiv m_{t+1}$ is the stochastic discount factor. This is a specific form of the general equation (1.2).

Viewed in this way, all asset pricing models amount to alternative ways of connecting the stochastic discount factor to the data. In principle, the consumption-based model is a complete answer to all asset pricing questions and it can be applied to the valuation of any uncertain cash flow. Given a functional form for utility, numerical values for parameters, and a statistical model for the conditional distribution of consumption and payoffs (in practice only data on consumption and returns are available), any asset can be priced. However, the Consumption-based Capital Asset Pricing Model[2] (CCAPM), which builds on the exposition above assuming a representative agent who consumes aggregate consumption, works poorly in practice[3]. Possible explanations for the failure of the model include measurement errors in consumption data, use of wrong utility functions, de-linking of consumption and asset returns at high frequencies because of the existence of transactions costs, and the use of the extreme notion of perfect risk sharing behind the use of aggregate consumption. This empirical finding motivates alternative asset pricing models, that is, different specific forms of equation (1.2) other than equation (1.3). These alternative models have featured such ideas as non-separabilities in utility functions to capture habit formation[4], or completion of the basic consumption- based model to substitute out for consumption in terms of other variables or factors, in the hope that these measure marginal utility directly in a better way. The latter approach gives rise to factor pricing models, which are popular in empirical work.

The discussion above provides the theoretical justification for the identification of appropriate multiple factors. These should be plausible proxies for marginal utility. In lay terms, these are events that describe whether typical investors are happy or unhappy. Using mathematical notation, factors should be variables for which the following expression is a reasonable and economically interpretable approximation:

$$\beta \frac{u'(c_{t+1})}{u'(ct)} \approx c + \beta_a f_{t+1}^a + \beta_b f_{t+1}^b + \cdots$$

where f are the 'factors', c is a constant and $\beta_a, \beta_b, \ldots$ are parameters which measure sensitivities to factors $f^a, f^b, \ldots$. These parameters should not be confused with the β on the left-hand side of the equation which captures impatience to the time dimension. As such, variables that indicate the current state of the economy, for example returns on broad-based portfolios, interest rates, GDP growth, investment, and other macroeconomic magnitudes, qualify as factors. Moreover, consumption and marginal utility respond to news. If a change in some variable today signals high income in future, then consumption rises now by permanent income logic. Thus, variables that forecast the future state of the economy, as reflected in changes in income or investment opportunity sets, or in future macroeconomic variables, also qualify as factors. Such variables include the term premium, asset returns and the dividend to price ratio.

---

[2] Rubinstein (1976), Lucas (1978), Breeden (1979), Grossman and Shiller (1981), Mehra and Prescott (1985).

[3] Mehra and Prescott (1985).

[4] Constantinides (1990), Abel (1990), Campbell and Cochrane (1999).

The view of factors as intuitively motivated proxies for marginal utility growth is sufficient for providing the link with current empirical work. All factor pricing models are derived as specializations of the consumption-based model using additional assumptions that allow one to proxy for marginal utility growth from some other variables. In the theoretical literature there exist various derivations of factor pricing models, the most important of which invoke the following analyses:

1. General equilibrium models with linear specification for the production technology, where consumption is substituted out for other endogenous variables. Examples of such models are the following:
   ■ CAPM (Sharpe (1964), Lintner (1965b)).
      In this context, $m_{t+1} = a + \beta_R w R^W_{t+1}$ where R^W is the rate of return on a claim to total wealth proxied by indices such as the NYSE or FTSE. The CAPM is derived from the basic consumption-based model in a number of ways by imposing one of the following additional assumptions: (1) a two-period quadratic utility function, (2) two periods, exponential utility function and normal returns, (3) an infinite horizon, quadratic utility function and independently and identically distributed returns, or (4) a logarithmic utility function.
   ■ Intertemporal CAPM (Merton (1973)).
      In this context, additional factors (over and above the return on the market) arise from investors' demands to hedge uncertainty about future investment opportunities. Investors are unhappy when the news is that future returns are lower, and prefer stocks that do well on such news thereby hedging the reinvestment risk. Thus, equilibrium expected returns depend on covariation with news of future returns, as well as covariation with the current market return. These additional factors may be any state variables that forecast shifts in the investment opportunity set, that is, changes in the distribution of future returns or income.
2. Law of one price and constraints on the volatility of the stochastic discount factors.
   This environment gives rise to the Arbitrage Pricing Theory (APT) model by Ross (1976), where factors are assumed to account for the common variation in asset returns. The proxies used can be returns on broad-based portfolios derived from a factor analysis of the return covariance matrix. This is a very useful model providing many insights into both the theoretical and empirical aspects of multifactor asset pricing analysis. It is presented in detail and used in subsequent chapters of this thesis.
3. Existence of non-asset income.
   Current theorizing allows for non-asset income unlike older models, for example the CAPM. It is now recognized that leisure and consumption are separable and that all sources of income including labour income correspond to traded securities. Investors with labour income will prefer assets that do not fall in recessions. Expected returns may thus depend on additional betas that capture distress or recession factors, for example labour market conditions[5], house values, fortunes of small businesses or other non-marketed assets.

[5] Jagannathan and Wang (1996), Reyfman (1997).

To complete the discussion regarding the operation of multiple risk factors in financial markets, section 1.2 surveys the empirical literature on this subject.

1.2   Empirical evidence of existence of multiple factors

Early empirical tests of the CAPM by Lintner (1965a) using individual stocks were not a great success, as the slope of the capital market line was found to be flatter than predicted by theory. Miller and Scholes (1972) diagnosed the problem as betas being measured with error. Consequently, Fama and McBeth (1973) and Black et al. (1972) grouped stocks into portfolios as portfolio betas are better measured and portfolios have lower residual variance. With this development the CAPM proved very successful in empirical work: strategies or characteristics that seemed to give high average returns turned out to have high betas. The first significant failure of the CAPM was the 'small firm effect' documented in Banz (1981).

In the meantime, the search for multiple factors in returns was also taking place. The Fama and French (1993, 1996) three-factor model (market, small market value minus big market value portfolio, high/book market minus low book/market portfolio) was tested and was found to successfully explain the average returns of size and book market sorted portfolios, and also of other strategies. Although no satisfactory theory explains this empirical phenomenon, these findings may suggest that the Fama and French factors are proxies or mimicking portfolios of some macroeconomic 'distress' or 'recession' factor. This operates independently of the market and carries a different premium than general market risk. One of the first studies investigating and documenting the relationship between multiple factors and asset returns was the one by Chen et al. (1986) for the US financial market. Since then a score of studies, for example McElroy and Burmeister (1988), Poon and Taylor (1991), Clare and Thomas (1994), Jagannathan and Wang (1996), Reyfman (1997) and others, have identified the effects of such magnitudes as labour income, industrial production, inflation and other news variables. These are easier to motivate theoretically than the Fama and French factors.

Section 1.3 discusses the identity and measurement of potential factors employed to explain asset returns, the econometric methodology in producing empirical estimates, and econometric problems that may be encountered in the search for numerical estimates of the sensitivities to risk factors and the prices of risk.

1.3   Estimation of factor pricing models

From the discussion on the theory and empirical evidence in sections 1.1 and 1.2, multiple factors can be:

1. Statistically derived returns on portfolios of traded assets.
   In this case, portfolios that represent factors are built from a comprehensive sample data set of asset returns. Factor analysis and principal components are the two main statistical methods that can be used towards this end. The number of factors can

be determined but the extracted factors are difficult to interpret, because they are non-unique linear combinations of more fundamental underlying economic forces.
2. Variables justified theoretically on the argument that they capture economy-wide systematic risks.

■ Macroeconomic and financial state variables.
Naturally, this approach provides us with a readily economic interpretation of sensitivities and risk premia. This is highly desirable given that one fundamental problem in both macroeconomics and finance is to explain asset returns with events in the aggregate economy. A representative study is Chen et al. (1986), one of the first empirical attempts to relate asset returns to macroeconomic factors in a way that is relevant to the analysis in this thesis. The main macro-economic factors that were used and that successfully explained asset returns were industrial production growth (measured by the difference in the logarithms of a production index), unanticipated inflation (difference in the logarithms of a consumer/retail price index), term premium (yield spread between long-term and short-term maturity government bonds) and default premium (yield spread between corporate high-grade and low-grade bonds).

■ Returns on portfolios of traded assets based on firm characteristics. The Fama and French (1993, 1996) methodology discussed in section 1.2 falls under this category.

In general, factors must be close to unpredictable (no serial correlation), as they proxy for marginal utility growth and this is unpredictable with a constant interest rate. With highly predictable factors, the model will counterfactually predict large interest rate variation. In empirical work, the use of right units, that is, growth rather than levels, returns rather than prices, and differences in returns, ensures that this condition is satisfied most of the time.

Regarding the number of factors, theory should be the guide, but it is not yet clear on this point. Studies like Lehmann and Modest (1988) and Connor and Korajczyk (1988) show that there is little sensitivity in the results in going from five to ten to fifteen statistical factors. This suggests that up to five factors may be adequate, a view which is also reinforced by the results in Roll and Ross (1980). Nevertheless, it can be argued that the issue of the pure number of pricing factors is not a meaningful question, because of the equivalence theorems[6] between stochastic discount factor and beta representations of factor models. A more specific example, in the context of the Intertemporal CAPM, would be that a single consumption factor could serve as a single state variable in place of the numerous state variables presumed to drive it.

As shown below, the economic multiple factor model is written in terms of an expected return-beta representation, which is equivalent to a linear model for the discount factor,

$$E(R^i) = \gamma + \beta_{i,1}\lambda_1 + \beta_{i,2}\lambda_2 + \cdots + \beta_{i,k}\lambda_k \quad i = 1, \cdots, N, \tag{1.4}$$

where R^i is the return on asset i, E is the expectation operator, γ is a constant (the return on a zero-beta portfolio), β is the contemporaneous exposure of asset i to factor

[6] These theorems are discussed extensively throughout Cochrane (2001).

risk k and λ is the price of risk exposure to factor k or the risk premium associated with factor k.

If a risk-free asset with return R^f exists, we can impose $R^f = \gamma$ and examine factor models using excess returns directly. The economic model in equation (1.4) becomes:

$$E(R^{ei}) = \beta_{i,1}\lambda_1 + \beta_{i,2}\lambda_2 + \cdots + \beta_{i,k}\lambda_k \quad i = 1, \ldots, N \tag{1.5}$$

where R^{ei} is the excess return on asset i.

The model in equation (1.5) is estimated by the two following statistical equations:

$$R_t^{ei} = a_i + b_{i,1}f_t^1 + b_{i,2}f_t^2 + \cdots + b_{i,k}f_t^k + \epsilon_t^i \quad t = 1, 2, \ldots, T \tag{1.6}$$

$$E(R^{ei}) = c + b_{i,1}\lambda_1 + b_{i,2}\lambda_2 + \cdots + b_{i,k}\lambda_k + \varepsilon_t^i \quad i = 1, 2, \ldots, N \tag{1.7}$$

where $b_{i,k}$ is the contemporaneous exposure of asset i to risk factor k estimated as the time-series regression coefficient of excess return R^{ei} on the factors f in the time-series regression equation (1.6), f measures 'good' or 'bad' states of the world, that is, riskiness, a_i is the asset specific intercept in the time-series regression (1.6), c is the intercept in the cross-sectional regression (1.7) and ϵ and ε are the usual error terms.

Many techniques have been used in the literature on empirical estimation of factor pricing models. However, all of these techniques can be seen as special cases of the Generalized Method of Moments (GMM) estimation procedure. Maximum Likelihood (ML) estimation is a special case of GMM whereby given a statistical description of the data, it prescribes which moments are statistically more informative and estimates parameters that make the observed data most likely. With appropriate assumptions, ML justifies both time-series and cross-sectional Ordinary Least Squares (OLS) regressions. In a traditional setup of normal and identically and independently distributed (iid) returns, it is hard to beat the efficiency and simplicity of linear regression methods. However, the promise of GMM lies in its ability to circumvent model misspecifications and to transparently handle non-linear or otherwise complex models, especially those including conditioning information.

In general, the beta pricing equation (1.4) is a restriction on expected returns, and thus imposes a restriction on intercepts in the time-series regression. Depending on the data, the model can be estimated using either time-series regressions only, or a two-pass regression methodology.

In the special case in which the factors are themselves excess returns (for example, in the CAPM), the restriction is that the time-series regression intercepts in equation (1.6) should all be zero. Factors have a beta of one on themselves and zero on all other factors, as the model applies to the factors as well, so that $\lambda_k = E(f^k)$, and thus the risk premia can be measured directly rather than through regression. All that remains is to estimate the time-series equation (1.6) for each asset, which gives the same results as ML if the error is normally iid over time and independent of the factors. The factors can be individually or jointly tested for significance using standard univariate or multivariate formulae, provided that these have been theoretically specified. With empirically derived factors such tests are not useful because they are not unique. The assumption of normal and iid errors is strong but has often been used in the literature despite the fact that asset returns are not normally distributed or iid. They have fatter tails than normal, they are heteroscedastic (times of high and low volatilities), they are autocorrelated and predictable from a variety of variables, especially at large horizons. The restrictive assumption of normality can be relaxed in a GMM framework. However, monthly returns are approximately normal and iid.

Estimation of cross-sectional regressions can be used whether the factors are returns or not. In this case, the estimation methodology becomes two-step as in Black et al. (1972). First, the time-series equation (1.6) is estimated for each asset using all of the data to find estimates b of the true β for each asset, and second, the cross-sectional equation (1.7) is estimated across assets to obtain estimates of the factor risk premia (λ). Estimates b from the first step are used as the independent variables and the true expectation of returns is replaced by the time-series average returns. In this case, the model's implication is that c should be zero, which can be tested using standard formulae.

This methodology suffers from a potential Error-In-Variables (EIV) problem, because sensitivities are estimated in the first step and then used as independent variables in the second step. This results in biased estimators in small samples and overstated precision of estimates.

A historically important procedure, popular in empirical work, was developed in Fama and McBeth (1973) in an attempt to overcome this problem. Elaborate portfolio grouping procedures based on individual assets' betas are used to minimize measurement error and estimate the sensitivities with increased precision. Beta estimates are obtained by time-series regressions using part of the data. Instead of then estimating a single cross-sectional regression with the sample averages, a cross-sectional regression is run at each time period. Parameters (intercept c and risk premia λ) are estimated as the average of the cross-sectional regression estimates. The model is tested by using the standard error of these cross-sectional regression estimates. Lintzenberger and Ramaswamy (1979) and Shanken (1982) have also developed methodologies to reflect the EIV problem by adjusting the standard errors of the estimates directly.

Another problem in the cross-sectional regression is that it is likely that returns across assets will be correlated and/or heteroscedastic, so that the OLS estimators will be inefficient. A potential solution to this problem is to use Generalized Least Squares (GLS) to estimate and test the cross-sectional regression in the second step, which is also asymptotically equivalent to the Maximum Likelihood (ML) estimation method. In fact, with the ML approach the EIV problem discussed above is eliminated because all parameters (b and λ) are estimated simultaneously.

Acknowledging the importance of these problems and the power of GLS and ML methods, the econometric analysis in this thesis is based on the McElroy and Burmeister (1988) method of estimation of multifactor asset pricing models. The models are formulated and estimated as restricted nonlinear seemingly unrelated regressions (NLSUR). The application of the NLSUR methodology is asymptotically equivalent to ML. The methodology is free from the important econometric limitations inherent in the more traditional two-step econometric estimation methods discussed, as the risk premia and the asset sensitivities to the risk factors are estimated jointly. In this way, the EIV problem from two-step estimation is avoided and potential problems resulting from the presence of correlation and/or heteroscedasticity in the cross-section of returns are addressed.

In practice, however, GLS and ML estimation methods, including the McElroy and Burmeister (1988) procedure, suffer from different limitations. A concern about stationarity over time of the factor model parameters restricts the length of the time series (T). As in empirical work the potential universe of assets is typically large, the number of assets (N) may exceed the number of time periods $(N > T)$. This renders the error variance-covariance matrix singular so that the ML and GLS estimators are undefined unless additional structure is imposed on the variance-covariance matrix (for example, that it is diagonal) or a reduced set of securities or portfolios is used. Moreover, as N increases, a greater number of covariance terms must be estimated so the validity of the asymptotic properties of the GLS and ML estimators can be questioned. Another limitation is the computational complexity of GLS and ML methods.

In empirical work on asset pricing tests, it has been usual practice to sort assets into portfolios based on a particular attribute of the assets. In addition to avoiding the problem of the singularity of the variance-covariance matrix as a result of the reduction in the number of assets, this has ensured that idiosyncratic risks of individual assets are diversified away. Size, estimated beta and book-to-market ratio have all been commonly used for sorting assets into portfolios (Fama and French (1993), Gibbons et al. (1989), Jagannathan and Wang (1996)). However, this may create other problems such as loss of information due to aggregation. Lo and MacKinlay (1990) point out that sorting without regard to the data generating process may lead to spurious correlation between the attributes and the estimated pricing errors. Berk (2000) shows that sorting assets into portfolios can lead to bias toward rejecting the model when asset pricing tests are implemented within the portfolio. In an empirical investigation of these issues, Lo (2001) also finds that portfolios formed by assets sorted on the basis of different attributes pick up different risks and can give rise to different asset pricing inference. In an effort to overcome some of these problems, Hwang and Satchell (1999) develop the 'average F-test' which imposes the condition of diagonality on the variance-covariance matrix to provide a testing methodology based on individual assets.

Bibliography

Abel, A. (1990). Asset prices under habit formation and catching up with the Joneses. *American Economic Review Papers and Proceedings*, 80:38–42.

Banz, R. (1981). The relationship between return and market value of common stocks. *Journal of Financial Economics*, 9:3–18.

Berk, J. (2000). Sorting out sorts. *Journal of Finance*, 55:407–427.

Black, F., Jensen, M., and Scholes, M. (1972). The Capital Asset Pricing Model: Some empirical tests. In Jensen, M. C., editor, *Studies in the theory of capital markets*. Praeger, New York.

Breeden, D. (1979). An intertemporal asset pricing model with stochastic consumption and investment opportunities. *Journal of Financial Economics*, 7:265–296.

Campbell, J. and Cochrane, J. (1999). By force of habit: A consumption-based explanation of aggregate stock market behaviour. *Journal of Political Economy*, 107:205–251.

Chen, N. F., Roll, R., and Ross, S. A. (1986). Economic forces and the stock market. *Journal of Business*, 59(3):383–403.

Clare, A. D. and Thomas, S. H. (1994). Macroeconomic factors, the APT and the UK stock market. *Journal of Business Finance and Accounting*, 21(3): 309–330.

Cochrane, J. (2001). *Asset pricing*. Princeton University Press, Princeton, NJ.

Connor, G. and Korajczyk, R. A. (1988). Risk and return in an equilibrium APT: Application of a new test methodology. *Journal of Financial Economics*, 21:255–290.

Constantinides, G. (1990). Habit formation: A resolution of the equity premium puzzle. *Journal of Political Economy*, 98:519–543.

Fama, E. and French, K. (1993). Common risk factors in the returns on stocks and bonds. *Journal of Financial Economics*, 33:3–56.

Fama, E. and French, K. (1996). Multifactor explanations of asset-pricing anomalies. *Journal of Finance*, 47:426–465.

Fama, E. and McBeth, J. (1973). Risk, return and equilibrium: Empirical tests. *Journal of Political Economy*, 71:607–636.

Gibbons, M., Ross, S., and Shanken, J. (1989). A test of the efficiency of a given portfolio. *Econometrica*, 57:1121–1152.

Grossman, S. and Shiller, R. (1981). The determinants of the variability of stock market prices. *American Economic Review*, 71:222–227.

Hansen, L. and Jagannathan, R. (1991). Restrictions on intertemporal marginal rates of substitution implied by asset returns. *Journal of Political Economy*, 99:225–262.

Hwang, S. and Satchell, S. (1999). Improved testing for the efficiency of asset pricing theories in linear factor models. *Financial Econometrics Research Centre*. Working paper. City University Business School.

Jagannathan, R. and Wang, Z. (1996). The conditional CAPM and the cross-section of expected returns. *Journal of Finance*, 51:3–53.

Lehmann, B. and Modest, D. (1988). The empirical foundations of the APT. *Journal of Financial Economics*, 21:213–254.

Lintner, J. (1965a). Security prices, risk and maximal gains from diversification. *Journal of Finance*, 20:587–615.

Lintner, J. (1965b). The valuation of risky assets and the selection of risky investment in stock portfolios and capital budgets. *Review of Economics and Statistics*, 47:13–37.

Lintzenberger, R. and Ramaswamy, K. (1979). The effects of dividends on common stock prices: Theory and empirical evidence. *Journal of Financial Economics*, 7:163–195.

Lo, A. and MacKinlay, A. (1990). Data snooping biases in tests of financial asset pricing models. *Review of Financial Studies*, 3:431–467.

Lo, K.-M. (2001). Implication of method of portfolio formation on asset pricing tests. *Unpublished manuscript*.

Lucas, R. (1978). Asset prices in an exchange economy. *Econometrica*, 46:1429–1446.

McElroy, M. B. and Burmeister, E. (1988). Arbitrage Pricing Theory as a restricted non-linear multivariate regression model. *Journal of Business and Economic Statistics*, 6(1):29–42.

Mehra, R. and Prescott, E. (1985). The equity premium: A puzzle. *Journal of Monetary Economics*, 15:145–161.

Merton, R. C. (1973). An Intertemporal Capital Asset Pricing Model. *Econometrica*, 41:867–887.

Miller, M. and Scholes, M. (1972). Rate of return in relation to risk: A re-examination of some recent findings. In Jensen, M. C., editor, *Studies in the theory of capital markets*. Praeger, New York.

Poon, S. and Taylor, J. (1991). Macroeconomic factors and the UK stock market. *Journal of Business Finance and Accounting*, 18(5):619–636.

Reyfman, A. (1997). *Labour market risk and expected asset returns*. PhD thesis, University of Chicago. Cited in Cochrane (2001).

Roll, R. and Ross, S. (1980). An empirical investigation of the Arbitrage Pricing Theory. *Journal of Finance*, 35:1073–1103.

Ross, S. A. (1976). The Arbitrage Theory of Capital Asset Pricing. *Journal of Economic Theory*, 13:341–360.

Rubinstein, M. (1976). The valuation of uncertain income streams and the pricing of options. *Bell Journal of Economics*, 7:407–425.

Shanken, J. (1982). The Arbitrage Pricing Theory: Is it testable. *Journal of Finance*, 37:1129–1140.

Sharpe, W. (1964). Capital asset prices: A theory of market equilibrium under conditions of risk. *Journal of Finance*, 19:425–442.

Shiller, R. (1982). Consumption, asset markets and macroeconomic fluctuations. *Carnegie-Rochester Conference Series on Public Policy*, 17:203–238.

2 Estimating UK factor models using the multivariate skew normal distribution

C. J. Adcock[*]

Abstract

This chapter describes a factor model, which is derived using the multivariate skew normal distribution. This is an attractive model for applications in finance because it is a tractable multivariate distribution which includes skewness. The model posits that asset returns and factors have a joint multivariate skew normal distribution. The factor model itself is derived formally from conditional distribution of asset returns given factors. This provides several new theoretical insights into the relationship between asset returns and factors. Most notable of these is that the sensitivity of asset returns to factors is not measured by the conventional regression coefficients. Another interesting feature is that the factor model contains a component that is a non-linear function of the factor values. According to results of this study of UKFTSE250 stocks, the multivariate skew normal distribution offers an improved fit when compared to the use of the multivariate normal distribution. The MSN factor model offers different measures of sensitivity to the linear effects of the chosen factors as well as a time-varying non-linear component.

2.1 Introduction

Linear factor models are used universally within the finance community. They have a long and distinguished pedigree which dates back to major theoretical papers, like those by Sharpe (1964) and Ross (1976). In the 1960s and 1970s, factor models were the subject of papers by many authors, including King (1966) and Rosenberg and his co-workers, see Rosenberg and Marathe (1975, 1976), to name but three examples. In the past two decades, there has been a large number of papers which, in essence, build empirical factor models. The paper by Jacobs and Levy (1988) is a well-known example, as are papers by Arnott et al. (1990) and Jones (1990). More recently, interest in linear factor models has enjoyed a revival, spurred on by the lively debate in the 1990s about the so-called 'Death of Beta'. Papers by Mei (1993), Roll and Ross (1994), Fama (1996), Fama and French (1995, 1996), and Barber and Lyon (1997) are just a few examples of studies that employ factor models and which were prompted by the work of Fama and French (1992).

The majority of papers which are concerned with linear factor models propose a relationship of the general form:

$$R = \sum_{j=1}^{n} \beta_j X_j + \varepsilon \tag{2.1}$$

[*] The University of Sheffield, UK.

In this notation R denotes the return on an asset. The X_j are the values of the explanatory factors and ε is the unobserved residual return, which is assumed to have zero expected value. The coefficient β_j measures the sensitivity of returns to factor j. In this formulation, the term under the summation sign represents the expected value of R conditional on the given values of the factors $\{X_j\}$. The method of estimation depends mainly on the assumptions made about the probability distribution of the unobserved residual returns. In many models of this form, estimation is done by ordinary least squares (OLS) or by one of its many variants. The implication of OLS-based methods, namely that the errors are normally distributed, has consequences for the unconditional distribution of the returns R. If it may also be assumed that the factors have a multivariate normal distribution, then standard manipulations show that the unconditional distribution of R is also normal. This is an important theoretical result. It means that if returns and factors have a joint multivariate normal distribution, then the factor model is linear *a fortiori*. No other form is correct.

It is accepted that the preceding paragraph describes a completely fictitious world, as least as far as finance is concerned. Returns are not normally distributed. Empirical evidence dating back several decades, see, for example, the well-known papers by Mandelbrot (1963) and Blattberg and Gonedes (1974), among many others, make it clear that returns on many financial assets exhibit both kurtosis and skewness. The issue that arises is how best to modify the model at equation (2.1) to account for this. A common approach is to retain the linear conditional expected value and to model kurtosis and skewness by specifying other distributions for the errors. In principle, it is then straightforward to compute the unconditional distribution and hence the unconditional expected value of returns by integrating over the distribution of the factors. This is potentially an attractive approach. It allows the investigator to specify distributions of choice for the errors. From an empirical perspective, this is clearly a potentially useful thing to be able to do. It also preserves the linear 'regression' relationship between returns and factors. The benefit of this is that the estimated beta coefficients have familiar interpretations. A side effect of this approach is that the unconditional distribution of returns may take an unusual form. It may lack tractability. Higher moments may not exist. Computations that require integration, such as Value at Risk and Conditional Expected Loss, may not admit closed form solutions. Pedersen and Satchell (2000) give an indication of some of the complications.

In this chapter, I propose that the appropriate starting point for a factor model is to specify the joint multivariate probability distribution of returns and factors. The factor model is then given by the expression for the conditional expected value of returns given the factor values. For the world of the multivariate normal distribution, this gives the linear factor model and the whole range of familiar techniques based on OLS and related methods. A tractable linear factor model also arises if returns and factors jointly follow the multivariate Student distribution. The factor model will also be linear under other members of the class of elliptically symmetric distributions, but not necessarily tractable in other respects. When returns and possibly factors are skewed it is clearly necessary to depart from multivariate normality and from elliptical symmetry in general.

The specific purpose of this chapter is to use the multivariate skew normal, henceforth MSN, distribution as a vehicle for deriving factor models. From the name, it will be clear that this multivariate probability distribution explicitly incorporates skewness.

Manipulation of the MSN distribution gives a factor model that is the correct expression for expected returns conditional on factor values. As is shown below, in the MSN world, the factor model is generally non-linear in the factor values. This is an interesting theoretical property of the model. Since the CAPM is just a one factor model, it means that the MSN market model is also non-linear. Adcock and Shutes (2001) give details of this property. The non-linearity has the potential, at least, to explain departures from the security market line.

As described below, the MSN distribution and its univariate form have been known for some time. The earliest known work is due to Roberts (1966) and the multivariate form of the distribution was introduced by Azzalini and Dalla Valle (1996). In recent years, there has been substantial development of related multivariate skewed distributions, with notable papers by Azzalini and Capitanio (2003), Branco and Dey (2001), Sahu et al. (2003) and Wang et al. (2002). In finance, there have been numerous studies of skewness in returns. Papers that are concerned with modelling skewness include works by Chunhachinda et al. (1997), Fernandez and Steel (1998), Theodossiou (1998), Peiro (1999) and Harvey and Siddique (2000). To date, exploitation of the MSN distribution in finance has been relatively limited. The paper by Adcock and Shutes (2001) is concerned with portfolio selection and with the theoretical aspects of the market model. Harvey et al. (2002) report an extensive empirical study of portfolio selection under the MSN distribution. Adcock (2003) reports an empirical study of the market model for UKFTSE100 stocks.

The structure of this chapter is as follows. Section 2.2 describes the multivariate skew normal distribution and its basic properties. Section 2.3 describes the properties of an MSN factor model which is derived from the conditional distribution of returns given factors. As well as the MSN model, the corresponding equations for a factor model based on the multivariate normal distribution are given. Section 2.4 summarizes the return and factor data used and the forms of model that are estimated. Section 2.5 describes an empirical study of UKFTSE250 stocks and section 2.6 concludes. Vectors and matrices appear in bold font. Other notation is that in common use. The computations were carried out using S-plus. More detailed results are available from the author on request.

2.2 The multivariate skew normal distribution and some of its properties

The multivariate skew normal, henceforth MSN, distribution was introduced by Azzalini and Dalla Valle (1996) and is an extension of the univariate skew normal distribution which was originally due to Roberts (1966) and, separately, O'Hagan and Leonard (1976) and was developed in articles by Azzalini (1985, 1986). The standard form of the distribution may be obtained by considering the distribution of a random vector, $\mathbf{R}$ say, which is defined as:

$$\mathbf{R} = \mathbf{Y} + \lambda U$$

The vector $\mathbf{Y}$ has a full rank multivariate normal distribution with mean vector μ and variance-covariance matrix Σ. The scalar variable U, which is independent of $\mathbf{Y}$, has a standard normal distribution that is truncated below at zero. The vector λ is a vector of skewness parameters, which may take any real values.

For applications in finance, a modification of this distribution is employed, as reported in Adcock and Shutes (2001), henceforth A&S. The vectors $\mathbf{R}$, $\mathbf{Y}$ and λ are defined as above. The scalar variable U has a normal distribution with mean τ and variance 1 truncated below at zero. This modification generates a richer family of probability distributions. As will be shown later in this section, non-zero values τ appear to be a desirable feature of the model for theoretical reasons. In addition, the empirical evidence described below supports the view that inclusion of τ as a parameter to be estimated is a useful feature.

From the perspective of applications in finance, the variable U may be interpreted as a non-negative shock, which is unobserved, but which affects all variables. The lambda parameters measure sensitivity of each variable to this shock, whatever it may be. It should be noted that the idea of adding a skewness shock to a multivariate normally distributed vector of asset returns is not new. It is suggested in Simaan (1993), which predates A&S. Simaan's paper is, however, mainly concerned with the effect of the skewness shock on portfolio selection and is not concerned with a specific model for the probability distribution of U.

The probability distribution of $\mathbf{R}$ is MSN with parameters μ, Σ, λ and τ, denoted as:

$$\mathbf{R} \sim \text{MSN}\,(\mu, \Sigma, \lambda, \tau)$$

The probability density function of this distribution is:

$$g_R(\mathbf{r}) = \phi\left(\mathbf{r}; \mu + \lambda\tau, \Sigma + \lambda\lambda^T\right) \frac{\Phi\left(\dfrac{\tau + \lambda^T \Sigma^{-1}(\mathbf{r} - \mu)}{\sqrt{1 + \lambda^T \Sigma^{-1}\lambda}}\right)}{\Phi(\tau)};$$

where $\Phi(x)$ is the standard normal distribution function evaluated at x. The notation $\phi(\mathbf{x}; \omega, \mathbf{W})$ denotes the probability density function, evaluated at $\mathbf{x}$, of a multivariate normal distribution with mean vector ω and variance-covariance matrix $\mathbf{W}$. This density function, which is reported in A&S, is essentially Azzalini and Dalla Valle's (1996) result with a change of notation and generalization to accommodate a non-zero value of τ. The distribution of any sub-vector of $\mathbf{r}$, including the scalar R_i, is of the same form, based upon the corresponding sub-vectors of μ and λ and sub-matrix of Σ.

As noted in Adcock (2003), an interesting feature of this model is the limiting case when $\tau \to -\infty$. Using the usual approximation to $\Phi(x)$, $x > 0$, for large values of x[1], it may be shown that the above probability density function is well approximated by:

$$g_R(\mathbf{r}) = \phi(\mathbf{r}; \mu, \Sigma) \frac{|\tau|}{|\tau + \lambda^T \Sigma^{-1}(\mathbf{r} - \mu)|}$$

However, the values of this density function are sensitive to the vector $\Sigma^{-1}\lambda$. Even for large negative values of τ, the critical values of the univariate version of this distribution differ from those implied by the normal component of the density alone[2].

---

[1] This is $\Phi(x) \approx \frac{1}{x}e^{-\frac{1}{2}x^2}$, $x > 0$, see Abramowitz and Stegun (1965) for further details.

[2] This may be demonstrated using a suitable numerical method to integrate $g_R(\;)$.

As reported in A&S, the moment generating function of this distribution, with $\mathbf{t}$ denoting a p vector, is:

$$M_R(\mathbf{t}) = \exp\left[\mathbf{t}^T(\mu + \lambda\tau) + \frac{1}{2}\mathbf{t}^T\left(\Sigma + \lambda\lambda^T\right)\mathbf{t}\right]\frac{\Phi\left(\lambda^T\mathbf{t} + \tau\right)}{\Phi(\tau)};$$

The first two (multivariate) moments are given by:

$$E[\mathbf{R}] = \mu + \lambda\{\tau + \xi_1(\tau)\}$$
$$V[\mathbf{R}] = \Sigma + \lambda\lambda^T\{1 + \xi_2(\tau)\}$$

where:

$$\xi_k(x) = \frac{\partial^k \ln \Phi(x)}{\partial x^k}, \quad k = 1, 2, \ldots$$

The coskewness of three variables, i, j and k say, is:

$$S[r_i, r_j, r_k] = \lambda_i\lambda_j\lambda_k\xi_3(\tau),$$

and the cokurtosis of these with variable l is:

$$K[r_i, r_j, r_k, r_l] = \lambda_i\lambda_j\lambda_k\lambda_l\xi_4(\tau)$$

Skewness and kurtosis of a single variable are therefore, respectively:

$$SK[r_i] = \lambda_{i_i}^3\xi_3(\tau), \quad KU[r_i] = \lambda_{i_i}^4\xi_4(\tau)$$

A standardized measure of skewness is:

$$sk = \frac{SK}{|KU|^{\frac{3}{4}}} = \frac{\xi_3(\tau)}{|\xi_4(\tau)|^{\frac{3}{4}}}$$

It follows from this equation that a theoretical limitation of the MSN model is that this ratio is fixed for all assets. However, it is better that the ratio be determined by the data under investigation rather than being preset being specifying that τ equals zero or indeed equals any other fixed value.

An implication of the moment generating function is that the distribution of a linear function of the elements of $\mathbf{R}$, $\mathbf{w}^T\mathbf{R}$ say, is also of the above MSN form, albeit in one dimension, with scalar parameters $\mathbf{w}^T\mu$, $\mathbf{w}^T\Sigma\mathbf{w}$, $\mathbf{w}^T\lambda$ and τ, respectively. If the vector $\mathbf{R}$ denotes asset returns and $\mathbf{w}$ denotes portfolio weights, then the return on the portfolio is univariate skew normal as long as the quantity $\mathbf{w}^T\lambda$ does not equal zero. When $\mathbf{w}^T\lambda = 0$, portfolio return has a normal distribution.

2.3   Conditional distributions and factor models

As stated in the introduction, a factor model is correctly obtained by considering the probability distribution of asset returns given the values of the factor variables. When returns $\mathbf{R}$ and factors $\mathbf{X}$ are multivariate normal with mean vector μ partitioned as:

$$\mu = \begin{bmatrix} \mu_R \\ \mu_X \end{bmatrix};$$

and variance covariance matrix Σ partitioned as:

$$\Sigma = \begin{bmatrix} \Sigma_{RR} & \Sigma_{RX} \\ \Sigma_{XR} & \Sigma_{XX} \end{bmatrix};$$

the conditional distribution of the vector of returns $\mathbf{R}$ given factors $\mathbf{X}$ is also multivariate normal:

$$\mathbf{R}|\mathbf{X} \sim \mathrm{N}(\mu_{R|X}, \Sigma_{R|X});$$

where:

$$\Sigma_{R|X} = \Sigma_{RR} - \Sigma_{RX}\Sigma_{XX}^{-1}\Sigma_{XR}$$

$$\mu_{R|X} = \mu_R + \Sigma_{RX}\Sigma_{XX}^{-1}(\mathbf{X} - \mu_X) = \mu_R + \mathbf{B}(\mathbf{X} - \mu_X), \text{say} \qquad (2.2)$$

The matrix $\mathbf{B}$ is a matrix of factor coefficients, which will be referred to as the beta matrix. These equations legitimize the use of linear factor models. Furthermore, when the conditional VC matrix $\Sigma_{R|X}$ is assumed to be diagonal they also legitimize the use of OLS on each asset separately. However, the formulae above mean that the diagonality assumption is unnecessary. It is only necessary to estimate μ and Σ, from which estimates of the beta matrix $\mathbf{B}$ may be computed.

For the MSN distribution, it is well known, see Azzalini and Dalla Valle (1996) for details, that the conditional distributions are also of the MSN form. The vector of skewness parameters is written in partitioned form as:

$$\lambda = \begin{bmatrix} \lambda_R \\ \lambda_X \end{bmatrix}$$

If the joint distribution of returns $\mathbf{R}$ and factors $\mathbf{X}$ is $\mathrm{MSN}(\mu, \Sigma, \lambda, \tau)$, then the conditional distribution of $\mathbf{R}$ given $\mathbf{X}$ is:

$$\mathbf{R}|\mathbf{X} \sim \mathrm{MSN}(\mu_{R|X}, \Sigma_{R|X}, \lambda_{R|X}, \tau_{R|X})$$

The parameters are defined as follows:

$$\tau_{R|X} = \frac{\tau + \lambda_X^T\Sigma_{11}^{-1}(\mathbf{X} - \mu_X)}{\sqrt{1 + \lambda_X^T\Sigma_{11}^{-1}\lambda_X}}$$

$$\lambda_{R|X} = \frac{\lambda_R - \Sigma_{RX}\Sigma_{XX}^{-1}\lambda_X}{\sqrt{1 + \lambda_X^T\Sigma_{XX}^{-1}\lambda_X}}$$

$$\Sigma_{R|X} = \Sigma_{RR} - \Sigma_{RX}\Sigma_{XX}^{-1}\Sigma_{XR}$$

$$\mu_{R|X} = \mu_R + \Sigma_{RX}\Sigma_{XX}^{-1}(X - \mu_X)$$

It should be noted that both $\tau_{R|X}$ and $\mu_{R|X}$ are time varying through their dependence on the given factor values X. Perusal of the expressions for the moments given in section 2.2 makes it clear that conditional moments are also time varying.

In this notation, the conditional mean vector of R given X is:

$$E[R|X] = \mu_{R|X} + \lambda_{R|X}\left\{\tau_{R|X} + \xi_1(\tau_{R|X})\right\}$$

Following A&S, rearrangement gives:

$$E[R|X] = \mu_R + \lambda_R\tau + \Delta(X - \mu_X - \lambda_X\tau) + \lambda_{R|X}\xi_1(\tau_{R|X})$$

where the matrix Δ is defined as:

$$\Delta = \left(\Sigma_{RX} + \lambda_R\lambda_X^T\right)\left(\Sigma_{XX} + \lambda_X\lambda_X^T\right)^{-1} \tag{2.3}$$

Further rearrangement gives the following alternative expression for the conditional mean:

$$E[R|X] = E[R] + \Delta(X - E[X]) + \lambda_{R|X}\left\{\xi_1(\tau_{R|X}) - \frac{1}{\sqrt{1 + \lambda_X^T\Sigma_{XX}^{-1}\lambda_X}}\xi_1(\tau)\right\}$$

This differs from the conventional factor model based on the multivariate normal distribution in two ways. First, the matrix Δ in the linear component has a different definition from the beta matrix B given above. Thus the linear sensitivity of asset returns to the factors in the model will be different from that in the model based on the normal distribution. Second, there is a component of the conditional expected value which is non-linear through the dependence of the argument $\tau_{R|X}$ of $\xi_1()$ on X, the vector of factors[3].

There are two special cases to consider. The first corresponds to the situation when all the X factors have a multivariate normal distribution, i.e. λ_X is a zero vector. In this case, the conditional expected value reduces to:

$$E[R|X] = E[R] + B(X - E[X])$$

The matrix B is as defined above, although it should be noted that it depends on sub-matrices of Σ, which itself is a matrix of parameters in the MSN distribution and

[3] It is readily shown that the expected value of the non-linear term is zero.

cannot in general be interpreted as a variance-covariance matrix. The second special case arises when:

$$\lambda_{R|X} = 0$$

In this case, the conditional distribution of asset returns given the factors is multivariate normal. It has the same expected value equation as that immediately preceding. This case is of methodological interest. It means that a theoretically correct linear factor model can arise when the joint multivariate distribution of returns and factors is not elliptically symmetric.

2.4   Data model choice and estimation

The data used in this study is based on weekly prices from Datastream for the securities that were constituents of the FTSE250 index as at 1 February 2000 and which had available price data since July 1990, thus giving 500 observations on each stock. This gave a total of 175 securities. Four factors were used in the study. The first was return on the FTSE250 index itself. The other three factors are: dividend yield of the FTA All Share, a measure of interest rate spread and expected inflation[4]. These factors are either the same or similar to those used in Lovatt and Parikh (2000).

Three models were estimated. These are:

1. MVN – standard multivariate normal distribution for which the ML estimators of the vector of expected returns and the VC matrix are the usual sample values.
2. MSN(1) – multivariate skew-normal model with all parameters being unrestricted.
3. MSN(2) – multivariate skew normal model in which dividend yield of the FTA, spread and expected inflation are assumed to comply with the usual OLS regression assumption of normality. That is, they each have skewness parameter value set to zero.

Maximum Likelihood Estimates of the parameters of each MSN model were computed using the EM algorithm.

2.5   Empirical study

This section summarizes the results of the empirical study defined in the previous section. To save space, only key findings are given. Further detail is available from the author on request.

2.5.1   Basic return statistics

Table 2.1 shows basic statistics for the 175 FTSE250 stocks included in this study. The first row of the table shows summary statistics for the 175 sample average weekly

---

[4] The data provided were originally computed on a monthly basis. They were converted to weekly frequency by assuming no change in the monthly value until the end of the following month.

Table entries are decimals shown to 4 decimal places, computed for
175 stocks as defined in section 2.4, using 500 weekly observations
from 10 July 1990 to 1 February 2000.

	Avg	Vol	Min	Max
Average	0.0018	0.0013	−0.0032	0.0076
Volatility	0.0355	0.0153	0.0090	0.1072
Min	−0.2638	0.1459	−1.1632	−0.0317
Median	0.0003	0.0009	0.0000	0.0046
Max	0.2745	0.2719	0.0745	3.0582

Legend for columns
Avg   Average value of each row computed over
        175 securities as defined in section 2.4.
Vol   Volatility of each row.
Min   Minimum value of each row.
Max   Maximum value of each row.

Legend for rows
Average Mean weekly return of each security computed
         over 500 weeks from 10 July 1990 to 1 February
         2000.
Volatility Volatility of weekly returns.
Min   Minimum weekly return.
Med   Median weekly return.
Max   Maximum weekly return.

Table 2.1 Basic statistics for weekly returns

returns computed over 500 weeks from 10 July 1990 to 1 February 2000. The first
column gives the average of all 175 individual averages, which is 0.0018 or 0.18%
per week, equivalent to an overall average return of almost 10% per annum. The
remaining three columns, titled Vol, Min and Max give an indication of the variability
of the sample average returns. The following four rows of the table give the same
summary information for the sample volatility, minimum, median and maximum
of each security. For example, the average of all median weekly returns is 0.0003
or 0.03%.

Table 2.2 gives an analysis of the skewness and kurtosis of returns of each stock,
based on the Bera-Jarque test. This well-known test for normality is based on a statistic
which comprises two components, one representing skewness and the other kurtosis.
Under the null hypothesis, the Bera-Jarque test statistic is distributed as Chi-squared
with 2 degrees of freedom and each component is independently distributed as Chi-
squared with 1 degree of freedom. Although Chi-squared tests based on 1 degree of
freedom have low power, this decomposition gives an initial indication of the extent
of skewness in stock returns. The Bera-Jarque test and its two components and the
corresponding probabilities were computed for all 175 stocks. The counts, which are
as shown in Table 2.2, indicate that a substantial number of securities in the FTSE250
index exhibit skewness, 144 out of 175 have a skewness p-value of 5% or less. It may

Computed using 500 weekly observations on 175
stocks from 10 July 1990 to 1 February 2000. Table
entries are counts.

Probability	BJskewp	Bjkurtp	BJprob
<0.1%	125	175	175
0.1–1%	12	0	0
1–5%	7	0	0
5–10%	3	0	0
>10%	28	0	0

Legend
Probability   Probability range.
BJskewp   Probability for the skewness component of
                     the Bera-Jarque test.
BJkurt   Probability for the kurtosis component of
                     the Bera-Jarque test.
BJskewp   Probability for the Bera-Jarque test.

Table 2.2 Analysis of skewness and kurtosis of returns
based on the Bera-Jarque test

also be noted that all stocks exhibit kurtosis, although this is not a specific concern of
this study.

Table 2.3 shows basic statistics for the four factors used in the model. The first factor
is the weekly return on the FTSE250 index itself. The other three factors are as defined
in section 2.4. For each factor, panel A of the table gives the overall average value and
other basic statistics. Panel B of the table gives the value of the Bera-Jarque test and
its p-value, as well the decomposition into the skewness and kurtosis components. As
the entries in panel B indicate, there is skewness as well as kurtosis in all four factors.
This is taken to be an indication that the appropriate multivariate skew normal model
to use is the version with all skewness parameters unrestricted.

2.5.2   Overall model fit

As described in section 2.4, three multivariate models were estimated for these data.
Models (2) and (3) were compared with model (1) using the likelihood ratio test. For
each test, the null hypothesis is that returns follow a multivariate normal distribution.
The degrees of freedom of the Chi-squared test are equal to the number of unrestricted
skewness parameters in the model. The values of the likelihood ratio test statistics for
comparing models (2) and (3) with model (1) are shown in panel A of Table 2.4. As
the table shows, the null hypothesis of multivariate normality is rejected in favour of
both MSN alternatives.

Using the data shown in the table, it is straightforward to compute a likelihood ratio
test in which MSN(1) is compared to MSN(2). The degrees of freedom for this test
are equal to 3, the number of restricted factors. As the entries in panel B show, the

Table entries are decimals shown to 4 decimal places, computed for 4 factors as defined in section 2.4, using 500 weekly observations from 10 July 1990 to 1 February 2000.

	FTSE250	FTDY	SPREAD	EXCPM
Panel A				
Avg	0.0026	4.2954	0.5923	5.6054
Vol	0.0225	1.0420	2.0337	3.3877
Min	−0.2184	0.0000	−3.6200	0.0000
Median	0.0035	4.2700	0.4600	4.8000
Max	0.1272	7.0300	5.6400	16.4000
Panel B				
BJskew	287.9189	5.4207	19.2867	436.4770
BJskewp	0.0000	0.0199	0.0000	0.0000
BJkurt	8027.9715	23.4304	15.1280	190.9083
BJkurtp	0.0000	0.0000	0.0001	0.0000
Bjtest	8315.8903	28.8511	34.4147	627.3853
Bjprob	0.0000	0.0000	0.0000	0.0000

Legend for panel B

BJskew	Value of the skewness component of the BJ test.
BJskewp	Corresponding p-value.
BJkurt	Value of the kurtosis component of the BJ test.
BJkurtp	Corresponding p-value.
Bjtest	Value of the BJ test.
BJprob	Corresponding p-value.

Table 2.3 Basic statistics and Bera-Jarque test values for return on the FTSE250 and other factors

Table entries shown to 2 decimal places, computed using 500 weekly observations from 10 July 1990 to 1 February 2000.

Model	Likelihood ratio statistic	dof	p-value (%)
Panel A – MSN models vs multivariate normal			
MSN(1)	262.45	179	0.00
MSN(2)	235.87	176	0.00
Panel B – MSN(1) vs MSN(2)			
MSN(1)	26.60	3	0.00

Table 2.4 Likelihood ratio tests for two multivariate skew normal models

restricted model is rejected in favour of the unrestricted model. Given the values of the Bera-Jarque test skewness components for the three factors shown in Table 2.3, this result is perhaps to be expected.

2.5.3   Comparison of parameter estimates

This section is devoted to a presentation of some of the parameters of the unrestricted MSN model and to a comparison with the parameters of the multivariate normal model. To avoid what would otherwise be a lengthy presentation, material relating to the restricted MSN model is omitted. The comparison focuses on the differences concerned with the coefficients of the return on the FTSE250 index. A comparison of the coefficients of the other factors may also be obtained from the author.

Table 2.5 shows a summary of the estimated beta coefficients from the MVN model and the estimated delta coefficients from the MSN(1) model corresponding to the return on the FTSE250 index. The beta coefficients are as defined at equation (2.2), the delta coefficients at equation (2.3). As the table indicates, values of delta are on average about 5% higher than values of beta. However, as shown by the volatility and other statistics, delta is more volatile. It ranges between -0.22 and 3.3, whereas beta takes values in the range 0.40 to 2.0. The correlation between beta and delta is about 0.60. A scatter plot of the beta and delta values is shown in Figure 2.1. This suggests that procedures that employ delta are likely to produce different results than the same procedure based on the betas.

Larger differences would be likely if, as is often the case in professional circles, procedures were based on ranks. Figure 2.2 shows a scatter plot of the ranks corresponding to beta and delta. Although the rank correlation coefficient is 0.60, it is clear from the scatter plot that there are a number of quite substantial changes of ordering. This is supported by an OLS regression of the delta ranks on the beta ranks, for which the fitted equation is $\text{RANK}_{\text{delta}} = 0.35 + 0.6\text{RANK}_{\text{beta}}$.

Table entries shown to 4 decimal places, computed using 500 weekly observations from 10 July 1990 to 1 February 2000.

	MVN – beta	MSN(1) – delta
Avg	0.9917	1.0584
Vol	0.2855	0.6581
Min	0.3981	−0.2195
Median	0.9487	0.9963
Max	2.0030	3.3021

Table 2.5 Summary of estimated MVN betas and MSN(1) deltas coefficient for return on the FTSE250 index

Computed using 500 weekly observations from 10 July 1990 to 1 February 2000.

Figure 2.1 Scatter plot of MV normal betas vs MSN(2) deltas for FTSE250 returns

Computed using 500 weekly observations from 10 July 1990 to 1 February 2000.

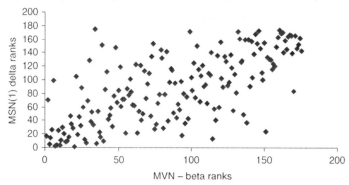

Figure 2.2 Scatter plot of ranks of MV normal betas vs ranks of MSN(2) deltas for FTSE250 returns

2.5.4   Skewness parameters

Table 2.6 shows a summary of the estimated values of the skewness parameter lambda. Also shown in the table is the corresponding summary for the conditional MSN model in which the distribution of asset returns is modelled conditional on given values of all four factors. The table indicates that on average the conditioning process reduces the values of the skewness parameters: averages of 0.033 and 0.002, respectively. Perusal of the minimum and maximum values indicates that the conditioning effect is more marked for assets with positive skewness in the unconditional model. However, this may be because only 26 of the 175 assets have negative skewness in the original model. An OLS regression of the conditional lambdas against the unconditional values indicates that the reduction in values is systematic. The fitted equation is:

$$\lambda_c = -0.01 + 0.36\lambda_U, \ R^2 = 0.95$$

Table entries shown to 4 decimal places, computed
using 500 weekly observations from 10 July 1990 to
1 February 2000.

	MSN(1) – lambda	Conditional lambda
Avg	0.0327	0.0018
Vol	0.0360	0.0133
Min	−0.0362	−0.0259
Median	0.0283	−0.0004
Max	0.1582	0.0494

Table 2.6 Summary statistics for estimated values of
the skewness parameter: unconditional and conditional
cases

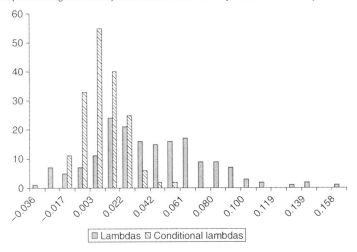

Computed using 500 weekly observations from 10 July 1990 to 1 February 2000.

Lambdas Conditional lambdas

Figure 2.3 Histograms of estimated skewness parameter: unconditional and conditional cases

with both estimated model coefficients being significantly different from zero. A histogram of the both sets of values is shown in Figure 2.3.

2.5.5 Tau and time-varying conditional variance

For the MSN(1) unconditional model, the estimated value of tau is −28.97. As shown in section 2.3, the value of tau conditional on given factors is time varying. A graph of the conditional values is shown in Figure 2.4.

It is clear from the graph that the conditioning variables have a systematic effect on the time series of conditional tau. Compared to the unconditional estimated value of nearly −29, the conditional estimated values range between −8.5 and −15.1. This is perhaps not of great interest when viewed in isolation; however, the implication

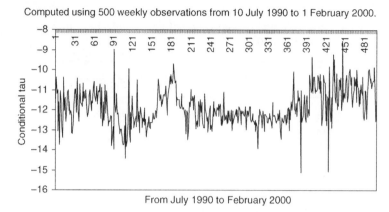

Figure 2.4 Sketch of time series of estimated values of $\tau_{R|X}$

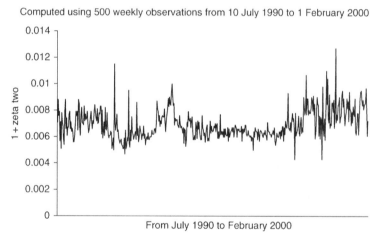

Figure 2.5 Sketch of time series of estimated values of $1 + \xi_2(\tau_{R|X})$

for the conditional variance-covariance matrix of asset returns is of more significance. As noted in section 2.3, the conditional VC matrix has a time-varying component in which all elements are proportional to

$$1 + \xi_2(\tau_{R|X})$$

A sketch of this function is shown in Figure 2.5. It is interesting to note that there is visual evidence of volatility clustering. Indeed, fitting an auto-regressive model to the time series $1 + \xi_2(\tau_{R|X})$ indicates a high degree of serial correlation. The implication of this is that the conditional MSN model may be an additional tool to be used to account for the volatility clustering that is so well known in financial asset returns.

2.6 Conclusions

According to the result of this study of UKFTSE250 stocks, the multivariate skew normal distribution offers an improved fit when compared to the use of the multivariate normal distribution. The MSN factor model offers different measures of sensitivity to the linear effects of the chosen factors as well as a time-varying non-linear component. The effect of the non-linear component is to make the higher conditional moments of asset returns time varying.

Planned developments of this work include use of the model for portfolio selection.

Acknowledgement

It is a pleasure to thank David Lovatt who kindly provided the factor data used in this study.

References

Abramowitz, M. and Stegun, I. (1965). *Handbook of Mathematical Functions*, New York: Dover.

Adcock, C. J. (2003). Capital asset pricing for UK stocks under the multivariate skew normal distribution. In Review.

Adcock, C. J. and Shutes, K. (2001). Portfolio selection based on the multivariate-skew normal distribution. In Skulimowski, A., editor. *Financial Modelling*, Krakow: Progress & Business Publishers.

Arnott, R. D., Kelso, C. M., Kiscadden, S., and Macedo, R. (1990). Forecasting factor returns: An intriguing possibility. *JPM*, Fall: 28–35.

Azzalini, A. (1985). A class of distributions which includes the normal ones. *Scandinavian Journal of Statistics*, 12:171–178.

Azzalini, A. (1986). Further results on a class of distributions which includes the normal ones. *Statistica*, 46:199–208.

Azzalini, A. and Dalla Valle, A. (1996). The multivariate skew-normal distribution. *Biometrika*, 83:715–726.

Azzalini, A. and Capitanio, A. (2003). Distributions generated by perturbation of symmetry with emphasis on a multivariate skew t-distribution. *Journal of the Royal Statistical Society*, Series B, 65:367–390.

Branco, M. D. and Dey, D. K. (2001). A general class of multivariate skew-elliptical distributions. *Journal of Multivariate Analysis*, 79:99–113.

Barber, B. M. and Lyon, J. D. (1997). Firm size, book-to-market ratio and security returns. *Journal of Finance*, 52:875–885.

Blattberg, R. and Gonedes, N. (1974). A comparison of the stable and Student distributions as statistical models for stock prices. *Journal of Business*, 47:244–280.

Chunhachinda, P., Dandapani, K., Hamid, S., and Prakash, A. J. (1997). Portfolio selection and skewness: Evidence from international stock markets. *Journal of Banking and Finance*, 21:143–167.

Fama, E. (1996). Multifactor portfolio efficiency and multifactor asset pricing. *Journal of Financial and Quantitative Analysis*, 31:441–465.

Fama, E. and French, K. R. (1992). The cross-section of expected stock returns. *Journal of Finance*, 47:427–465.

Fama, E. and French, K. R. (1995). Size and book-to-market factors in earnings and returns. *Journal of Finance*, 50:131–155; *Journal of Finance*, 49:1579–1593.

Fama, E. and French, K. R. (1996). Multifactor explanations of asset pricing anomalies. *Journal of Finance*, 51:55–84.

Fernandez, C. and Steel, M. F. J. (1998). On Bayesian models of fat tails and skewness. *Journal of the American Statistical Association*, 93:359–371.

Harvey, C. R., Leichty, J. C., Leichty, M. W., and Muller, P. (2002). Portfolio selection with higher moments. Working Paper.

Harvey, C. R. and Siddique, A. (2000). Conditional skewness in asset pricing tests. *Journal of Finance*, 55:1263–1295.

Jacobs, B. L. and Levy, K. N. (1988). Disentangling equity return regularities: New insights and investment opportunities. *Financial Analysts Journal*, 44, May–June.

Jones, R. C. (1990). Designing factor models for different types of stock: What's good for the goose ain't always good for the gander. *Financial Analysts Journal*, 46, March–April:25–30.

King, B. F. (1966). Market and industry factors in stock price behaviour. *Journal of Business*, 39:139–190.

Lovatt, D. and Parikh, A. (2000). Stock returns and economic activity: The UK case. *European Journal of Finance*, 6:280–297.

Mandelbrot, B. (1963). The variation of certain speculative prices. *Journal of Business*, 36:394–341.

Mei, J. (1993). Explaining the cross-section of returns via a multi-factor APT model. *Journal of Financial and Quantitative Analysis*, 28:331–346.

O'Hagan, A. and Leonard, T. (1976). Bayes estimation subject to uncertainty about parameter constraints. *Biometrika*, 63:201–203.

Pedersen, C. S. and Satchell, S. E. (2000). Small sample analysis of performance measures in the asymmetric response model. *Journal and Financial and Quantitative Analysis*, 35:425–450.

Peiro, A. (1999). Skewness in financial returns. *Journal of Banking and Finance*, 23:847–862.

Roberts, C. (1966). A correlation model useful in the study of twins. *Journal of the American Statistical Association*, 61:1184–1190.

Roll, R. and Ross, S. A. (1994). On the cross-sectional relation between expected returns and betas. *Journal of Finance*, 49:101–121.

Rosenberg, B. and Marathe, V. (1975). The prediction of investment risk: Systematic and residual risk. Working Paper No. 21, IBER.

Rosenberg, B. and Marathe, V. (1976). Common factors in security returns: Microeconomic determinants and macroeconomic correlates. Working Paper No. 44, IBER.

Ross, S. A. (1976). The arbitrage theory of capital asset pricing. *Journal of Economic Theory*, 13:341–360.

Sahu, S. K., Dey, D. K., and Branco, M. D. (2003). A new class of multivariate skew distributions with applications to Bayesian regression models. *The Canadian Journal of Statistics*, 31:129–150.

Sharpe, W. F. (1964). Capital asset prices: A theory of market equilibrium under conditions of risk. *Journal of Finance*, 19:425–442.

Simaan, Y. (1993). Portfolio selection and asset pricing – Three parameter framework. *Management Science*, 39(5):568–587.

Theodossiou, P. (1998). Financial data and the skewed generalized T distribution. *Management Science*, 44:1650–1661.

Wang, J., Boyer, J., and Genton, M. G. (2002). On the skew symmetric representation of multivariate distributions. Working Paper.

3 Misspecification in the linear pricing model

Ka-Man Lo[*]

Abstract

This chapter compares the performance of multivariate F test and average F test under misspecification. In particular, two misspecifications with autocorrelated factors and time-varying factor loadings are considered. The linear factor pricing literature uses a noncentral F distribution to evaluate the extent of misspecification. However, one central finding in this chapter that under the two forms of misspecification considered, the test statistic does not follow a noncentral F distribution. A simulation study is conducted to gauge the extent of the misspecification. Another finding is that the average F test is more sensitive to misspecification than the multivariate F test.

3.1 Introduction

Linear factor models are at the heart of asset management. Knowing the effect of misspecifying the linear factor pricing model is of paramount importance. Arbitrage pricing theory states that the expected return of an asset is a linear function of k factors. However, the theory itself, unlike the CAPM theory, does not state which k factors should be included. Thus empirical researchers have little theoretical guidance as to what factors to include in the linear factor model. In this context, it is important to ask the question 'What is the potential damage if the model is misspecified?' The standard practice in the literature is to evaluate the distortion in the size and the power of the multivariate F under misspecification. The multivariate F test was proposed by Gibbons et al. (1989). One central result in the literature is that given a set of relevant factors is omitted, the test statistic follows a noncentral F distribution.

This chapter examines the performance of the multivariate F test and the average F test, proposed by Hwang and Satchell (2000), under misspecification. In particular, it analyzes two forms of misspecification. The first form is that the factors are auto-correlated and the second is that the factor loadings are time varying. This chapter finds that, contrary to the literature, the test statisitic does not follow a noncentral F distribution under these two forms of misspecification.

Both the multivariate F test and the average F test are used in testing the linear factor model posed in the regression framework with a system of equations. One

[*] I am indebted to my thesis advisors, John Knight and Stephen Sapp, for their help.

prerequisite of implementing the multivariate F test is that the number of time series observations is required to be greater than the number of assets included in the test. This restriction is quite stringent when we are testing a large portfolio while trying to maintain stationarity with five or ten years of monthly observations. The average F test is a response to this constraint by imposing a diagonality constraint on the disturbance covariance matrix. Consequently, the only constraint this test needs to satisfy is that the number of time series observations is larger than the number of factors. If the factors describe the expected returns of the assets well and the disturbances of individual assets are less correlated with each other, the power of the average F test is good even if the number of assets is large.

The major problem of applying either of these tests is that there is little theoretical guidance on the number of factors and the identity of factors. As a result, we run great risk of misspecifying the model. One form of misspecification is omitting a set of relevant factors in the correctly specified model. Another form of misspecification is falsely to assume stationarity when the factor loadings vary with time. For the multivariate F test, the conventional way to gauge the extent of misspecification is to use the noncentral F distribution to evaluate the bias (as in Chapter 6 of Campbell et al. (1997)). However, it is shown in this chapter that using the noncentral F distribution to judge the extent of bias is misleading under the two forms of misspecification studied here. In these cases, the test statistics do not follow a noncentral F distribution. For the average F test, the diagonality assumption is violated in either cases of misspecification. Another finding of this chapter is that the distortion in the average F test is more severe than the multivariate F test under misspecification.

The next section provides a brief review of the Arbitrage Pricing Theory and a general discussion of the multivariate F test and the average F test. The third section examines the distribution of the multivariate F test statistics under misspecification and is divided into two subsections: one subsection examines the case in which a set of relevant factors is omitted from estimation, the other subsection examines the case of falsely assuming constant factor loadings. Although this section examines only the distribution of the multivariate F test under misspecification, it gives us a handle on the magnitude of violation of diagonality assumption in the average F test. The fourth section investigates the extent of bias of the two tests via simulation. The last section concludes.

3.2   Framework

3.2.1   Arbitrage Pricing Theory

Arbitrage Pricing Theory was developed by Ross (1976). Assume the return generating process for N assets are described by the following linear system of equations at any particular time t,

$$r_t = a_t + B_t f_t + \varepsilon_t \tag{3.1}$$

$$E\left(\varepsilon_t \mid f_t\right) = 0$$

$$E\left(\varepsilon_t \varepsilon_t' \mid f_t\right) = \Sigma$$

where r is an $N \times 1$ vector of asset returns at time t, a is an $N \times 1$ vector of constants, B_t is an $N \times K$ matrix of factor loadings, each row of B_t describes an asset's 'responsiveness' to one unit change in the factor realization, f, a $K \times 1$ vector. The central theme of Arbitrage Pricing Theory is that in the absence of arbitrage, conditional on the information at time $t - 1$, the expected returns of the assets are approximately a linear function of k factor risk premia, λ_k.

$$E\left(r_t \mid \Omega_{t-1}\right) \approx i\lambda_0 + B_t\lambda_k$$

and with the presence of a riskless asset,

$$E\left(r_t - r_{ft} \mid \Omega_{t-1}\right) \approx B_t\left(\lambda_k - r_f\right) \tag{3.2}$$

in which Ω_{t-1} represents the information set at time $t - 1$ and λ_k represents the return of holding one unit of the kth factor risk. Various papers have imposed additional assumptions to make the pricing equation exact. Examples are Connor (1984) and Ingersoll (1984). This chapter will discuss only the case where exact pricing equation holds and a risk-free asset exists so that the multivariate F test is applicable and equation (3.2) holds. One important implication is $a_t = 0$ if (3.1) is expressed in excess return.

There are two points worth our attention about the arbitrage pricing model. The first point is that, unlike the CAPM, the arbitrage pricing theory in its original form does not relate asset returns to any specific set of pricing factors. The identities of the factors are unknown. This lack of theoretical underpinning poses some difficulties in estimating the model. It is possible that we omit a set of relevant factors which is in the return generating process. The first form of misspecification this chapter examines is the omission of relevant factors. Two alternative generating processes for the factors are investigated: (1) the factors are independent serially and (2) they are autocorrelated.

The second point is that the traditional arbitrage pricing model is basically a static model. It is assumed in the traditional APT model that the factor loadings remain constant through time. It means

$$E\left(r_t - r_{ft} \mid \Omega_{t-1}\right) = B\left(\lambda_k - r_f\right) \tag{3.3}$$

However, it is very probable that factor loadings are time varying. Consequently, the second form of misspecification this chapter investigates is the effect of falsely imposing stationarity of the factor loadings. In particular, we examine the case that factor loadings is a linear function of the conditioning information in time $t - 1$.

3.2.2   Multivariate F test used in linear factor model

This section provides a brief review of the multivariate F tests and discusses its advantages and shortcomings. We assume that factor loadings are constant in this section. Assuming that risk-free asset exists, the linear pricing model we want to test is

$$R^e = 1_T a' + fB + E \tag{3.4}$$

It is a system of equations with N assets and each asset has T time series observations. R^e is a $T \times N$ matrix of excess returns. The ith column of R^e represents T time series observations of the ith individual asset's excess return. f is a $T \times k$ matrix of excess factor portfolio returns. Similarly, the kth column represents T time series observations of factor k. B is a $k \times N$ matrix of factor loadings. E is a $T \times N$ matrix of disturbance terms, each row of which is *iid* $N(0, \Sigma)$, implying that the N disturbances are independent serially. Arbitrage Pricing Theory, together with the existence of a riskless asset, implies that

$$a = 0_N \qquad (3.5)$$

Equation (3.5) forms the null hypothesis in testing.

The first paper which proposes a multivariate test on the linear asset pricing framework is Gibbons et al. (1989). They utilize distributions of $\hat{a}$ and $\hat{\Sigma}$ to form the multivariate F test. $\hat{a}$ and $\hat{\Sigma}$ are the OLS or MLE estimates of the intercepts and the variance-covariance matrix of the disturbances of the N asset returns equations. Under the assumptions of equation (3.4) and conditional on the realization of the k factors, the estimates of the intercepts $\hat{a}$ follow multivariate normal distribution

$$\hat{a} \sim N\left(a, \frac{1 + \bar{f}'\hat{\Omega}^{-1}\bar{f}}{T}\Sigma\right) \qquad (3.6)$$

where

$$\bar{f} = \frac{1}{T}f'1_T$$

and

$$\hat{\Omega} = \frac{1}{T}\left(f - 1_T\bar{f}'\right)'\left(f - 1_T\bar{f}'\right)$$

$\bar{f}$ is a $k \times 1$ vector of sample mean of the k factors and $\hat{\Omega}$ is the sample covariance matrix of the k factors. The estimated covariance matrix $\hat{\Sigma}$ follows central Wishart distribution with $T - K$ degrees of freedom and the parameter matrix $(1/T)\Sigma$,

$$\hat{\Sigma} \sim W\left(T - K, \frac{1}{T}\Sigma\right) \qquad (3.7)$$

Under (3.6) and (3.7), applying theorem (3.2.13) in Muirhead (1983), the multivariate F test Gibbons et al. proposed is given by

$$W = \frac{(T - N - K)}{N} \frac{1}{1 + \bar{f}'\hat{\Omega}^{-1}\bar{f}}\hat{a}'\hat{\Sigma}^{-1}\hat{a} \qquad (3.8)$$

The test statistic, W, follows a central F distribution unconditionally with N and $T - N - K$ degrees of freedom under the null. Under the alternative, it follows a noncentral F distribution, conditional on the realization of the k factors, with the same degrees of freedom and the noncentrality parameter given by,

$$\frac{T}{1 + \bar{f}'\hat{\Omega}^{-1}\bar{f}}a'\Sigma^{-1}a$$

As shown in Gibbons et al. (1989), the multivariate F test has a nice economic intuition: it is the distance between the ex-post price of risk and the price of the portfolio. However, there is a disadvantage of this test: it has very low power when the number of assets, N, is large. It is not implementable if the number of assets is larger than the number of time series observations. It is because when $N > T - k$, $\hat{\Sigma}$ becomes singular and is not invertible.

3.2.3 Average F test used in linear factor model

Hwang and Satchell (2000) relax the restriction of $T > N + k$ by imposing diagonality assumption on the covariance matrix of the disturbances such that the disturbances are uncorrelated cross-sectionally. It means Σ is specified as a diagonal matrix such that

$$\Sigma = diag\left(\sigma_1^2, \sigma_2^2, \ldots, \sigma_N^2\right)$$

The average F test is given by

$$AF = \sum_{i=1}^{N} T\left(1 + \bar{f}'\hat{\Omega}^{-1}\bar{f}\right)^{-1} \frac{\hat{a}_i^2}{\hat{\sigma}_j^2} \tag{3.9}$$

where $\hat{\sigma}_j^2$ is the unbiased estimate of asset j residual variance, i.e.,

$$\hat{\sigma}_j^2 = \frac{1}{T - K - 1} \sum_{t=1}^{T} \left(R_{j,t} - \hat{a}_j - f_t\hat{B}_j\right)^2$$

Each term in the summation in equation (3.9), $T\left(1 + \bar{f}'\hat{\Omega}^{-1}\bar{f}\right)^{-1}\hat{a}_i^2/\hat{\sigma}_j^2$, is distributed as $F(1, T - K - 1)$. As long as $T > K + 1$, the average F test can be implemented. The intuition of the average F test is that given the residual risks between assets are uncorrelated, the optimal weight of the individual asset's pricing error is its own variance. So we can implement OLS on each asset equation, average their estimated pricing deviation, $\hat{a}_i$, weighted by their estimated variances and see how precisely the factors priced the set of assets. The assumption of diagonality holds well when the k factors in asset pricing equations explain all common variation in asset returns. However, the average F test does not perform well if the off-diagonal elements of the disturbance covariance matrix are not small enough. In the case of omitting a set of relevant factors, the factor loadings and the factor risks of the omitted factors systematically affect the disturbance covariance matrix.

3.3 Distribution of the multivariate F test statistics under misspecification

In this section, we study the distribution of the multivariate F test under misspecification. We examine two cases of misspecification: (1) omitting a set of relevant factors from estimation and (2) falsely imposing stationarity of factor loadings when they are time varying.

We will examine the distribution of the multivariate F test under misspecification via studying the distributions of $\hat{a}$ and $\hat{\Sigma}$. In this way, we can see whether the distributions of $\hat{a}$ and $\hat{\Sigma}$ satisfy the assumptions leading to the multivariate F test. This section serves another purpose: in the process of examining the distribution of $\hat{\Sigma}$, we can see the extent of deviation from the diagonality assumption of residuals, which is essential in applying the average F test. To facilitate analysis, we adopt the assumption that the factors in the return generating equations follow a multivariate normal distribution.

3.3.1   Exclusion of a set of factors from estimation

We now examine the effect on the distribution of the test statistics of a set of relevant factors being omitted from estimation. It is assumed that the factor loadings are constant through time. We examine two cases for the generating process of factors: in the first case, the factors are cross-sectionally correlated but they are time independent. In the second case, the time independence assumption is relaxed so factors are both autocorrelated and cross-sectionally correlated.

Assume a risk-free rate exists. Suppose that in the correctly specified model, asset returns are described by two sets of excess factor portfolio returns, f_1 and f_2. They are of dimension $T \times k_1$ and $T \times k_2$ respectively. The return equations of the set of N assets are then written as

$$R^e = 1_T a' + f_1 B_1 + f_2 B_2 + E$$

where B_1 $(k_1 \times N)$ and B_2 $(k_2 \times N)$ are the factor loadings of the first and the second set of factors respectively. The ith column of B_1 and B_2 represents the ith individual asset's sensitivity to marginal change in f_1 and f_2. The disturbance terms are represented by the matrix E which is of dimension $T \times N$. E' has a covariance matrix of $I_T \otimes \Sigma$. Now suppose that only the first set of factors is included in estimation, so that the excess asset returns are misspecified as

$$R^e = 1_T a'_m + f_1 B_1 + E_m$$

In this equation, both the intercept terms and the disturbance matrix are different from the correctly specified model. The intercepts are given by

$$1_T a'_m = 1_T a' + \mu'_2 1_T B_2$$

where $\mu_2 = E(f_2)$ and it is a $k_2 \times 1$ vector of factor means of the omitted factors. The disturbances matrix is given by

$$E_m = E + (f_2 - \mu'_2 1_T) B_2$$

Let $\bar{f}_1$ be the $k_1 \times 1$ vector of sample mean of factors included in estimation and similarly let $\bar{f}_2$ be the $k_2 \times 1$ vector of sample mean of missing factors. Hwang and

Satchell (2000) examine the distribution of the intercept estimates in the case where factors are orthogonal and they are non-autocorrelated, which results in

$$\hat{a}_m \sim N\left(a + B_2'\mu_2, \frac{1}{T}\left(1 + \bar{f}_1'\bar{f}_1\right)[B_2'B_2 + \Sigma]\right)$$

3.3.1.1 Factors serially independent

We now examine the case where the factors are assumed to be contemporaneously correlated with each other but are non-autocorrelated. Assume that the factors, like the disturbances, are *iid* over time and they follow multivariate normal distribution. The k factors at any time t are distributed as

$$\begin{bmatrix} f_{1t} \\ f_{2t} \end{bmatrix} \sim N(\mu, \Omega)$$

$$\mu = \begin{pmatrix} \mu_1 \\ \mu_2 \end{pmatrix}, \quad \Omega = \begin{bmatrix} \Omega_{11} & \Omega_{12} \\ \Omega_{21} & \Omega_{22} \end{bmatrix}$$

where μ_1 are $k_1 \times 1$ and μ_2 are $k_2 \times 1$, Ω_{11} are $k_1 \times k_1$ and Ω_{22} are $k_2 \times k_2$. All the parameter values, μ and Ω, are identical over time. While normally this may seem to be a restrictive assumption, it produces tractable results and provides a framework to generalize to the more complicated cases later.

Distribution of $\hat{a}_m$

Proposition 3.1 *Conditional on the realization of the included factors, the distribution of $\hat{a}_m$ is given by*

$$\hat{a}_m \sim N\left(a + B_2'\mu_2 - B_2'\Omega_{21}\Omega_{11}^{-1}\mu_1, \frac{1}{T}\left(1 + \bar{f}_1'\hat{\Omega}_{11}^{-1}\bar{f}_1\right)\right.$$
$$\left. \times \left[B_2'\left(\Omega_{22} - \Omega_{21}\Omega_{11}^{-1}\Omega_{12}\right)B_2 + \Sigma\right]\right) \quad (3.10)$$

where Ω_{11}^{-1} is the inverse of the covariance of the included factors.

See the appendix for proof. Distribution of the intercepts differs from the orthogonal factor case in two aspects: (1) for the mean of $\hat{a}_m$, there is an adjustment term, $B_2'\Omega_{21}\Omega_{11}^{-1}\mu_1$, and (2) for the covariance of $\hat{a}_m$, the factor loadings of the omitted factors are weighted by the conditional covariance matrix of the omitted factors, $\Omega_{22} - \Omega_{21}\Omega_{11}^{-1}\Omega_{12}$.

Distribution of $\hat{E}_m$ Hwang and Satchell (2000) stopped short of analyzing the statistical properties of $\hat{\Sigma}_m = (1/T)\hat{E}_m'\hat{E}_m$, the estimator of covariance matrix of disturbance under missing factors. We start with examining the distribution of $\hat{E}_m$. Define $F_1 = [1_T \quad f_1]$, then $\hat{E}_m$ can be written as,

$$\hat{E}_m = \left(I_T - F_1\left(F_1'F_1\right)^{-1}F_1'\right)R^e \quad (3.11)$$

$$= \left(I_T - F_1\left(F_1'F_1\right)^{-1}F_1'\right)\left(\left(f_2 - \bar{f}_2\right)B_2 + E\right)$$

The expected value of $\hat{E}_m$, μ_m, conditional on factor realization f_1, is given by

$$\mu_m = \left(I_T - F_1 \left(F_1' F_1 \right)^{-1} F_1' \right) E \left(f_2 \mid f_1 \right) B_2 \tag{3.12}$$

$$= \left(I_T - F_1 \left(F_1' F_1 \right)^{-1} F_1' \right) \left(1_T \mu_2' + \left(f_1 - 1_T \mu_1' \right) \Omega_{11}^{-1} \Omega_{21} \right) B_2$$

$$= 0_{T \times N}$$

The covariance matrix of $\hat{E}_m$, Σ_m, conditional on f_1, is given by

$$\Sigma_m = \left(B_2' \left(\Omega_{22} - \Omega_{21} \Omega_{11}^{-1} \Omega_{12} \right) B_2 + \Sigma \right) \otimes \left(I_T - F_1 \left(F_1' F_1 \right)^{-1} F_1' \right) \tag{3.13}$$

We now show that with correlated but non-autocorrelated factors, the inner products of $\hat{E}_m$ follow central Wishart distribution.

$$H \hat{E}_m \sim N \left(0_{T \times N}, \left(B_2' \left(\Omega_{22} - \Omega_{21} \Omega_{11}^{-1} \Omega_{12} \right) B_2 + \Sigma \right) \otimes I_T \right)$$

where

$$H H' = \left(I_T - F_1 \left(F_1' F_1 \right)^{-1} F_1' \right) \text{ and } H' H = I_{T - K_1}$$

Applying Theorem 3.1.4 in Muirhead (1982), $T \hat{\Sigma}_m$ follows central Wishart distribution with $T - K_1$ degrees of freedom and the parameters matrix $B_2' \left(\Omega_{22} - \Omega_{21} \Omega_{11}^{-1} \Omega_{12} \right) B_2 + \Sigma$.

$$\hat{E}_m' \hat{E}_m = T \hat{\Sigma}_m \sim W \left(T - K_1, \left(B_2' \left(\Omega_{22} - \Omega_{21} \Omega_{11}^{-1} \Omega_{12} \right) B_2 + \Sigma \right) \right) \tag{3.14}$$

Distribution of the F test statistics   As $\hat{a}_m$ is independent of $\hat{E}_m$, the test statistic follows an F distribution under null. If the factors have joint means of zero, the multivariate F test follows an unconditional central F distribution under the null, with k_2 more degrees of freedom, under null in the denominator. It results in a larger test statistic, under which the null is more likely to be rejected. If the number of missing factors is relatively small, the bias in the multivariate F test statistic is probably marginal. On the other hand, if the factors have positive means, the multivariate F test under the null follows a noncentral F instead of a central F distribution. The noncentrality parameter under null is given by

$$\delta = \varphi \left(B_2' \mu_2 - B_2' \Omega_{21} \Omega_{11}^{-1} \mu_1 \right)' \left[B_2' \left(\Omega_{22} - \Omega_{21} \Omega_{11}^{-1} \Omega_{12} \right) B_2 + \Sigma \right]^{-1}$$

$$\times \left(B_2' \mu_2 - B_2' \Omega_{21} \Omega_{11}^{-1} \mu_1 \right) \tag{3.15}$$

with $\varphi = T / \left(1 + \bar{f}_1' \hat{\Omega}^{-1} \bar{f}_1 \right)$. See the appendix for the derivation of the noncentrality parameter. We are going to examine the extent of the bias under various situations in the simulation section.

	r^e_{mt}	SMB_t	HML_t
A. Univariate summary statistics			
mean	0.57	0.078	0.408
standard error	4.559	3.313	3.071
B. Correlation matrix			
r^e_{mt}	1	0.264	−0.447
SMB_t	0.264	1	−0.298
HML_t	−0.447	−0.298	1
C. Cross-autocorrelation matrix; Jan 1971–Dec 2000			
r^e_{mt-1}	0.045	0.205	−0.009
SMB_{t-1}	0.118	0.056	−0.052
HML_{t-1}	−0.03	−0.053	0.168
D. Cross-autocorrelation matrix; Jan 1971–Dec 1980			
r^e_{mt-1}	0.018	0.236	−0.045
SMB_{t-1}	0.076	0.161	−0.168
HML_{t-1}	0.003	−0.048	0.153
E. Cross-autocorrelation matrix; Jan 1981–Dec 1990			
r^e_{mt-1}	0.121	0.326	−0.081
SMB_{t-1}	0.139	0.095	−0.034
HML_{t-1}	−0.063	−0.096	0.166
F. Cross-autocorrelation matrix; Jan 1991–Dec 2000			
r^e_{mt-1}	−0.031	0.11	0.089
SMB_{t-1}	0.156	−0.026	0.014
HML_{t-1}	−0.032	−0.035	0.17

Table 3.1 Summary Statistics of Excess Market Return, SMB and HML

3.3.1.2 Factors autocorrelated

In this section, we relax the assumption of factors being time independent. To motivate our discussion, Table 3.1 shows monthly first order cross-autocorrelation of the three empirical indices used as factors in the factor pricing models in Fama and French (1993, 1996). The indices are value-weighted market index, SMB and HML using stocks from NYSE, Amex and NASDAQ. SMB is the monthly return on a portfolio of small stocks minus the monthly return on a portfolio of large stocks. HML is the return on a portfolio of high book-to-market stocks minus the return on a portfolio of low book-to-market stocks. We follow Fama and French (1993) and call SMB the size factor and HML the book-to-market factor. Panel D to Panel F show three ten-year spans of cross-autocorrelation. Many of the elements are quite large. The book-to-market factor's first order autocorrelation is well above 10% in all three ten-year spans. The cross-autocorrelation between the size factor at t and the excess market return at $t-1$ is all over 25% in all three ten-year spans. Panel C shows cross-autocorrelation for a thirty-year span. It depicts roughly the same pattern.

Assume the k factors have time-varying means and they are autocorrelated. Further, assume that the set of factors jointly follows multivariate normal distribution over time such that

$$\left(\begin{array}{c} vec(f_1) \\ vec(f_2) \end{array} \right) \sim N(U, \Phi)$$

$$U = \left(\begin{array}{c} vec(\mu_1) \\ vec(\mu_2) \end{array} \right), \Phi = \left[\begin{array}{cc} \Phi_{11} & \Phi_{12} \\ \Phi_{21} & \Phi_{22} \end{array} \right]$$

where μ_1 is $T \times k_1$ and μ_2 is $T \times k_2$ vector of means, $k = k_1 + k_2$. Each column of μ_i, $i = 1, 2$, represents the time-varying mean of each factor. Φ represents the variance-covariance matrix of the $k_1 + k_2$ factors. Each of $\Phi_{ij}, i, j = 1, 2$, is of dimension $Tk_i \times Tk_j$ so that each Ω_{ij} represents a covariance matrix of autocorrelated factors. To simplify algebra and make the analysis tractable, we assume that

$$\Phi = \Omega \otimes A$$

$$\Omega = \left[\begin{array}{cc} \Omega_{11} & \Omega_{12} \\ \Omega_{21} & \Omega_{22} \end{array} \right]$$

where Ω is of dimension $(k_1 + k_2) \times (k_1 + k_2)$ and depicts the cross-sectional correlation between factors. What this assumption essentially says is that each factor and their covariances have the same time series behavior, represented by the matrix A. Under this setting, the distribution of the omitted set of relevant factors conditional on the set of included factors is given by

$$vec(f_2) \mid vec(f_1) \sim N \left(\mu_{2|1}, \Omega_{2|1} \right) \tag{3.16}$$

$$\mu_{2|1} = vec(\mu_2) + \left(\Omega_{21} \Omega_{11}^{-1} \otimes A \right) (vec(f_1) - vec(\mu_1))$$

$$\Omega_{2|1} = \left(\Omega_{22} - \Omega_{21} \Omega_{11}^{-1} \Omega_{12} \right) \otimes A$$

Distribution of $\hat{a}$

Proposition 3.2 *The joint distribution of the estimators of the intercepts, $\hat{a}$, is given by*

$$\hat{a}_m \sim N(\mu_a, \Sigma_a) \tag{3.17}$$

where $\mu_a = a + B_2' u_2 + B_2' \Omega_{21} \Omega_{11}^{-1} (f_1 - \mu_1)' A \left(1_T g_1 + f_1 g_2' \right)$

$$\Sigma_a = \left(1_T g_1 + f_1 g_2' \right)' A \left(1_T g_1 + f_1 g_2' \right) \left[B_2' \left(\Omega_{22} - \Omega_{21} \Omega_{11}^{-1} \Omega_{12} \right) B_2 \right]$$
$$+ \frac{1}{T} \left(1 + \bar{f}_1' \hat{\Omega}_{11}^{-1} \bar{f}_1 \right) \Sigma$$

with

$$g_1 = \frac{1}{T} \left(1 + \bar{f}_1' \hat{\Omega}_{11}^{-1} \bar{f}_1 \right)$$

$$g_2 = -\frac{1}{T} \bar{f}_1' \hat{\Omega}_{11}^{-1}$$

See the appendix for proof. Unlike the case in which factors are independent serially, the factor realizations, f_1, are weighted by the time series adjustment matrix A in both the means and the variance-covariance matrix of $\hat{a}$. Another point worth mentioning is that the variance-covariance matrix of $\hat{a}$ is no longer a product of just two terms. Instead, it is the summation of two terms: a term involving the conditional covariance matrix of the omitted factors and a term involving the covariance matrix of the disturbances. It introduces complication into the formation of test statistics which will be explained in the section after next.

Distribution of $\hat{E}_m$ The distribution of $\hat{E}_m$, unlike the *iid* case, has a nonzero mean. The estimated covariance matrix of the residuals, $\hat{\Sigma}_m = (1/T)\hat{E}'_m\hat{E}_m$, no longer follows central Wishart distribution. To see this, define $F_1 = [1_T \quad f_1]$ and $M_f = (I_T - F_1(F'_1 F_1)^{-1} F'_1)$. Distribution of $\hat{E}_m$ is given by

$$\hat{E}_m \sim N(\mu_E, \Sigma_m) \tag{3.18}$$

in which

$$\mu_E = E\left(\hat{E}_m \mid f_1\right) = M_f E\left(f_2 \mid f_1\right) B_2 \tag{3.19}$$

$$= M_f \left(\mu_2 + A\left(f_1 - \mu_1\right)\Omega_{11}^{-1}\Omega_{12}\right) B_2$$

Notice that both μ_2 and μ_1 do not lie in the span of M_f if the factor means are time varying. Even if the factors have the same mean over time, unless A is an identity matrix, terms involving f_1 are not annihilated by M_f. Therefore, $\hat{E}_m$ has a nonzero mean and the sign of its elements depends on the realization of the included factors. The covariance matrix of the disturbances is given by

$$\Sigma_m = \left[B'_2\left(\Omega_{22} - \Omega_{21}\Omega_{11}^{-1}\Omega_{12}\right)B_2\right] \otimes M_f A M_f + \Sigma \otimes M_f \tag{3.20}$$

Like the covariance matrix of the estimated intercept, Σ_a, Σ_m is a sum of two terms: a term involving the covariance matrix of the factors and a term involving the covariance matrix of the disturbances. The only difference between Σ_a and Σ_m is that both terms in Σ_m are projected off the span of the factors.

Distribution of the F test statistics   The multivariate F test statistic no longer follows a central F under the null or a noncentral F under the alternative. Because $\hat{E}_m$ has a nonzero mean, $\hat{\Sigma}_m = (1/T)\hat{E}'_m\hat{E}_m$ follows a variant of noncentral Wishart distribution (since there is no obvious way to factorize Σ_m into $\Sigma^* \otimes I_T$, the covariance matrix of the residuals does not strictly follow noncentral Wishart distribution). As a result, unlike the non-autocorrelated factor case, the density function of

$$\frac{(T - N - K)}{N} \frac{1}{1 + \bar{f}'\hat{\Omega}^{-1}\bar{f}} \hat{a}'\hat{\Sigma}^{-1}\hat{a}$$

is unknown and must be estimated via simulation.

3.3.2 Time-varying factor loadings

The last form of misspecification examined in this chapter is where factor loadings are time varying but researchers wrongly assume stationarity. A lot of work in the literature has documented the presence of time-varying risk premium, resulting in the fluctuation of parameters over time. Examples of work in this area are Jagannathan and Wang (1996), Hodrick and Zhang (2001), and Lettau and Ludvigson (2001). Suppose the expected return of assets follows the following equation,

$$E\left(r_t - r_{ft} \mid \Omega_{t-1}\right) = B_t \left(\lambda_k - r_f\right) \tag{3.21}$$

but we assume B_t is constant so that

$$E\left(r_t - r_{ft} \mid \Omega_{t-1}\right) = B \left(\lambda_k - r_f\right) \tag{3.22}$$

is falsely assumed to be true. Inference using equation (3.21) requires specification of the evolution of the factor loadings, B_t. Following Cochrane (2001), we assume the factor loading for any asset i evolves according to the following linear function,

$$a_{it}(z_{t-1}) = a_i' z_{t-1} \tag{3.23}$$
$$b_{it}(z_{t-1}) = b_i' z_{t-1}$$

where z_{t-1} is a $(q+1) \times 1$ vector of random variables and $z_{t-1} = [1, z_{1t-1}, \ldots, z_{qt-1}]'$, with q the number of scaled factors. The parameters a and b are of the same dimension $1 + q$. For example, in a single factor model ($k = 1$) and a single scaled factor case, $q = 1$, the return for any asset i is generated by the following equation,

$$r_{it} = a_{i0} + a_{i1}z_{t-1} + (b_{i0} + b_{i1}z_{t-1})f_{1t} + \varepsilon_t$$
$$= a_{i0} + a_{i1}z_{t-1} + b_{i0}f_{1t} + b_{i1}z_{t-1}f_{1t} + \varepsilon_t$$

A one factor model in the stationary case becomes a three factor model. We call z_{t-1}s the scaled factors and they can be interpreted as signals in period $t-1$ that capture changes in the factor loadings in period t. Under this assumption, factor loadings in time t varies linearly with scaled factors in period $t-1$.

We examine the case in which there is only one scaled factor with $z = (z_0, z_1, \ldots, z_{T-1})'$. For ease of exposition, we assume that the scale factor is independent of the factors, f_1. In matrix form, the return equations of the N assets are given by

$$R^e = 1_T a_0' + diag(z)1_T a_1' + f_1 B_0 + diag(z)f_1 B_1 + E \tag{3.24}$$

where $diag(z)$ represents a diagonal matrix with diagonal elements given by z. By falsely imposing stationarity on the factor loadings, the model estimated becomes

$$R^e = 1_T a_m' + f_1 B_m + E_m$$

So we are essentially dealing with the case of missing factors as in the last section. The missing factors in this case are, however, the scaled original factors. Distribution of the scaled factor, z, is given by,

$$z \sim N(\mu_z, \Phi)$$

$$\mu_z = \left(\mu_{z0}, \mu_{z1}, \ldots, \mu_{z(T-1)}\right)$$

$$\Phi = \begin{bmatrix} \phi_{00} & \cdots & \phi_{0(T-1)} \\ \vdots & \ddots & \vdots \\ \phi_{(T-1)0} & \cdots & \phi_{(T-1)(T-1)} \end{bmatrix}$$

To simplify notation and facilitate the analysis, define $Y = (1_T a_1' + f_1 B_1)$, a matrix of dimension $T \times N$. Each row of Y, Y_t, represents one time series observation of dimension $1 \times N$ and is given by

$$Y_t = a_1' + f_{1t} B_1$$

in which f_{1t} is a $1 \times k_1$ vector. Furthermore, let $G = (1_T a_1' + f_1 B_1)' diag(z) = Y' diag(z)$. The distribution of $vec(G)$ is given by

$$vec(G) \sim N(\mu_G, \Lambda)$$

$$\mu_G = vec\left(Y' diag\left(\mu_z\right)\right)$$

$$\Lambda = \begin{bmatrix} \phi_{00} Y_1' Y_1 & \phi_{01} Y_1' Y_2 & \cdots & \phi_{0(T-1)} Y_1' Y_T \\ \phi_{10} Y_2' Y_1 & \phi_{11} Y_2' Y_2 & \cdots & \phi_{1(T-1)} Y_2' Y_T \\ \vdots & & \ddots & \vdots \\ \phi_{(T-1)0} Y_T' Y_1 & \cdots & \cdots & \phi_{(T-1)(T-1)} Y_T' Y_T \end{bmatrix}$$

Distribution of $\hat{a}_m$ Distribution of the OLS estimates of the pricing errors, a_m, becomes,

$$\hat{a}_m \sim N(\mu_a, \Sigma_a) \tag{3.25}$$

$$\mu_a = a + Y' diag(\mu_z)\left(1_T g_1 + f_1 g_2'\right)$$

$$= a + \left(1_T a_1' + f_1 B_1\right) diag\left(\mu_z\right)\left(1_T g_1 + f_1 g_2'\right)$$

$$\Sigma_a = \left(\left(1_T g_1 + f_1 g_2'\right)' \otimes I_N\right) \Lambda \left(\left(1_T g_1 + f_1 g_2'\right) \otimes I_N\right)$$

$$+ \frac{1}{T}\left(1 + \bar{f}_1' \hat{\Omega}_{11}^{-1} \bar{f}_1\right) \Sigma$$

The joint mean of $\hat{a}_m$ now includes factors scaled by the mean of the scale factor in each time period. Likewise, each element in the first term of Σ_a is a function of a weighted sum of covariances of scaled factors at time t.

Distribution of $\hat{E}$ The distribution of $\hat{E}$ is given by

$$\hat{E}_m \sim N(\mu_E, \Sigma_m) \tag{3.26}$$

$$\mu_E = M_f diag(\mu_z) Y$$

$$\Sigma_m = (M_f \otimes I_N)\Lambda(M_f \otimes I_N) + M_f \otimes \Sigma$$

Means of the disturbances are given by the projection off the linear space of the included factors scaled by the mean of the scaled factor. If the mean of the scale factor is constant, μ_E is a matrix of zeros.

Distribution of the F test statistics   We discuss one special case here. One may think that if the scaled factors are time independent, distribution of test statistics should be similar to the omitted factor case discussed in section (3.3.1.1). Thus one may reach the conclusion that in the case of a time independent scaled factor, the test statistics should follow the central F distribution under the null or the noncentral F distribution under the alternative. We will examine whether this is true here. Suppose the scaled factor, z_{t-1}, has the same mean and variance and is serially uncorrelated,

$$\hat{a}_1 \sim N(\mu_{a1}, \Sigma_{a1}) \qquad (3.27)$$

$$\mu_{a1} = a + \mu_z a_1$$

$$\Sigma_{a1} = \left((1_T g_1 + f_1 g_2')' \otimes I_N \right) \Lambda^* \left((1_T g_1 + f_1 g_2') \otimes I_N \right)$$

$$\qquad + \frac{1}{T} \left(1 + \bar{f}_1' \hat{\Omega}_{11}^{-1} \bar{f}_1 \right) \Sigma$$

here μ_z is a scalar and $\Lambda^* = diag \left(\phi_{00} Y_1' Y_1, \phi_{11} Y_2' Y_2, \dots, \phi_{(T-1)(T-1)} Y_T' Y_T \right)$. The distribution of $\hat{E}$ in this case is given by

$$\hat{E}_1 \sim N(\mu_E, \Sigma_m) \qquad (3.28)$$

$$\mu_{E1} = 0_{T \times N}$$

$$\Sigma_{m1} = (M_f \otimes I_N) \Lambda^* (M_f \otimes I_N) + M_f \otimes \Sigma$$

Although $\hat{E}_1$ has a joint mean of zeros, $\hat{\Sigma}_m = (1/T)\hat{E}_m' \hat{E}_m$ does not follow central Wishart distribution, since there is no obvious way to factorize Σ_m into $I_T \otimes \tilde{\Sigma}$. Therefore, even in this simplified setting, the multivariate F test statistic does not follow a central F distribution under the null or a noncentral F distribution under the alternative.

3.4   Simulation study

3.4.1   Design

In this section, we examine the effect of omitting relevant factors on the performance of the multivariate F test and average F test. This simulation exercise uses 60 time series observations and 25 assets, as in many empirical studies. The reason for using these numbers of time series observations and assets is to maintain the stationarity of factor loadings in empirical work. We are going to examine three forms of misspecification:

1. The factors are independent serially.
2. The factors are autocorrelated.
3. The factor loadings are time varying.

For the first two forms of misspecification, values of the parameters are extracted from the Fama and French (1993) three factor model. The three factors included in

asset	a	b_{mkt}	b_{SMB}	b_{HML}
1	−0.34	1.46	1.46	−0.29
2	−0.12	1.02	1.26	0.08
3	−0.05	0.95	1.19	0.26
4	0.01	0.91	1.17	0.4
5	0	0.96	1.23	0.62
6	−0.11	1.11	1	−0.52
7	−0.01	1.06	0.98	0.01
8	0.08	1	0.88	0.26
9	0.03	0.97	0.73	0.46
10	0.02	1.09	0.89	0.7
11	−0.11	1.12	0.76	−0.38
12	0.04	1.02	0.65	0
13	−0.04	0.98	0.6	0.32
14	0.05	0.97	0.48	0.51
15	0.05	1.09	0.66	0.68
16	0.09	1.07	0.37	−0.42
17	−0.22	1.08	0.33	0.04
18	−0.08	1.04	0.29	0.3
19	0.03	1.05	0.24	0.56
20	0.13	1.18	0.41	0.74
21	0.21	0.96	−0.17	−0.46
22	−0.05	1.02	−0.12	0
23	0.13	0.98	−0.23	0.21
24	−0.05	0.99	−0.17	0.57
25	−0.16	1.06	−0.05	0.76

Table 3.2 Factor loadings of the three
factors and the pricing errors

our simulation are the excess market return, f_m, the return on size factor, f_s, and the return on book-to-market factor, f_b. Table 3.1 gives the summary statistics of the three factors[1]. Panel A gives the sample means and the sample standard errors of the three factors. The excess market return factor has the highest mean, 0.57, and it is the most volatile with standard error equaling 4.559. The size factor has the lowest sample mean, 0.078. Panel B gives the correlation between the factors. The book-to-market factor is negatively correlated with both the excess market return and the size factor. We use the sample means and sample covariances of the three factors as the parameter values of factors' means and covariances in the simulation. Values of factor loadings a, b_b, b_s, and b_m come from Fama and French (1993) and are shown in Table 3.2.

The basic asset pricing equation we examine is

$$R^e = 1_T a' + f_b b_b' + f_s b_s' + f_m b_m' + E \qquad (3.29)$$

[1] The data of the three factors was downloaded from Kenneth French's website. The sample period is January 1971 to December 2000.

As excess market return is very unlikely to be excluded from the asset pricing model, we examine two cases: (1) the book-to-market factor being omitted and (2) both the book-to-market factor and size factor are omitted. For the first case, the pricing equation under correct specification is generated by,

$$R^e = 1_T a' + f_b(cb_b)' + f_s b'_s + f_m b'_m + E \qquad (3.30)$$

We vary the constant c to examine the extent of distortion in the size and the power of the two tests when the factor omitted becomes more important. For the second case, we examine the effect of omitting both the size factor and the book-to-market factor with the three factors autocorrelated to different degrees. The details of the procedure are explained below.

3.4.2 Factors serially independent

In the case that the factors are independent serially, simulation for the multivariate F test is relatively easy: bias in the size and the power of the multivariate F test depends on the noncentrality parameter alone. For the average F test, as distribution of $\hat{a}$ and $\hat{\Sigma}$ are independent, we can generate them separately.

We consider two specifications for the distribution of residuals in this case of misspecification. They are the following,

1. Each row of E is assumed to be *iid* $N(0, I_N)$.
2. Each row of E is assumed to be *iid* $N(0, \Sigma)$ where

$$
\Sigma = \begin{bmatrix}
1 & \rho & \cdots & \rho \\
\rho & 1 & & \vdots \\
\vdots & & \ddots & \rho \\
\rho & \cdots & \rho & 1
\end{bmatrix}
$$

The covariance of asset i and asset j, $i \neq j$, is equal to ρ and is assumed to be equal across assets. We consider four values of ρ. They are 0, 0.1, 0.5 and 0.8.

The multivariate F test The distribution of the multivariate F test is determined by the noncentrality parameter δ. The noncentrality parameter δ is given by

$$\delta = \varphi a' \Sigma^{-1} a$$

and with φ defined as

$$\varphi = \frac{T}{1 + \bar{f}' \hat{\Omega}^{-1} \bar{f}}$$

There are six possible values of the noncentrality parameter given that a set of relevant non-autocorrelated factors is omitted. φ is assumed to be the same in all six cases. Under the null hypothesis, the multivariate F test follows a noncentral F distribution only if the omitted factors have positive means. We do not examine the situation in which the omitted factor means are zero because the test statistics distribution in that case follows a central F distribution under the null. The only two possibilities that the multivariate F follows a noncentral F distribution under the null are the following:

1. The set of factors under correct specification are correlated with positive means. The noncentrality parameter δ is given by

$$\delta = \varphi \left(B'_2 \mu_2 - B'_2 \Omega_{21} \Omega_{11}^{-1} \mu_1 \right)' \left[B'_2 \left(\Omega_{22} - \Omega_{21} \Omega_{11}^{-1} \Omega_{12} \right) B_2 + \Sigma \right]^{-1}$$
$$\times \left(B'_2 \mu_2 - B'_2 \Omega_{21} \Omega_{11}^{-1} \mu_1 \right) \tag{3.31}$$

2. The set of factors under correct specification are orthogonal to each other with positive means. The noncentrality parameter δ is given by

$$\delta = \varphi \left(B'_2 \mu_2 \right)' \left[B'_2 B_2 + \Sigma \right]^{-1} \left(B'_2 \mu_2 \right) \tag{3.32}$$

Under the alternative hypothesis, the multivariate F test follows noncentral F distribution and the four cases considered in this chapter are:

1. The set of factors under correct specification are orthogonal with zero means. The noncentrality parameter δ is given by

$$\delta = \varphi a' \left[B'_2 B_2 + \Sigma \right]^{-1} a \tag{3.33}$$

2. The set of factors under correct specification are correlated with zero means. The noncentrality parameter δ is given by

$$\delta = \varphi a' \left[B'_2 \left(\Omega_{22} - \Omega_{21} \Omega_{11}^{-1} \Omega_{12} \right) B_2 + \Sigma \right]^{-1} a \tag{3.34}$$

3. The set of factors under correct specification are correlated with positive means. The noncentrality parameter δ is given by

$$\delta = \varphi \left(a + B'_2 \mu_2 - B'_2 \Omega_{21} \Omega_{11}^{-1} \mu_1 \right)' \left[B'_2 \left(\Omega_{22} - \Omega_{21} \Omega_{11}^{-1} \Omega_{12} \right) B_2 + \Sigma \right]^{-1}$$
$$\times \left(a + B'_2 \mu_2 - B'_2 \Omega_{21} \Omega_{11}^{-1} \mu_1 \right) \tag{3.35}$$

4. The set of factors under correct specification are orthogonal with positive means. The noncentrality parameter δ is given by

$$\delta = \varphi \left(a + B'_2 \mu_2 \right)' \left[B'_2 B_2 + \Sigma \right]^{-1} \left(a + B'_2 \mu_2 \right) \tag{3.36}$$

Each distribution is simulated by 10 000 replications. For replication, we first calculate the value of δ from the parameter values. Then one noncentral variable $x(\delta)$ is generated by

$$x(\delta) = \frac{\sum_{i=1}^{N} \chi^2(1, \delta/N)/N}{\sum_{j=1}^{T-N-2} \chi^2(1)/T - N - 2}$$

with $N = 25$ and $T = 60$.

The average F test Corresponding to the case of the multivariate F test, we can study four cases each under the null and under the alternative. Each case is described by a pair of distributions, $\hat{a}_m$ and $\hat{\Sigma}_m$. Unlike the multivariate F test, we will study two cases in which the factor means are zero. This is because even if factor means are zero under the null, the disturbance covariance matrix is not diagonal. The factor loadings of the omitted factors affect the disturbance covariance matrix.

Below are the four cases that we are going to study. To avoid repetition, it is understood that under null a is equal to an $N \times 1$ vector of zeros.

1. The set of factors under correct specification have zero means and they are correlated

$$\hat{a}_m \sim N\left(a, \frac{1}{T}\left(1 + \bar{f}_1'\hat{\Omega}_{11}^{-1}\bar{f}_1\right)\left[B_2'\left(\Omega_{22} - \Omega_{21}\Omega_{11}^{-1}\Omega_{12}\right)B_2 + \Sigma\right]\right)$$

$$T\hat{\Sigma}_m \sim W\left(T - K_1, \left(B_2'\left(\Omega_{22} - \Omega_{21}\Omega_{11}^{-1}\Omega_{12}\right)B_2 + \Sigma\right)\right)$$

2. The set of factors under correct specification have zero means and they are orthogonal

$$\hat{a}_m \sim N\left(a, \frac{1}{T}\left(1 + \bar{f}_1'\hat{\Omega}_{11}^{-1}\bar{f}_1\right)\left[B_2'B_2 + \Sigma\right]\right)$$

$$T\hat{\Sigma}_m \sim W\left(T - K_1, \left(B_2'B_2 + \Sigma\right)\right)$$

3. The set of factor means under correct specification have nonzero means and they are correlated

$$\hat{a}_m \sim N\left(a + B_2'\mu_2 - B_2'\Omega_{21}\Omega_{11}^{-1}\mu_1, \frac{1}{T}\left(1 + \bar{f}_1'\hat{\Omega}_{11}^{-1}\bar{f}_1\right)\right.$$
$$\left. \times \left[B_2'\left(\Omega_{22} - \Omega_{21}\Omega_{11}^{-1}\Omega_{12}\right)B_2 + \Sigma\right]\right)$$

$$T\hat{\Sigma}_m \sim W\left(T - K_1, \left(B_2'\left(\Omega_{22} - \Omega_{21}\Omega_{11}^{-1}\Omega_{12}\right)B_2 + \Sigma\right)\right)$$

4. The set of factor means under correct specification have nonzero means and they are orthogonal

$$\hat{a}_m \sim N\left(a + B_2'\mu_2, \frac{1}{T}\left(1 + \bar{f}_1'\hat{\Omega}_{11}^{-1}\bar{f}_1\right)\left[B_2'B_2 + \Sigma\right]\right)$$

$$T\hat{\Sigma}_m \sim W\left(T - K_1, \left(B_2'B_2 + \Sigma\right)\right)$$

Each replication is based on a draw from $\hat{a}_m$ and a draw from $T\hat{\Sigma}_m$. Each element of $\hat{a}_m$ is squared. Diagonal elements of $T\hat{\Sigma}_m$ are divided by $T - K_1 - 1$ to form $\hat{\sigma}_j^2$. One replication of the average F test is generated by

$$AF = \sum_{i=1}^{N} T\left(1 + \bar{f}'\hat{\Omega}^{-1}\bar{f}\right)^{-1}\frac{\hat{a}_i}{\hat{\sigma}_j^2}$$

Each case is simulated by 10 000 replications.

3.4.3   Factors autocorrelated

For factors which are autocorrelated, the conditional distribution of $\hat{a}_m$ is a function of the realization of the included factors, f_1. We use the average of four five-year monthly samples from January 1981 to December 2000 as realization of f_1 in the simulation. Two cases of f_1 are considered. In the first case, f_1 includes both the excess market return factor and the size factor. In the second case, f_1 includes only the excess market return factor.

One replication of $\hat{a}_m$ and $\hat{\Sigma}_m$ is obtained by first generating a replication of omitted factors from its conditional distribution as in equation (3.37),

$$vec(f_2) \mid vec(f_1) \sim N\left(\mu_{2|1}, \Omega_{2|1}\right)$$

$$\mu_{2|1} = vec(\mu_2) + \left(\Omega_{21}\Omega_{11}^{-1} \otimes A\right)\left(vec(f_1) - vec(\mu_1)\right)$$

$$\Omega_{2|1} = \left(\Omega_{22} - \Omega_{21}\Omega_{11}^{-1}\Omega_{12}\right) \otimes A$$

where f_1 indicates the included factors and A is specified as

$$A = \begin{bmatrix} 1 & \rho & \rho^2 & \cdots & \rho^{T-1} \\ \rho & 1 & \rho & & \rho^{T-2} \\ \vdots & & \ddots & & \vdots \\ \rho^{T-2} & & & \ddots & \rho \\ \rho^{T-1} & \rho^{T-2} & \cdots & \rho & 1 \end{bmatrix}$$

We consider four values of the autocorrelation coefficient, ρ: 0, 0.1, 0.3 and 0.5 so that we can examine the effect of omitting autocorrelated factors on the size and the power of the test. A replication of excess return of N asset, R^e, is generated by the equation,

$$R^e = 1_T a' + f_1 b_1' + f_2 b_2' + E$$

in which elements in E are assumed to be normally distributed and independent of each other. We get the estimates $\hat{a}_m$ and $\hat{\Sigma}_m$ from the misspecified equation

$$R^e = 1_T a_m' + f_1 b_1' + E_m$$

We can then construct one replication of the multivariate F test statistics by the equation

$$W = \frac{(T - N - k_1)}{N} \frac{1}{1 + \bar{f}_1' \hat{\Omega}_{11}^{-1} \bar{f}_1} \hat{a}_m' \hat{\Sigma}_m^{-1} \hat{a}_m$$

and one replication of the average F test statistics by the equation

$$AF = \sum_{i=1}^{N} \frac{T}{N} \left(1 + \bar{f}_1' \hat{\Omega}_{11}^{-1} \bar{f}_1\right)^{-1} \frac{\hat{a}_i}{\hat{\sigma}_j^2}$$

where $\hat{\sigma}_j^2$ is the jth diagonal element of $\hat{\Sigma}_m$ scaled by a factor of $T/(T - k_1 - 1)$. This process is repeated 10 000 times.

	r^e_{mt}	cay
Correlation Matrix		
r^e_{mt}	1	0.151577
cay	0.151577	1
Univariate summary statistics		
Mean	0.57	0.381
Standard errors	4.559	0.015
Autocorrelation	0.045	0.879

Table 3.3 Summary statistics of the scaled factor

3.4.4 Time-varying factor loadings

The scaled factor that we use is the log of the consumption–wealth ratio as in Lettau and Ludvigson (2001). Following Lettau and Ludvigson (2001), we denote the log of the consumption–wealth ratio at time t as cay_t. The summary statistics of cay are given in Table 3.3. The sampling period is the same as the other three factors used in this study: from January 1971 to December 2000. The sample mean of excess market return is slightly higher than cay but the standard deviation is much higher, indicating that the excess market return is more volatile than cay. cay exhibits a much higher degree of first order autocorrelation, 0.8721, than that of the excess market return, 0.0496.

In our simulation study, the return of asset i is generated by

$$r^e_{it} = \alpha_{it} + f^e_{mt}\beta_{imt} + e_{it}$$

where

$$\beta_{imt} = b_{i0} + b_{i1}cay_{t-1}$$
$$\alpha_{it} = a_{i0} + a_{i1}cay_{t-1}$$

so that the return of asset i is given by

$$r^e_{it} = a_{i0} + a_{i1}cay_{t-1} + (b_{i0} + b_{i1}cay_{t-1})f^e_{mt} + e_{it}$$

The disturbance, e_{it}, is assumed to be a normally distributed *iid* random variable. For the parameter values of the factor loadings of the N assets, a_{i0}, a_{i1}, b_{i0} and b_{i1}, we use the same factor loadings as in the case of the previous two forms of misspecification. The purpose of using the same factor loadings is that it facilitates comparison across different forms of misspecification. We set $a_{i0} = a$, $b_{i0} = b_m$, $a_{i1} = b_s$ and $b_{i1} = b_b$. In this way, the factor loading of excess market return, b_{i0}, is the same as that in Fama and French's three factors specification.

The simulations of the distributions of the multivariate F test statistics and the average F test statistics under the null hypothesis and the alternative hypothesis are similar to the autocorrelated factor case. The only difference is that the conditioning factor is generated independently of the excess market return factor. The misspecified equation includes only the excess market return, which is the average of four five-year monthly samples from January 1981 to December 2000. Two specifications of *cay* are examined: (i) *cay* is assumed to be serially independent,

$$cay_t = c\mu + \xi_t$$

The disturbance, ξ_t, is normally distributed with standard deviation equal to the sample counterpart of *cay*, 0.015. The value of μ is set equal to the sample mean of *cay*. We vary the constant, c, to examine the effect of a larger scaled factor mean on the size and the power of the two tests. Five values of c are considered: 0, 0.1, 0.3, 0.5 and 1. (ii) Because the standard error of *cay* is small compared to the standard error of the excess market return, we enlarge the standard error of *cay* to examine the effect of a more volatile scale factor. In this case, *cay* is also assumed to be serially independent,

$$cay_t = \mu + \nu\xi_t$$

The disturbance, ξ_t, is normally distributed with standard error, ν. Six values of ν are considered: 0.015, 0.075, 0.15, 0.75, 1.5 and 3. (iii) *cay* follows the univariate AR(1) process. Five AR(1) processes are considered. In each AR(1) process of *cay*, we use a different value of the mean and vary the value of the autocorrelation coefficient to examine the effect of autocorrelation. Five values of the mean are considered: the sample mean of *cay* is multiplied by the constants 0, 0.1, 0.3, 0.5 and 1 so that $\mu_1 = 0 \cdot \mu, \mu_2 = 0.1 \cdot \mu, \ldots, \mu_5 = \mu$. More specifically, the *i*th AR(1) process is generated by the following equation

$$cay_t = (1 - \rho)\mu_i + \rho cay_{t-1} + \xi_t,$$

where ρ is the autocorrelation coefficient. The values of ρ considered are: 0, 0.1, 0.3 and 0.879. The last value, 0.879, is the sample autocorrelation coefficient of *cay*. Each simulation is generated by 10 000 replications.

3.4.5   Simulation results

3.4.5.1   Factors serially independent

Book-to-market factor missing   Table 3.4 shows the size and power of the multivariate F test and the average F test with the book-to-market factor omitted and the covariance of disturbances an identity matrix. The value of the factor loadings of the book-to-market factor is multiplied by c, where c takes the values 0.1, 1, 2, 5 and 10. Under the null hypothesis, the size of the multivariate F test is between 5% and 7.76%. The average F test exhibits a much larger size distortion. With the three factors' means set to zero, the size of the average F test when factor loadings are large is about 4 times larger than that in the correctly specified model. With nonzero factor means, the size distortion is even larger: in the case with correlated factors, the size of the average F test is 61.46% when the book-to-market factor loading is enlarged by tenfold.

   Under the alternative hypothesis, the power of the multivariate F test is quite stable with the book-to-market factor omitted from estimation. It stays within the range

	Null				Alternative			
	F test		AF test		F test		AF test	
	Test statistics	Size	Test statistics	Size	Test statistics	Power	Test statistics	Power
Panel A: $\mu = 0_k$, factors correlated								
$c = 0.1$			1.61	5.94	3.10	42.77	2.70	66.25
$c = 1$			2.48	16.16	3.10	42.56	3.02	33.83
$c = 2$			3.17	18.61	3.10	42.56	3.42	25.15
$c = 5$			3.49	20.29	3.10	42.56	3.64	23.12
$c = 10$			3.56	20.29	3.10	42.56	3.64	21.62
Panel B: $\mu = \bar{f}$, factors correlated								
$c = 0.1$	1.87	5.42	1.67	7.70	3.17	45.64	2.76	70.48
$c = 1$	2.00	7.64	5.64	54.28	3.26	48.91	6.52	71.32
$c = 2$	2.00	7.72	7.59	58.34	3.25	48.84	8.15	66.29
$c = 5$	2.00	7.75	8.89	59.98	3.25	48.74	9.25	62.40
$c = 10$	2.00	7.76	9.33	61.46	3.25	48.69	9.42	60.64
Panel C: $\mu = 0$, factors orthogonal								
$c = 0.1$			1.60	5.55	3.10	42.75	2.69	66.62
$c = 1$			2.62	17.05	3.10	42.56	3.10	31.51
$c = 2$			3.20	18.84	3.10	42.56	3.41	24.60
$c = 5$			3.53	20.14	3.10	42.56	3.64	23.04
$c = 10$			3.70	20.35	3.10	42.56	3.72	21.57
Panel D: $\mu = \bar{f}$, factors orthogonal								
$c = 0.1$	1.84	5.00	1.64	6.71	3.14	44.39	2.72	68.84
$c = 1$	1.89	5.79	4.26	33.72	3.16	45.19	4.92	49.96
$c = 2$	1.89	5.79	5.27	37.38	3.16	45.09	5.78	44.32
$c = 5$	1.89	5.79	5.98	39.12	3.16	45.03	6.12	40.68
$c = 10$	1.89	5.79	6.51	39.48	3.16	45.01	6.19	38.91

Table 3.4 Size and power of tests with HML omitted and Σ an identity matrix

of 40% to 50% for all four values of c. The power of the average F test in general drops with larger omitted factor loading. With larger c, the factor loadings of the omitted factor dominate and the power of the test converges towards that of the size of the test.

Table 3.5 shows the size and power of the two tests with the book-to-market factor omitted and covariance of disturbances correlated to different extents. The distortion in size of the multivariate F test is a little larger than the case with uncorrelated disturbances. The size of the multivariate F test is between 6.13% to 8.02%. For the average F test, the distortion in size is much greater than the multivariate F test. The distortion of size is greatest when the factors have nonzero means and are correlated. The size of the average F test is between 53% and 55%.

	Null				Alternative			
	F test		AF test		F test		AF test	
	Test statistics	Size	Test statistics	Size	Test statistics	Power	Test statistics	Power
Factors correlated, $\mu = 0_k$								
$\rho = 0$			2.51	15.91	3.12	42.78	3.04	33.25
$\rho = 0.1$			2.58	16.73	3.21	45.92	3.04	32.62
$\rho = 0.5$			2.83	18.55	4.20	77.77	3.29	33.57
$\rho = 0.8$			3.09	20.28	7.56	99.77	3.65	33.14
Factors correlated, $\mu = \bar{f}$								
$\rho = 0$	2.02	7.93	5.73	54.11	3.28	48.64	6.44	70.72
$\rho = 0.1$	2.02	7.93	5.58	53.50	3.39	52.76	6.42	71.61
$\rho = 0.5$	2.02	7.98	5.94	53.55	4.39	81.85	6.56	70.12
$\rho = 0.8$	2.03	8.02	6.14	53.60	7.74	99.81	6.73	69.43
Factors orthogonal, $\mu = 0_k$								
$\rho = 0$			2.70	16.99	3.12	42.78	3.10	30.47
$\rho = 0.1$			2.68	17.00	3.21	45.92	3.15	30.88
$\rho = 0.5$			2.86	19.83	4.20	77.77	3.32	32.62
$\rho = 0.8$			3.20	21.22	7.56	99.77	3.59	31.99
Factors orthogonal, $\mu = \bar{f}$								
$\rho = 0$	1.93	6.13	4.33	34.70	3.19	45.10	4.93	49.64
$\rho = 0.1$	1.93	6.13	4.42	34.99	3.28	48.52	4.96	51.27
$\rho = 0.5$	1.93	6.14	4.43	35.09	4.28	79.55	5.02	51.48
$\rho = 0.8$	1.93	6.15	4.74	36.05	7.63	99.79	5.21	51.23

Table 3.5 Size and power of tests with HML omitted and non-diagonal elements in Σ positive

The power of the multivariate F test seems to be sensitive to changes in the correlation of disturbance. The power of the multivariate F test increases quite quickly as the disturbances become more correlated with each other. On the other hand, the power of the average F test remains more or less the same in each case.

Book-to-market factor and the size factor missing Intuitively, if more factors are omitted from the estimation, we would expect the magnitude of specification bias to be larger. However, it does not seem to be true in every circumstance. Comparing Table 3.5 with Table 3.6, the power of the multivariate F test with two factors missing is lower than that with just one factor missing. The same applies to the average F test. It seems that the interaction of the factor loadings of the omitted factors of the N assets cancelled out some effect on the power of the test.

3.4.5.2 Factors autocorrelated

Book-to-market factor missing Table 3.7 shows the size and the power of tests in the case that the book-to-market factor is omitted and the factors under correct specification are autocorrelated. The size of the multivariate F test increases as the

	Null				Alternative			
	F test		AF test		F test		AF test	
	Test statistics	Size	Test statistics	Size	Test statistics	Power	Test statistics	Power
Factors correlated, $\mu = 0_k$								
$\rho = 0$			2.94	19.74	2.98	36.61	3.03	24.36
$\rho = 0.1$			2.96	20.03	3.04	40.91	3.10	24.10
$\rho = 0.5$			3.05	20.86	3.96	71.84	3.25	23.80
$\rho = 0.8$			3.09	20.34	6.91	99.43	3.27	24.49
Factors correlated, $\mu = \bar{f}$								
$\rho = 0$	2.02	7.62	4.09	41.91	3.10	42.34	4.15	45.49
$\rho = 0.1$	2.02	7.99	4.13	42.62	3.18	47.14	4.11	45.71
$\rho = 0.5$	2.01	7.98	4.19	41.60	4.08	75.80	4.27	44.57
$\rho = 0.8$	2.01	7.83	4.30	40.42	7.20	99.68	4.33	45.00
Factors orthogonal, $\mu = 0_k$								
$\rho = 0$			2.93	20.04	2.94	36.80	3.11	24.06
$\rho = 0.1$			2.89	19.49	3.06	40.75	3.07	23.52
$\rho = 0.5$			2.96	20.70	3.93	72.46	3.14	23.90
$\rho = 0.8$			3.08	20.65	6.95	99.54	3.23	24.57
Factors orthogonal, $\mu = \bar{f}$								
$\rho = 0$	1.94	6.19	3.91	33.23	3.02	39.71	3.80	35.50
$\rho = 0.1$	1.93	6.42	3.68	32.78	3.13	43.80	3.79	35.70
$\rho = 0.5$	1.93	6.20	3.80	32.78	4.05	72.78	3.84	34.69
$\rho = 0.8$	1.95	6.54	3.86	33.03	7.08	99.52	3.99	35.94

Table 3.6 Size and power of tests with HML and SMB omitted and non-diagonal elements in Σ positive

autocorrelation coefficient increases. With $\rho = 0.5$ in the case of zero factor means, the size of the multivariate F test is 9%, which is 4% higher than the correct size. Together with the effect of nonzero factor means, the size of the multivariate F test goes up to 11.6% with $\rho = 0.5$. For the average F test, the size of the test goes up from 15.94% to 44.64% as ρ increases from 0 to 0.5 with zero factor means. With nonzero factor means, the variation in the size of the average F test is much smaller: the size of the test goes up from about 53% to about 55%.

The general pattern of results of the power of the two tests is the same as that of the size of tests. The power of the multivariate F test is greater as ρ enlarges: the test power in the case of zero factor means increases by nearly 6% and the test power in the case of nonzero factor means increases by nearly 4% as ρ increases from 0 to 0.5. For the average F test, the power of the test in the case of nonzero factor means again does not vary much as factors become more autocorrelated: the power of the test for the four autocorrelation coefficients is between 68% to 71%.

Book-to-market factor and the size factor missing   Table 3.8 shows the size and power of tests in the case that two factors are omitted and the factors under correct

	Null				Alternative			
	F test		AF test		F test		AF test	
	Test statistics	Size	Test statistics	Size	Test statistics	Power	Test statistics	Power
$\mu = 0_k$								
$\rho = 0$	1.85	5.04	2.53	15.94	3.11	42.94	3.05	33.12
$\rho = 0.1$	1.88	5.46	2.89	19.43	3.12	43.65	3.33	36.30
$\rho = 0.3$	1.92	6.02	4.12	29.53	3.14	44.61	4.56	45.65
$\rho = 0.5$	2.07	9.00	7.14	44.64	3.30	48.78	7.57	58.14
$\mu = \bar{f}$								
$\rho = 0$	2.01	7.95	5.67	53.63	3.27	48.94	6.47	70.86
$\rho = 0.1$	2.04	8.31	6.14	54.00	3.31	48.65	6.97	70.35
$\rho = 0.3$	2.09	9.36	7.42	53.95	3.35	50.34	8.23	68.78
$\rho = 0.5$	2.21	11.59	9.38	55.14	3.45	52.59	10.11	69.00

Table 3.7 Size and power of tests with HML omitted and the three factors autocorrelated

specification are autocorrelated. The effect of autocorrelation seems to become bigger as more factors are omitted. The size of the multivariate F test is more than two times larger with $\rho = 0.5$ than the size of the test with $\rho = 0$. The increase in the size of the average F test is also larger than the case with just one omitted factor. In the nonzero factor mean case, the size of the average F test goes up from 42.54% ($\rho = 0$) to 61.56% ($\rho = 0.5$) with two factors being omitted while the size varies between 53% to about 55% with only one factor being omitted.

The power of the two tests with two omitted factors is shown in the last four columns of Table 3.8. The power of the multivariate F test with two omitted factors is lower in both cases than the power of the test with only one omitted factor. Another feature is that the increase in the power of the multivariate F test in the two omitted factor case is greater than that in the one omitted factor case. For example, in the zero mean factor case, the increase in the power of the multivariate F test is about 11% in the two omitted factor case while the increase in power is about 6% in the one omitted factor case as the autocorrelation coefficient increases. The power of the average F test is also more responsive to changes in autocorrelation in the two omitted factor case than in the single omitted factor case. For example, in the nonzero factor means case, the power of the average F test increases from 45.68% to 64.89% in the two omitted factor case while that of the single omitted factor case varies between 68% to 71%.

3.4.5.3 Time-varying factor loadings

Table 3.9 shows the size and power of test with non-autocorrelated scaled factor, *cay*, being omitted. It shows the effect of a larger mean of *cay*, holding standard deviation equal to the value of its counterpart. The size of both tests increases as the mean of

	Null				Alternative			
	F test		AF test		F test		AF test	
	Test statistics	Size	Test statistics	Size	Test statistics	Power	Test statistics	Power
$\mu = 0_k$								
$\rho = 0$	1.85	5.12	2.82	19.63	2.94	35.92	3.04	23.55
$\rho = 0.1$	1.88	5.58	3.35	24.97	2.98	37.48	3.58	29.72
$\rho = 0.3$	2.00	7.61	5.17	40.17	3.04	40.35	5.18	44.38
$\rho = 0.5$	2.31	13.52	8.60	60.14	3.31	47.71	8.58	64.05
$\mu = \bar{f}$								
$\rho = 0$	2.01	7.67	4.13	42.54	3.10	42.96	4.14	45.68
$\rho = 0.1$	2.04	8.68	4.66	45.94	3.14	43.84	4.71	49.50
$\rho = 0.3$	2.12	9.99	6.07	53.28	3.24	46.66	6.10	56.21
$\rho = 0.5$	2.33	14.10	8.85	61.56	3.37	49.81	8.81	64.89

Table 3.8 Size and power of tests with HML and SMB omitted and the three factors autocorrelated

	Null				Alternative			
	F test		AF test		F test		AF test	
	Test statistics	Size	Test statistics	Size	Test statistics	Power	Test statistics	Power
$\mu_1 = 0$	1.97	6.84	1.71	9.46	3.30	49.52	2.89	76.85
$\mu_1 = 0.1\mu_{cay}$	2.02	8.07	1.80	12.88	3.13	44.77	2.75	71.29
$\mu_1 = 0.3\mu_{cay}$	2.72	28.64	2.39	49.39	3.39	52.16	2.95	78.71
$\mu_1 = 0.5\mu_{cay}$	3.98	72.55	3.52	93.77	4.21	77.74	3.64	96.11
$\mu_1 = 1\mu_{cay}$	9.83	100.00	8.23	100.00	8.98	99.99	7.49	100.00

Table 3.9 Size and power of test with serially independent scaled factor omitted: the effect of scale factor mean

the scaled factor is multiplied by a larger number. The distortion in the size of the multivariate F test, 6.84%, is not big with the mean of *cay* set equal to zero but it quickly increases as the mean approaches its sample value. With the scaled mean value equal to half of the sample value, the size of the multivariate F test goes up to 72.55%. The pattern of distortion in the size of the average F test is similar to the case of the multivariate F test, though the average F test exhibits a larger size than the multivariate F test for all values of the mean considered. The power of both tests also increases as

	Null				Alternative			
	F test		AF test		F test		AF test	
	Test statistics	Size	Test statistics	Size	Test statistics	Power	Test statistics	Power
$\delta_1 = 0.015$	9.83	100.00	8.23	100.00	8.98	99.99	7.49	100.00
$\delta_2 = 0.075$	9.11	99.98	8.15	100.00	8.34	99.98	7.44	100.00
$\delta_3 = 0.15$	7.46	99.78	8.11	100.00	7.02	99.65	7.36	100.00
$\delta_4 = 0.7$	3.05	37.63	6.48	94.18	3.81	64.68	5.77	93.52
$\delta_5 = 1.5$	2.34	14.25	4.95	59.60	3.34	49.99	4.57	57.08
$\delta_6 = 3$	2.08	9.27	4.01	35.08	3.19	45.58	3.86	33.29

Table 3.10 Size and power of test with serially independent scaled factor omitted: the effect of scale factor volatility

the mean of *cay* becomes larger, with the power of the average F test greater than the multivariate F test for all mean values considered.

Table 3.10 shows the effect of a more volatile *cay*. As *cay* becomes more volatile, the size and power of both tests drop. Recalling that v is the standard error of *cay*, with $v = 3$, which is near to the standard error of the book-to-market factor, the size and power of the multivariate F test is 9.27% and 45.58% respectively. Both the size and power are larger than the case with two factors being omitted and the disturbance covariance an identity matrix, with the size equal 7.62% and the power equal to 42.34%. However, the size and power of the average F test with $v = 3$ is 35.08% and 33.29%. Both values are lower than that in the case with two factors being omitted and disturbance covariance an identity matrix with size equal to 41.91% and power equal to 45.49%. This finding suggests that omitting the scale factor tends to enlarge the size and power on the multivariate F test but shrink the size and power of the average F test.

Table 3.11 shows the size and the power of tests with correlated *cay*. The first panel shows the case in which the AR(1) process is generated with mean equal to zero. Unlike the case with autocorrelated factors, both the size and the power of the two tests, with zero mean, do not increase as the autocorrelation coefficient, ρ, increases: the size of the multivariate F test stays close to 6% while the power of test stays near to 50%. As the mean of *cay* increases to $\mu_3 = 0.3\mu$ and $\mu_4 = 0.5\mu$, the size of both the multivariate F test and the average F test decreases as the scaled factor becomes more autocorrelated. This result is contrary to the result of omitting an autocorrelated factor, in which case the size of the test increases as ρ increases. The power of the multivariate F test in these two cases ($\mu_3 = 0.3\mu$ and $\mu_4 = 0.5\mu$) also decrease as ρ increases. For the last panel in which the mean of the scaled factor is equal to the sample mean, the size and the power of the two tests for all values of ρ are all higher than 99%. It seems that the mean of the scaled factor accentuates the effect of ρ and keeps the size and power of tests large as ρ increases.

Another feature of Table 3.11 is that the size and the power of the average F test is greater than that of the multivariate F test. The size of the average F test is around

	Null				Alternative			
	F test		AF test		F test		AF test	
	Test statistics	Size	Test statistics	Size	Test statistics	Power	Test statistics	Power
$\mu_1 = 0$								
$\rho_{cay} = 0$	1.93	6.34	1.72	9.62	3.28	49.94	2.88	76.41
$\rho_{cay} = 0.1$	1.94	6.27	1.72	9.40	3.35	50.47	2.90	76.37
$\rho_{cay} = 0.3$	1.93	6.59	1.76	10.54	3.31	49.08	2.87	77.23
$\rho_{cay} = 0.5$	1.95	6.44	1.72	9.49	3.30	50.06	2.88	76.31
$\rho_{cay} = 0.879$	1.95	6.70	1.74	10.15	3.35	50.05	2.91	76.81
$\mu_2 = 0.1\mu_{cay}$								
$\rho_{cay} = 0$	2.06	8.52	1.80	12.52	3.17	43.75	2.77	70.61
$\rho_{cay} = 0.1$	2.03	8.10	1.81	13.31	3.13	43.96	2.78	70.80
$\rho_{cay} = 0.3$	2.02	7.99	1.79	12.50	3.18	44.30	2.75	71.13
$\rho_{cay} = 0.5$	2.06	8.76	1.80	13.49	3.17	44.34	2.77	70.58
$\rho_{cay} = 0.879$	2.01	7.78	1.80	12.54	3.18	44.37	2.76	71.76
$\mu_3 = 0.3\mu_{cay}$								
$\rho_{cay} = 0$	2.70	28.24	2.39	48.33	3.37	51.76	2.93	78.37
$\rho_{cay} = 0.1$	2.70	27.42	2.39	48.50	3.31	51.80	2.93	78.33
$\rho_{cay} = 0.3$	2.70	27.64	2.37	47.81	3.41	52.14	2.93	77.11
$\rho_{cay} = 0.5$	2.66	27.06	2.37	47.36	3.39	51.68	2.94	78.46
$\rho_{cay} = 0.879$	2.50	21.73	2.25	38.67	3.28	48.43	2.84	75.45
$\mu_4 = 0.5\mu_{cay}$								
$\rho_{cay} = 0$	4.00	72.72	3.49	93.89	4.22	76.84	3.65	95.95
$\rho_{cay} = 0.1$	3.99	72.73	3.49	93.48	4.24	77.88	3.67	95.78
$\rho_{cay} = 0.3$	4.00	72.29	3.46	93.38	4.18	76.82	3.62	95.75
$\rho_{cay} = 0.5$	3.96	70.10	3.45	92.59	4.17	76.79	3.58	94.64
$\rho_{cay} = 0.879$	3.45	56.74	3.14	84.58	3.82	68.16	3.37	91.74
$\mu_5 = \mu_{cay}$								
$\rho_{cay} = 0$	9.81	100.00	8.21	100.00	8.99	99.97	7.57	100.00
$\rho_{cay} = 0.1$	9.90	100.00	8.20	100.00	8.83	99.99	7.52	100.00
$\rho_{cay} = 0.3$	9.76	99.99	8.10	100.00	8.84	100.00	7.43	100.00
$\rho_{cay} = 0.5$	9.37	99.99	7.98	100.00	8.54	99.97	7.32	100.00
$\rho_{cay} = 0.879$	7.29	99.82	6.74	100.00	6.82	99.60	6.22	100.00

Table 3.11 Size and power of test with scaled factor omitted: scaled factor autocorrelated

3% higher than that of the multivariate F test while the power of the average F test is around 25% higher than its counterpart for all autocorrelation values.

3.5 Conclusion

This chapter is the first systematic study of misspecification in the linear pricing model. In particular, it analyzes the effect of omitting relevant factors which are autocorrelated and the effect of assuming time-varying factor loadings to be constant. Under these two forms of misspecification, the test statistic does not follow an F distribution under the null or a noncentral F distribution under the alternative. In the case that a set of autocorrelated factors are omitted, the size of the test is increasing in the degree of autocorrelation. The test is biased towards overrejecting the null hypothesis.

In the case that the time-varying factor loadings are assumed constant, three cases are analyzed. In the first case, the effect of the volatility of the scaled factor is studied. We find that a more volatile scaled factor leads to a drop in the power of the test. Thus the test's ability to distinguish between the null and the alternative decreases as the volatility of the scaled factor increases. In the second case, the effect of the mean of the scaled factor is examined. As the mean of the scaled factor increases, the size of the test rises rapidly. As a result, the test is biased towards rejecting the null. In the third case, the effect of a more autocorrelated scaled factor is analyzed. It is found that both the size and power of test, unlike the case of omitting autocorrelated factors, are not too sensitive to the changes of autocorrelation. Both the size and the power of test in this case are driven by the mean of the scaled factor. The test, as in the second case, tends to overreject the null.

The findings indicate that, contrary to the practice in the literature, the use of a noncentral F distribution to evaluate the extent of misspecification is not correct. The implication is that if we suspect a set of factors are omitted and we want to evaluate the extent of misspecification, we should check for the presence of autocorrelation of factors and the stationarity of factor loadings. If they exist, we should then use a simulation-based approach, as this chapter does, to evaluate the effect of misspecification.

Lastly, this chapter studies the effect of misspecification on the average F test. It is found that the distortion in the average F test is more severe than the multivariate F test under misspecification. Thus, although the average F test offers a way out of the degree of freedom constraint, it should be applied cautiously. In particular, it would be desirable to find a way to justify theoretically the factors used in the return equations. This would in turn justify the diagonality assumption of the covariance of disturbances matrix, which is of critical importance in implementing the average F test.

Appendix: Proof of proposition 3.1 and proposition 3.2

The distribution of the omitted set of relevant factors conditional on the set of included factors is given by

$$vec(f_2) \mid vec(f_1) \sim N\left(\mu_{2|1}, \Omega_{2|1}\right) \tag{3.37}$$

$$\mu_{2|1} = vec(\mu_2) + \left(\Omega_{21}\Omega_{11}^{-1} \otimes A\right)\left(vec(f_1) - vec(\mu_1)\right)$$

$$\Omega_{2|1} = \left(\Omega_{22} - \Omega_{21}\Omega_{11}^{-1}\Omega_{12}\right) \otimes A$$

in which A is a matrix of dimension $T \times T$. If the factors are uncorrelated over time, then $A = I_T$.

We first derive the distribution of $\hat{a}_m$. $\hat{a}_m$ is given by the following expression

$$\hat{a}'_m = \begin{bmatrix} 1 & 0 \end{bmatrix} \begin{bmatrix} 1'_T 1_T & 1'_T f_1 \\ f'_1 1_T & f'_1 f_1 \end{bmatrix}^{-1} \begin{bmatrix} 1'_T \\ f'_1 \end{bmatrix} R^e \tag{3.38}$$

$$= \begin{bmatrix} 1 & 0 \end{bmatrix} \begin{bmatrix} \dfrac{1}{T} + \dfrac{1}{T}\bar{f}'_1\hat{\Omega}_{11}^{-1}\bar{f}_1 & -\dfrac{1}{T}\bar{f}'_1\hat{\Omega}_{11}^{-1} \\ \dfrac{1}{T}\hat{\Omega}_{11}^{-1}\bar{f}_1 & \dfrac{1}{T}\hat{\Omega}_{11}^{-1} \end{bmatrix} \begin{bmatrix} 1'_T \\ f'_1 \end{bmatrix} R^e$$

$$= \left\{ \left[\dfrac{1}{T} + \bar{f}'_1\hat{\Omega}_{11}^{-1}\bar{f}_1\right]1'_T - \dfrac{1}{T}\bar{f}'_1\hat{\Omega}_{11}^{-1}f'_1 \right\} R^e$$

Let

$$C = \left[\dfrac{1}{T} + \dfrac{1}{T}\bar{f}'_1\hat{\Omega}_{11}^{-1}\bar{f}_1\right]1'_T - \dfrac{1}{T}\bar{f}'_1\hat{\Omega}_{11}^{-1}f'_1$$

in which C has the following properties

1. $C1_T = 1$
2. $Cf_1 = 0_{1 \times k_1}$
3. $CC' = \left[\dfrac{1}{T} + \dfrac{1}{T}\bar{f}'_1\hat{\Omega}_{11}^{-1}\bar{f}_1\right]$

Substituting $R^e = 1_T a' + f_1 B_1 + f_2 B_2 + E$ into (3.38) and utilizing property (1) and property (2) of C, we have

$$\hat{a}_m = a + B'_2 f'_2 C' + E'C'$$

The mean of $\hat{a}_m$, μ_a, is given by

$$\mu_a = a + \left(B'_2 \otimes C\right)vec(1_T u_2) + \left(B'_2\Omega_{21}\Omega_{11}^{-1} \otimes CA\right)\left(vec(f_1 - 1_T u_1)\right)$$

$$= a + B'_2 u_2 + B'_2\Omega_{21}\Omega_{11}^{-1}\left(f_1 - 1_T \mu'_1\right)' AC'$$

In the case that factors are independent over time, μ_a is given by

$$\mu_a = a + B'_2 u_2 + B'_2\Omega_{21}\Omega_{11}^{-1}\mu_1$$

The variance-covariance matrix of $\hat{a}_m$ is given by

$$\Sigma_a = (B_2' \otimes C)\left[\left(\Omega_{22} - \Omega_{21}\Omega_{11}^{-1}\Omega_{12}\right) \otimes A\right](B_2 \otimes C') + (I_T \otimes C)[\Sigma \otimes I_T](I_T \otimes C')$$

Using property (3) of C, we have

$$\Sigma_a = CAC'\left[B_2'\left(\Omega_{22} - \Omega_{21}\Omega_{11}^{-1}\Omega_{12}\right)B_2\right] + \frac{1}{T}\left(1 + \bar{f}_1'\hat{\Omega}_{11}^{-1}\bar{f}_1\right)\Sigma$$

In the case that factors are independent over time, Σ_a is given by

$$\Sigma_a = \frac{1}{T}\left(1 + \bar{f}_1'\hat{\Omega}_{11}^{-1}\bar{f}_1\right)\left[B_2'\left(\Omega_{22} - \Omega_{21}\Omega_{11}^{-1}\Omega_{12}\right)B_2 + \Sigma\right] \tag{3.39}$$

In addition, in the case that factors are independent over time, the test statistics follow a noncentral F distribution under the alternative. The noncentrality parameter, δ, is just a quadratic function of μ_a, weighted by the inverse of Σ_a. That is

$$\delta = \varphi\left(B_2'\mu_2 - B_2'\Omega_{21}\Omega_{11}^{-1}\mu_1\right)'\left[B_2'\left(\Omega_{22} - \Omega_{21}\Omega_{11}^{-1}\Omega_{12}\right)B_2 + \Sigma\right]^{-1}$$
$$\times \left(B_2'\mu_2 - B_2'\Omega_{21}\Omega_{11}^{-1}\mu_1\right) \tag{3.40}$$

with $\varphi = T/(1 + \bar{f}_1'\hat{\Omega}^{-1}\bar{f}_1)$.

Next we derive the distribution of $\hat{E}_m$. Define $F_1 = [1_T \quad f_1]$ and $M_f = (I_T - F_1(F_1'F_1)^{-1}F_1')$. The residual matrix, $\hat{E}_m$, is given by

$$\hat{E}_m = M_f R^e$$
$$= M_f (f_2 B_2 + E)$$

The mean of $\hat{E}_m$ is given by

$$vec(\mu_E) = (B_2' \otimes M_f)\left(\Omega_{21}\Omega_{11}^{-1} \otimes A\right)(vec(f_1 - 1_T u_1))$$
$$= \left(B_2'\Omega_{21}\Omega_{11}^{-1} \otimes M_f A\right)(vec(f_1 - 1_T u_1))$$

As a result,

$$\mu_E = M_f\left(\mu_2 + A(f_1 - \mu_1)\Omega_{11}^{-1}\Omega_{12}\right)B_2$$

The covariance matrix of $\hat{E}_m$ is given by

$$\Sigma_m = (B_2' \otimes M_f)\left[\left(\Omega_{22} - \Omega_{21}\Omega_{11}^{-1}\Omega_{12}\right) \otimes A\right](B_2 \otimes M_f)$$
$$+ (I \otimes M_f)[\Sigma \otimes I_T](I \otimes M_f)$$
$$= \left[B_2'\left(\Omega_{22} - \Omega_{21}\Omega_{11}^{-1}\Omega_{12}\right)B_2\right] \otimes M_f A M_f + \Sigma \otimes M_f$$

4 Bayesian estimation of risk premia in an APT context

Theofanis Darsinos and Stephen E. Satchell[*][†]

Abstract

Recognizing the problems of estimation error in computing risk premia via arbitrage pricing, this chapter provides a Bayesian methodology for estimating factor risk premia and hence equity risk premia for both traded and non-traded factors. Some illustrative calculations based on UK equity are also provided.

4.1 Introduction

The calculation of factor-risk premia is one of the major contributions of Arbitrage Pricing Theory as espoused by Ross (1976) and Ingersoll (1987). In this literature, two cases are considered; when the factors are traded portfolios and when they are not (see, for example, Campbell et al. (1997)). While practitioner-oriented models focus on the former, the academic literature is more concerned with the latter (see Burmeister and McElroy (1988)). There are considerable problems in estimating factor-risk premia, as discussed in Pitsillis and Satchell (2001), Pitsillis (2002), and elsewhere. To alleviate some of the estimation problems, we consider a Bayesian approach to estimation, so that prior information can be utilized to improve accuracy. Many authors (see, for example, Polson and Tew (2000), Ericsson and Karlsson (2002)) have shown that Bayesian approaches to linear factor models and portfolio theory have been successful in reducing some of the excess variability in the data.

Regarding the choice of factors, interest rates, returns on broadbased portfolios one of which, typically, approximates the market portfolio, growth in consumption as tabulated, for example, from inflationary data, production and other macroeconomic variables that measure the state of the economy are potential risks that are rewarded in the stock market and could be included in a factor model. Furthermore, variables that signal changes in the future, such as term premiums, credit spreads, etc., are also reasonable to include (see Ericsson and Karlsson (2002)). Our focus is on the case of non-traded factors, so that our factors are macroeconomic ones. Several authors have used macroeconomic variables as factors (see, for example, Jagannathan and Wang (1996), Reyfman (1997)). Chen et al. (1986) test whether innovations in macroeconomic variables are risks that are rewarded in the stock market. Included variables are: the spread between long and short interest rates, expected and unexpected inflation,

[*] Faculty of Economics, University of Cambridge, UK.
[†] We thank Marios Pitsillis for providing us with the data for the empirical application in this chapter.

industrial production, the spread between high- and low-grade bonds, market portfolio, aggregate consumption and oil prices. Other macroeconomic variables have also been considered.

Fama and French (1992, 1993, 1996) advocate a model with the market return, the return of small less big stocks (SMB) and the spread between high and low book-to-market stocks (HML) as factors. However, although empirically very successful, the non-diversifiable risk that is proxied by the returns of the HML and SMB is not clear.

The structure of this chapter is as follows. In section 4.2 we briefly introduce the general APT framework. Section 4.2.1 outlines the excess return generating process when factors are traded portfolios and suggests how a Bayesian estimation framework can be utilized in this case. Section 4.2.2 considers the case of non-traded or macroeconomic factors and section 4.3 derives the prior and posterior estimates for the (non-traded) factor-risk premia. In section 4.4 we provide an empirical application to illustrate how the methodology developed here could be utilized in practice. Concluding comments follow in section 4.5.

4.2 The general APT framework

4.2.1 The excess return generating process (when factors are traded portfolios)

We have N assets. Then for each asset i, its excess return x^i is generated by:

$$x^i = \sum_{j=1}^{K} \beta_{ij} f_j + \varepsilon^i \tag{4.1}$$

where

$$f = (f_1, \ldots, f_K)'$$
$$b_i = (\beta_{i1}, \ldots, \beta_{iK})'$$
$$E(\varepsilon^i) = 0$$
$$E(f\varepsilon^i) = 0$$

The f_js are the factors, K factors in total. The β_{ij} are the betas or factor loadings, and the ε^is are white noise errors. Exact factor pricing implies that in the case of traded factors the intercept term in the factor model (i.e. equation (4.1)) is zero. In this case the risk premia on the factors λ_k can be estimated directly from the sample means of the excess returns on the traded portfolios that constitute the factors. Thus

$$\hat{\lambda}_k = \overline{x}_k$$

x_k represents expected excess return from the portfolio that mimics perfectly factor k. Note that as the sample size n increases we expect

$$\overline{x}_k \sim N\left(\mu_k, \frac{\sigma_k^2}{n}\right)$$

via the usual central limit theorems.

$N(\cdot)$ denotes the Normal distribution. μ_k and σ_k^2 are the mean and variance respectively of the factor mimicking portfolio for factor k. For this model, unlike the case where factors are non-traded, the APT restriction $\mu^i = \sum \beta_{ij} \lambda_j$ holds exactly upon taking the expected value of equation (4.1).

4.2.1.1   A Bayesian framework

When portfolios are factors it is quite straightforward to introduce a Bayesian framework in the estimation of risk premia. This case strongly resembles the popular Black-Litterman model used in tackling asset management problems (see Black and Litterman (1991, 1992)).

We wish to obtain the posterior probability density function (pdf) for μ_k which will then gives us directly a posterior estimate for the risk premium λ_k. We assume that observations on x_k are drawn from a normal population with unknown mean μ_k and known variance σ_k^2. As regards a prior pdf for μ_k we assume using standard Bayesian methodology (see, for example, Zellner (1971), Bauwens et al. (1999)) that

$$
\mu_{Prior} = \begin{pmatrix} \mu_1 \\ \vdots \\ \mu_K \end{pmatrix} \sim N \left[\begin{pmatrix} \tilde{\mu}_1 \\ \vdots \\ \tilde{\mu}_K \end{pmatrix}, \begin{pmatrix} \tilde{\sigma}_1^2 & \cdots & 0 \\ \vdots & \ddots & 0 \\ 0 & 0 & \tilde{\sigma}_K^2 \end{pmatrix} \right]
$$

The values of these parameters are assigned by the investigator on the basis of his/her initial information. Prior values of risk premia are simply in this case

$$
\lambda_{Prior} = \begin{pmatrix} \lambda_1 \\ \vdots \\ \lambda_K \end{pmatrix} = \begin{pmatrix} \tilde{\mu}_1 \\ \vdots \\ \tilde{\mu}_K \end{pmatrix}
$$

Then using Bayes's theorem to combine the likelihood function with the prior pdf to obtain the posterior pdf for μ_k ($k = 1, \ldots, K$) we have that

$$
\mu_k^{Posterior} \sim N \left(\frac{\bar{x}_k \left(\sigma_k^2/n \right)^{-1} + \tilde{\mu}_k \left(\tilde{\sigma}_k^2 \right)^{-1}}{\left(\sigma_k^2/n \right)^{-1} + \left(\tilde{\sigma}_k^2 \right)^{-1}}, \frac{1}{\left(\sigma_k^2/n \right)^{-1} + \left(\tilde{\sigma}_k^2 \right)^{-1}} \right)
$$

Hence a posterior estimate of the risk premium, λ_k, for factor k is given by the mean of $\mu_k^{Posterior}$.

Extensions for the cases of correlated factors and/or factors where the variance-covariance matrix of the factor mimicking portfolios is unknown and stochastic are straightforward to derive. For example, a diffuse prior (i.e. $pdf(\mu, \Sigma) \propto |\Sigma|^{-(k+1)/2}$) or a Normal-Inverted Wishart prior (i.e. $pdf(\mu|\Sigma) \sim$ Normal and $pdf(\Sigma) \sim$ Inverted

Wishart) both lead to matrixvariate t distributions for the posterior (i.e. $pdf(\mu|\Sigma) \sim$ matrixvariate t). See, for example, Satchell and Scowcroft (2000) for an illustration on incorporating stochastic volatility in Black–Litterman type models.

4.2.2 The excess return generating process (when factors are macroeconomic variables or non-traded portfolios)

This time for each asset i, the excess return x^i is generated by:

$$x^i = \mu_i + \sum_{j=1}^{K} \beta_{ij} f_j + \varepsilon^i \qquad (4.2)$$

$$= \mu_i + b_i' f + \varepsilon^i$$

$$= a_i' h + \varepsilon^i$$

where $h = (f_1, \ldots, f_K, 1)'$, $a_i = (\beta_{i1}, \ldots, \beta_{iK}, \mu_i)'$, $E(\varepsilon^i) = 0$, $E(f\varepsilon^i) = 0$.

The factors f_js are now constructed so that they have zero mean (they are in fact factor deviations from their mean) and μ_i denotes the expected excess return for asset i (i.e. $\mu_i = E(x^i)$). To generalize the above setting for our N assets we write:

$$
\begin{bmatrix} x^1 \\ \vdots \\ x^N \end{bmatrix} =
\begin{bmatrix} \beta_{1,1} & \cdots & \beta_{K,1} & \mu_1 \\ \vdots & \ddots & \vdots & \vdots \\ \beta_{1,N} & \cdots & \beta_{K,N} & \mu_N \end{bmatrix}
\begin{bmatrix} f_1 \\ \vdots \\ f_K \\ 1 \end{bmatrix} +
\begin{bmatrix} \varepsilon^1 \\ \vdots \\ \varepsilon^N \end{bmatrix}
$$

$$\Rightarrow$$

$$x = A'h + \varepsilon \qquad (4.3)$$

where

$$\varepsilon \sim NID_N(0, \Psi), \qquad (4.4)$$

NID: Independent Normal, Ψ is the positive-definite $N \times N$ residual variance-covariance matrix and A is the regression coefficients matrix:

$$
A = \begin{bmatrix} B \\ \mu' \end{bmatrix} =
\begin{bmatrix} \beta_{1,1} & \cdots & \beta_{1,N} \\ \vdots & \ddots & \vdots \\ \beta_{K,1} & \cdots & \beta_{K,N} \\ \mu_1 & \cdots & \mu_N \end{bmatrix} \qquad (4.5)
$$

The matrix version of the above multivariate regression for T observations is:

$$
\underset{T \times N}{X} = \underset{T \times (K+1)}{H} \times \underset{(K+1) \times N}{A} + \underset{T \times N}{E}
$$

$$
= [F, i_T] \begin{bmatrix} B \\ \mu' \end{bmatrix} + E \qquad (4.6)
$$

where $E \sim MN_{T \times N}(0, \Psi \otimes I_T)$ and X, H, and E are obtained by stacking the row vectors x', h', and ε' respectively. MN denotes a matrixvariate normal distribution[1]. F is obtained by stacking together f' and is the factor data matrix.

4.2.3 Obtaining the (K × 1) vector of risk premia λ

The APT pricing relationship is

$$E(x^i) = \mu_i = \lambda_1 \beta_{i1} + \cdots + \lambda_K \beta_{iK} = b_i' \lambda \tag{4.7}$$

where $\lambda = (\lambda_1, \ldots, \lambda_K)'$; i.e. a $K \times 1$ vector of factor-risk premia. We write this as an equality although it is only approximately equal in the case of non-traded factors. This then implies that

$$\mu = B' \lambda \tag{4.8}$$

μ is an $(N \times 1)$ vector of expected excess returns for our N assets and B is a $(K \times N)$ matrix of betas. Then the best (cross-sectional) linear predictor for the column vector of excess returns μ is obtained when

$$E\left[B(\mu - B' \lambda) \right] = 0 \tag{4.9}$$

This implies that

$$E[B\mu] - E\left[BB' \right] \lambda = 0$$

$$\lambda = \left[E(BB') \right]^{-1} E[B\mu] \tag{4.10}$$

where

$$E\left(BB'\right) = \begin{bmatrix} \sum\limits_{i=1}^{N} \left[Var(\beta_{1,i}) + \left[E\left(\beta_{1,i}\right) \right]^2 \right] & \cdots & \sum\limits_{i=1}^{N} \left[Cov(\beta_{1,i}, \beta_{K,i}) + E(\beta_{1,i})E(\beta_{K,i}) \right] \\ \vdots & \ddots & \vdots \\ \sum\limits_{i=1}^{N} \left[Cov(\beta_{1,i}, \beta_{K,i}) + E(\beta_{1,i})E(\beta_{K,i}) \right] & \cdots & \sum\limits_{i=1}^{N} \left[Var(\beta_{K,i}) + \left[E\left(\beta_{K,i}\right) \right]^2 \right] \end{bmatrix}$$

$$\Rightarrow$$

$$E\left(BB'\right) = \begin{bmatrix} tr\,\Omega_{11} + \sum\limits_{i=1}^{N} \left[E(\beta_{1,i}) \right]^2 & \cdots & tr\,\Omega_{1K} + \sum\limits_{i=1}^{N} E(\beta_{1,i})E(\beta_{K,i}) \\ \vdots & \ddots & \vdots \\ tr\,\Omega_{1K} + \sum\limits_{i=1}^{N} E(\beta_{1,i})E(\beta_{K,i}) & \cdots & tr\,\Omega_{KK} + \sum\limits_{i=1}^{N} \left[E\left(\beta_{K,i}\right) \right]^2 \end{bmatrix}$$

---

[1] See the appendix for a definition of the matrixvariate Normal distribution. For more information we refer the reader to Bauwens et al. (1999).

and

$$
E[B\mu] = \begin{bmatrix} \sum\limits_{i=1}^{N} \left[Cov\left(\beta_{1,i},\mu_i\right) + E\left(\beta_{1,i}\right)E\left(\mu_i\right) \right] \\ \vdots \\ \sum\limits_{i=1}^{N} \left[Cov(\beta_{K,i},\mu_i) + E(\beta_{K,i})E(\mu_i) \right] \end{bmatrix}
$$

$$
= \begin{bmatrix} tr\,\Omega_{1\mu} + \sum\limits_{i=1}^{N} E(\beta_{1,i})E(\mu_i) \\ \vdots \\ tr\,\Omega_{K\mu} + \sum\limits_{i=1}^{N} E(\beta_{K,i})E(\mu_i) \end{bmatrix}
$$

(4.11)

Note that the Ωs are $N \times N$ matrices obtained from the $(K+1)N \times (K+1)N$ variance-covariance matrix Σ_A of the regression coefficients matrix A:

$$
\Sigma_A = \begin{bmatrix} \Omega_{11} & \cdots & \Omega_{1K} & \Omega_{1\mu} \\ \vdots & \ddots & \vdots & \vdots \\ \Omega_{K1} & \cdots & \Omega_{KK} & \Omega_{K\mu} \\ \Omega_{\mu1} & \cdots & \Omega_{\mu K} & \Omega_{\mu\mu} \end{bmatrix}
$$

(4.12)

4.3 Introducing a Bayesian framework using a Minnesota prior (Litterman's prior)

We start by assuming that the residual variance-covariance matrix Ψ defined in equation (4.13) is fixed and diagonal:

$$
\Psi = \begin{bmatrix} \psi_{11} & 0 & \cdots & 0 \\ 0 & \psi_{22} & \cdots & 0 \\ \vdots & \cdots & \ddots & \vdots \\ 0 & 0 & \cdots & \psi_{NN} \end{bmatrix}
$$

(4.13)

This of course implies that the diagonal elements of Ψ need to be specified. We shall follow the empirical Bayes approach where the ψ_{ii} are replaced by s_i^2, the sample residual variance estimates.

It is possible to relax the assumption that Ψ is fixed and diagonal and work with Ψ non-diagonal. This is the approach followed by Chamberlain and Rothschild (1983), Ingersoll (1984) and Connor and Korajczyk (1993). These authors allow for non-diagonality in the variance-covariance matrix which will disappear as N gets large. The strict factor model we assume is more in line with practitioner factor models where the emphasis is on making clear the distinction between systematic risk (through common factors) and idiosyncratic risk (stock-specific risk). In any case we shall outline the appropriate extensions to our results when Ψ is non-diagonal.

4.3.1 Prior estimates of the risk premia

In Bayesian statistics, parameters are treated as random variables and are assigned probability distributions. We assume that the prior distribution of the regression parameters is

$$A \backsim MN \left[Vec\widetilde{A}, \widetilde{\Sigma} \right] \tag{4.14}$$

where MN denotes the matrixvariate Normal distribution (see the appendix for a definition). $Vec\widetilde{A}$ denotes the prior mean of A and $\widetilde{\Sigma}$ the prior variance-covariance matrix of the regression parameters. In partitioned form we have

$$\begin{bmatrix} B \\ \mu' \end{bmatrix} \backsim MN \left[\begin{pmatrix} Vec\widetilde{B} \\ \widetilde{\mu} \end{pmatrix}, \begin{bmatrix} \Theta_{BB} & \Theta_{B\mu} \\ \Theta_{\mu B} & \Theta_{\mu\mu} \end{bmatrix} \otimes I_N \right] \tag{4.15}$$

where we assume that

$$\Theta_{BB} = \begin{bmatrix} \theta_{11} & \cdots & \theta_{1K} \\ \vdots & \ddots & \vdots \\ \theta_{K1} & \cdots & \theta_{KK} \end{bmatrix}$$

i.e. a $(K \times K)$ matrix and

$$\Theta_{B\mu} = \begin{bmatrix} \theta_{1\mu} \\ \vdots \\ \theta_{K\mu} \end{bmatrix}$$

i.e. a $(K \times 1)$ column vector and $\theta_{\mu\mu}$ is a scalar. This assumption implies that equation (4.12) above is specialized so that $\Omega_{11} = \theta_{11}I_N$, $\Omega_{12} = \theta_{12}I_N, \ldots$, etc. To clarify what this means, we shall consider a simple example. Suppose we have a classic Fama and French three factor model (i.e. $K = 3$: market portfolio, size ranking, and book-to-market ratio). Then for each stock we have betas for each of these three factors. Assuming that $\Omega_{11} = \theta_{11}I_N$ is tantamount to assuming that all the betas with respect to the market are drawn from a common population with variance θ_{11}. Likewise $\Omega_{12} = \theta_{12}I_N$ means that the betas from the market and the size factors have a common covariance θ_{12}. Such an assumption is both helpful for interpretation and also leads to empirical Bayes analysis. Similar assumptions are made for the means. In particular we assume that the betas of all assets with respect to each factor k are drawn from a common population with mean $\tilde{\beta}_k$. Thus

$$Vec\widetilde{B} = \begin{bmatrix} \tilde{\beta}_1 & \cdots & \tilde{\beta}_1, \cdots, \tilde{\beta}_K & \cdots & \tilde{\beta}_K \end{bmatrix}'$$

$$= \begin{bmatrix} \tilde{\beta}_1 & \cdots & \tilde{\beta}_K \end{bmatrix}' \otimes i_N$$

and finally

$$\tilde{\mu} = \begin{bmatrix} \mu_0 & \cdots & \mu_0 \end{bmatrix}' = \mu_0 \otimes i_N$$

We stress that the above assumptions are standard in Bayesian finance and particularly helpful in understanding cross-sectional analyses. So changes in θ_{11} would represent a change in the volatility exposure of factor 1.

4.3.1.1 Standard Bayesian case (prior independence between B and μ; i.e. $\Theta_{B\mu} = 0$)

Here we assume that $\Theta_{B\mu} = 0$. This prior assumption would be held by an investor who was sceptical that the β_{ij}s influenced μ^i and expresses a disbelief in linear factor modelling and the APT. Sub-cases where a subset of $\Theta_{B\mu}$ is set to zero could also be considered.

The prior estimate for the risk premium vector λ is then obtained from equation (4.10), where

$$
E(BB') = \begin{bmatrix} N\theta_{11} + \sum_{i=1}^{N} \left[E(\beta_{1,i})\right]^2 & \cdots & N\theta_{1K} + \sum_{i=1}^{N} E(\beta_{1,i})E(\beta_{K,i}) \\ \vdots & \ddots & \vdots \\ N\theta_{1K} + \sum_{i=1}^{N} E(\beta_{1,i})E(\beta_{K,i}) & \cdots & N\theta_{KK} + \sum_{i=1}^{N} \left[E\left(\beta_{K,i}\right)\right]^2 \end{bmatrix}
$$

and

$$
E[B\mu] = \begin{bmatrix} \sum_{i=1}^{N} E(\beta_{1,i})E(\mu_i) \\ \vdots \\ \sum_{i=1}^{N} E(\beta_{K,i})E(\mu_i) \end{bmatrix}
$$

We therefore obtain:

$$
\lambda_{prior} = \begin{bmatrix} \theta_{11} + \tilde{\beta}_1^2 & \cdots & \theta_{1K} + \tilde{\beta}_1\tilde{\beta}_K \\ \vdots & \ddots & \vdots \\ \theta_{1K} + \tilde{\beta}_1\tilde{\beta}_K & \cdots & \theta_{KK} + \tilde{\beta}_K^2 \end{bmatrix}^{-1} \begin{bmatrix} \tilde{\beta}_1\mu_0 \\ \vdots \\ \tilde{\beta}_K\mu_0 \end{bmatrix}
\tag{4.16}
$$

This can be expanded as

$$
\lambda_{prior} = \left[\Theta_{BB} + Vec(\tilde{B})Vec(\tilde{B})'\right]^{-1} Vec(\tilde{B})\mu_0
\tag{4.17}
$$

$$
= \Theta_{BB}^{-1} Vec(\tilde{B})\mu_0 - \frac{\Theta_{BB}^{-1} Vec(\tilde{B}) Vec(\tilde{B})' \Theta_{BB}^{-1} Vec(\tilde{B})\mu_0}{1 + Vec(\tilde{B})'\Theta_{BB}^{-1} Vec(\tilde{B})}
$$

$$
= \frac{1}{1 + Vec(\tilde{B})'\Theta_{BB}^{-1} Vec(\tilde{B})} \Theta_{BB}^{-1} Vec(\tilde{B})\mu_0
$$

Thus comparative statics are easy to calculate. We can, for example, compute $\partial\lambda/\partial\mu_0$, $\partial\lambda/\partial\Theta_{BB}$, $\partial\lambda/\partial Vec(\tilde{B})$.

For example, for the CAPM case where the only factor is the market portfolio, we have that the prior estimate of the risk premium is

$$
\lambda_1 = \frac{\tilde{\beta}_1\mu_0}{\theta_{11} + \tilde{\beta}_1^2}
$$

$\tilde{\beta}_1$ is the prior estimate of the market beta, μ_0 is the prior mean of the excess return assigned by the investigator to be common for all assets, θ_{11} is the prior variance of $\tilde{\beta}_1$. Also

$$\frac{\partial \lambda}{\partial \mu_0} = \frac{\tilde{\beta}_1}{\theta_{11} + \tilde{\beta}_1^2}$$

When we have two factors we get:

$$\lambda_{prior} = \begin{bmatrix} \lambda_1 \\ \lambda_2 \end{bmatrix} = \begin{bmatrix} \dfrac{\left(\theta_{22} + \tilde{\beta}_2^2\right)(\mu_0\tilde{\beta}_1) - (\theta_{12} + \tilde{\beta}_1\tilde{\beta}_2)(\mu_0\tilde{\beta}_2)}{\left(\theta_{11} + \tilde{\beta}_1^2\right)\left(\theta_{22} + \tilde{\beta}_2^2\right) - \left(\theta_{12} + \tilde{\beta}_1\tilde{\beta}_2\right)^2} \\ \dfrac{\left(\theta_{11} + \tilde{\beta}_1^2\right)(\mu_0\tilde{\beta}_2) - (\theta_{12} + \tilde{\beta}_1\tilde{\beta}_2)(\mu_0\tilde{\beta}_1)}{\left(\theta_{11} + \tilde{\beta}_1^2\right)\left(\theta_{22} + \tilde{\beta}_2^2\right) - (\theta_{12} + \tilde{\beta}_1\tilde{\beta}_2)^2} \end{bmatrix}$$

We can proceed similarly for three or more factors.

4.3.1.2 General case (prior dependence between B and μ; i.e. $\Theta_{B\mu} \neq 0$)

That there is no cross-sectional dependence, a priori, between a given beta and the mean excess return seems highly unlikely given the nature of many practitioner processes and their possible knowledge of asset pricing theory. Typical processes involve sorting by factor exposure or variable, so fund managers will believe that high growth leads to high return. Here we generalize the above setting to allow for the more realistic case of prior dependence between B and μ. We therefore assume that $\Theta_{B\mu} = [\theta_{1\mu}, \ldots, \theta_{K\mu}]' \neq 0$. The general formula for the prior estimate for the factor-risk premium now becomes

$$\lambda_{prior} = \frac{1}{1 + Vec(\tilde{B})'\Theta_{BB}^{-1}Vec(\tilde{B})}\Theta_{BB}^{-1}\left(Vec(\tilde{B})\mu_0 + \Theta_{B\mu}\right)$$

From this we can now write very easily the analytic formulae for the prior estimates of the one factor case (i.e. CAPM), two factors, etc. For example, the risk premium for the one factor CAPM case is now

$$\lambda_1 = \frac{\theta_{1\mu} + \tilde{\beta}_1\mu_0}{\theta_{11} + \tilde{\beta}_1^2}$$

with $\theta_{1\mu}$ being the prior covariance between $\tilde{\beta}_1$ and μ_0. Similarly the risk premium for the two factor case with prior dependence between B and μ is obtained from

$$\lambda_{prior} = \begin{bmatrix} \lambda_1 \\ \lambda_2 \end{bmatrix} = \begin{bmatrix} \dfrac{\left(\theta_{22} + \tilde{\beta}_2^2\right)(\theta_{1\mu} + \mu_0\tilde{\beta}_1) - (\theta_{12} + \tilde{\beta}_1\tilde{\beta}_2)(\theta_{2\mu} + \mu_0\tilde{\beta}_2)}{\left(\theta_{11} + \tilde{\beta}_1^2\right)\left(\theta_{22} + \tilde{\beta}_2^2\right) - (\theta_{12} + \tilde{\beta}_1\tilde{\beta}_2)^2} \\ \dfrac{(\theta_{11} + \tilde{\beta}_1^2)(\theta_{2\mu} + \mu_0\tilde{\beta}_2) - (\theta_{12} + \tilde{\beta}_1\tilde{\beta}_2)(\theta_{1\mu} + \mu_0\tilde{\beta}_1)}{\left(\theta_{11} + \tilde{\beta}_1^2\right)\left(\theta_{22} + \tilde{\beta}_2^2\right) - (\theta_{12} + \tilde{\beta}_1\tilde{\beta}_2)^2} \end{bmatrix}$$

Extensions for three or more factors are straightforward to obtain.

4.3.2 *Posterior estimates of the risk premia*

We now turn to deriving the posterior estimates of the risk premia. If the prior distribution of the regression coefficients matrix A is as in (4.14), then the posterior distribution of A is (see, for example, Kadiyala and Karlsson (1997)):

$$A \sim MN\left[VecA_p, \Sigma_p\right]$$

where

$$\Sigma_p = \left[(\widetilde{\Sigma}^{-1} + ((H'H)^{-1} \otimes \Psi)^{-1})\right]^{-1} \tag{4.18}$$

$$= \left(\widetilde{\Sigma}^{-1} + ((H'H) \otimes \Psi^{-1})\right)^{-1}$$

$$= (\widetilde{\Sigma}^{-1} + \widehat{\Sigma}^{-1})^{-1}$$

(Note that $\widehat{}$ denotes a sample estimate and $\widetilde{}$ denotes a prior estimate) and

$$VecA_p = \Sigma_p\left((\widetilde{\Sigma}^{-1} \times Vec\widetilde{A}) + ((H'H)^{-1} \otimes \Psi)^{-1} \times Vec[(H'H)^{-1}H'X]\right)$$

$$= \Sigma_p\left((\widetilde{\Sigma}^{-1} \times Vec\widetilde{A}) + (\widehat{\Sigma}^{-1} \times Vec\widehat{A})\right)$$

Now to write Σ_p and $VecA_p$ in partitioned form note first that

$$H = [F, i_T] \Rightarrow$$

$$H'H = \begin{bmatrix} F'F & F'i_T \\ i'_T F & i'_T i_T \end{bmatrix}$$

$$= \begin{bmatrix} F'F & 0 \\ 0 & T \end{bmatrix}$$

where we have assumed by construction that the factors have zero sample mean (i.e. $F'i_T$ and $i'_T F = 0$). Therefore

$$\Sigma_p = \left(\begin{bmatrix} \Theta_{BB} & \Theta_{B\mu} \\ \Theta_{\mu B} & \theta_{\mu\mu} \end{bmatrix} \otimes I_N\right]^{-1} + \begin{bmatrix} F'F & 0 \\ 0 & T \end{bmatrix} \otimes \Psi^{-1}\right)^{-1} \tag{4.19}$$

4.3.2.1 Standard Bayesian case (prior independence between B and μ; i.e. $\Theta_{B\mu} = 0$)

Turning to the posterior estimates of the mean and variance, with prior independence we get the following simplifications (for detailed calculations see the appendix):

$$\Sigma_p = \begin{bmatrix} [\Theta_{BB}^{-1} \otimes I_N + F'F \otimes \Psi^{-1}]^{-1} & 0 \\ 0 & [\theta_{\mu\mu}^{-1} \times I_N + T \times \Psi^{-1}]^{-1} \end{bmatrix} \tag{4.20}$$

and

$$VecA_p = \begin{bmatrix} VecB_p \\ \mu_p \end{bmatrix}$$

$$= \begin{bmatrix} \left[\Theta_{BB}^{-1} \otimes I_N + F'F \otimes \Psi^{-1} \right]^{-1} \times \left\{ \left(\Theta_{BB}^{-1} \otimes I_N \right) Vec\tilde{B} + |F'F \otimes \Psi^{-1}|Vec\hat{B} \right\} \\ \left[\theta_{\mu\mu}^{-1} \times I_N + T \times \Psi^{-1} \right]^{-1} \times \left\{ \left(\theta_{\mu\mu}^{-1} \times I_N \right) \tilde{\mu} + T\Psi^{-1}\hat{\mu} \right\} \end{bmatrix}$$

The estimates for the risk premium vector λ now follow straightforwardly from the procedure outlined in section 4.2.3.

4.3.2.2 General case (prior dependence between B and μ; i.e. $\Theta_{B\mu} \neq 0$)

When there is prior dependence between B and μ things get a bit more complicated. We know that

$$\Sigma_p = \left(\left[\begin{array}{cc} \Theta_{BB} & \Theta_{B\mu} \\ \Theta_{\mu B} & \theta_{\mu\mu} \end{array} \right] \otimes I_N \right]^{-1} + \left[\begin{array}{cc} F'F & 0 \\ 0 & T \end{array} \right] \otimes \Psi^{-1} \right)^{-1}$$

This can now be written as

$$\Sigma_p = \left(\left[\begin{array}{cc} \Theta_{BB}^{-1} \left(I + \Theta_{B\mu} \Xi_2 \Theta_{\mu B} \Theta_{BB}^{-1} \right) & -\Theta_{BB}^{-1}\Theta_{B\mu}\Xi_2 \\ -\Xi_2\Theta_{\mu B}\Theta_{BB}^{-1} & \Xi_2 \end{array} \right] \otimes I_N + \left[\begin{array}{cc} F'F & 0 \\ 0 & T \end{array} \right] \otimes \Psi^{-1} \right)^{-1}$$

where

$$\Xi_2 = \left(\theta_{\mu\mu} - \Theta_{\mu B}\Theta_{BB}^{-1}\Theta_{B\mu} \right)^{-1}$$

From this we have (see the appendix) that the posterior variance-covariance in partitioned form is:

$$\Sigma_p = \begin{bmatrix} \Sigma_{p11} & \Sigma_{p12} \\ \Sigma_{p21} & \Sigma_{p22} \end{bmatrix}$$

where

$$\Sigma_{p11} = V_{11}^{-1} \left(I + \Upsilon_2 \left(V_{22} - \Upsilon_2 V_{11}^{-1}\Upsilon_2 \right)^{-1} \Upsilon_2' V_{11}^{-1} \right)$$

$$\Sigma_{p12} = -V_{11}^{-1}\Upsilon_2 \left(V_{22} - \Upsilon_2 V_{11}^{-1}\Upsilon_2 \right)^{-1}$$

$$\Sigma_{p21} = \Sigma_{p12}'$$

$$\Sigma_{p22} = \left(V_{22} - \Upsilon_2 V_{11}^{-1}\Upsilon_2 \right)^{-1}$$

with

$$\Upsilon_1 = \left[\Theta_{BB}^{-1} \left(I + \Theta_{B\mu} \Xi_2 \Theta_{\mu B} \Theta_{BB}^{-1} \right) \right] \otimes I_N$$

$$\Upsilon_2 = \left[-\Theta_{BB}^{-1}\Theta_{B\mu}\Xi_2 \right] \otimes I_N$$

$$\Upsilon_3 = \Xi_2 \times I_N$$

and

$$V_{11} = \Upsilon_1 + \left(F'F \otimes \Psi^{-1} \right)$$

$$V_{22} = \Upsilon_3 + T\Psi^{-1}$$

Similarly the posterior estimates for the regression coefficients are given by (see the appendix)

$$VecA_p = \Sigma_p \left((\tilde{\Sigma}^{-1} \times VecA) + (\hat{\Sigma}^{-1} \times Vec\hat{A}) \right)$$

$$= \left[\begin{array}{c} VecB_p \\ \mu_p \end{array} \right]$$

where

$$VecB_p = \left(\Sigma_{p11}\Upsilon_1 + \Sigma_{p12}\Upsilon_2' \right) VecB + \Sigma_{p11} \left[F'F \otimes \Psi^{-1} \right] Vec\hat{B}$$

$$+ (\Sigma_{p12}\Upsilon_3 - \Sigma_{p11}\Upsilon_2)\underline{\mu} + \Sigma_{p12}T\Psi^{-1}\hat{\mu}$$

and

$$\mu_p = \left(\Sigma_{p21}\Upsilon_1 + \Sigma_{p22}\Upsilon_2' \right) VecB + \Sigma_{p21} \left[F'F \otimes \Psi^{-1} \right] Vec\hat{B}$$

$$+ (\Sigma_{p22}\Upsilon_3 - \Sigma_{p21}\Upsilon_2)\underline{\mu} + \Sigma_{p22}T\Psi^{-1}\hat{\mu}$$

Now that we have obtained the posterior estimates for Σ_p and $VecA_p$ in partitioned form it is straightforward to obtain the risk premium vector λ following the procedure of section 4.2.3.

4.3.2.3 Extensions of the Minnesota prior

The Bayesian framework introduced above used the Minnesota prior. It is possible to generalize this framework by allowing for a non-diagonal variance-covariance matrix and/or by taking Ψ to be unknown. Possibilities include using a Normal-Wishart prior, a Normal-Diffuse prior (introduced by Zellner (1971)) or an extended Natural Conjugate Prior (see Dreze and Richard (1983)). For the latter two priors no closed form solution for the posterior moments exist, and numerical methods such as importance sampling or Gibbs sampling are required (see Kadiyala and Karlsson (1997)). An additional possibility is to maintain the assumption of a diagonal Ψ matrix while taking the diagonal elements to be unknown. Independent inverse gamma priors on the diagonal elements then lead to marginal multivariate t priors and posteriors for the parameters of each equation.

4.4 An empirical application

We now present an empirical application of our methodology, using non-traded factors. Our use of several observed macroeconomic risk factors to explain asset returns can be justified by the newest generation of empirical research, as summarized, for example, in Cochrane (2001). One of the earliest examples of applying macroeconomic risks in the APT is the paper by Chen et al. (1986) analyzing the pricing of such factors in the US market. Recognizing the ability of investors to diversify and the co-movements of asset prices, the authors suggest the presence of pervasive or systematic influences as the likely source of investment risk. In particular Chen et al. find that (1) unanticipated changes in the expected level of production, (2) unanticipated shifts in the shape of the term structure, (3) changes in default premiums and (4) unexpected inflation are risks that are significantly priced in the US market. By contrast, risks stemming from unanticipated changes in the market portfolio, aggregate consumption and oil prices were found not to be priced by the authors.

4.4.1 Data

The choice of candidate macroeconomic factors in this chapter is largely inspired by Chen et al. (1986) and is a subset of the factors presented in Antoniou et al. (1998). All data for measuring the macroeconomic factors are obtained from Datastream. In addition, data on total monthly logarithmic returns for UK stocks are also obtained from Datastream. Our sample spans a period of five years, starting from the end of November 1993 until the end of September 1998. The sample comprises 66 stocks from the FTSE100 Index on which data are available throughout the sample period. Thus there is bound to be some survivorship bias. The overall sample mean of excess returns for the 66 stocks over our sample period is calculated to be 16.7% (annualized).

Apart from spanning the space of returns, the most important property required of appropriate factor measures is that they cannot be predictable from their own past. To avoid problems caused by the potential presence of autocorrelation in the variables, simple ARIMA models were fitted to pre-whiten the series. It has to be noted, however, that although this procedure is designed to avoid spurious correlation, it carries a danger of possible misspecification. Given finite samples, the fitted ARIMA models can only be approximations to the true data generating process. The measurement of the risk factors used in our empirical application is explained below.

4.4.1.1 Industrial Production (Ind. Prod.)

In line with Chen et al., we use the monthly growth rate in industrial production. This is defined as:

$$MP_t = \ln IP_t - \ln IP_{t-1}$$

where IP denotes industrial production. We use the UKINPRODG Datastream series defined as the 'UK industrial production – total production vol.'. An AR(1) model was used to derive the innovations in industrial production.

4.4.1.2 Inflation (Infl.)

We use the difference in the logarithm of the consumer price index (CPI) to capture the effect of the inflation factor, as follows:

$$IR_t = \ln CPI_t - \ln CPI_{t-1}$$

We use the series UKRP…F defined as the 'UK Retail Price Index NADJ'. An ARMA model was used to derive the unexpected component of this series.

4.4.1.3   Market risk premium (Market)

To capture the effect of the market risk premium factor, we use the difference in the returns on the equity market (EM) and the government bond market (BM) in line with the definition of the risk premium in Datastream:

$$RP_t = \left[\ln EM_t - \ln EM_{t-1}\right] - \left[\ln BM_t - \ln BM_{t-1}\right]$$

We use the FTALLSH(RI) series defined as the 'FTSE All share – Total Return Index' and the series FTAGOVT(RI) defined as the 'FTA Government All Stocks – Total return Index'. An AR(1) model was used to derive the innovations in this series.

4.4.1.4   Term Structure (Term Str.)

To capture the effect of unanticipated shifts in the term structure, in line with the approach followed in the literature we use the spread between long-term (LTR) and short-term interest rates (STR):

$$TS_t = LTR_t - STR_t$$

We use the first difference in the logarithm of the series BMUK30Y(RI) defined as the 'UK Benchmark 30 Years DS Government Index – Total Return Index' and the series LDNT3BM defined as the 'UK Treasury Bill Discount 3 month – Middle Rate'.

4.4.2   Results

4.4.2.1   Empirical Bayesian approach as prior

We start by employing an empirical Bayesian approach in specifying our prior (hyper)parameters of section 4.3.1. We first estimate equation (4.2):

$$x^i = \mu_i + \sum_{j=1}^{K} \beta_{ij} f_j + \varepsilon^i$$

using OLS regression for each of the 66 stocks in our portfolio. Next, the prior parameter μ_0 is calculated as the mean of the intercepts from our estimated regressions

$$\mu_0 = \frac{1}{N}\sum_{i=1}^{N} \hat{\mu}_i$$

(The symbol $\hat{\ }$ denotes an OLS estimate.) Similarly the prior parameters $\left[\begin{array}{ccc} \tilde{\beta}_1 & \cdots & \tilde{\beta}_K \end{array}\right]$ are calculated as the means of the estimated factor βs. Thus

$$\tilde{\beta}_k = \frac{1}{N}\sum_{i=1}^{N} \hat{\beta}_{ik} \forall k \in (1,\ldots,K)$$

Finally Θ_{BB}, $\theta_{\mu\mu}$, and $\Theta_{B\mu}$ are assigned values taken from the cross-sectional variance-covariance matrix of the estimated μs (intercepts) and βs (see, for example, Table 4.2 in the appendix where we report the estimated cross-sectional correlation matrix of μs and βs). Prior and posterior estimates for the risk premia are next derived using the two sub-cases presented in sections 4.3.1 and 4.3.2 (see Table 4.4 in the appendix). Note that for the sub-case where by construction we assume prior independence between B and μ (see sections 4.3.1.1 and 4.3.2.1) $\Theta_{B\mu} = 0$.

4.4.2.2   CAPM as prior

We now make the assumption that we are CAPM advocates and we want to incorporate this in our prior information. This effectively means that we construct our priors so that we now have $\tilde{\beta}_{\text{Market}} = 1$ and $\tilde{\beta}_1, \ldots, \tilde{\beta}_K = 0$, $\forall k \neq$ Market. For the remaining hyperparameters we continue to use the empirical Bayes approach arising from the procedure of estimating unconstrained regressions outlined in the previous section. However, we note that since in this case our prior information implies the exclusion of certain regressors another possibility would be to compute the remaining hyperparameters by estimating constrained least squares regressions.

We estimate risk premia both with and without the assumption of prior independence between μ and B. Our results are exhibited in the appendix. In particular Table 4.1 reveals the correlation structure between our factors; notable are the high correlation between Industrial Production and Inflation (positive) and Industrial Production and the Term Structure (negative). Table 4.2 reports the pattern of cross-sectional OLS betas and mean excess returns for our 66 stocks. Table 4.3 reports our beta results.

Correlation	Ind. Prod.	Infl.	Market.	Term Str.
Ind. Prod.	1.000	0.275	0.075	−0.207
Infl.	0.275	1.000	0.090	−0.066
Market	0.075	0.075	1.000	−0.067
Term Str.	−0.207	−0.066	−0.067	1.000

Table 4.1 Correlation structure of macroeconomic factors

Correlation	$\hat{\mu}$	$\hat{\beta}_{Ind.\ Prod.}$	$\hat{\beta}_{Infl.}$	$\hat{\beta}_{Market}$	$\hat{\beta}_{Term\ Str.}$
$\hat{\mu}$	1.000	−0.247	−0.124	0.054	−0.027
$\hat{\beta}_{Ind.\ Prod.}$	−0.247	1.000	−0.355	0.050	0.297
$\hat{\beta}_{Infl.}$	−0.124	−0.355	1.000	−0.178	0.008
$\hat{\beta}_{Market}$	0.054	0.050	−0.178	1.000	−0.264
$\hat{\beta}_{Term\ Str.}$	−0.027	0.297	0.008	−0.264	1.000

Table 4.2 Cross-sectional correlation of means and betas

	Emp. Bayes prior $(\Theta_{\mu B} \neq 0)$	Emp. Bayes prior $(\Theta_{\mu B} = 0)$	CAPM prior $(\Theta_{\mu B} \neq 0)$	CAPM prior $(\Theta_{\mu B} = 0)$
Prior values				
$\tilde{\mu}$ (intercept)	19.2%	19.2%	19.2%	19.2%
$\tilde{\beta}_{\text{Ind. Prod.}}$	0.079	0.079	0	0
$\tilde{\beta}_{\text{Infl.}}$	−2.295	−2.295	0	0
$\tilde{\beta}_{\text{Market}}$	0.030	0.030	1	1
$\tilde{\beta}_{\text{Term Str.}}$	−0.185	−0.185	0	0
Posterior estimates (means)				
$\bar{\mu}_p$ (intercept)	18.8%	18.8%	18.3%	18.8%
$\bar{\beta}_{p\text{Ind. Prod.}}$	0.095	0.094	−0.101	−0.101
$\bar{\beta}_{p\text{Infl.}}$	−2.217	−2.221	−0.563	−0.563
$\bar{\beta}_{p\text{Market}}$	0.033	0.033	0.664	0.664
$\bar{\beta}_{p\text{Term Str.}}$	−0.189	−0.189	−0.005	−0.005

Table 4.3 Mean prior and posterior values of regression coefficients

	Emp. Bayes prior $(\Theta_{\mu B} \neq 0)$	Emp. Bayes prior $(\Theta_{\mu B} = 0)$	CAPM prior $(\Theta_{\mu B} \neq 0)$	CAPM prior $(\Theta_{\mu B} = 0)$
Prior estimates				
$\tilde{\lambda}_{\text{Ind. Prod.}}$	−0.022	+0.005	−0.002	−0.002
$\tilde{\lambda}_{\text{Infl.}}$	−0.017	−0.011	+0.001	+0.001
$\tilde{\lambda}_{\text{Mkt risk prem.}}$	−0.032	−0.060	+0.182	0.180
$\tilde{\lambda}_{\text{Term str.}}$	−0.182	−0.228	+0.043	+0.042
Posterior estimates				
$\lambda_{p\text{Ind. Prod.}}$	−0.016	+0.002	−0.008	−0.008
$\lambda_{p\text{Infl.}}$	−0.017	−0.013	+0.0005	+0.0005
$\lambda_{p\text{Mkt risk prem.}}$	−0.033	−0.053	+0.249	+0.253
$\lambda_{p\text{Term str.}}$	−0.236	−0.268	+0.049	+0.049

Table 4.4 Prior and posterior estimates of the risk premia (annualized)

Imposing the restriction $\Theta_{\mu B} = 0$ has little impact on the results. Using the empirical Bayes prior leads to very little Bayesian updating; our prior and posterior estimates are essentially equal. However, imposition of the CAPM prior leads to posterior estimates of betas that are smaller in magnitude for inflation than before, while (unsurprisingly) increasing substantially the role of the market. Industrial Production has changed little while Term Structure has more or less disappeared. Turning to Table 4.4, the market risk premia with a CAPM prior are now positive except for industrial production

$\mu = B'\lambda$	Prior	Posterior
Emp. Bayes prior ($\Theta_{\mu B} \neq 0$)	6.9%	8.1%
Emp. Bayes prior ($\Theta_{\mu B} = 0$)	6.5%	7.9%
CAPM prior ($\Theta_{\mu B} \neq 0$)	18.2%	16.9%
CAPM prior ($\Theta_{\mu B} = 0$)	18.0%	16.6%

Overall annualized SAMPLE mean excess return of stocks over the period 11/93-9/98: 16.7%.

Table 4.5 Overall prior and posterior excess return premiums ($\mu = B'\lambda$) (annualized)

and are dominated by the market risk premium. Finally in Table 4.5 we compute the mean overall prior and posterior return premium arising from the APT relationship $\mu = B'\lambda$. Purists might make a case for transforming the posterior joint distributions to derive the distribution of the posterior risk premium and then calculating our mean. However, since our results are essentially the same whether we impose the prior that $\Theta_{\mu B} = 0$ or $\Theta_{\mu B} \neq 0$, we thought this would add unnecessary complications. Our final result of a CAPM posterior of 16.6% ($\Theta_{\mu B} \neq 0$) or 16.9% ($\Theta_{\mu B} = 0$) can be compared with the overall annualized sample mean excess return of stocks in the period of 16.7%. This compares favorably with the empirical Bayes posterior estimates of about 8% and also with the CAPM estimate of about 18%.

4.5　Conclusion

This chapter has set out to illustrate how to use Bayesian methods to compute factor-risk premia in an APT framework for both cases of traded and non-traded factors. Using a sample of UK stocks from 1993 to 1998 we found evidence that a CAPM prior seemed to produce more data consistent results than an empirical Bayes approach. However, since our CAPM prior still retains some empirical Bayes hyperparameters based on the APT, a role of importance for the CAPM versus the APT, is by no means conclusive. In fact, our results suggest that a Bayesian mixture of CAPM as prior and APT as the data generating process outperforms both classical cases of CAPM or APT alone.

One case not considered here, or indeed elsewhere in the literature, is the important hybrid case where some factors are traded while some are not.

References

Antoniou, A., Garrett, I., and Priestley, R. (1998). Macroeconomic variables as common pervasive risk factors and the empirical content of the arbitrage pricing theory. *Journal of Empirical Finance*, 221–240.

Bauwens, L., Lubrano, M., and Richard, J.-F. (1999). *Bayesian inference in dynamic econometric models*. Advanced texts in econometrics, Oxford University Press.

Black, F. and Litterman, R. (1991). Global asset allocation with equities, bonds and currencies. Goldman Sachs and Co., October.

Black, F. and Litterman, R. (1992). Global portfolio optimization. *Financial Analysts Journal*, Sept–Oct:28–43.

Burmeister, E. and McElroy, M. (1988). Joint estimation of factor sensitivities and risk premia for the Arbitrage Pricing Theory. *Journal of Finance*, 43: 721–733.

Campbell, J., Lo, A., and MacKinlay, C. (1997). *The Econometrics of Financial Markets*. Princeton University Press, Princeton, NJ.

Chamberlain, G. and Rothschild, M. (1983). Arbitrage, factor structure, and mean-variance analysis on large asset markets. *Econometrica*, 51:1281–1304.

Chen, N., Roll, R., and Ross, S. (1986). Economic forces and the stock market. *Journal of Business*, 59:383–403.

Cochrane, J. (2001). *Asset Pricing*. Princeton University Press, Princeton, NJ.

Connor, G. and Korajczyk, R. (1993). A test for the number of factors in an approximate factor model. *Journal of Finance*, 48:1263–1291.

Dreze, J. and Richard, J.-F. (1983). Bayesian analysis of simultaneous equations. In Griliches, Z. and M. Intriligator, editors, *Handbook of Econometrics, Vol. I*, Chap. 9. Amsterdam: North-Holland.

Ericsson, J. and Karlsson, S. (2002). Selection of Factors in a Multifactor Pricing Model: A Bayesian Model Selection Approach. Mimeo.

Fama, E. and French, K. (1992). The cross-section of expected stock returns. *Journal of Finance*, 47:427–465.

Fama, E. and French, K. (1993). Common risk factors in the return of stocks and bonds. *Journal of Financial Economics*, 33:3–56.

Fama, E. and French, K. (1996). Multifactor explanations for asset pricing anomalies. *Journal of Finance*, 51:55–94.

Ingersoll, J. (1984). Some results in the theory of arbitrage pricing. *Journal of Finance*, 39:1021–1039.

Ingersoll, J. (1987). *Theory of Financial Decision Making*. Rowman & Littlefield, NJ.

Jagannathan, R. and Wang, Z. (1996). The conditional CAPM and the cross-section of expected returns. *Journal of Finance*, 51:3–53.

Kadiyala, K. R. and Karlsson, S. (1997). Numerical methods for estimation and inference in Bayesian VAR-models. *Journal of Applied Econometrics*, 12:99–132.

Pitsillis, M. (2002). *Econometric Analysis of National and International Risk Premia*. PhD thesis, University of Cambridge, UK.

Pitsillis, M. and Satchell, S. (2001). Improving the estimates of risk premia – application in the UK financial market. DAE working paper, University of Cambridge.

Polson, N. G. and Tew, B. V. (2000). Bayesian portfolio selection: An empirical analysis of the S&P 500 index 1970–1996. *Journal of Business and Economic Statistics*, 18:164–173.

Reyfman, A. (1997). *Labor market risk and expected asset returns*. PhD thesis, University of Chicago.

Ross, S. A. (1976). The Arbitrage Theory of Capital Asset Pricing. *Journal of Economic Theory*, 13:341–360.

Satchell, S. and Scowcroft, A. (2000). A demystification of the Black–Litterman model: Managing quantitative and traditional portfolio construction. *Journal of Asset Management*, 1(2):138–150.

Zellner, A. (1971). *An introduction to Bayesian inference in econometrics*. Wiley, New York.

Appendix

Definition of the matrixvariate Normal distribution

Let X and $VecX$ denote a $p \times q$ random matrix and its pq-dimensional column expansion respectively. X is said to have a matrixvariate Normal distribution with parameters $M \in \Re^{p \times q}$, $P \in C_p$, and $Q \in C_q$ (C_n denotes the set of $n \times n$, positive definite symmetric matrices)

$$X \sim MN_{p \times q}(VecM, Q \otimes P)$$

if and only if

$$VecX \sim N_{pq}(VecM, Q \otimes P)$$

(this denotes a multivariate normal distribution).

Therefore its density function is given by

$$f_{MN}^{p \times q}(X|M, Q \otimes P) = C_{MN}^{-1}(P, Q; p, q) \times \exp\left\{-\tfrac{1}{2}tr[Q^{-1}(X - M)'P^{-1}(X - M)]\right\}$$

where

$$C_{MN}(P, Q; p, q) = \left[(2\pi)^{pq} |P|^q |Q|^p\right]^{1/2}$$

Posterior risk premia calculations

Prior independence (i.e. $\Theta_{\mu B} = 0$)

$$\Sigma_p = \left(\begin{bmatrix} \Theta_{BB}^{-1} \otimes I_N + F'F \otimes \Psi^{-1} & 0 \\ 0 & \theta_{\mu\mu}^{-1} \times I_N + T \times \Psi^{-1} \end{bmatrix}\right)^{-1}$$

$$\Rightarrow$$

$$\Sigma_p = \begin{bmatrix} \Sigma_{p11} & 0 \\ 0 & \Sigma_{p22} \end{bmatrix} = \begin{bmatrix} [\Theta_{BB}^{-1} \otimes I_N + F'F \otimes \Psi^{-1}]^{-1} & 0 \\ 0 & [\theta_{\mu\mu}^{-1} \times I_N + T \times \Psi^{-1}]^{-1} \end{bmatrix}$$

and

$$VecA_p = \begin{bmatrix} VecB_p \\ \mu_p \end{bmatrix} = \begin{bmatrix} \Sigma_{p11}\left\{\left(\Theta_{BB}^{-1} \otimes I_N\right) Vec\tilde{B} + [F'F \otimes \Psi^{-1}]Vec\widehat{B}\right\} \\ \Sigma_{p22}\left\{(\theta_{\mu\mu}^{-1} \times I_N)\tilde{\mu} + T\Psi^{-1}\hat{\mu}\right\} \end{bmatrix}$$

$$= \begin{bmatrix} \left[\Theta_{BB}^{-1} \otimes I_N + F'F \otimes \Psi^{-1}\right]^{-1} \times \left\{\left(\Theta_{BB}^{-1} \otimes I_N\right) Vec\tilde{B} + [F'F \otimes \Psi^{-1}]Vec\widehat{B}\right\} \\ [\theta_{\mu\mu}^{-1} \times I_N + T \times \Psi^{-1}]^{-1} \times \left\{(\theta_{\mu\mu}^{-1} \times I_N)\tilde{\mu} + T\Psi^{-1}\hat{\mu}\right\} \end{bmatrix}$$

Prior dependence (i.e. $\Theta_{\mu B} \neq 0$)

$$
\Sigma_p = \left(\begin{bmatrix} \left[\Theta_{BB}^{-1} \left(I + \Theta_{B\mu} \Xi_2 \Theta_{\mu B} \Theta_{BB}^{-1} \right) \right] \otimes I_N & \left[-\Theta_{BB}^{-1} \Theta_{B\mu} \Xi_2 \right] \otimes I_N \\ \left[-\Xi_2 \Theta_{\mu B} \Theta_{BB}^{-1} \right] \otimes I_N & \Xi_2 \times I_N \end{bmatrix} \right.
$$

$$
\left. + \begin{bmatrix} F'F \otimes \Psi^{-1} & 0 \\ 0 & T \times \Psi^{-1} \end{bmatrix} \right)^{-1}
$$

$$
= \begin{bmatrix} \Upsilon_1 + (F'F \otimes \Psi^{-1}) & \Upsilon_2 \\ \Upsilon_2' & \Upsilon_3 + T\Psi^{-1} \end{bmatrix}^{-1}
$$

where

$$
\Upsilon_1 = \left[\Theta_{BB}^{-1} \left(I + \Theta_{B\mu} \Xi_2 \Theta_{\mu B} \Theta_{BB}^{-1} \right) \right] \otimes I_N
$$

$$
\Upsilon_2 = \left[-\Theta_{BB}^{-1} \Theta_{B\mu} \Xi_2 \right] \otimes I_N
$$

$$
\Upsilon_3 = \Xi_2 \times I_N
$$

Now let

$$
V_{11} = \Upsilon_1 + \left(F'F \otimes \Psi^{-1} \right)
$$

$$
V_{22} = \Upsilon_3 + T\Psi^{-1}
$$

The posterior variance-covariance in partitioned form is therefore:

$$
\Sigma_p = \begin{bmatrix} V_{11} & \Upsilon_2 \\ \Upsilon_2' & V_{22} \end{bmatrix}^{-1}
$$

$$
= \begin{bmatrix} V_{11}^{-1} \left(I + \Upsilon_2 \left(V_{22} - \Upsilon_2 V_{11}^{-1} \Upsilon_2 \right)^{-1} \Upsilon_2' V_{11}^{-1} \right) & -V_{11}^{-1} \Upsilon_2 \left(V_{22} - \Upsilon_2 V_{11}^{-1} \Upsilon_2 \right)^{-1} \\ -\left(V_{22} - \Upsilon_2 V_{11}^{-1} \Upsilon_2 \right)^{-1} \Upsilon_2' V_{11}^{-1} & \left(V_{22} - \Upsilon_2 V_{11}^{-1} \Upsilon_2 \right)^{-1} \end{bmatrix}
$$

$$
= \begin{bmatrix} \Sigma_{p11} & \Sigma_{p12} \\ \Sigma_{p21} & \Sigma_{p22} \end{bmatrix}
$$

where

$$
\Sigma_{p11} = V_{11}^{-1} \left(I + \Upsilon_2 \left(V_{22} - \Upsilon_2 V_{11}^{-1} \Upsilon_2 \right)^{-1} \Upsilon_2' V_{11}^{-1} \right)
$$

$$
\Sigma_{p12} = -V_{11}^{-1} \Upsilon_2 \left(V_{22} - \Upsilon_2 V_{11}^{-1} \Upsilon_2 \right)^{-1}
$$

$$
\Sigma_{p21} = \Sigma_{p12}'
$$

$$
\Sigma_{p22} = \left(V_{22} - \Upsilon_2 V_{11}^{-1} \Upsilon_2 \right)^{-1}
$$

Similarly

$$VecA_p = \Sigma_p \left((\tilde{\Sigma}^{-1} \times VecA) + (\hat{\Sigma}^{-1} \times Vec\hat{A}) \right)$$

$$= \Sigma_p \left(\begin{bmatrix} \Upsilon_1 & \Upsilon_2 \\ \Upsilon_2' & \Upsilon_3 \end{bmatrix} \times \begin{bmatrix} VecB \\ \underline{\mu} \end{bmatrix} + \begin{bmatrix} F'F \otimes \Psi^{-1} & 0 \\ 0 & T \times \Psi^{-1} \end{bmatrix} \times \begin{bmatrix} Vec\hat{B} \\ \hat{\mu} \end{bmatrix} \right)$$

$$= \Sigma_p \left(\begin{bmatrix} \Upsilon_1 VecB - \Upsilon_2\underline{\mu} \\ \Upsilon_2' VecB + \Upsilon_3\underline{\mu} \end{bmatrix} + \begin{bmatrix} [F'F \otimes \Psi^{-1}]Vec\hat{B} \\ T\Psi^{-1}\hat{\mu} \end{bmatrix} \right)$$

$$= \begin{bmatrix} \Sigma_{p11} & \Sigma_{p12} \\ \Sigma_{p21} & \Sigma_{p22} \end{bmatrix} \times \begin{bmatrix} \Upsilon_1 VecB - \Upsilon_2\underline{\mu} + [F'F \otimes \Psi^{-1}]Vec\hat{B} \\ \Upsilon_2' VecB + \Upsilon_3\underline{\mu} + T\Psi^{-1}\hat{\mu} \end{bmatrix}$$

$$= \begin{bmatrix} VecB_p \\ \mu_p \end{bmatrix}$$

where

$$VecB_p = \Sigma_{p11} \times \left\{ \Upsilon_1 VecB - \Upsilon_2\underline{\mu} + [F'F \otimes \Psi^{-1}]Vec\hat{B} \right\}$$
$$+ \Sigma_{p12} \times \left\{ \Upsilon_2' VecB + \Upsilon_3\underline{\mu} + T\Psi^{-1}\hat{\mu} \right\}$$
$$= \Sigma_{p11}\Upsilon_1 VecB - \Sigma_{p11}\Upsilon_2\underline{\mu} + \Sigma_{p11} \left[F'F \otimes \Psi^{-1} \right] Vec\hat{B}$$
$$+ \Sigma_{p12}\Upsilon_2' VecB + \Sigma_{p12}\Upsilon_3\underline{\mu} + \Sigma_{p12}T\Psi^{-1}\hat{\mu}$$
$$\Rightarrow$$
$$VecB_p = \left(\Sigma_{p11}\Upsilon_1 + \Sigma_{p12}\Upsilon_2' \right) VecB + \Sigma_{p11} \left[F'F \otimes \Psi^{-1} \right] Vec\hat{B}$$
$$+ (\Sigma_{p12}\Upsilon_3 - \Sigma_{p11}\Upsilon_2)\underline{\mu} + \Sigma_{p12}T\Psi^{-1}\hat{\mu}$$

and

$$\mu_p = \Sigma_{p21} \times \left\{ \Upsilon_1 VecB - \Upsilon_2\underline{\mu} + [F'F \otimes \Psi^{-1}]Vec\hat{B} \right\}$$
$$+ \Sigma_{p22} \times \left\{ \Upsilon_2' VecB + \Upsilon_3\underline{\mu} + T\Psi^{-1}\hat{\mu} \right\}$$
$$= \Sigma_{p21}\Upsilon_1 VecB - \Sigma_{p21}\Upsilon_2\underline{\mu} + \Sigma_{p21} \left[F'F \otimes \Psi^{-1} \right] Vec\hat{B}$$
$$+ \Sigma_{p22}\Upsilon_2' VecB + \Sigma_{p22}\Upsilon_3\underline{\mu} + \Sigma_{p22}T\Psi^{-1}\hat{\mu}$$
$$\Rightarrow$$
$$\mu_p = (\Sigma_{p21}\Upsilon_1 + \Sigma_{p22}\Upsilon_2') VecB + \Sigma_{p21} \left[F'F \otimes \Psi^{-1} \right] Vec\hat{B}$$
$$+ (\Sigma_{p22}\Upsilon_3 - \Sigma_{p21}\Upsilon_2)\underline{\mu} + \Sigma_{p22}T\Psi^{-1}\hat{\mu}$$

5 Sharpe style analysis in the MSCI sector portfolios: a Monte Carlo integration approach[1]

George A. Christodoulakis[*]

Abstract

We examine a decision-theoretic Bayesian framework for the estimation of Sharpe style portfolio weights of the MSCI sector returns. Following van Dijk and Kloek (1980) an appropriately defined prior density of style weights can incorporate non-negativity and other constraints. We use factor-mimicking portfolios as proxies to global style factors such as Value, Growth, Debt and Size. Our computational approach is based on the Monte Carlo Integration (MCI) of Kloek and van Dijk (1978) for the estimation of the posterior moments and distribution of portfolio weights. MCI provides a number of advantages, such as a flexible choice of prior distributions, improved numerical accuracy of the estimated parameters, the use of inequality restrictions in prior distributions and exact inference procedures. Our empirical findings suggest that, contrary to existing evidence, style factors do explain the MSCI sector portfolio returns for the particular sample period. Further, non-negativity constraints on portfolio weights were found to be binding in all cases.

5.1 Introduction

The Style Analysis introduced by Sharpe (1988, 1992) is probably the most popular portfolio performance attribution methodology. It is based on the simple idea that asset returns can be attributed to the returns of investment management style factors such as *value* and *size*. In its original form, relevant style factors should form a (non-hedge) portfolio which replicates the returns of the asset under assessment, thus style factor coefficients should be positive and sum to unity.

Given time-series data of asset and style factor returns, style analysis forms a constrained linear regression problem without intercept. The least squares estimation of the style portfolio weights – the regression coefficients – under linear *equality* constraints is a typical quadratic programming problem with closed-form solution and known distribution for the estimator, thus it has become a standard practice. When linear *inequality* constraints are imposed to ensure non-negative portfolio weights, it is not possible to obtain a closed-form solution, thus Judge and Takayama (1966)

---

[1] Reprinted from *Operational Research: An International Journal*, 2003, Vol. 2, Iss. 2, pp. 122–137, with the permission of HELORS.
[*] Bank of Greece and Sir John Cass Business School, City University London, 106 Bunhill Row, London ECI, UK, gchristodoulakis@bankofgreece.gr

proposed a modified simplex algorithm for an iterative solution of the inequality-constrained quadratic program. In univariate regression, the style coefficient estimator has a truncated normal distribution if the regression error is normally distributed. However, when there are more than two independent variables, it can be very difficult to obtain the desired sampling distributions using standard methods. One could at most assess the superiority or inferiority of the solution versus the maximum likelihood estimator using the results of Judge and Yancey (1986).

In this chapter we adopt a Bayesian perspective to formally impose the inequality parameter restrictions, in the form of a prior probability density of the model parameters. The latter is then combined with the sampling information as captured by the likelihood function to provide the joint posterior density function of the model parameters. For a normal linear model, the posterior density is a function of a multivariate t, thus making the analytical calculation of functions of the parameters difficult. We use Monte Carlo Integration (MCI) as proposed by Kloek and van Dijk (1978) and van Dijk and Kloek (1980) and further studied by Geweke (1986). This methodology is sufficiently general, allowing the computation of the posterior distribution of arbitrary functions of the parameters of interest and enables exact inference procedures that are impossible to treat in a sampling-theoretic approach. We apply this methodology on monthly MSCI country and sector returns and such style factor mimicking portfolios as *value*, *growth*, *debt* and *size*, from 1988 until 1998.

The structure of the chapter is as follows. In the next section we develop our Bayesian MCI methodological framework for style analysis under both equality and inequality constraints. Section 5.3 is devoted to the analysis and interpretation of our empirical results on monthly MSCI data. We conclude and provide thoughts on future research in section 5.4.

5.2 Methodology

Following the seminal work of Sharpe (1988, 1992) our portfolio returns Y can be attributed to a number of style factors X such that

$$Y = X\beta + U$$

s.t.

$$1'\beta = 1 \quad \text{and} \quad \beta \geq 0 \tag{5.1}$$

where Y is a vector of T observations of portfolio returns, X a matrix of T observations for K style factor returns, β a vector of K style factor betas, 1 is a vector of units and $U \sim N(0, \sigma^2 I)$. The least squares estimation of β in the above model is a constrained quadratic program. The solution under equality constraints is available in closed form and its distributional properties known. When inequality constraints are imposed in addition, the solution requires iterative optimization, see Judge and Takayama (1966), but the distributional properties of the estimator are not known. Davis (1978) provides a solution for the latter problem which requires that one knows which constraints are binding, an implausible assumption for Sharpe style analysis. One solution to that problem is to view the style regression from a Bayesian perspective and impose the parameter restrictions in the form of information encapsulated in the prior distribution. Then, using the posterior distribution one can estimate moments and other functions of the style parameters by means of Monte Carlo Integration.

5.2.1 A Bayesian decision-theoretic approach

Implementing the Bayesian-Monte Carlo Integration approach, we first impose the equality constraint by restating model (5.1) in deviation form from the kth style return

$$Y^* = X^*\beta^* + U^*$$

s.t.

$$1'\beta^* \leq 1 \quad \text{and} \quad \beta \geq 0 \tag{5.2}$$

where tth elements of the new variables are $y_t^* = y_t - x_{k,t}$ and $x_{i,t}^* = x_{i,t} - x_{k,t}$, where $i = 1,\ldots,K-1$ is the ith column of X. Now β^* is a vector of $K-1$ elements and the Kth beta can be obtained from $1 - 1'\beta^*$. In our standard Bayesian framework β^* is formally treated as a random variable in population and all elements of X^* are independent of each other and of U, β^* and σ^2. Then, by Bayes law the posterior density of β^* and σ^2 is given by

$$\text{Posterior}\left(\beta^*,\sigma^2 | Y^*, X^*\right) = \text{Likelihood}\left(\beta^*,\sigma^2 | Y^*, X^*\right) \times \text{Prior}\left(\beta^*,\sigma^2\right)$$

which is the product of the likelihood function and the prior density. Following van Dijk and Kloek (1980) our prior is composed of an improper uninformative component regarding σ^2 and an informative one regarding β^*, which for style analysis it captures our prior knowledge $1'\beta^* \leq 1$ and $\beta^* \geq 0$. By independence

$$\text{Prior}\left(\beta^*,\sigma^2\right) = \sigma^{-1}q\left(\beta^*\right) \tag{5.3}$$

where

$$q(\beta^*) = \begin{cases} 1 & \text{if } 1'\beta^* \leq 1 \quad \text{and} \quad \beta^* \geq 0 \\ 0 & \text{otherwise} \end{cases}$$

Under multivariate normality for U, it can be shown that the likelihood function is proportional to

$$L\left(\beta^*,\sigma | Y^* X^*\right) \propto \sigma^{-T} \exp\left\{-\frac{1}{2\sigma^2}\left[v\hat{\sigma}^2 + (\beta^* - b)'X'^*X^*(\beta^* - b)\right]\right\}$$

where $v\hat{\sigma}^2 = (Y^* - X^*b)'(Y^* - X^*b)$, $b = (X'^*X^*)^{-1}X'^*Y^*$ is the OLS estimator and $v = T - K + 1$. Combining the likelihood and the prior density yields a joint posterior density function which is proportional to

$$\text{Posterior}\left(\beta^*,\sigma | Y^*, X^*\right) \propto \sigma^{-(T+1)} \exp\left\{-\frac{1}{2\sigma^2}\left[v\hat{\sigma}^2 + (\beta^* - b)'X'^*X^*(\beta^* - b)\right]\right\}$$

$$\times q\left(\beta^*\right)$$

Standard analysis[2] to integrate σ out yields the marginal posterior probability density function of vector β^*, which is recognized as a multivariate t density with mean zero, variance $(\lambda/(\lambda-2)\hat{\sigma}^2)X'^*X^*$ and λ degrees of freedom

$$\text{Posterior}\left(\beta^*|Y^*,X^*\right) = c\left[\lambda + \frac{(\beta^*-b)'X'^*X^*(\beta^*-b)}{\hat{\sigma}^2}\right]^{-\frac{1}{2}(\lambda+K-1)} \times q(\beta^*)$$

(5.4)

where

$$c = \frac{\lambda^{\frac{\lambda}{2}}\Gamma\left[\frac{1}{2}(\lambda+K-1)\right]}{\pi^{\frac{K-1}{2}}\Gamma\left[\frac{\lambda}{2}\right]\det\left(\hat{\sigma}^2(X'^*X^*)^{-1}\right)^{\frac{1}{2}}}$$

and $\Gamma(.)$ is the gamma function.

5.2.2   Estimation by Monte Carlo integration

We shall follow the methodology proposed by Kloek and van Dijk (1978) and further studied by van Dijk and Kloek (1980). For any function $g(.)$, the point estimator of $g(\beta^*)$ is given by

$$E(g(\beta^*)|Y^*X^*) = \frac{\int g(\beta^*)\text{Posterior}\left(\beta^*|Y^*X^*\right)d\beta^*}{\int \text{Posterior}\left(\beta^*|Y^*X^*\right)d\beta^*}$$

The numerical implementation of the above estimator using Monte Carlo procedures requires the specification of a density function $I(\beta^*)$ from which random draws of β^* will be drawn; this is called *importance function* and is a proxy to the posterior density with convenient Monte Carlo properties. We can then have

$$E(g(\beta^*)|Y^*X^*) = \int \left(\frac{g(\beta^*)\,\text{Posterior}\left(\beta^*|Y^*X^*\right)}{I(\beta^*)}\right)I(\beta^*)d\beta^*$$

where the expectation is now taken over $I(\beta^*)$. Let $\beta_1^*, \beta_2^*, \ldots, \beta_N^*$ be a set of N random draws from $I(\beta^*)$, then we can prove that

$$\lim_{N\to\infty}\frac{1}{N}\sum_{i=1}^{N}\frac{g\left(\beta_i^*\right)\text{Posterior}\left(\beta_i^*|Y^*X^*\right)}{I(\beta_i^*)} = E(g(\beta^*)|Y^*X^*)$$

(5.5)

apart from a normalizing constant which can be calculated separately. Since $I(\beta^*)$ is supposed to be a proxy to the posterior distribution, the standard Bayesian analysis of the normal linear model in section 5.2.1 suggests that we could choose the multivariate t density. In this case our MCI estimator will be reduced to

$$\frac{1}{N}\sum_{i=1}^{N}g(\beta_i^*)q(\beta_i^*)$$

(5.6)

---

[2] See Judge et al. (1985).

In our Monte Carlo procedure we generate multivariate t-distributed vectors β_i^* as follows. We first derive the Cholesky decomposition of the OLS estimator covariance matrix such that

$$AA' = \hat{\sigma}^2 (X'^* X^*)^{-1}$$

and then generate a $K-1$ vector z_i of independent standard normal random variables. Then the ith replication of β_i^* will be

$$\beta_i^* = b + Az_i$$

drawn from a $(K-1)$-variate normal density. This can be converted to a t-distributed draw, by generating a λ vector w_i of independent standard normal variables and writing

$$\beta_i^* = b + Az_i \left(\frac{\lambda}{w_i' w_i} \right)^{\frac{1}{2}} \tag{5.7}$$

which is t-distributed with λ degrees of freedom. Thus our parameter estimates can now be obtained using (5.5) and $g(\beta_i^*) = \beta_i^*$. Similarly we can obtain estimates of higher moments of β^* or any other functions of interest.

The Bayesian MCI approach offers exact inference which is discussed in van Dijk and Kloek (1980), Geweke (1986) and Kim et al. (2000). In a different context, Lobosco and DiBartolomeo (1997) pointed out the problem of the lack of a precision measure for the style regression coefficients and proposed an approximate method based on Taylor expansions. However, the latter approach is valid only in the special case in which none of the true style coefficients are zero or one, thus excluding empirically relevant cases. Kim et al. (2000) also apply the results of Andrews (1999) and develop a comparable Bayesian method to obtain statistically valid distributions and confidence intervals regardless of the true values of style weights.

5.3 Style analysis in the MSCI sector portfolios[3]

We apply the Bayesian MCI approach to perform Sharpe style analysis for capitalization- and equally weighted portfolio returns, representing the sectors of Morgan Stanley Capital International universe from 1988 until 1998. Our data set is identical to the one used by Hall et al. (2002) and Christodoulakis and Satchell (2002), thus making some direct comparisons possible. Briefly, our time series consist of 120 data points for 1154 stocks, thus our data matrix of equity returns is 120×1154. The MSCI universe we use is drawn from twenty-one countries and nine sectors, where the nine sectors are regrouped to six: Basic Industries, Capital Goods, Consumer Goods, Energy, Financial, and the Other group (Resources, Transport, Utilities and Other Sectors). An inspection of the data uncovers substantial differences

---

[3] I would like to thank Steve Satchell and Soosung Hwang for providing the data set.

in the value and the number of equities in different sectors. This arises naturally for a number of reasons. It is therefore useful to consider value-weighted returns versus equally weighted returns. A natural value weighting scheme would be to consider, at each point in time, the value of the ith stock relative to the value of the group of stocks within its sector. In particular

$$w_{i,t}^k = \frac{S_{i,t}^k}{\sum_{i=1}^{N^k} S_{i,t}^k}$$

where k denotes the kth sector, N^k is the number of stocks in the kth sector, $S_{i,t}^k$ is the US dollar market value of equity i in the kth sector and $\sum_{i=1}^{N^k} S_{i,t}^k = 1$ for all k.

Since style factors are typically latent, we use *style factor mimicking portfolios* (FMPs) as a proxy. That is we construct portfolios of assets that mimic the style factors themselves in that their returns are designed to be highly correlated with the (unobservable) factor values or their equilibrium risk premiums. The theory of factor mimicking portfolios is discussed in Huberman et al. (1987), Lehman and Modest (1988) and Connor and Linton (2000). In constructing FMPs, for each factor X_i the entire MSCI universe is ranked according to an attribute of X_i. As in Hall et al. (2002) and Christodoulakis and Satchell (2002), we use style attributes for Value, Growth, Debt and Size defined using observable company data[4]. For each attribute, X_a, an equally weighted hedge portfolio is then constructed which is long the top n-tile and short the bottom n-tile of the MSCI universe ranked by X_a. The resulting hedge portfolio is the factor-mimicking portfolio of factor X. A better diversification is produced for small n, thus our data set is constructed for $n = 3$. Some data providers construct style indices based on measures which attribute Growth, say, to non-Value stocks. In contrast to the latter approach we prefer a dual sort, thus recognizing stocks that are 'growth at the right price', i.e. cheap (Value) Growth stocks.

We have set the number of Monte Carlo replications equal to 10^6 and have used GAUSS language as our computational platform. In performing MCI we need to specify the importance function $I(\beta_i^*)$. A first candidate is the multivariate t distribution as dictated by standard Bayesian analysis of the normal regression model with an uninformative volatility prior. We specify its parameters by adopting the OLS estimators b and $\hat{\sigma}^2(X'^*X^*)^{-1}$ and experimenting with λ. We found our results to be insensitive to the choice of λ, so we set $\lambda = 4$. We also found it was not necessary to multiply $\hat{\sigma}^2(X'^*X^*)^{-1}$ by any constant as van Dijk and Kloek (1980) mention in page 315. Our normalization constant in equation (5.5) is obtained by setting $g = 1$ in (5.5) and taking the inverse.

We present our empirical results for the six capitalization- and value-weighted MSCI sector portfolios in Tables 5.1 to 5.6. For comparison reasons we also report OLS and equality-restricted OLS estimates. We observe that unrestricted OLS produces Value and Growth portfolio weights that violate both the positivity and equality constraints in all six sector portfolios. Equality-restricted OLS still violates the positivity but to a lesser extent, primarily for the Value factor.

---

[4] For the explicit definition see Christodoulakis and Satchell (2002).

	OLS		OLS restricted		Bayesian Monte Carlo integration				
	Beta	Std error	Beta	Std error	Beta	Std error	Skew	Kurtosis	B-J stat.
β_v^c	−0.1458	0.0209	0.0494	0.2009	0.2574	0.1883	0.7477	2.9115	166.4
β_v^e	0.0305	0.0195	0.3359	0.1919	0.2786	0.2011	0.6977	2.7880	179.8
β_g^c	−1.0434	0.0426	−0.3779	0.2816	0.2244	0.1758	0.9509	3.4066	280.4
β_g^e	−1.2444	0.0397	−0.2033	0.2690	0.2150	0.1760	0.9883	3.4611	371.9
β_s^c	0.5222	0.0278	0.7256	0.2819	0.1310	0.1083	1.3381	5.0076	830.1
β_s^e	0.2955	0.0259	0.6137	0.2692	0.1054	0.0940	1.6101	6.1976	1859
β_d^c	0.5493	0.0008	0.6029	0.0865	0.3873	0.2228	0.1936	2.1110	69.73
β_d^e	0.1700	0.0078	0.2537	0.0826	0.4010	0.2318	0.1563	2.0657	87.64

Note: (c) capitalization weighted, (e) equally weighted, (v) value, (g) growth, (s) size, (d) debt, 10^6 replications.

Table 5.1 Basic Industries, 1988–1998

	OLS		OLS restricted		Bayesian Monte Carlo integration				
	Beta	Std error	Beta	Std error	Beta	Std error	Skew	Kurtosis	B-J stat.
β_v^c	−0.5714	0.0179	−0.2725	0.1770	0.2669	0.2034	0.6148	2.2711	19.83
β_v^e	−0.2260	0.0175	0.0917	0.1742	0.2360	0.1883	0.9584	3.4135	175.7
β_g^c	−0.6752	0.0364	0.3441	0.2481	0.2530	0.2030	0.9369	3.2782	34.83
β_g^e	−1.0714	0.0356	0.0118	0.2442	0.2365	0.1953	1.1146	3.8451	259.7
β_s^c	0.0624	0.0238	0.3739	0.2483	0.1012	0.1003	1.6857	6.2235	211.2
β_s^e	0.2000	0.0232	0.5311	0.2445	0.0926	0.0967	2.1739	9.0893	2558
β_d^c	0.4725	0.0072	0.5545	0.0762	0.3790	0.2413	0.3297	2.0854	12.34
β_d^e	0.2782	0.0070	0.3653	0.0750	0.4349	0.2454	0.0495	1.9605	49.83

Note: (c) capitalization weighted, (e) equally weighted, (v) value, (g) growth, (s) size, (d) debt, 10^6 replications.

Table 5.2 MSCI Capital Goods, 1988–1998

Inspecting our results from the Bayesian Monte Carlo Integration approach, we observe that this methodology always produces positive portfolio weights which sum to unity. Since the MCI results are based on the empirical posterior density of the β^* vector, it is flexible enough to produce estimates of more complicated functions than the mean. In particular, Tables 5.1 to 5.6 report estimates of standard errors, skewness and kurtosis coefficients as well as the Bera–Jarque normality statistic. It is evident that most of the beta coefficients are highly non-normal exhibiting positive skewness and in some cases excess kurtosis. There is only one case in which normality cannot be

	OLS		OLS restricted		Bayesian Monte Carlo integration				
	Beta	Std error	Beta	Std error	Beta	Std error	Skew	Kurtosis	B-J stat.
β_v^c	−0.6730	0.0150	−0.4514	0.1467	0.2251	0.1977	1.2277	4.2956	74.82
β_v^e	−0.3765	0.0153	−0.1382	0.1510	0.2030	0.1745	1.1098	3.7228	233.6
β_g^c	−0.0174	0.0305	0.7383	0.2057	0.2721	0.2101	0.7939	4.2956	24.68
β_g^e	−0.4242	0.0313	0.3884	0.2116	0.2460	0.1974	0.9097	3.1606	143.0
β_s^c	0.1481	0.0199	0.3790	0.2059	0.1024	0.1035	1.7552	6.4459	234.9
β_s^e	0.2492	0.0204	0.4975	0.2118	0.0860	0.0856	1.9238	8.0499	1728
β_d^c	0.2732	0.0060	0.3340	0.0632	0.4005	0.2477	0.1656	1.9433	11.90
β_d^e	0.1869	0.0061	0.2522	0.0650	0.4650	0.2402	−0.045	2.0654	37.81

Note: (c) capitalization weighted, (e) equally weighted, (v) value, (g) growth, (s) size, (d) debt, 10^6 replications.

Table 5.3 MSCI Consumer Goods, 1988–1998

	OLS		OLS restricted		Bayesian Monte Carlo integration				
	Beta	Std error	Beta	Std error	Beta	Std error	Skew	Kurtosis	B-J stat.
β_v^c	−0.6238	0.0167	−0.2088	0.1733	0.2067	0.1637	1.0315	3.7633	692.30
β_v^e	−0.4408	0.0180	−0.0331	0.1844	0.2179	0.1693	0.9241	3.3913	504.06
β_g^c	−1.0485	0.0340	0.3666	0.2429	0.2144	0.1697	0.9453	3.3659	530.61
β_g^e	−1.3722	0.0367	0.0179	0.2585	0.2248	0.1776	0.9340	3.3608	511.26
β_s^c	0.2886	0.0222	0.7212	0.2431	0.3102	0.1339	−0.017	2.8026	5.7456
β_s^e	0.4928	0.0240	0.9177	0.2588	0.2577	0.1286	0.3057	3.1525	56.076
β_d^c	0.0072	0.0067	0.1210	0.0746	0.2687	0.1724	0.4473	2.4532	157.31
β_d^e	−0.0141	0.0072	0.0976	0.0794	0.2995	0.1880	0.4072	2.4255	140.30

Note: (c) capitalization weighted, (e) equally weighted, (v) value, (g) growth, (s) size, (d) debt, 10^6 replications.

Table 5.4 MSCI Energy, 1988–1998

rejected, namely the weight of *size* style factor for the capitalization-weighted energy sector portfolio. Also, a small number of style portfolio weights exhibit non-normality to a smaller extent compared to the majority of weights, e.g. the *value* factor weight for the capital goods sector and the *debt* factor for consumer goods and capital goods, due to platikurtosis.

The Bayesian MIC values of the *value* and *growth* factor weights for our six different portfolios range from 0.20 to 0.27 for both the capitalization- and equally weighted portfolios. Similarly, the *size* style weight takes values from 0.08 to 0.31 while the *debt*

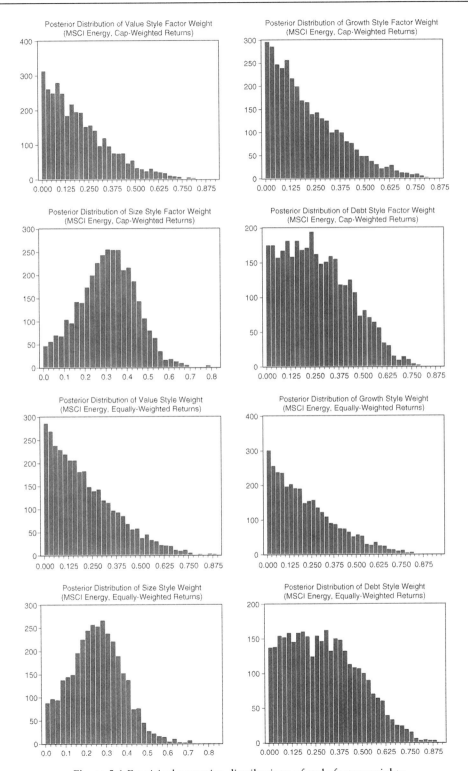

Figure 5.1 Empirical posterior distributions of style factor weights

	OLS		OLS restricted		Bayesian Monte Carlo Integration				
	Beta	Std error	Beta	Std error	Beta	Std error	Skew	Kurtosis	B-J stat.
β_v^c	−0.6947	0.0198	−0.5659	0.1888	0.2137	0.1707	0.9687	3.4139	292.07
β_v^e	−0.4466	0.0175	−0.1557	0.1728	0.2083	0.1747	1.0972	3.7558	756.55
β_g^c	−0.2324	0.0403	0.2067	0.2646	0.2687	0.1952	0.7178	2.8463	155.14
β_g^e	−0.6233	0.0356	0.3686	0.2423	0.2477	0.1943	0.8932	3.1602	451.87
β_s^c	0.7166	0.0263	0.8508	0.2649	0.1851	0.1228	0.8937	4.3954	382.62
β_s^e	0.3305	0.0232	0.6337	0.2425	0.1058	0.0894	1.6719	7.1986	4046
β_d^c	0.4731	0.0079	0.5084	0.0813	0.3325	0.2084	0.3581	2.2777	77.002
β_d^e	0.0736	0.0070	0.1533	0.0744	0.4382	0.2362	−0.040	1.9649	151.40

Note: (c) capitalization weighted, (e) equally weighted, (v) value, (g) growth, (s) size, (d) debt, 10^6 replications.

Table 5.5 MSCI Financials, 1988–1998

	OLS		OLS restricted		Bayesian Monte Carlo Integration				
	Beta	Std error	Beta	Std error	Beta	Std error	Skew	Kurtosis	B-J stat.
β_v^c	−0.5608	0.0165	−0.2758	0.1634	0.2088	0.1709	1.0630	3.6624	294.62
β_v^e	−0.3842	0.0165	0.0130	0.1703	0.2316	0.1797	0.9523	3.3994	625.03
β_g^c	−0.7548	0.0335	0.2172	0.2290	0.2389	0.1895	0.8549	2.9717	173.73
β_g^e	−1.1676	0.0336	0.1867	0.2387	0.2301	0.1846	0.9415	3.2998	599.99
β_s^c	0.3311	0.0219	0.6282	0.2293	0.1039	0.0907	1.5919	6.4776	1320.8
β_s^e	0.2687	0.0219	0.6826	0.2390	0.1231	0.0905	1.2536	5.3875	1978.1
β_d^c	0.3521	0.0066	0.4303	0.0703	0.4485	0.2332	−0.049	2.0008	59.915
β_d^e	0.0088	0.0066	0.1177	0.0733	0.4151	0.2247	0.0342	2.0392	153.13

Note: (c) capitalization weighted, (e) equally weighted, (v) value, (g) growth, (s) size, (d) debt, 10^6 replications.

Table 5.6 MSCI Other Sectors, 1988–1998

factor takes values from 0.09 to 0.46. Thus, contrary to existing evidence presented in Hall et al. (2002) our approach presents evidence that style factors do explain the return performance of the MSCI sector portfolios fairly uniformly for the period 1988 to 1998.

Our exact inference procedure provides easily constructed confidence intervals for the point parameter estimates. The latter can take the form of a Bayesian Highest Posterior Density (HPD) interval (L, U) which, for a given confidence level

$1 - a$, is given by the shortest interval over which the cumulative posterior probability equals $1 - a$. Following Kim et al. (2000) the interval (L, U) is given by $(0, \beta^*_{i,1-a})$ if posterior$(0|Y^*, X^*) >$ posterior$(\beta^*_{i,1-a}|Y^*, X^*)$ where $\beta^*_{i,1-a}$ is the value of factor weight at which the cumulative posterior probability equals $1 - a$. Further, if posterior$(0|Y^*, X^*) =$ posterior$(\beta^*_{i,1-a}|Y^*, X^*)$ then the shortest interval (L, U) can be found numerically. We graph the empirical posterior distribution for the four style factor weights on the MSCI Energy sector[5]. An inspection uncovers clearly the effects of the non-negativity constraints which appear to be binding in all eight cases, thus truncating the posterior density of the beta coefficients. Note that the effect of the truncation is smaller for the *size* style factor which also deviated less from the normal distribution.

5.4 Conclusions

We have presented a framework for Sharpe style analysis in the MSCI sector portfolios from 1988 to 1998. Following Kloek and van Dijk (1978) and van Dijk and Kloek (1980) we consider style portfolios from a Bayesian perspective and can formally incorporate non-negativity constraints for the beta coefficients through a appropriately specified prior density function. We can estimate any function of the parameters of interest using the Monte Carlo Integration method. The framework allows for exact inference procedures that have been further studied in an asymptotic framework by Kim et al. (2000). Also, Andrews (1999) provides an asymptotically valid inference procedure for parameters on the boundary.

Contrary to existing studies, our empirical results provide evidence for a relatively uniform significance of style factors in determining the MSCI sector portfolio returns for the given sample period. We also observe that non-negativity constraints are strikingly binding in the majority of the cases, thus truncating the posterior distribution of beta coefficients. In a few cases beta coefficients can be well represented by normal densities.

Future research involves the development of an MCI methodology for betas and volatility that follows conditionally stochastic processes over time as in Christodoulakis and Satchell (2002). This approach would maintain the normality assumption in its conditional form while allowing for unconditional non-normality, see Geweke (1989) and Koop (1994) for similar work in the ARCH volatility framework.

References

Andrews, D. W. K. (1999). Estimation when the Parameter in on the Boundary. *Econometrica*, 67:1341–1383.

Christodoulakis, G. A. and Satchell, S. E. (2002). On the Evolution of Global Style Factors in the MSCI Universe of Assets. *International Transactions in Operational Research*, 9(5):643–660.

---

[5] Because of space requirements we do not present distribution graphs for the remaining five portfolios. However, these are available from the author upon request.

Connor, G. and Linton, O. (2000). Semiparametric Estimation of a Characteristic-based Factor Model of Stock Returns. Working Paper, Department of Accounting and Finance, LSE, University of London, UK.

Davis, W. W. (1978). Bayesian Analysis of the Linear Model Subject to Linear Inequality Constraints. *Journal of the American Statistical Association*, 78:573–579.

Geweke, J. (1986). Exact Inference in the Inequality Constrained Normal Linear Regression Model. *Journal of Applied Econometrics*, 1:127–141.

Geweke, J. (1989). Exact Predictive Densities in Linear Models with ARCH Disturbances. *Journal of Econometrics*, 40:63–86.

Hall, A. D., Hwang, S., and Satchell, S. E. (2002). Using Bayesian Variable Selection Methods to Choose Style Factors in Global Stock Return Models. *Journal of Banking and Finance*, Forthcoming.

Huberman, G., Shmuel, A., and Stambaugh, R. F. (1987). Mimicking Portfolios and Exact Arbitrage Pricing. *Journal of Finance*, 42:1–10.

Judge, G. G. and Takayama, T. (1966). Inequality Restrictions in Regression Analysis. *Journal of the American Statistical Association*, 61:166–181.

Judge, G. G. and Yancey, T. A. (1986). *Improved Methods of Inference in Econometrics*. Amsterdam, North Holland.

Judge, G. G., Griffiths, W. E., Hill, R. C., Lutkepohl, H., and Lee, T. C. (1985). *The Theory and the Practice of Econometrics*. New York, Wiley.

Kim, T.-H., Stone, D., and White, H. (2000). *Asymptotic and Bayesian Confidence Intervals for Sharpe Style Weights*. University of California, San Diego, Department of Economics Working Paper 2000–27.

Kloek, T. and van Dijk, H. K. (1978). Bayesian Estimates of Equation System Parameters: An Application of Integration by Monte Carlo. *Econometrica*, 46(1):1–19.

Koop, G. (1994). Bayesian Semi-nonparametric ARCH Models. *Review of Economics and Statistics*, 76(1):176–181.

Lehman, B. N. and Modest, D. M. (1988). The Empirical Foundations of the Arbitrage Pricing Theory. *Journal of Financial Economics*, 21(2):213–254.

Lobosco, A. and DiBartolomeo, D. (1997). Approximating the Confidence Intervals for Sharpe Style Weights. *Financial Analysts Journal*, July–August:80–85.

Sharpe, W. F. (1988). Determining the Fund's Effective Asset Mix. *Investment Management Review*, November–December:59–69.

Sharpe, W. F. (1992). Asset Allocation: Management Style and Performance Measurement. *Journal of Portfolio Management*. 18:7–19.

van Dijk, H. K. and Kloek, T. (1980). Further Experience in Bayesian Analysis Using Monte Carlo Integration. *Journal of Econometrics*, 14:307–328.

6 Implication of the method of portfolio formation on asset pricing tests

Ka-Man Lo[*]

Abstract

This chapter investigates the issues of portfolio formation and asset pricing tests. Work in empirical finance starts with grouping individual stocks into portfolios based on a particular attribute of the stocks. This chapter also examines the effect of this practice and whether using individual stocks solves the problem of grouping. Canadian stock return data is used. Three asset pricing tests, the multivariate F test, the average F test and a robust specification test by Hansen and Jagannathan (1997) are considered. It is found that (i) grouping of stocks based on different attributes can give different asset pricing inference using the same pool of stocks, (ii) using individual assets introduces a survivorship problem and (iii) the three asset pricing tests can give different inference on the same model specification. A simulation study is implemented to study the robustness of different asset pricing tests to the spurious correlation. It is found that the GMM-based J_t test is more robust to spurious correlation.

6.1 Introduction

One universal practice in any asset pricing test is to sort stocks into portfolios based on a particular attribute of the stocks. Size, estimated beta and book-to-market ratio are some of the most common attributes used in sorting stocks (see e.g. Fama and French (1992, 1993); Gibbons et al. (1989); Jagannathan and Wang (1996). There are two reasons for sorting stocks into portfolios to implement asset pricing tests: first, grouping stocks into portfolios diversifies away idiosyncratic risks of individual stocks. Second, the cross-section of individual stocks is very often larger than the number of time-series observations available. To make estimation feasible, it is necessary to group stocks into portfolios. The theoretical implication of using an attribute correlated with stocks' return has been examined by Berk (2000) and Lo and MacKinlay (1990). Lo and MacKinlay (1990) point out that sorting without regard to the data generating process may lead to spurious correlation between the attributes and the estimated pricing errors. They advocate using data from a different sampling period to avoid data-snooping bias. Berk (2000) shows that sorting assets into portfolios using

---

[*] I am indebted to my thesis advisors, John Knight and Stephen Sapp, for their help. I also wish to thank Robin Carter, Joel Fried, Lynda Kalaf and participants of CEA and NFA conference for helpful comments and suggestions.

an attribute can lead to bias toward rejecting the model when asset pricing tests are implemented within the portfolio. Since grouping of stocks is unavoidable in an empirical context, this chapter studies whether different attributes used in sorting the same pool of stocks would lead to different asset pricing inference[1]. This issue is important because if different attributes used in sorting leads to different asset pricing inference, we have no way to judge whether a set of factors statistically prices a pool of stocks. Another issue examined here concerns the asset pricing test used. Many asset pricing tests exist in the literature. As the asset pricing inference depends on the asset pricing test used, this chapter also examines whether different asset pricing tests would lead to the same inference.

This chapter is divided into two broad sections: an empirical study and a simulation study. In the first part, it examines empirically, using Canadian stock return data, the following three related questions: (1) Does sorting stocks into portfolios based on different attributes yield different asset pricing inference? (2) If sorting stocks does have an effect on inference, does using individual stocks (if possible) solve the problems associated with sorting? (3) Do different asset pricing tests give the same inference? In this study, two attributes, size and estimated betas, are used in grouping stocks into portfolios. It is found that portfolios formed by stocks sorted by different attributes pick up different risks and they can give different asset pricing inference. One special feature of this study is that the pricing of individual assets' returns is examined through the average F test proposed by Hwang and Satchell (1997). It is found that, although using individual stocks avoids issues associated with sorting, it introduces a survivorship bias problem. Regarding the third question, three asset pricing tests are considered. The three tests are the multivariate F test, the average F test and a robust specification test developed by Hansen and Jagannathan (1997). The first two tests are based on the regression framework. The robust specification test is based on the stochastic discount factor framework. We find that the three tests can lead to different inferences due to the different definition of pricing errors and the weighting of pricing errors in the three tests.

Canadian stock return data are used to create a modified version of the three factors used in Fama and French (1996). The three factors in Fama and French (1996) are excess market return, SMB and HML. SMB is defined as the difference between the return of a portfolio of small firms and the return of a portfolio of large firms. HML is defined as the difference in return between a portfolio of high book-to-market firms and a portfolio of low book-to-market firms. The latter two factors are 'empirical' in the sense that there is no solid economic theory to explain why those factors should price assets. They are thought to approximate some unknown risks. Canadian stock return data are used because there is relatively little work examining Canadian stock return with Fama and French factors. Elfakhani et al. (1998) examine the pricing of Canadian stocks using Fama and French's three factors. However, their study uses a two-stage cross-section regression method, which is prone to error-in-variables problems. Griffin (2001) compares the performance of country-specific and the global

---

[1] Lo and MacKinlay (1990) implemented two independent empirical studies using beta-sorted and size-sorted portfolios. However, their study does not study the asset pricing inference of using different attributes within the same pool of stocks. The two empirical studies in their paper are of different sampling interval and different pool of stocks. Also, the two attributes used in their paper are in sample so as to show the data-snooping bias in testing. This chapter uses attributes which are obtained prior to the sampling interval to avoid data-snooping issues.

version of Fama and French's three factor model with Canada being one of the domestic models examined.

The second part of this chapter is a simulation study which examines the effect of different sorting criteria. In a controlled experiment, this simulation study shows how sorting by size of stock and estimated beta of stock can lead to different conclusions. The emphasis of this simulation study is quite different from the Lo and Mackinlay's simulation study. Instead of focusing on the effect of suprious correlation between sorting criteria and estimation error, our simulation study studies the robustness of different tests to the supurious correlation. We examine three tests: the multivariate F test, the average F test and the J_T test, which is based on the stochastic discount factor framework. More specifically, our study extends Lo and MacKinlay's simulation study in two ways: (1) it examines the robustness of the average F test and the stochastic discount factor framework to the spurious correlation between the sorting criteria and the estimation error and (2) it provides a more detailed study on the GRS test on beta-sorted portfolios.

The rest of the chapter is organized as follows: Section 6.2 presents the model specification. Section 6.3 examines the implementation of the multivariate F test, the average F test and the robust specification test. Section 6.4 explains the construction of the variables and the data sources. Section 6.5 presents the empirical results. Section 6.6 is the simulation study. Section 6.7 concludes.

6.2   Models

6.2.1   Asset pricing frameworks

We focus on linear pricing relationships and examine asset pricing in both the traditional regression framework and the stochastic discount factor framework using GMM. For asset pricing posed in the traditional regression framework, assets' excess returns are linear functions of k factors' return.

$$r_{it} - r_{ft} = \alpha + \beta_{1,i}f_{1t} + \beta_{2,i}f_{2t} + \cdots + \beta_{k,i}f_{kt} + \epsilon_{it} \tag{6.1}$$

$$i = 1, \ldots, n \quad t = 1, \ldots, T$$

where n is the number of assets and T is the number of time-series observations. If a linear combination of the k factors is efficient, the expected return linear beta relation holds, i.e.,

$$E(r_{it} - r_{ft}) = \beta_{1,i}E(f_{1t}) + \beta_{2,i}E(f_{2t}) + \cdots + \beta_{k,i}E(f_{kt}) \quad i = 1, \ldots, n \tag{6.2}$$

r_{it} is the asset return and r_{ft} is the risk-free rate so that $r_{it} - r_{ft}$ is the excess return at time t, hereafter denoted as r_{it}^e. f_{jt} is the factor return of factor j at time t. $\beta_{j,i}$ is factor j's loading of asset i. The assumptions such that equation (6.2) holds are: (1) r_{it} and f_{jt} are stationary and spherically distributed, (2) ϵ_{it} is iid. with zero mean, and (3) each $\beta_{j,i}$ is constant through time. Both equation (6.1) and equation (6.2) can be put into linear regression framework using their sample counterpart. We will use equation (6.1) and linear regression to implement the multivariate F test and the average F test.

Asset pricing in the stochastic discount framework is based on the Euler equation, which is the first order condition of the investor's utility maximization problem. Denoting m_t as the stochastic discount factor and r_{it} as the simple net return, the Euler equation states that

$$E[m_t(1 + r_{it})|\Omega_{t-1}] = 1, \qquad i = 0, \ldots, n \quad r_{0t} = r_f \tag{6.3}$$

in which Ω_{t-1} is the investor's information set at time $t-1$. Denoting r_{it}^e as the simple excess return, the Euler equation becomes

$$E[m_t r_{it}^e|\Omega_{t-1}] = 0, \qquad i = 1, \ldots, n \tag{6.4}$$

This representation is unfortunately too general to estimate, thus we will examine the linear discount factor model, i.e.

$$m_t = a + b_1 f_{1t} + b_2 f_{2t} + \cdots + b_k f_{kt} \tag{6.5}$$

in which a is normalized to 1. Substituting equation (6.5) into equation (6.4), all parameters can be estimated and inference can be drawn in the GMM framework with the n moment conditions.

6.2.2 Specifications to be tested

Excess market return, size factor return and book-to-market factor return are constructed from Canadian securities. The last two factors, the size factor and the book-to-market factor, are modified versions of SMB and HML from Fama and French (1993). The reasons for the modifications will be explained in section 6.4. Three models are examined: the first model is a standard CAPM model with the excess market return as the only factor:

$$r_{it}^e = \alpha_i + \beta_{m,i} r_{mt}^e + \epsilon_{it}, \qquad i = 1, \ldots, n \tag{6.6}$$

in which r_{it}^e represents the excess return of asset i at time t, r_{mt}^e is excess of market return at time t and $\beta_{m,i}$ is the factor loading of asset i. α_i is interpreted as the pricing error of asset i: if excess market return is the only source of risk in pricing r_{it}^e, then α_i should be equal to zero. In the stochastic discount factor framework, the linear discount factor is given by

$$m_t = a + b_m r_{mt}^e \tag{6.7}$$

b_m is the change in the intertemporal marginal rate of substitution with respect to unit change in excess market return.

The second model contains two factors: excess market return and size factor return. The excess return of asset i is generated by the following equation,

$$r_{it}^e = \alpha_i + \beta_{m,i} r_{mt}^e + \beta_{s,i} r_{st} + \epsilon_{it}, \qquad i = 1, \ldots, n \tag{6.8}$$

in which r_{st} is the return of size factor at time t and $\beta_{s,i}$ is the factor loading of size factor of asset i. In the stochastic discount factor framework, the discount factor is given by

$$m_t = a + b_m r^e_{mt} + b_s r_{st} \qquad (6.9)$$

The third model uses three factors with the book-to-market factor return as the additional factor. The excess return of asset i is generated by,

$$r^e_{it} = \alpha_i + \beta_{m,i} r^e_{mt} + \beta_{s,i} r_{st} + \beta_{bk,i} r_{bkt} + \epsilon_i, \qquad i = 1,\ldots,n \qquad (6.10)$$

in which r_{bkt} is the return of book-to-market factor at time t and $\beta_{bk,i}$ is the factor loading of book-to-market factor of asset i. The linear discount factor counterpart is given by

$$m_t = a + b_m r^e_{mt} + b_s r_{st} + b_{bk} r_{bkt} \qquad (6.11)$$

6.3 Implementation

Three tests are implemented. The multivariate F test and the average F test are based on the linear regression framework: each of the n asset returns is specified as a linear function of the k factor returns. In the stochastic discount factor framework, the stochastic discount factor is assumed to be a linear function of the k factor returns and the parameters are estimated via the n moment conditions using the GMM with the weighting matrix advocated by Hansen and Jagannathan (1997).

6.3.1 Multivariate F test

Both the multivariate F test and the average F test start with the following multivariate linear regression:

$$r^e_{it} = \alpha_i + \beta_{1,i} f_{1t} + \beta_{2,i} f_{2t} + \cdots + \beta_{k,i} f_{kt} + \epsilon_{it} \qquad i = 1,\ldots,n \qquad (6.12)$$
$$= \alpha_i + \beta_i f_t + \epsilon_{it}$$

where β_i is a $1 \times k$ vector of factor loadings of asset i and f_t is a $k \times 1$ vector of the k factor returns at time t. If the expected return of asset i is linear in betas, i.e. a linear combination of the k factors is on the efficient frontier, then

$$E(r^e_{it}) = \beta_{1,i} E(f_1) + \beta_{2,i} E(f_2) + \cdots + \beta_{ki,} E(f_k) \qquad i = 1,\ldots,n \qquad (6.13)$$

Equation (6.12) and equation (6.13) imply that α, the $n \times 1$ vector of n asset pricing errors, is jointly equal to zero.

Assuming that the random error, ϵ_{it}, is normally distributed, together with assumptions stated in the first section, the multivariate F test is given by

$$W = \frac{(T - n - k)}{n} \cdot \frac{1}{(1 + \hat{\mu}'_k \widehat{\Omega}_k \hat{\mu}_k)} \hat{\alpha}' \widehat{\Sigma}^{-1} \hat{\alpha} \qquad (6.14)$$

where

$$\hat{\Sigma} = \frac{1}{T} \sum_{t=1}^{T} \left(r_t^e - \hat{\alpha} - \hat{\beta} f_t \right) \left(r_t^e - \hat{\alpha} - \hat{\beta} f_t \right)'$$

$$\hat{\mu}_k = \frac{1}{T} \sum_{t=1}^{T} f_t$$

$$\hat{\Omega}_k = \frac{1}{T} \sum_{t=1}^{T} (f_t - \hat{\mu}_k) (f_t - \hat{\mu}_k)'$$

where r_t^e is a vector of $n \times 1$ asset excess returns at time t, f_t is a vector of $k \times 1$ factor returns at time t and $\hat{\mu}_k$ is the $k \times 1$ vector of sample means of the k factor returns. $\hat{\alpha}$ is an $n \times 1$ vector of OLS estimates of intercepts of the n assets. $\hat{\beta}$ is an $n \times k$ matrix of loadings.

The multivariate F test follows an F distribution with n and $T - n - k$ degrees of freedom. An advantage of this test is that it is intuitive. It is a linear combination of the estimated second moment of the pricing errors, weighted by their variances and covariances. As explained in Gibbons et al. (1989), the test gives a weighted measure of how much the whole set of assets deviated from their correct price. However, this test has one shortcoming: the number of time-series observations has to be greater than the number of assets included in the test. To maintain stationarity of the factor loadings, β, empirical work usually uses a relatively short time series and hence T is often less than $n + k$. To overcome this problem, assets are usually grouped into portfolios according to some characteristics of the assets, thereby ensuring that $n + k$ is less than T. However, the implicit assumption in this aggregation into portfolios is that no information is lost.

6.3.2 Average F test

The average F test is given by

$$S = \frac{T}{n} \sum_{j=1}^{n} \frac{\hat{\alpha}_j^2}{\hat{\sigma}_j^2}$$

where

$$\hat{\sigma}_j^2 = \sum_{t=1}^{T} \left(r_{it}^e - \hat{\alpha}_j - f_t \hat{\beta}_j \right)^2 / (T - k - 1)$$

The average F test is made up of a sum of n components, each of which follows F distribution with 1 and $(T - k - 1)$ degrees of freedom. It is a special case of the multivariate F test in that the correlation of disturbances, σ_{ij}^2, of two different assets is assumed to be zero. Under this assumption, the average F test has a great advantage that the number of assets is not constrained by the number of time-series observations in implementing the test. As long as the number of time-series observations is greater than the number of factors, we can put any desired number of assets in the test. The practice of grouping assets into portfolios and the potential problem associated with it can be avoided.

On the other hand, the assumption that $E[\epsilon\epsilon']$ being diagonal cannot always hold exactly. This is especially so if some subset of factors is missed so that the loadings run systematically into the non-diagonal elements of the variance-covariance matrix. In the arbitrage pricing theory framework, where the identity of factors is not specified, there is a potential risk that the diagonality assumption is violated and hence invalidating the application of the test. Another shortcoming of the average F test is that it induces survivorship bias problems. The time span used in a typical asset pricing test is usually equal to or more than five years. To conduct the average F test, only individual assets with up to or more than five years of complete return information can be put into the test. The average F test may end up testing whether a set of factors prices a set of surviving stocks.

As the average F test hinges on the assumption that the disturbances are being uncorrelated with each other, it would be of interest to test whether the disturbance covariance matrix is diagonal. The likelihood ratio test is not implementable in testing individual assets because the residual covariance matrix is singular when the number of individual assets is greater than the number of time-series observations. Here we use a simulation-based exact LM test proposed by Dufour and Kalaf (2001). The standard LM zero correlation test asymptotically follows $\chi^2_{(N(N-1)/2)}$. It is given by the following expression

$$\xi_{LM} = T \sum_{i=1}^{N} \sum_{j=1}^{i-1} \bar{r}_{ij}^2$$

in which

$$\bar{r}_{ij} = \frac{\hat{w}_i' \hat{w}_j}{\left[(\hat{w}_i' \hat{w}_i)(\hat{w}_j' \hat{w}_j) \right]^{1/2}}$$

and $\hat{w}_i$ is the $T \times 1$ vector of residuals of regression i given by

$$\hat{w}_i = M(X)u_i$$

with $M(X) = I_T - X(X'X)^{-1}X'$ and u_i is a $T \times 1$ vector of disturbance of regression i. In a simulation-based exact LM test, the distribution of the disturbance, u_i, is specified in the simulation. We assume that the distribution of the disturbance follows normal distribution and the T elements are assumed to be independent of each other. It is shown in Dufour and Kalaf (2001) that the distribution of the LM test does not involve any unknown parameter under the null hypothesis that the disturbance variance-covariance matrix is diagonal. The distribution of LM statistics of each specification is generated by 20 000 replications.

6.3.3   Stochastic discount factor using GMM with Hansen and Jagannathan distance

GMM minimizes pricing errors. In the stochastic discount framework, the pricing errors are defined as,

$$g_{iT} = \left(\frac{1}{T}\right) \sum_{t=1}^{T} \left(m_t r_{it}^e\right) \qquad i = 1, \ldots, n \tag{6.15}$$

Given we assume that $m_t = a + b_1 f_{1t} + b_2 f_{2t} + \cdots + b_k f_{kt}$, the pricing errors are given by

$$g_{iT} = \left(\frac{1}{T}\right) \sum_{t=1}^{T} \left((a + b_1 f_{1t} + b_2 f_{2t} + \cdots + b_k f_{kt}) r_{it}^e\right) \qquad i = 1, \ldots, n \tag{6.16}$$

where a is normalized to 1. The GMM framework minimizes a quadratic form of pricing errors

$$g_T' W g_T$$

where g_T is an $n \times 1$ vector of pricing errors and W is a weighting matrix. The GMM estimator takes a particularly simple form when g_T is a linear function of the factors. The estimator $\hat{b}$ is given by

$$\hat{b} = [d' W_T d]^{-1} d' W_T \bar{r}^e \tag{6.17}$$

where d in equation (6.17) is given by

$$d = \frac{1}{T} R^{e\prime} f$$

and R^e is a matrix of excess return of dimension $T \times n$. The ith column of R^e is the excess return of asset i.

$$R^e = r_1^e \ldots r_n^e$$

We follow Hansen and Jagannathan (1997) and choose the weighting matrix as

$$W_T = \left(\frac{1}{T} \sum_{t=1}^{T} r_t^e r_t^{e\prime}\right)^{-1}$$

and the Hansen and Jagannathan distance (HJ), δ, is given by

$$Dist(\delta) = \left(g_T' W_T g_T\right)^{1/2} \tag{6.18}$$

where

$$W_T = \left(\frac{1}{T} \sum_{t=1}^{T} r_t^e r_t^{e\prime}\right)^{-1} \tag{6.19}$$

There are two advantages of using W_T as the weighting matrix. First, it has good intuition. The distance $(g'_T W_T g_T)^{1/2}$, in its population moment, is the largest pricing error. Second, it is invariant across models. All specifications use the same weighting matrix and thus the weighting of pricing errors is not affected by the noise of factors in the model. In this way, the comparison of model fit across specifications is more objective.

It is shown in Jagannathan and Wang (1996) that the asymptotic distribution of $T[Dist(\delta)]^2$ is given by

$$T[Dist(\delta)]^2 \sim \sum_{i=1}^{n-k} \lambda_i \chi_{(1)}^2, T \to \infty \tag{6.20}$$

The λ_is are the $n - k$ positive eigenvalues of the following matrix,

$$A = S^{1/2}G^{-1/2}\left(I_n - G^{-1/2\prime}D\left[D'G^{-1}D\right]D'G^{-1/2}\right)G^{-1/2\prime}S^{1/2}$$

where S is the variance-covariance matrix of the pricing errors, G^{-1} is the weighting matrix, W_T, $S^{1/2}$ and $G^{1/2}$ are the Cholesky decomposition of S and G. D is an $N \times k$ matrix of rank k. Matrix A has a nice interpretation: it is the variance of weighted pricing errors not explained by d, which is the second moment of excess return and factors. In application, matrix A is constructed by using sample counterparts of S and W. As a result, the distribution of $T[Dist(\delta)]^2$ depends on the sample and it changes with the sample and the model specification. Consequently, comparing p-values across models is meaningless.

6.3.4 A look at the pricing errors under different tests

It will be of interest to have a detailed look at what pricing errors the three tests are measuring. The pricing errors of tests using the regression framework are given by:

$$\hat{\alpha}_i = \bar{r}_i^e - \frac{1}{T}1'_T f\hat{\beta}_i \quad \text{for } i = 1, 2, \ldots, n \tag{6.21}$$

where

$$\hat{\beta}_i = \left[\left(f - \hat{\mu}'_k 1_T\right)'\left(f - \hat{\mu}'_k 1_T\right)\right]^{-1}\left(f - \hat{\mu}'_k 1_T\right)'\left(r_i^e - \bar{r}_i^e\right)$$

where $\bar{r}_i^e$ are sample average of excess return of asset i, f is a $T \times k$ matrix of factor returns and $\hat{\mu}_k$ is the $k \times 1$ vector of sample mean of factor returns. The $\hat{\alpha}_i$s are the pricing errors that the multivariate F test and the average F test are measuring. The major difference between the two tests is that the pricing errors are weighted by different weighting matrices. For the multivariate F test, the weighting matrix is the inverse of the second moment matrix of residuals of n assets, $\hat{\Sigma}^{-1}$, which is defined by:

$$\hat{\Sigma} = \frac{1}{T}\hat{E}'\hat{E}$$

with

$$\widehat{E} = \hat{\epsilon}_1 \ \hat{\epsilon}_2 \ \dots \ \hat{\epsilon}_n$$

For the average F test, the weighting matrix is the diagonal elements of $\widehat{\Sigma}$, scaled by $T/(T - k - 1)$.

The pricing error of asset i using the stochastic discount factor is given by

$$g_i = \bar{r}_i^e - \frac{1}{T} r_i^{e\prime} f \hat{b} \qquad (6.22)$$

where

$$\hat{b} = [d' W_T d]^{-1} d' W_T \bar{r}^e$$

$$d = \frac{1}{T} R^{e\prime} f \qquad (6.23)$$

and

$$R^e = r_1^e \dots r_n^e$$

$\bar{r}^e$ is an $n \times 1$ vector of sample mean for the n assets. Notice that $\hat{b}$, unlike $\hat{\beta}_i$, is constant across assets. Intuitively, $\hat{b}$ measures the overall marginal impact on the means of n excess returns given a unit change in the covariance of excess return and factor return.

The major difference between the pricing errors of the regression-based approach and the stochastic discount factor approach is in the second term of the pricing error equations. For $\hat{\alpha}_i$, the second term is the sum of the mean factor return, weighted by the loading of factors on each individual asset. For g_i, the second term is the sum of second moment of excess return and factors, weighted by b, which measures how important is each second moment. The interpretation of $\hat{\alpha}_i$ is 'residuals not explained by the k factors' whereas that of g_i is 'residuals not explained by the covariances of excess return and the k factors'.

In addition, the pricing errors of the three tests are weighted very differently. For the stochastic discount factor approach, the pricing errors are weighted by W_T, which is invariant across specifications. For the regression-based approach, the pricing errors are weighted by a function of $\widehat{\Sigma}$, which is different across specifications. The pricing errors of the multivariate F test are weighted by the inverse of $\widehat{\Sigma}$ while those of the average F test are weighted by the inverse of $diag(\widehat{\Sigma})$. Since $\widehat{\Sigma}$ is a function of the factors included in a model, there is a potential problem that a 'noisy' factor downweights the pricing errors and a researcher may falsely conclude that the model with the 'noisy' factor performs better.

6.4   Variables construction and data sources

6.4.1   Data sources

This study uses monthly data from January 1981 to December 2000. The twenty-year sample is divided into four subsamples, each consisting of five consecutive years of data. Two data sets are used. Toronto Stock Exchange Database and Datastream. Asset returns, the value-weighted market return, the equally weighted market return, the 91 days T-bill rate, shares outstanding and price of assets are obtained from the Toronto Stock Exchange Database. The monthly return of 91 days T-bill rate is used as the risk-free rate. Book-to-market ratio of stocks is obtained from Datastream.

6.4.2 Independent variables: excess market return, size return factor and book-to-market return factor

Two types of excess market return, defined as the market return minus the risk-free rate, are used: equally weighted excess market return and value-weighted market return. The two excess market monthly returns summary statistics in the four sub-samples are given in Table 6.1 and Table 6.2. The sub-sample means of equally weighted excess market return in the 1980s are a little lower than their value-weighted counterpart. The situation reverses in the 1990s, with the subsample means of equally weighted excess market return higher than that of the value-weighted excess market return. The equally weighted excess market return seems to be more volatile than the value-weighted excess market return. Its standard deviation is higher in all of the sub-samples. In the last subsample, the monthly standard deviation of the equally weighted excess market return is nearly 3% larger than its value-weighted counterpart.

SMB in Fama and French (1993) is constructed by splitting assets ranked on their size into two equal groups: small and big. SMB is the return of portfolio of small size stocks minus the return of portfolio of big size stocks. HML in their paper is constructed by using the top 30% and bottom 30% of assets ranked on their book-to-market ratio to form two portfolios: one with high book-to-market ratio stocks and one with low book-to-market ratio stocks. HML is then formed by subtracting the return of the portfolio of low book-to-market ratio assets from the return of the portfolio of high book-to-market ratio assets. The construction of the two factors

	$r_{m,e}^{e*}$	$r_{m,v}^{e*}$	Size	Book-to-market
Sample mean				
1981–1985	−0.483	−0.151	−2.053	
1986–1990	−0.459	−0.242	−1.080	
1991–1995	1.844	0.373	1.194	0.857
1996–2000	1.603	1.258	−1.086	1.777
Standard deviation				
1981–1985	6.5397	5.4068	5.683	
1986–1990	5.6982	4.8447	4.4768	
1991–1995	4.8109	2.9192	5.3926	3.1172
1996–2000	8.1399	5.2287	7.201	4.2436

$*r_{m,e}^{e}$: equally weighted excess market return.
$*r_{m,v}^{e}$: value-weighted excess market return.

Table 6.1 Statistics of factors: sample mean and standard deviation

	Value-weighted market return				Equally weighted market return		
	$r^e_{m,v}$	Size	Book-to-market		$r^e_{m,e}$	Size	Book-to-market
1981–1985							
$r^e_{m,e}$	1.000	0.307		$r^e_{m,e}$	1.000	0.676	
Size	0.307	1.000		Size	0.676	1.000	
1986–1990							
$r^e_{m,e}$	1.000	0.165		$r^e_{m,e}$	1.000	0.520	
Size	0.165	1.000		Size	0.520	1.000	
1991–1995							
$r^e_{m,v}$	1.000	0.136	0.021	$r^e_{m,e}$	1.000	0.685	0.185
Size	0.136	1.000	0.336	size	0.685	1.000	0.336
Bk-to-mkt	0.021	0.336	1.000	Bk-to-mkt	0.185	0.336	1.000
1996–2000							
$r^e_{m,v}$	1.000	0.197	0.182	$r^e_{m,e}$	1.000	0.488	0.283
Size	0.197	1.000	0.464	Size	0.488	1.000	0.464
Bk-to-mkt	0.182	0.464	1.000	Bk-to-mkt	0.283	0.464	1.000

Table 6.2 Statistics of factors: correlation

is not symmetric: SMB is formed by dividing assets in the sample at any year t into two groups while HML is formed by dividing assets in the sample at any year t into three groups.

We use modified versions of SMB and HML as empirical factors in this study. Hereafter, the modified version of SMB is referred to as the size factor and the modified version of HML is referred to as the book-to-market factor. The monthly return of the size factor in year t is based on asset returns sorted on the size of Canadian stocks in year t. Assets are sorted according to their size at year t and are divided into three groups, each with one-third of the assets usable in year t. The three portfolios represent the average monthly return of small, medium and large firms. The size factor is formed by subtracting the equally weighted return of the large firms' portfolio from the equally weighted return of the small firms' portfolio[2]. The reason for dividing size-sorted assets into three instead of two equal groups is that we want the empirical factor to have enough variations to be correlated with the unknown risk and yet we would like the portfolio to have sufficient assets so that assets' idiosyncratic risk is diversified away. Table 6.3 shows the monthly sample mean and standard deviation of the Canadian size factor using the two proportions. The sample mean of the size factor formed by the 1/3 proportion has uniformly higher standard deviations and

[2] The size factor return in this study is constructed by two equally weighted portfolios instead of two value-weighted portfolios. This is because the value-weighted portfolio of large firms is dominated by a couple of large firms throughout the sampling period. For example, the weight of IBM in the portfolio of large firms is near to or above 30% from 1981 to 1991. Since we want the idiosyncratic risks to be diversified away, equally weighted size factor return is constructed.

	Mean		Standard deviation	
	1/3 proportion	1/2 proportion	1/3 proportion	1/2 proportion
1981	−5.373	−3.295	4.949	3.499
1982	−1.653	−1.384	4.571	3.019
1983	−2.041	−1.629	9.126	7.126
1984	−1.901	−1.560	2.975	2.379
1985	0.701	0.446	3.898	3.008
1986	−0.222	0.096	3.612	2.757
1987	1.126	0.786	5.698	3.940
1988	−2.917	−2.320	4.195	3.636
1989	−1.318	−1.147	4.629	3.471
1990	−2.069	−1.674	3.469	2.769
1991	0.539	0.397	4.750	4.011
1992	4.330	3.488	7.940	5.447
1993	2.785	2.530	4.867	3.965
1994	−1.088	−0.319	3.409	2.399
1995	−0.595	−0.433	3.453	2.449
1996	0.935	0.798	5.053	4.039
1997	−3.932	−3.057	5.150	4.193
1998	−2.696	−1.901	4.899	3.533
1999	0.723	0.649	5.603	3.903
2000	−0.458	−1.087	12.271	8.211

Table 6.3 Size factor return statistics created by different proportion

except in a couple of cases, larger absolute sample means than size factor formed by the 1/2 proportion. Summary statistics of monthly size factor return of Canada are given in Table 6.1 and Table 6.2. Three out of four monthly subsample means are negative. Another notable feature of the size factor return is that it is more correlated with the equally weighted excess market return than with the value-weighted excess market return. The correlation between size factor return and equally weighted excess market return is close to or above 0.5 while the correlation between size factor return and value-weighted excess market return is lower than 0.2.

The book-to-market factor of Canada is created similarly as the size factor, using 1/3 of the assets ranked top on the book-to-market ratio and 1/3 of the assets ranked bottom on the book-to-market ratio. Table 6.4 shows sample mean and standard deviation of the book-to-market factor constructed by the 1/3 proportion and the proportion used in Fama and French (1993). The difference in sample mean, except in 1983, is lower than 0.5% and the standard deviation of using the proportion in Fama and French (1993) is not uniformly higher than the standard deviation of using the 1/3 proportion. Therefore, for symmetry and reduction of idiosyncratic risk, we use the 1/3 proportion in constructing the book-to-market factor. The book-to-market factor starts from the 1990s, as the number of assets with book-to-market ratio information before 1987 is less than 50. Summary statistics of book-to-market factor are given in

	Mean		Standard deviation	
	1/3 proportion	1/2 proportion	1/3 proportion	1/2 proportion
1991	1.687	1.584	3.816	3.322
1992	0.852	1.151	3.392	3.760
1993	0.560	1.391	3.179	3.980
1994	−0.310	−0.285	2.892	3.095
1995	1.495	1.639	2.190	2.249
1996	0.978	1.121	2.438	2.453
1997	−0.700	−0.954	3.422	3.361
1998	2.269	2.342	3.396	3.215
1999	2.670	2.610	3.000	2.953
2000	3.667	4.016	6.781	7.104

Table 6.4 Book-to-market factor return statistics created by different proportion

Time	$r^e_{m,e}$	$r^e_{m,v}$	Size factor	Book-to-market factor
1981	−4.198	−2.378	−5.373	
1982	−0.620	−0.597	−1.653	
1983	2.126	1.858	−2.041	
1984	−1.810	−0.786	−1.901	
1985	2.087	1.150	0.701	
1986	0.682	0.215	−0.222	
1987	0.603	−0.023	1.126	
1988	−1.234	0.191	−2.917	
1989	−0.018	0.645	−1.318	
1990	−2.331	−2.236	−2.069	
1991	1.121	0.116	0.539	1.687
1992	2.476	−0.497	4.330	0.852
1993	5.517	1.906	2.785	0.560
1994	−0.813	−0.301	−1.088	−0.310
1995	0.922	0.642	−0.595	1.495
1996	5.329	1.910	0.935	0.978
1997	−0.022	1.500	−3.932	−0.700
1998	−1.678	−0.047	−2.696	2.269
1999	2.909	2.448	0.723	2.670
2000	1.477	0.481	−0.458	3.667

Table 6.5 Monthly mean returns of the three factors

Time	$r_{m,e}^e$	$r_{m,v}^e$	Size factor	Book-to-market factor
1981	6.414	6.357	4.949	
1982	8.788	7.534	4.571	
1983	6.635	4.064	9.126	
1984	4.547	4.304	2.975	
1985	3.835	3.504	3.898	
1986	3.037	2.973	3.612	
1987	10.397	8.619	5.698	
1988	3.838	3.278	4.195	
1989	2.672	2.609	4.629	
1990	5.256	4.420	3.469	
1991	4.883	2.604	4.750	3.816
1992	5.604	1.841	7.940	3.392
1993	4.667	3.221	4.867	3.179
1994	3.527	3.568	3.409	2.892
1995	3.211	2.897	3.453	2.190
1996	10.766	3.600	5.053	2.438
1997	5.830	4.804	5.150	3.422
1998	7.754	7.367	4.899	3.396
1999	5.277	4.455	5.603	3.000
2000	9.267	5.647	12.271	6.781

Table 6.6 Monthly standard errors of the three factors
returns

Table 6.1 and Table 6.2. Both monthly subsample means are positive. Like the size factor return, the book-to-market factor return is more correlated with the equally weighted excess market return than with the value-weighted excess market return.

6.4.3 Dependent variables: size-sorted portfolios, beta-sorted portfolios and individual assets

The dependent variable in each of the three models will be the return associated with size-sorted portfolios, beta-sorted portfolios and individual assets. It has been recognized that sorting of assets according to their characteristics can lead to bias in estimation. Lo and MacKinlay (1990) point out that sorting without regard to the data generating process may lead to spurious correlation between the characteristics and the estimated pricing errors. Berk (2000) shows that sorting assets into portfolios can lead to bias toward rejecting the model. However, the critique of Berk (2000) is not exactly applicable in this study for two reasons. First, his paper examines how sorting of assets affects pricing within the sorted portfolios. Second, none of the regression framework tests in this study regress return on factor loading and thus the errors-in variables problem is avoided.

We use asset returns data from stocks which are listed for five consecutive years on the Toronto Stock Exchange. This is the minimum time span required for implementing the average F test with individual assets.

Size-sorted portfolios Monthly return of size sorted portfolios at t are obtained by sorting asset returns according to the size of individual assets at $t-1$. Size is defined as the market value of a stock. This implies that only stocks which have complete return and size information for at least two years are included. Thus, the survivorship bias existed, though it is minimal compared to the use of individual assets. The reason for using size information in the previous time period is explained by Lo and MacKinlay (1990). Under the assumption of time independence, characteristics in the last period are uncorrelated with the returns in the next period. Using the characteristics in the last period decreases spurious correlation between the characteristics and the estimates of pricing errors, $\hat{\alpha}$. Ten size portfolios are formed by dividing the set of assets usable at time t into ten equal groups according to their size. Summary statistics of size-sorted portfolios are shown in Table 6.7 and Table 6.8. Table 6.7 shows the monthly mean and standard deviation of size-sorted portfolios in each subsample. For all subsamples, in general the standard deviation of a portfolio decreases as size of stocks in a portfolio increases. The portfolio containing the smallest firms has the highest standard deviation and the portfolio containing the largest firms is the least volatile in all four subsamples. Another special feature of the data is that through the 1980s the difference between the return of the three portfolios with the largest firms and the return of the three portfolios with the smallest firms is positive while this situation reverses in the 1990s. Table 6.8 shows the correlation matrix of size-sorted portfolios. The correlation between portfolios of near percentile is quite high and decreases as the percentile of portfolios becomes farther apart.

	1981–1985		1986–1990		1991–1995		1996–2000	
	Mean	Std	Mean	Std	Mean	Std	Mean	Std
1 (smallest)	−1.120	10.861	0.068	8.271	2.616	7.741	3.039	13.314
2	−0.564	8.425	−0.147	6.840	1.557	5.596	0.939	8.880
3	−0.933	7.281	−0.346	6.466	1.802	6.106	−0.476	8.091
4	0.435	5.993	−0.317	6.280	0.844	5.142	−0.165	6.607
5	0.449	6.433	−0.128	5.474	1.037	4.002	−0.829	6.151
6	0.525	6.437	−0.056	5.244	0.773	3.863	0.269	5.726
7	0.498	5.844	0.147	5.572	0.545	3.467	0.601	5.350
8	1.114	5.206	0.468	4.767	0.659	3.736	0.188	5.379
9	0.651	6.158	0.746	5.168	0.730	3.498	0.769	5.163
10	1.284	5.108	0.539	4.672	0.949	3.032	1.304	4.413

Table 6.7 Summary statistics of size-sorted portfolios returns: sample mean and standard deviation

0

1.000	0.832	0.781	0.646	0.679	0.627	0.602	0.494	0.509	0.468
0.832	1.000	0.846	0.744	0.787	0.747	0.729	0.643	0.659	0.592
0.781	0.846	1.000	0.734	0.819	0.729	0.738	0.651	0.656	0.587
0.646	0.744	0.734	1.000	0.740	0.724	0.723	0.683	0.683	0.608
0.679	0.787	0.819	0.740	1.000	0.824	0.820	0.791	0.779	0.676
0.627	0.747	0.729	0.724	0.824	1.000	0.872	0.849	0.846	0.793
0.602	0.729	0.738	0.723	0.820	0.872	1.000	0.887	0.889	0.841
0.494	0.643	0.651	0.683	0.791	0.849	0.887	1.000	0.885	0.840
0.509	0.659	0.656	0.683	0.779	0.846	0.889	0.885	1.000	0.890
0 0.468	0.592	0.587	0.608	0.676	0.793	0.841	0.840	0.890	1.000

Table 6.8 Summary statistics of size-sorted portfolios returns: correlation

Beta-sorted portfolios   We also sort assets into portfolios according to their estimated betas. The estimated beta of asset i is obtained by running the following regression using excess asset returns and excess market return in the previous two years,

$$r_{is}^e = \alpha_i + \beta_{m,i} r_{ms}^e + \epsilon_{is} \qquad s = t - 24, t - 23, \ldots, t - 1$$

with r_{ms}^e, the excess market return, as independent variable. Assets are grouped according to their estimated market beta, $\hat{\beta}_{m,i}$. The portfolio with the highest beta is the one that contains assets most correlated with the market in the previous two years. Therefore only stocks which have complete return information for three consecutive years are included. For the beta-sorted portfolios, we only examine the latter three subsamples of five-year monthly returns. The summary statistics for the beta-sorted portfolios is shown in Table 6.9 and Table 6.10 . Table 6.9 shows the mean and standard deviation of beta-sorted portfolios in each subsample. There is no obvious relationship between a beta sorted portfolio and standard deviation of the portfolios. In general, volatility first decreases and then increases. The portfolio which contains the largest estimated betas is the most volatile. Table 6.10 shows the correlation matrix of the portfolios.

Individual assets   The final type of dependent variable used in the study is excess return on individual assets. An asset is included if it existed through any subsample period. In other words, only stocks which have complete return information for five consecutive years are included. The number of assets included in the average F tests is 142 (in 1981–1985 subsample), 163 (in 1986–1990 subsample), 195 (in 1991–1995 subsample) and 292 (in 1996–2000 subsample) respectively. The sample means of individual assets at each year from 1981 to 2000 are given in Table 6.11. They are compared to the sample means of the beta-sorted portfolios and the size-sorted portfolios. Sample mean of year t is defined as the monthly mean return of an equal weight portfolio in individual assets, size-sorted portfolios or beta-sorted portfolios in year t. In general, the sample means of individual assets are higher than the other two sample means. Sample means of the individual assets are higher than the other two portfolios in 16 out of 20 years. It seems that there is possibly survivorship problems since only assets with five consecutive years of returns are included in the average F test.

	1986–1990		1991–1995		1996–2000	
	Mean	Std	Mean	Std	Mean	Std
1 (smallest)	0.543	6.541	1.457	4.718	0.982	6.537
2	0.519	5.905	0.518	3.241	1.467	4.933
3	0.255	5.409	1.004	3.634	1.062	5.166
4	0.501	5.089	0.648	3.879	1.107	5.087
5	−0.039	5.374	0.921	3.745	0.536	4.867
6	0.063	5.657	0.854	4.592	1.147	6.418
7	0.047	5.328	0.798	4.374	−0.085	5.950
8	0.216	6.399	0.674	4.798	0.829	7.909
9	−0.683	6.537	1.303	6.025	−0.068	7.468
10	−0.995	7.029	2.190	6.531	−0.451	12.369

Table 6.9 Summary statistics of beta-sorted portfolios returns: sample mean and standard deviation

									0
1.000	0.531	0.612	0.671	0.710	0.711	0.664	0.653	0.691	0.611
0.531	1.000	0.763	0.589	0.696	0.594	0.552	0.507	0.605	0.461
0.612	0.763	1.000	0.731	0.783	0.705	0.732	0.680	0.733	0.558
0.671	0.589	0.731	1.000	0.795	0.778	0.800	0.786	0.749	0.595
0.710	0.696	0.783	0.795	1.000	0.780	0.800	0.721	0.752	0.619
0.711	0.594	0.705	0.778	0.780	1.000	0.826	0.766	0.782	0.713
0.664	0.552	0.732	0.800	0.800	0.826	1.000	0.786	0.803	0.716
0.653	0.507	0.680	0.786	0.721	0.766	0.786	1.000	0.806	0.663
0.691	0.605	0.733	0.749	0.752	0.782	0.803	0.806	1.000	0.742
0 0.611	0.461	0.558	0.595	0.619	0.713	0.716	0.663	0.742	1.000

Table 6.10 Summary statistics of beta-sorted portfolios returns: correlation

The dispersion of individual assets is also examined. With over 100 individual assets in each subsample, we need to define a measure to summarize the dispersion of the set of individual assets. In this study, dispersion is defined as dispersion from the monthly mean of excess market return at year t. Let $\bar{r}^e_{mt}$ denote the monthly mean of excess market return of year t.

$$\bar{r}^e_{mt} = \frac{\sum_{s=1}^{12} r^e_{mt,s}}{12}$$

s being a month in year t.

Time	Individual assets	Size-sorted portfolios	Beta-sorted portfolios
1981	−1.822	−2.852	
1982	1.162	0.605	
1983	2.457	2.088	
1984	−0.631	−0.765	
1985	1.944	2.093	
1986	1.477	0.920	0.708
1987	1.308	0.895	0.865
1988	0.382	0.143	0.140
1989	1.048	0.902	0.821
1990	−2.493	−2.372	−2.321
1991	2.010	0.918	0.899
1992	0.764	0.538	0.274
1993	3.606	3.608	3.363
1994	−0.109	−0.515	−0.402
1995	1.437	1.207	1.050
1996	3.363	2.462	2.410
1997	0.662	−0.412	−0.258
1998	−1.110	−1.542	−1.459
1999	1.992	1.376	1.523
2000	0.781	0.936	1.046

Table 6.11 Mean of individual assets returns, size-sorted portfolios returns and beta-sorted portfolios returns

The dispersion of the set of individual assets in a subsample is defined as

$$d(individual\ assets) = \frac{1}{n}\sum_{i=1}^{n}\left(\frac{\sum_{s=1}^{12}\left(r_{it,s}^{e} - \bar{r}_{mt}^{e}\right)^2}{12}\right)$$

For comparison purposes, the dispersion of the size-sorted portfolios and the beta-sorted portfolios are also computed. Table 6.12 shows the dispersion of the individual assets, the size-sorted portfolios and the beta-sorted portfolios. It seems that the dispersion of individual assets is particularly high in the recession in early 1980s and 1990s. It is also high in 1987 and particularly in the latter half of the 1990s. The dispersion of the size-sorted portfolios and the beta-sorted portfolios are also high around these time periods but not quite as persistent as the individual assets. The rise of dispersion in the late 1990s may be related to the fact that it became more common for firms with no earnings record to become listed. Evaluation of the long-term earnings prospect of these firms is difficult and it leads to higher idiosyncratic risk in individual firms. As a result the dispersion of the set of individual assets from mean of excess market return increases in the latter 1990s.

	Individual assets	Size-sorted portfolios	Beta-sorted portfolios
1981	11.189	7.142	
1982	13.828	8.554	
1983	10.209	6.364	
1984	9.311	5.292	
1985	9.985	4.523	
1986	10.813	3.798	4.122
1987	13.630	9.684	9.381
1988	8.881	4.138	4.191
1989	8.753	3.366	3.701
1990	10.728	5.208	5.451
1991	11.631	5.138	5.122
1992	10.992	4.440	4.180
1993	11.463	4.462	4.378
1994	8.952	3.839	3.947
1995	9.156	3.920	3.898
1996	13.144	4.862	4.601
1997	13.634	6.384	6.117
1998	15.752	8.303	8.225
1999	17.330	5.496	5.367
2000	16.929	8.031	7.563

Table 6.12 Mean of individual assets returns,
size-sorted portfolios returns and beta-sorted
portfolios returns

6.5   Result and discussion

6.5.1   Formation of W_T

Before moving on to discuss the results, we first examine the weighting matrix used in the stochastic discount factor approach, W_T. Two versions of W_T are calculated. The first version follows the conventional practice and uses excess return in each subsample to obtain W_T at that subsample period. The second version uses the whole sample to create W_T and then uses it as the weighting matrix in each subsample. The reason for using the W_T created from the whole sample is that it is robust to changes in W_T through subsamples and allows us to compare the performance in each model across subsamples.

The prerequisite of calculating the HJ distance is that the weighting matrix, $W_T = \left(\frac{1}{T} \sum_{t=1}^{T} r_t^e r_t^{e\prime} \right)^{-1}$, exists. This requires that the inner product of excess return, $\frac{1}{T} \sum_{t=1}^{T} r_t^e r_t^{e\prime}$, is invertible. We use a measure suggested by Belsley et al. (1980), the condition number, to measure the extent of multicollinearity of $\frac{1}{T} \sum_{t=1}^{T} r_t^e r_t^{e\prime}$. The condition number is defined by

$$\gamma = \left(\frac{\lambda_{\max}}{\lambda_{\min}}\right)^{1/2}$$

in which $\lambda_{\max}$ is the largest characteristic root and $\lambda_{\min}$ is the smallest characteristic root of $\frac{1}{T}\sum_{t=1}^{T} r_t^e r_t^{e'}$. For the W_T created by the whole sample, the condition number of $\frac{1}{T}\sum_{t=1}^{T} r_t^e r_t^{e'}$ of the size-sorted portfolios is 12.70 and that of the beta-sorted portfolios is 8.39. The invertibility of inner product of excess return in both portfolios seems not to be a problem. For the W_T created by subsample, the table below shows the condition number of inner product of excess return in each subsamples.

	1981–1985	1986–1990	1991–1995	1996–2000
Size-sorted portfolios	17.12	17.97	12.21	15.10
Beta-sorted portfolios		11.02	8.27	11.09

It can be seen that the condition numbers of the size-sorted portfolio is in general higher than the condition numbers in the whole sample case. The largest is near 18. It implies that the inner product matrix is possibly hard to invert and, as pointed out in Cochrane (2001), the weight of pricing errors of different assets varies greatly. The condition number of the beta-sorted portfolios is smaller than that of the size-sorted portfolios and we can be more confident in the weight it assigns to pricing errors.

6.5.2 Model 1

Regression-based approach Table 6.13 depicts the results of the regression-based tests of the first specification in which the only factor is the excess market return. It shows that different ways of forming portfolios can give different results. With value-weighted excess market return, the size-sorted portfolios are rejected while the beta-sorted portfolios have a p-value of 6% for the multivariate F test in the 1996–2000 subsample. With equally weighted excess market return, there is also a large difference in the F test's p-values of the size-sorted and beta-sorted portfolios in the 1986–1990 subsample: the size-sorted portfolios have a p-value of 5% while that of the beta-sorted portfolios reaches 41%.

The average F test result is given in the second and fourth columns. The results of the size-sorted and beta-sorted portfolios with the value-weighted excess market return are similar: both sets of portfolios in the 1981–1985 subsample, the 1986–1990 subsample and the 1996–2000 subsample have very low p-values while the 1991–1995 subsample is not rejected in 5% significance levels. The results of the two sets of attribute-sorted portfolios with the equally weighted excess market return are also similar with higher p-values in the 1986–1990 subsample and low p-values in the 1990s. For individual assets with both the value-weighted excess market return and the equally weighted excess market return, all subsamples have p-values higher than 20%. The significance of the average F test results depends on the assumption

	Value-weighted r^e_{mkt}				Equally weighted r^e_{mkt}			
	Multi. F test		Average F test		Multi. F test		Average F test	
	Test stat.	p-value	Test stat.	p-value	Test stat.	p-value	Test stat.	p-value
Size-sorted portfolio								
1981–1985	1.377	21.500	2.913	0.000	2.146	3.500	2.725	0.000
1986–1990	1.874	7.000	2.233	2.000	1.996	5.000	1.542	14.000
1991–1995	0.767	65.500	1.081	40.000	1.231	29.000	3.699	0.000
1996–2000	3.204	0.000	4.102	0.000	3.260	0.000	3.726	0.000
Beta-sorted portfolio								
1986–1990	1.484	17.000	2.508	0.500	1.053	41.000	1.672	10.000
1991–1995	0.997	45.500	0.721	72.000	1.398	20.500	3.576	0.000
1996–2000	1.926	6.000	2.442	1.000	2.313	2.500	2.154	2.500
Individual assets								
1981–1985			1.383	20.500			1.333	23.000
1986–1990			1.380	20.500			1.343	22.500
1991–1995			0.960	50.000			0.912	54.500
1996–2000			1.174	33.000			1.277	26.500

Table 6.13 Regression-based results of model 1

of the residual covariance matrix being diagonal. Table 6.14 shows the result of the simulation-based LM zero correlation test. Regardless of the types of excess market return used, model 1 in all subsamples is rejected. It indicates that the assumption of disturbances being uncorrelated is violated.

Table 6.15 and Table 6.16 depict the individual regression results of the beta-sorted portfolios and Table 6.17 and Table 6.18 depict the individual regression results of the size-sorted portfolios. Three features in the four tables are quite interesting. First, the tables show the cause of the difference in p-values of the size-sorted and beta-sorted portfolios. Table 6.15 to Table 6.18 give a hint of why, with value-weighted excess market return, the beta-sorted portfolios have a p-value of 6% but size-sorted portfolios are rejected in the multivariate F test in the 1996–2000 subsample. In Table 6.15 and Table 6.17, the absolute magnitude of the $\hat{\alpha}$s in the beta-sorted portfolios, with the exception of the last portfolio, are in general lower than those in the size-sorted portfolios. The t-statistics of $\hat{\alpha}$s in the beta-sorted portfolios are also lower than that in the size-sorted portfolios, which implies that the $\hat{\alpha}$s in the beta-sorted portfolios are less significantly different from zero. This suggests that value-weighted excess market return has greater explanatory power for the beta-sorted portfolios returns than the size-sorted portfolios returns.

The second feature is that the R^2 of the size-sorted portfolios with value-weighted excess market return in general decreases with the size of assets. Portfolios containing the largest assets have the highest R^2. It indicates that the excess market return prices

	Size-sorted portfolios		Beta-sorted portfolios		Individual assets	
	Test stat.	p-value	Test stat.	p-value	Test stat.	p-value
Value-weighted r^e_{mkt}						
1981–1985	403.08	0.00			17287.67	0.00
1986–1990	299.33	0.00	182.60	0.00	24823.62	0.00
1991–1995	400.88	0.00	176.49	0.00	26644.11	0.00
1996–2000	742.64	0.00	719.43	0.00	78879.84	0.00
Equally weighted r^e_{mkt}						
1981–1985	341.38	0.00			18968.03	0.00
1986–1990	347.36	0.00	211.19	0.00	29131.79	0.00
1991–1995	413.65	0.00	319.04	0.00	30591.19	0.00
1996–2000	749.97	0.00	664.12	0.00	81853.05	0.00

Table 6.14 Exact LM test of zero correlation of disturbance covariance matrix

Portfolio	1	2	3	4	5	6	7	8	9	10
1986–1990										
α	−0.02	−0.05	−0.32	−0.09	−0.62	−0.50	−0.53	−0.34	−1.23	−1.55
$t(\alpha)$	−0.03	−0.12	−1.05	−0.32	−2.01	−1.59	−1.93	−0.71	−2.56	−2.63
β_m	1.09	1.05	1.02	0.97	1.00	1.06	1.02	1.10	1.12	1.12
$t(\beta_m)$	10.11	12.42	15.99	17.12	15.66	16.26	18.00	11.05	11.20	9.19
adj. R^2	0.63	0.72	0.81	0.83	0.81	0.82	0.85	0.67	0.68	0.59
1991–1995										
α	0.55	−0.33	0.10	−0.27	−0.01	−0.17	−0.20	−0.34	0.18	1.12
$t(\alpha)$	1.10	−1.08	0.32	−0.82	−0.04	−0.50	−0.59	−0.82	0.34	1.68
β_m	0.95	0.78	0.94	0.99	1.02	1.27	1.19	1.22	1.54	1.38
$t(\beta_m)$	5.54	7.50	8.98	8.58	9.90	10.58	10.24	8.68	8.56	6.04
adj. R^2	0.33	0.48	0.57	0.55	0.62	0.65	0.64	0.56	0.55	0.38
1996–2000										
α	−0.34	0.22	−0.19	−0.14	−0.77	−0.35	−1.55	−0.73	−1.69	−2.66
$t(\alpha)$	−0.48	0.50	−0.40	−0.30	−1.97	−0.60	−3.06	−0.89	−2.35	−2.04
β_m	0.76	0.70	0.71	0.70	0.75	0.90	0.88	0.95	1.00	1.46
$t(\beta_m)$	5.81	8.49	7.81	7.98	10.19	8.25	9.22	6.17	7.41	6.00
adj. R^2	0.36	0.55	0.50	0.51	0.64	0.53	0.59	0.39	0.48	0.37

Table 6.15 Individual regression results of beta-sorted portfolios returns in model 1:
value-weighted r^e_m

Portfolio	1	2	3	4	5	6	7	8	9	10
1986–1990										
α	0.17	0.12	−0.20	0.05	−0.49	−0.36	−0.39	−0.15	−1.05	−1.35
$t(\alpha)$	0.36	0.31	−0.51	0.15	−1.33	−0.99	−1.23	−0.37	−2.34	−2.57
β_m	0.97	0.92	0.79	0.80	0.81	0.87	0.85	0.99	0.98	1.02
$t(\beta_m)$	11.73	13.83	11.24	14.59	12.48	13.58	15.29	13.46	12.38	11.04
adj. R^2	0.70	0.76	0.68	0.78	0.72	0.76	0.80	0.75	0.72	0.67
1991–1995										
α	−0.48	−0.86	−0.44	−0.88	−0.65	−0.99	−0.99	−1.05	−1.05	−0.12
$t(\alpha)$	−1.12	−2.54	−1.15	−2.18	−1.76	−2.30	−2.43	−2.05	−2.02	−0.19
β_m	0.75	0.45	0.48	0.53	0.55	0.70	0.67	0.63	0.98	0.95
$t(\beta_m)$	9.00	6.74	6.42	6.70	7.64	8.32	8.40	6.35	9.58	7.58
adj. R^2	0.58	0.43	0.41	0.43	0.49	0.54	0.54	0.40	0.61	0.49
1996–2000										
α	−0.20	0.46	−0.04	0.07	−0.58	−0.17	−1.32	−0.70	−1.52	−2.67
$t(\alpha)$	−0.31	0.94	−0.09	0.14	−1.45	−0.30	−2.48	−1.01	−2.28	−2.52
β_m	0.51	0.40	0.46	0.42	0.47	0.59	0.54	0.73	0.68	1.16
$t(\beta_m)$	6.32	6.74	8.05	6.86	9.60	8.66	8.39	8.60	8.38	8.99
adj. R^2	0.40	0.43	0.52	0.44	0.61	0.56	0.54	0.55	0.54	0.58

Table 6.16 Individual regression results of beta-sorted portfolios returns in model 1: equally weighted r_m^e

large assets better than the small assets. Another possible explanation of this feature is that returns sorted on size in $t - 1$ are correlated with value-weighted market return at time t, which gives greater weight to large firms. If this is true, then there would be a problem of spurious correlation between the size factor and the estimates of α of the size-sorted portfolios. As this relation between size of firms and R^2 does not exist with the equally weighted excess market return, it seems that the size-sorted portfolio, constructed by sorting market value of firms at $t - 1$, is correlated with value-weighted excess market return and there may be spurious correlation between the size factor and the estimates of α of the size-sorted portfolios.

The third feature is that, independent of the type of the excess market return used, the R^2 of the two subsamples in the 1990s is lower than that of the 1980s for both the size-sorted portfolios and the beta-sorted portfolios. It is most noticeable in the 1996–2000 subsamples in Table 6.17 and Table 6.18: the R^2 of all regressions of the size-sorted portfolios on both types of excess market return are much lower than they were ten years earlier. Though the factor loadings of both types of excess market returns, β_m, remain significantly different from zero in the 1990s for both methods of forming portfolios, the significance of them decreases through the subsamples. It suggests that some other factors may be needed to price the factor.

One might conclude from the third panel of Table 6.13 that the two types of excess market return price the set of individual assets well. Table 6.19 shows a summary of the test statistics of individual assets returns in the first model for the four subsamples. The statistics of the set of individual assets' regressions examined in the two tables are

Portfolio	1	2	3	4	5	6	7	8	9	10
1981–1985										
α	−1.93	−1.38	−1.79	−0.45	−0.41	−0.32	−0.36	0.23	−0.20	0.41
$t(\alpha)$	−1.87	−2.23	−2.97	−0.96	−0.93	−1.05	−1.32	0.92	−0.93	2.46
β_m	1.39	1.30	1.05	0.89	1.02	1.12	1.02	0.90	1.10	0.92
$t(\beta_m)$	7.23	11.23	9.38	10.26	12.26	19.43	19.80	19.07	27.26	29.76
adj. R^2	0.46	0.68	0.60	0.64	0.72	0.86	0.87	0.86	0.93	0.94
1986–1990										
α	−0.43	−0.70	−0.91	−0.87	−0.71	−0.64	−0.41	−0.12	0.17	−0.06
$t(\alpha)$	−0.63	−1.28	−1.76	−1.98	−1.99	−2.29	−1.74	−0.69	0.91	−0.36
β_m	1.35	1.13	1.07	1.11	0.99	1.00	1.10	0.95	1.03	0.94
$t(\beta_m)$	9.58	9.99	9.89	12.10	13.29	17.22	22.44	25.44	26.06	29.56
adj. R^2	0.61	0.63	0.62	0.71	0.75	0.83	0.90	0.92	0.92	0.94
1991–1995										
α	1.57	0.61	0.75	−0.17	0.12	−0.16	−0.38	−0.29	−0.22	0.04
$t(\alpha)$	1.79	1.00	1.22	−0.36	0.32	−0.53	−1.54	−1.08	−1.09	0.26
β_m	1.33	1.05	1.35	1.24	0.98	1.03	0.99	1.06	1.06	0.96
$t(\beta_m)$	4.43	5.03	6.44	7.59	7.97	9.56	11.73	11.52	15.34	20.62
adj. R^2	0.24	0.29	0.41	0.49	0.51	0.61	0.70	0.69	0.80	0.88
1996–2000										
α	1.08	−0.79	−2.13	−1.67	−2.21	−1.07	−0.75	−1.11	−0.53	0.13
$t(\alpha)$	0.70	−0.86	−2.61	−2.70	−3.67	−1.99	−1.63	−2.21	−1.17	0.34
β_m	1.27	1.08	1.02	0.90	0.80	0.78	0.78	0.74	0.74	0.64
$t(\beta_m)$	4.38	6.31	6.69	7.81	7.13	7.66	9.06	7.86	8.70	8.99
adj. R^2	0.24	0.40	0.43	0.50	0.46	0.49	0.58	0.51	0.56	0.57

Table 6.17 Individual regression results of size-sorted returns portfolios in model 1: value-weighted r^e_m

the adjusted R^2, the t-statistics of $\hat{\alpha}$ and the t-statistics of $\hat{\beta}_m$. The mean, standard deviation, minimum and maximum of individual regression statistics and the percentage of t-statistics of estimates being significantly different from zero are examined. The statistics of the adjusted R^2 suggests that the fit of individual assets are much worse than the beta-sorted and size-sorted portfolios. It is especially so in the last subsample: half of the assets with equally weighted excess market return have adjusted R^2 lower than 0.058. It suggests that idiosyncratic risks of the individual assets are quite large and the high p-value of the average F test partly reflects the domination of this noise. Another feature of the table is that despite the idiosyncratic risks, the percentage of estimates $\hat{\beta}_m$ of factor loading of excess market return, being significantly different from zero, is quite high. Except for the 1991–1995 subsample, the percentage of estimates significantly different from zero is over 90% with value-weighted excess market return. The percentage is even higher with equally weighted excess market return, over 90% of the market factor loadings are significant in all subsamples. It shows that the two types of excess market return factor are sources of risk that most assets pick up.

Stochastic discount factor-based approach Table 6.20 shows the results of applying the stochastic discount method. The size-sorted portfolios and the beta-sorted portfolios have the biggest HJ distance and the lowest p-values in the last subsamples.

Portfolio	1	2	3	4	5	6	7	8	9	10
1981–1985										
α	−1.41	−0.99	−1.46	−0.17	−0.14	−0.06	−0.13	0.44	0.02	0.57
$t(\alpha)$	−2.25	−2.51	−3.49	−0.56	−0.37	−0.16	−0.37	1.31	0.04	1.38
β_m	1.50	1.21	1.01	0.84	0.88	0.90	0.81	0.70	0.79	0.62
$t(\beta_m)$	15.58	19.88	15.67	17.41	15.01	16.43	15.56	13.63	11.76	9.75
adj. R^2	0.80	0.87	0.81	0.84	0.79	0.82	0.80	0.76	0.70	0.61
1986–1990										
α	−0.16	−0.46	−0.71	−0.67	−0.55	−0.50	−0.29	−0.03	0.28	0.03
$t(\alpha)$	−0.31	−1.24	−1.72	−2.08	−1.80	−1.54	−0.77	−0.08	0.77	0.08
β_m	1.30	1.10	1.00	1.03	0.88	0.82	0.85	0.72	0.77	0.68
$t(\beta_m)$	14.51	16.66	13.81	18.06	16.33	14.09	12.94	12.23	12.10	10.93
adj. R^2	0.78	0.82	0.76	0.85	0.82	0.77	0.74	0.72	0.71	0.67
1991–1995										
α	−0.34	−0.75	−0.68	−1.28	−0.73	−0.85	−0.90	−0.79	−0.63	−0.26
$t(\alpha)$	−0.54	−1.66	−1.40	−2.98	−2.17	−2.32	−2.55	−1.98	−1.63	−0.75
β_m	1.30	0.95	1.04	0.85	0.66	0.58	0.49	0.49	0.44	0.35
$t(\beta_m)$	10.64	10.79	11.09	10.13	10.03	8.07	7.01	6.21	5.80	5.27
adj. R^2	0.66	0.66	0.67	0.63	0.63	0.52	0.45	0.39	0.36	0.31
1996–2000										
α	0.86	−0.77	−2.06	−1.46	−2.09	−0.91	−0.54	−0.82	−0.22	0.45
$t(\alpha)$	0.68	−1.01	−2.98	−2.37	−3.81	−1.75	−1.14	−1.43	−0.41	0.93
β_m	1.13	0.84	0.76	0.58	0.56	0.51	0.49	0.40	0.39	0.31
$t(\beta_m)$	7.28	9.11	9.04	7.75	8.38	8.03	8.37	5.76	5.90	5.20
adj. R^2	0.47	0.58	0.58	0.50	0.54	0.52	0.54	0.35	0.36	0.31

Table 6.18 Individual regression results of size-sorted returns portfolios in model 1: equally weighted r^e_m

The other subsamples are not rejected at the conventional significance level. This holds for both types of excess market return and both ways of forming W_T. This consistency of results is in contrast with the results in the multivariate F test: for the multivariate F test, the beta-sorted portfolios have a p-value of 41% while the size-sorted portfolios are marginally rejected at 5% significance level with equally weighted excess market return in the 1986–1990. There are two possible explanations for this discrepancy: first, since the p-value of $T[Dist(\delta)]^2$ is generated from a sample-dependent distribution, it may accidentally create a smaller difference in p-values than that of the multivariate F test. The second possible explanation is that, as mentioned before, the two tests are measuring different definitions of pricing errors and these pricing errors are weighted differently for the two tests. The discrepancy in p-values may reflect this fact.

Table 6.21 shows the estimates of model 1 in the stochastic discount framework. Panel A reports estimates of model 1 with value-weighted excess market return. Using subsample varying W_T, none of the estimates are significant. It implies that the value-weighted excess market return is not priced in all subsamples using the

	Mean	Stdc	Max	Min	Median	% of est.
Panel A: value-weighted market return						
1981–1985						
adj. R^2	0.28	0.14	0.62	−0.01	0.28	
$t(\alpha)$	0.23	1.22	3.73	−2.36	−0.02	10.56
$t(\beta_m)$	25.51	14.67	78.66	1.61	22.10	99.30
1986–1990						
adj. R^2	0.26	0.15	0.74	0.00	0.24	
$t(\alpha)$	0.04	1.05	2.78	−2.34	0.05	6.14
$t(\beta_m)$	25.04	18.19	96.72	1.70	21.29	99.39
1991–1995						
adj. R^2	0.13	0.11	0.52	−0.02	0.12	
$t(\alpha)$	0.27	1.03	5.04	−3.15	0.22	6.15
$t(\beta_m)$	10.19	8.85	44.10	−1.62	7.88	84.62
1996–2000						
adj. R^2	0.09	0.09	0.53	−0.02	0.07	
$t(\alpha)$	0.03	0.81	2.66	−2.87	−0.02	4.45
$t(\beta_m)$	8.87	8.11	75.00	−4.37	6.85	90.41
Panel B: equally weighted market return						
1981–1985						
adj. R^2	0.25	0.13	0.55	0.01	0.25	
$t(\alpha)$	0.36	1.13	3.62	−2.19	0.17	9.86
$t(\beta_m)$	25.97	11.47	59.13	3.25	25.69	100.00
1986–1990						
adj. R^2	0.22	0.11	0.63	0.03	0.21	
$t(\alpha)$	0.12	0.98	3.07	−1.95	0.08	2.45
$t(\beta_m)$	23.57	13.68	76.79	3.87	22.55	100.00
1991–1995						
adj. R^2	0.10	0.09	0.38	−0.02	0.08	
$t(\alpha)$	−0.25	0.95	3.67	−3.97	−0.20	5.13
$t(\beta_m)$	11.88	9.04	48.75	−2.58	9.99	91.79
1996–2000						
adj. R^2	0.08	0.07	0.34	−0.02	0.06	
$t(\alpha)$	0.14	0.85	3.15	−2.95	0.04	5.48
$t(\beta_m)$	10.85	8.16	56.07	−12.12	9.28	96.58

% of est.: percentage of estimates significantly different from zero
at 5% significance level.
Max: maxima of statistics.
Min: minima of statistics.

Table 6.19 Test statistics summary of individual assets returns in model 1

	Value-weighted r_m^e				Equally weighted r_m^e			
	Subsample W_T		Whole sample W_T		Subsample W_T		Whole sample W_T	
	HJ dist	p-value*	HJ dist	p-value*	HJ dist	p-value*	HJ dist	p-value*
Size portfolio								
1981–1985	0.47	37.43	0.52	17.03	0.45	46.98	0.50	34.55
1986–1990	0.48	30.40	0.38	35.11	0.47	35.90	0.35	69.52
1991–1995	0.36	63.38	0.34	53.01	0.29	73.23	0.29	72.77
1996–2000	0.61	5.09	0.78	1.49	0.62	3.31	0.79	0.23
Beta portfolio								
1986–1990	0.37	40.94	0.34	46.30	0.37	42.69	0.34	56.11
1991–1995	0.39	33.47	0.33	43.58	0.34	41.70	0.27	70.43
1996–2000	0.51	4.48	0.57	3.58	0.52	4.57	0.58	1.99

*p-value of $T(HJ - dist)^2$.
*r_m^e: excess market return.

Table 6.20 Stochastic discount factor-based results of model 1

	W_t created by subsample return				W_t created by whole sample return			
	Size portfolios		Beta portfolios		Size portfolios		Beta portfolios	
	b_m	$se(b_m)$	b_m	$se(b_m)$	b_m	$se(b_m)$	b_m	$se(b_m)$
Panel A: value-weighted excess market return								
1981–1985	−0.004	0.024			−0.014	0.026		
1986–1990	−0.016	0.024	−0.027	0.023	−0.024	0.024	−0.016	0.026
1991–1995	0.038	0.044	0.025	0.048	0.059	0.049	0.033	0.052
1996–2000	0.045	0.036	0.031	0.033	0.048	0.036	0.018	0.032
Panel B: equally weighted excess market return								
1981–1985	−0.021	0.020			−0.023	0.021		
1986–1990	−0.028	0.019	−0.025	0.019	−0.032	0.020	−0.012	0.022
1991–1995	0.048	0.021	0.046	0.022	0.055	0.024	0.049	0.025
1996–2000	0.025	0.019	0.008	0.019	0.024	0.018	0.002	0.020

Table 6.21 Parameter estimates of SDF framework in model 1

stochastic discount factor framework. Panel B shows the results with equally weighted excess market return. Using subsample varying W_T, the estimates in the 1991–1995 subsample for both the beta-sorted and the size-sorted portfolios are significant. The results using whole sample W_T in general confirms with the subsample varying W_T,

	1	2	3	4	5	6	7	8	9	10

Panel A: value-weighted excess market return

Size portfolio

	1	2	3	4	5	6	7	8	9	10
1981–1985	−1.99	−1.45	−1.84	−0.49	−0.46	−0.38	−0.42	0.19	−0.25	0.36
1986–1990	−0.27	−0.56	−0.78	−0.74	−0.59	−0.52	−0.28	−0.01	0.30	0.06
1991–1995	1.61	0.65	0.80	−0.11	0.16	−0.11	−0.33	−0.24	−0.17	0.08
1996–2000	1.00	−0.76	−2.02	−1.59	−2.09	−1.02	−0.72	−1.05	−0.51	0.11

Beta portfolio

	1	2	3	4	5	6	7	8	9	10
1986–1990	0.40	0.35	0.07	0.28	−0.23	−0.09	−0.13	0.08	−0.80	−1.11
1991–1995	0.69	−0.20	0.25	−0.12	0.15	0.03	−0.01	−0.14	0.42	1.33
1996–2000	−0.04	0.47	0.08	0.12	−0.46	−0.01	−1.17	−0.35	−1.25	−2.01

Panel B: equally weighted excess market return

Size portfolio

	1	2	3	4	5	6	7	8	9	10
1981–1985	−0.80	−0.50	−1.04	0.16	0.21	0.30	0.20	0.71	0.33	0.81
1986–1990	0.40	0.01	−0.27	−0.22	−0.16	−0.15	0.08	0.28	0.61	0.32
1991–1995	0.45	−0.13	−0.01	−0.67	−0.28	−0.44	−0.54	−0.44	−0.32	−0.03
1996–2000	0.75	−0.79	−2.03	−1.44	−2.05	−0.91	−0.56	−0.81	−0.24	0.41

Beta portfolio

	1	2	3	4	5	6	7	8	9	10
1986–1990	0.48	0.42	0.06	0.31	−0.22	−0.07	−0.11	0.17	−0.72	−1.00
1991–1995	0.05	−0.50	−0.09	−0.47	−0.24	−0.46	−0.47	−0.55	−0.33	0.50
1996–2000	0.34	0.88	0.45	0.51	−0.08	0.46	−0.73	0.07	−0.79	−1.42

Table 6.22 Pricing errors of stochastic discount factor framework in model 1

though the 1991–1995 subsample estimates with equally weighted excess market return are nearly significant.

Table 6.22 shows the pricing errors of the stochastic discount factor framework in model 1. One interesting fact is that with the value-weighted excess market return, the absolute magnitude of pricing errors decreases as the size of stocks in portfolios increases in the 1981–1985 subsample. It is similar to the relationship between the size-sorted portfolios' individual regressions' R^2 and the size of stocks in the regression framework. Another feature of this table is that for both the value-weighted excess market return and the equally weighted excess market return, the pricing errors of the size-sorted portfolios are in general larger than the beta-sorted portfolios in the last subsample. This aspect confirms with the results in the regression framework.

6.5.3 Model 2

Regression-based approach   Table 6.23 shows the result of model 2 with the two types of excess market return and the size factor return as independent variables. The first and third columns show the results of applying the multivariate F test. With value-weighted excess market return, the last subsample of the size-sorted portfolios is rejected at all significance levels but that of the beta-sorted portfolios has a p-value of 11.5%. Comparing Table 6.25 and Table 6.27, the estimates of αs of the size-sorted

	Value-weighted r^e_{mkt}				Equally weighted r^e_{mkt}			
	Multi. F test		Average F test		Multi. F test		Average F test	
	Test stat.	p-value	Test stat.	p-value	Test stat.	p-value	Test stat.	p-value
Size portfolio								
1981–1985	0.823	60.500	0.987	47.500	2.025	5.000	4.217	0.000
1986–1990	1.648	12.000	1.226	29.500	2.302	2.500	3.024	0.000
1991–1995	0.537	85.000	0.932	52.500	1.333	23.500	5.025	0.000
1996–2000	4.069	0.000	5.453	0.000	4.033	0.000	5.131	0.000
Beta portfolio								
1986–1990	1.145	34.500	1.395	20.000	1.251	28.000	2.594	0.500
1991–1995	0.810	61.500	0.960	50.000	2.281	2.500	4.439	0.000
1996–2000	1.668	11.500	1.527	14.500	1.931	6.000	1.487	16.000
Individual assets								
1981–1985			1.069	41.000			1.223	29.500
1986–1990			1.559	13.000			1.581	12.500
1991–1995			0.879	57.500			0.998	46.500
1996–2000			1.039	43.500			1.047	42.500

Table 6.23 Regression-based results of model 2

	Size portfolios		Beta portfolios		Individual assets	
	Test stat.	p-value	Test stat.	p-value	Test stat.	p-value
Value weighted r^e_{mkt}						
1981–1985	102.40	0.00			16728.10	0.00
1986–1990	137.67	0.00	96.00	0.01	20501.34	0.00
1991–1995	242.35	0.00	101.38	0.01	26075.62	0.00
1996–2000	865.54	0.00	594.09	0.00	76133.27	0.00
Equally weighted r^e_{mkt}						
1981–1985	135.97	0.00			16623.63	0.00
1986–1990	342.61	0.00	164.72	0.00	20373.89	0.00
1991–1995	333.20	0.00	272.07	0.00	27790.08	0.00
1996–2000	1026.82	0.00	755.04	0.00	75160.46	0.00

Table 6.24 Exact LM test of zero correlation of residual covariance matrix

Portfolio	1	2	3	4	5	6	7	8	9	10
1986–1990										
α	0.41	0.32	−0.23	0.05	−0.53	−0.29	−0.33	0.11	−0.7	−0.94
$t(\alpha)$	0.87	0.88	−0.75	0.18	−1.67	−0.96	−1.28	0.27	−1.77	−1.87
β_m	1.02	0.99	1	0.95	0.99	1.03	0.99	1.03	1.04	1.03
$t(\beta_m)$	10.49	13.33	15.63	17.06	15.32	16.61	18.63	11.92	12.82	10.08
β_s	0.41	0.35	0.08	0.13	0.09	0.2	0.19	0.44	0.51	0.58
$t(\beta_s)$	3.91	4.39	1.21	2.16	1.26	3.00	3.24	4.64	5.75	5.25
adj. R^2	0.7	0.79	0.81	0.84	0.81	0.84	0.87	0.76	0.79	0.72
1991–1995										
α	0.24	−0.44	0	−0.39	−0.19	−0.35	−0.44	−0.48	−0.29	0.49
$t(\alpha)$	0.51	−1.46	0.01	−1.14	−0.68	−1.03	−1.4	−1.17	−0.65	0.89
β_m	0.88	0.75	0.92	0.96	0.97	1.23	1.14	1.19	1.43	1.24
$t(\beta_m)$	5.48	7.34	8.79	8.40	10.11	10.63	10.72	8.52	9.49	6.65
β_s	0.28	0.11	0.09	0.1	0.16	0.16	0.22	0.13	0.42	0.57
$t(\beta_s)$	3.22	1.9	1.53	1.63	3.16	2.59	3.75	1.76	5.17	5.68
adj. R^2	0.43	0.51	0.58	0.56	0.67	0.68	0.7	0.57	0.69	0.59
1996–2000										
α	0.29	0.38	0.04	−0.18	−0.53	0.06	−1.32	−0.18	−1.2	−1.09
$t(\alpha)$	0.5	0.86	0.09	−0.38	−1.45	0.1	−2.66	−0.23	−1.82	−1.36
β_m	0.64	0.67	0.66	0.71	0.7	0.82	0.83	0.85	0.9	1.17
$t(\beta_m)$	5.94	8.14	7.51	7.85	10.16	8.27	8.93	5.96	7.32	7.72
β_s	0.44	0.11	0.16	−0.03	0.17	0.29	0.16	0.39	0.34	1.1
$t(\beta_s)$	5.61	1.88	2.57	−0.43	3.29	3.95	2.41	3.79	3.81	10.00
adj. R^2	0.58	0.57	0.55	0.51	0.69	0.63	0.62	0.5	0.58	0.77

Table 6.25 Individual regression results of beta-sorted portfolios returns in model 2: value-weighted r^e_{mkt}

portfolios are higher and more significantly different from zero than that of the beta-sorted portfolios in the last subsample. Mispricing is quite large for the size-sorted portfolio containing the smallest firms: $\hat{\alpha}_1$ equals 3.17 and the estimate is significant. It seems that in the last subsample with value-weighted excess market return, the beta-sorted portfolios pick up the excess market return risk and the size factor risk better than the size-sorted portfolios.

Another notable feature with value-weighted excess market return is that with the addition of the size factor, the size-sorted portfolios' $\hat{\alpha}$s, which were significantly different from zero in model 1, are no longer so in the 1981–1985 subsample. This can be seen from Table 6.27. In addition, the relationship between size and R^2 is not evident anymore. This indicates that the size factor raises the explanatory power and thus leads to a decline in the significance of the pricing errors.

Turning to the case with equally weighted excess market return, the size-sorted portfolios and beta-sorted portfolios again show contradictory results: the size-sorted portfolios have a p-value of 2.5% but the beta-sorted portfolios have a p-value of

Portfolio	1	2	3	4	5	6	7	8	9	10
1986–1990										
α	0.11	0.03	−0.52	−0.23	−0.82	−0.59	−0.62	−0.19	−1	−1.24
$t(\alpha)$	0.23	0.07	−1.41	−0.85	−2.49	−1.68	−2.12	−0.45	−2.15	−2.29
β_m	1	0.96	0.94	0.93	0.96	0.98	0.95	1.01	0.96	0.97
$t(\beta_m)$	10.22	12.35	12.61	16.63	14.54	13.82	16.14	11.64	10.25	8.94
β_s	−0.06	−0.1	−0.36	−0.31	−0.37	−0.26	−0.27	−0.05	0.06	0.13
$t(\beta_s)$	−0.51	−1.02	−3.78	−4.43	−4.41	−2.89	−3.54	−0.42	0.5	0.91
adj. R^2	0.69	0.76	0.74	0.84	0.79	0.78	0.83	0.75	0.72	0.67
1991–1995										
α	−0.52	−0.9	−0.5	−0.94	−0.69	−1.06	−1.03	−1.12	−1.08	−0.09
$t(\alpha)$	−1.26	−2.82	−1.39	−2.51	−1.93	−2.7	−2.61	−2.3	−2.07	−0.13
β_m	0.91	0.61	0.69	0.75	0.69	0.95	0.83	0.87	1.08	0.83
$t(\beta_m)$	8.21	7.06	7.11	7.41	7.26	9.01	7.79	6.71	7.71	4.84
β_s	−0.21	−0.21	−0.26	−0.28	−0.19	−0.33	−0.2	−0.31	−0.13	0.15
$t(\beta_s)$	−2.13	−2.74	−3.07	−3.16	−2.2	−3.49	−2.16	−2.69	−1.05	1.01
adj. R^2	0.6	0.49	0.48	0.5	0.52	0.61	0.57	0.46	0.61	0.49
1996–2000										
α	0.37	0.43	−0.03	−0.3	−0.57	0.01	−1.36	−0.45	−1.3	−1.22
$t(\alpha)$	0.58	0.83	−0.06	−0.6	−1.34	0.02	−2.44	−0.62	−1.88	−1.43
β_m	0.37	0.41	0.46	0.51	0.46	0.55	0.55	0.66	0.62	0.8
$t(\beta_m)$	4.35	5.95	6.92	7.67	8.24	7.02	7.39	6.91	6.75	7.07
β_s	0.32	−0.02	0.01	−0.21	0.01	0.1	−0.02	0.14	0.13	0.82
$t(\beta_s)$	3.36	−0.22	0.09	−2.76	0.14	1.15	−0.25	1.33	1.21	6.38
adj. R^2	0.49	0.42	0.51	0.5	0.6	0.56	0.53	0.56	0.54	0.75

Table 6.26 Individual regression results of beta-sorted portfolios returns in model 2: equally weighted r^e_{mkt}

28% in the 1986–1990 subsample. As shown in Table 6.26 and Table 6.28, pricing errors of the beta-sorted portfolios are not much lower than the size-sorted portfolios. Actually, four of the estimates of αs with the beta-sorted portfolios in the 1986–1990 subsample are larger than those of the size-sorted portfolios. The reason that the size-sorted portfolios are rejected is that nearly all of the size-sorted portfolios have better fit than the beta-sorted portfolios. The low p-value of the size-sorted portfolios mainly reflects a more powerful test. In the 1991–1995 subsample, the situation reverses: the size-sorted portfolios have a p-value of 23.5% but the beta-sorted portfolios have a p-value of 2.5%. The reason that the beta-sorted portfolios are rejected is that the beta-sorted portfolios, although they are less well fit than the size-sorted portfolios, have larger and more significant pricing errors and thus they have a lower p-value.

The second and fourth columns of Table 6.23 show the results of applying the average F test. With value-weighted excess market return, only the last subsample of the size-sorted portfolios is rejected. For the beta-sorted portfolios, all subsamples are not rejected, though the last subsample has a lower p-value. The results of the average F test are more in line with the multivariate F test with the addition of size factor than in model 1 with the value-weighted excess market return. One possible explanation is that

Portfolio	1	2	3	4	5	6	7	8	9	10
1981–1985										
α	0.75	0.12	−0.45	0.41	0.24	0.04	−0.1	0.3	−0.31	0.18
$t(\alpha)$	1.63	0.33	−1.11	1.09	0.59	0.15	−0.37	1.08	−1.35	1.17
β_m	0.96	1.06	0.84	0.75	0.91	1.06	0.98	0.89	1.11	0.95
$t(\beta_m)$	11.39	16.37	11.30	10.75	12.11	19.12	18.98	17.86	26.55	33.13
β_s	1.33	0.75	0.67	0.43	0.33	0.18	0.13	0.03	−0.05	−0.11
$t(\beta_s)$	16.64	12.18	9.50	6.45	4.55	3.48	2.64	0.64	−1.36	−4.06
adj. R^2	0.91	0.91	0.84	0.79	0.79	0.89	0.88	0.86	0.93	0.95
1986–1990										
α	0.57	0.1	−0.18	−0.3	−0.39	−0.54	−0.33	−0.22	0.13	−0.1
$t(\alpha)$	1.39	0.31	−0.53	−0.94	−1.21	−1.91	−1.38	−1.21	0.65	−0.62
β_m	1.2	1.01	0.96	1.02	0.94	0.98	1.09	0.96	1.04	0.95
$t(\beta_m)$	14.37	14.92	13.83	15.63	14.24	16.92	22.09	26.28	25.89	29.41
β_s	0.96	0.77	0.7	0.55	0.31	0.09	0.08	−0.09	−0.04	−0.04
$t(\beta_s)$	10.55	10.41	9.33	7.70	4.30	1.49	1.41	−2.20	−1.03	−1.14
adj. R^2	0.86	0.87	0.85	0.86	0.81	0.84	0.9	0.92	0.92	0.94
1991–1995										
α	0.45	−0.12	0.12	−0.57	−0.21	−0.29	−0.42	−0.31	−0.18	0.11
$t(\alpha)$	0.86	−0.29	0.26	−1.35	−0.71	−0.91	−1.65	−1.13	−0.88	0.8
β_m	1.07	0.89	1.2	1.15	0.91	1	0.98	1.05	1.07	0.98
$t(\beta_m)$	6.03	6.40	7.46	8.12	8.89	9.42	11.47	11.28	15.30	21.84
β_s	1.01	0.66	0.57	0.36	0.3	0.11	0.04	0.02	−0.03	−0.06
$t(\beta_s)$	10.54	8.80	6.48	4.64	5.41	1.92	0.76	0.39	−0.92	−2.67
adj. R^2	0.74	0.69	0.65	0.62	0.67	0.62	0.7	0.69	0.8	0.89
1996–2000										
α	3.17	0.3	−1.16	−1.2	−1.8	−0.88	−0.72	−1.29	−0.69	−0.11
$t(\alpha)$	4.56	0.51	−2.25	−2.19	−3.25	−1.64	−1.52	−2.58	−1.52	−0.32
β_m	0.87	0.88	0.84	0.82	0.73	0.74	0.78	0.77	0.77	0.69
$t(\beta_m)$	6.68	8.04	8.69	7.90	7.00	7.31	8.75	8.24	9.05	10.30
β_s	1.47	0.76	0.68	0.33	0.28	0.13	0.02	−0.13	−0.11	−0.17
$t(\beta_s)$	15.50	9.61	9.71	4.34	3.74	1.8	0.35	−1.88	−1.8	−3.48
adj. R^2	0.85	0.77	0.78	0.62	0.56	0.51	0.57	0.53	0.58	0.64

Table 6.27 Individual regression results of size-sorted portfolios returns in model 2: value-weighted r^e_{mkt}

assuming the size factor being a genuine factor in pricing assets, using excess market return alone in the first specification would mean misspecification. The factor loading of the size factor would run systematically into the variance-covariance matrix of the residuals. The average F test ignores this correlation of disturbances resulting from misspecification and uses misspecified weight in weighting the pricing errors. Thus, it leads to differences in inference between the multivariate F test and the average F test in the first model. Results in Table 6.24 confirm our conjecture. Although zero correlation

Portfolio	1	2	3	4	5	6	7	8	9	10
1981–1985										
α	0.05	−0.62	−1.04	−0.19	−0.45	−0.73	−0.83	−0.39	−1.11	−0.46
$t(\alpha)$	0.1	−1.5	−2.38	−0.55	−1.1	−2.33	−2.92	−1.67	−3.78	−1.56
β_m	1.02	1.09	0.87	0.85	0.99	1.12	1.04	0.98	1.16	0.96
$t(\beta_m)$	11.08	13.62	10.37	12.79	12.63	18.55	19.08	21.57	20.73	17.14
β_s	0.82	0.21	0.24	−0.01	−0.17	−0.38	−0.4	−0.47	−0.63	−0.58
$t(\beta_s)$	7.8	2.29	2.46	−0.12	−1.94	−5.49	−6.32	−9	−9.82	−8.98
adj. R^2	0.9	0.88	0.82	0.83	0.8	0.88	0.88	0.9	0.89	0.84
1986–1990										
α	0.22	−0.2	−0.45	−0.61	−0.68	−0.83	−0.64	−0.5	−0.17	−0.36
$t(\alpha)$	0.47	−0.55	−1.13	−1.83	−2.2	−2.97	−1.98	−2.44	−0.65	−1.27
β_m	1.12	0.98	0.88	1	0.94	0.97	1.01	0.93	0.98	0.86
$t(\beta_m)$	11.74	13.69	11.02	14.96	15.19	17.14	15.52	22.65	18.24	14.92
β_s	0.43	0.3	0.29	0.07	−0.14	−0.37	−0.4	−0.53	−0.51	−0.44
$t(\beta_s)$	3.52	3.31	2.8	0.82	−1.84	−5.16	−4.83	−10.16	−7.43	−5.98
adj. R^2	0.82	0.85	0.79	0.85	0.83	0.84	0.81	0.9	0.85	0.79
1991–1995										
α	−0.22	−0.68	−0.67	−1.32	−0.74	−0.92	−0.98	−0.88	−0.72	−0.35
$t(\alpha)$	−0.39	−1.6	−1.38	−3.08	−2.21	−2.83	−3.29	−2.53	−2.31	−1.28
β_m	0.87	0.73	1.02	0.97	0.71	0.83	0.76	0.78	0.76	0.66
$t(\beta_m)$	5.92	6.42	7.82	8.46	7.85	9.46	9.47	8.35	9.06	9.06
β_s	0.56	0.28	0.03	−0.15	−0.07	−0.32	−0.35	−0.38	−0.42	−0.39
$t(\beta_s)$	4.25	2.73	0.3	−1.46	−0.82	−4.12	−4.97	−4.54	−5.61	−6.08
adj. R^2	0.73	0.7	0.67	0.64	0.63	0.62	0.61	0.54	0.58	0.58
1996–2000										
α	3.13	0.22	−1.17	−1.17	−1.91	−1.01	−0.86	−1.37	−0.72	−0.11
$t(\alpha)$	4.21	0.36	−2.03	−1.87	−3.36	−1.86	−1.8	−2.58	−1.42	−0.26
β_m	0.58	0.6	0.54	0.51	0.52	0.53	0.56	0.53	0.51	0.44
$t(\beta_m)$	5.83	7.13	7.02	6.05	6.76	7.31	8.81	7.5	7.46	7.72
β_s	1.27	0.56	0.5	0.16	0.1	−0.06	−0.18	−0.31	−0.28	−0.31
$t(\beta_s)$	11.32	5.91	5.68	1.69	1.18	−0.69	−2.45	−3.88	−3.66	−4.86
adj. R^2	0.83	0.74	0.73	0.52	0.54	0.51	0.58	0.48	0.48	0.5

Table 6.28 Individual regression results of size-sorted portfolios returns in model 2: equally weighted r^e_{mkt}

of the disturbances is rejected in all specifications, the value of LM test statistics in most cases is much smaller than that in the excess market return specification.

The average F test has quite different results with equally weighted excess market return from those with value-weighted excess market return. The size-sorted portfolios in all of the subsamples are rejected at all significance level. Comparing Table 6.27 and Table 6.28, estimates of αs of the size-sorted portfolios in the first three subsamples with the equally weighted excess market return are generally larger than those with the value-weighted excess market return. The beta-sorted portfolios are also rejected in the 1986–1990 and 1991–1995 subsamples. Estimates of αs are larger than those with value-weighted excess market return in these two subsamples. As a result, the p-values of the average F test with equally weighted excess market return are much lower than their value-weighted counterpart in the first three subsamples.

The third panel of Table 6.23 shows the result of applying the average F test on the set of individual assets. All the subsamples are not rejected at 10% significance level, though the p-value (13%) of the 1985–1990 subsample is lower. It may seem that the lower p-value is a result of the October 1987 stock market crash, but removing the observation only improves the p-value by 0.5%. Table 6.29 and Table 6.30 show the summary of individual assets returns test statistics. With both types of excess market return, the adjusted R^2 improves a bit over the first model: both the mean and median of the equally weighted excess market return case move up by nearly 5%. A significant feature of these tables is that regardless of which excess market return we use, the individual assets pick up the size factor risk. The percentage of the size factor estimates

	Mean	Stdc	Max	Min	Median	% of est.
1981–1985						
adj. R^2	0.30	0.14	0.62	0.00	0.31	
$t(\alpha)$	0.25	0.96	3.01	−2.07	0.11	5.63
$t(\beta_m)$	23.46	14.54	73.95	0.42	20.41	98.59
$t(\beta_s)$	0.78	8.36	17.30	−27.82	1.37	83.10
1986–1990						
adj. R^2	0.31	0.14	0.74	0.02	0.31	
$t(\alpha)$	0.04	1.13	3.51	−2.60	0.11	6.75
$t(\beta_m)$	25.55	19.00	93.38	1.14	22.33	98.16
$t(\beta_s)$	0.00	10.41	39.84	−31.59	0.82	83.44
1991–1995						
adj. R^2	0.16	0.12	0.53	−0.03	0.15	
$t(\alpha)$	0.24	1.09	5.97	−3.05	0.13	8.21
$t(\beta_m)$	10.20	9.24	49.21	−2.08	7.55	84.10
$t(\beta_s)$	0.72	9.80	24.05	−34.74	2.07	77.44
1996–2000						
adj. R^2	0.14	0.11	0.52	−0.03	0.12	
$t(\alpha)$	−0.02	0.73	2.24	−2.86	0.03	1.71
$t(\beta_m)$	9.37	9.19	71.61	−3.89	6.70	85.96
$t(\beta_s)$	−2.62	11.70	21.53	−60.87	0.08	79.11

% of est.: percentage of estimates significantly different from zero at 5% significance level.
Max: maxima of statistics.
Min: minima of statistics.

Table 6.29 Test statistics summary of individual assets returns in model 2: value-weighted r^e_{mkt}

	Mean	Stdc	Max	Min	Median	% of est.
1981–1985						
adj. R^2	0.29	0.14	0.64	0.01	0.31	
$t(\alpha)$	−0.31	0.96	2.16	−2.65	−0.27	7.04
$t(\beta_m)$	21.33	13.09	74.42	−0.01	18.87	97.18
$t(\beta_s)$	−7.61	8.79	5.55	−34.25	−5.58	86.62
1986–1990						
adj. R^2	0.29	0.13	0.68	0.03	0.29	
$t(\alpha)$	−0.27	1.12	3.03	−3.10	−0.15	9.20
$t(\beta_m)$	23.83	16.70	78.30	1.41	20.54	98.16
$t(\beta_s)$	−6.89	10.98	27.08	−38.98	−6.22	84.66
1991–1995						
adj. R^2	0.13	0.10	0.43	−0.03	0.12	
$t(\alpha)$	−0.34	1.01	3.71	−4.33	−0.26	6.67
$t(\beta_m)$	10.42	8.86	40.05	−1.99	9.29	84.10
$t(\beta_s)$	−6.20	8.76	6.83	−41.58	−3.83	73.85
1996–2000						
adj. R^2	0.12	0.09	0.40	−0.03	0.11	
$t(\alpha)$	−0.04	0.72	2.31	−3.39	−0.02	1.71
$t(\beta_m)$	11.49	9.79	51.59	−2.80	8.89	89.73
$t(\beta_s)$	−4.96	10.34	14.72	−46.48	−2.37	80.14

% of est.: percentage of estimates significantly different from zero at 5% significance level.
Max: maxima of statistics.
Min: minima of statistics.

Table 6.30 Test statistics summary of individual assets returns in model 2: equally weighted r^e_{mkt}

being significantly different from zero in all subsamples is more than 70%. Another feature is about the t-statistics of the size factor in with value-weighted excess market return: the variance of the t-statistics is quite large relative to the sample mean. It implies that the individual assets in the case of the value-weighted excess market return response to changes in size factor vary greatly.

Stochastic discount factor-based approach   Table 6.31 show the HJ distance and the p-value of $T[Dist(\delta)]^2$ using the two versions of W_T. One feature of the results is that, regardless of the excess market return used, the beta-sorted portfolios in the last subsample are rejected at 5% significant level in both versions of W_T. It contrasts with the fact that the beta-sorted portfolios in the multivariate F test and the average F test in the last subsample are not rejected at 10% significance level. The difference of results using regression framework and stochastic discount framework will be discussed below. The second feature of the results is that the HJ distance of model 2 is lower than the HJ distance of model 1 in all subsamples using both versions of W_T.

	Value-weighted r_m^e				Equally weighted r_m^e			
	Subsample W_T		Whole sample W_T		Subsample W_T		Whole sample W_T	
	HJ dist	p-value*	HJ dist	p-value*	HJ dist	p-value*	HJ dist	p-value*
Size portfolio								
1981–1985	0.34	45.97	0.40	23.07	0.33	46.31	0.39	29.17
1986–1990	0.45	13.76	0.30	39.41	0.45	14.03	0.30	58.37
1991–1995	0.27	71.14	0.27	56.72	0.27	68.12	0.27	66.71
1996–2000	0.60	1.58	0.78	0.01	0.59	1.76	0.78	0.04
Beta portfolio								
1986–1990	0.35	41.18	0.33	36.62	0.35	39.95	0.33	47.28
1991–1995	0.23	90.28	0.20	91.78	0.24	88.76	0.21	95.20
1996–2000	0.48	3.00	0.53	3.68	0.49	2.61	0.53	1.49

*p-value of $T(HJ - dist)^2$.
r_m^e: excess market return.

Table 6.31 Stochastic discount factor-based results of model 2

It seems that the size factor helps in shrinking the distance between the true discount factor and the estimated factor. The third feature is that the stochastic discount factor-based results with the value-weighted excess market return and those with the equally weighted excess market return are quite consistent with each other. The HJ distance of the two types of excess market return are very close to each other. The difference in HJ distance between the two excess market returns is less than 0.01 in all subsamples.

Table 6.32 and Table 6.33 report the estimates and their significance in stochastic discount framework with the addition of the size factor. With value-weighted excess market return, the size factor coefficients of the size-sorted portfolios are significant in the 1981–1985 subsample and in the 1991–1995 subsample using both versions of W_T. The size factor coefficient of the size-sorted portfolios is nearly significant in the 1986–1990 subsample as well when the full sample is used to create W_T. For the beta-sorted portfolios, the size factor coefficient in the 1991–1995 subsample is significant with both versions of W_T. The results suggest that the size factor is priced in some subsamples.

Table 6.34 shows the pricing errors with the addition of the size factor. With value-weighted market return, pricing errors of the size-sorted portfolios reduce in the first three subsamples. The drop in mispricing (when compared to model 1) is greater than 1 in the three portfolios containing the smallest firms in the 1981–1985 subsample. It shows that the size factor risk in the case of value-weighted excess market return is essential in pricing small stocks in the early 1980s. The result is similar to the rise in adjusted R^2 in the size-sorted portfolios containing small stocks in the regression framework in the first subsample.

	Size portfolios				Beta portfolios			
	b_m	b_s	$se(b_m)$	$se(b_s)$	b_m	b_s	$se(b_m)$	$se(b_s)$
Panel A: value-weighted excess market return								
1981–1985	0.016	−0.0582	0.020	0.025				
1986–1990	−0.008	−0.043	0.023	0.031	−0.015	−0.042	0.025	0.040
1991–1995	0.023	0.0480	0.045	0.021	−0.041	0.0907	0.054	0.037
1996–2000	0.051	−0.017	0.037	0.018	0.042	−0.026	0.034	0.022
Panel B: equally weighted excess market return								
1981–1985	0.016	−0.0582	0.020	0.025				
1986–1990	−0.008	−0.043	0.023	0.031	−0.015	−0.042	0.025	0.040
1991–1995	0.023	0.0480	0.045	0.021	−0.041	0.0907	0.054	0.037
1996–2000	0.051	−0.017	0.037	0.018	0.042	−0.026	0.034	0.022

Table 6.32 Parameter estimates of model 2 using stochastic discount factor approach with W_T created by using subsample return

	Size portfolios				Beta portfolios			
	b_m	b_s	$se(b_m)$	$se(b_s)$	b_m	b_s	$se(b_m)$	$se(b_s)$
Panel A: value-weighted excess market return								
1981–1985	0.007	−0.0606	0.023	0.026				
1986–1990	−0.009	−0.061	0.022	0.033	−0.010	−0.021	0.027	0.045
1991–1995	0.033	0.0527	0.050	0.022	−0.041	0.0949	0.056	0.042
1996–2000	0.051	−0.005	0.038	0.018	0.040	−0.026	0.034	0.023
Panel B: equally weighted excess market return								
1981–1985	0.0141	−0.0704	0.0231	0.0295				
1986–1990	−0.0111	−0.0555	0.022	0.0372	−0.005	−0.0232	0.0272	0.0506
1991–1995	0.0196	0.0423	0.0483	0.0425	−0.0191	0.0997	0.047	0.0574
1996–2000	0.0406	−0.0206	0.025	0.0205	0.0282	−0.0355	0.0237	0.0241

Table 6.33 Parameter estimates of model 2 using stochastic discount factor approach with W_T created by using whole-sample return

Table 6.34 also gives a clue as to why the beta-sorted portfolios are rejected in the last subsample. With value-weighted excess market return, the addition of the size factor return reduces pricing errors in the most mispriced beta-sorted portfolios in the last subsample: the drop in mispricing is greater than 1 in portfolio 10, which contains the largest beta in the last subsample. However, the improvement in pricing errors of portfolio 7 and portfolio 9 seems to be relatively small. They remain close to 1 with the addition of the size factor. This is the main reason why the HJ distance remains large

	1	2	3	4	5	6	7	8	9	10

Panel A: value-weighted excess market return

Size portfolio

	1	2	3	4	5	6	7	8	9	10
1981–1985	0.44	−0.05	−0.53	0.27	0.12	−0.05	−0.17	0.20	−0.34	0.11
1986–1990	0.54	0.10	−0.17	−0.25	−0.31	−0.42	−0.20	−0.08	0.24	0.02
1991–1995	0.17	−0.26	0.01	−0.57	−0.24	−0.24	−0.35	−0.24	−0.10	0.17
1996–2000	2.14	−0.16	−1.46	−1.33	−1.85	−0.94	−0.73	−1.19	−0.65	−0.08

Beta portfolio

	1	2	3	4	5	6	7	8	9	10
1986–1990	0.60	0.51	0.02	0.27	−0.26	−0.04	−0.09	0.31	−0.47	−0.71
1991–1995	0.25	−0.18	0.33	−0.02	0.07	0.05	−0.15	−0.04	−0.16	0.24
1996–2000	0.41	0.50	0.19	−0.01	−0.33	0.23	−1.03	0.03	−0.90	−0.74

Panel B: equally weighted excess market return

Size portfolio

	1	2	3	4	5	6	7	8	9	10
1981–1985	0.35	−0.14	−0.59	0.16	0.01	−0.16	−0.27	0.09	−0.44	0.04
1986–1990	0.62	0.18	−0.10	−0.17	−0.23	−0.34	−0.13	−0.01	0.32	0.08
1991–1995	0.22	−0.23	0.04	−0.54	−0.21	−0.22	−0.32	−0.20	−0.06	0.22
1996–2000	1.96	−0.30	−1.51	−1.32	−1.96	−1.08	−0.90	−1.28	−0.70	−0.11

Beta portfolio

	1	2	3	4	5	6	7	8	9	10
1986–1990	0.48	0.39	−0.11	0.15	−0.39	−0.17	−0.21	0.20	−0.60	−0.82
1991–1995	0.26	−0.25	0.24	−0.11	−0.03	−0.06	−0.27	−0.17	−0.28	0.13
1996–2000	0.60	0.69	0.30	0.10	−0.19	0.40	−0.85	0.06	−0.75	−0.58

Table 6.34 Pricing errors of stochastic discount factor framework in model 2

with the addition of the size factor. Comparing the results to the regression framework, the regression fit of portfolio 7 and portfolio 9 of the beta-sorted portfolios in the last subsample is no worse than other portfolios: they rank fourth and fifth among the ten beta-sorted portfolios in terms of adjusted R^2. These differences in the magnitude of pricing errors between the two approaches may drive the difference in p-values of the regression approach tests and the stochastic discount factor test.

6.5.4 Model 3

Regression-based approach Table 6.35 shows results of the three factor model with the excess market return, the size factor return and the book-to-market factor return. We first discuss the results associated with value-weighted excess market return. For the multivariate F test, the general pattern of results is the same as that of the two factor model. Specification is not rejected for both the size-sorted portfolios and the beta-sorted portfolios at 10% significant levels in the 1991–1995 subsample. In 1996–2000 subsample, the p-value of the beta-sorted portfolios is again much higher than the size-sorted portfolio: the beta-sorted portfolios have a p-value of 62% but the size-sorted portfolios are rejected at all significance levels. For the individual assets, there is one interesting fact: the p-value of the average F test in the 1991–1995 subsample is actually

	Value-weighted r^e_{mkt}				Equally weighted r^e_{mkt}			
	Multi. F test		Average F test		Multi. F test		Average F test	
	Test stat.	p-value	Test stat.	p-value	Test stat.	p-value	Test stat.	p-value
Size portfolio								
1991–1995	0.503	87.500	1.015	45.000	1.371	22.000	5.191	0.000
1996–2000	3.417	0.000	3.601	0.000	3.385	0.000	3.535	0.000
Beta portfolio								
1991–1995	0.774	65.000	0.987	47.500	2.334	2.000	4.704	0.000
1996–2000	0.808	62.000	0.584	83.500	0.977	47.000	0.650	78.000
Individual assets								
1991–1995			0.912	54.500			1.074	40.500
1996–2000			1.013	45.500			0.994	47.000

Table 6.35 Regression-based results of model 3

lower than the two factor model. It suggests that the addition of the book-to-market factor adds noise rather than explanatory power to the model in that subsample.

We now turn to the case with equally weighted excess market return. For the multivariate F test, the results of the size-sorted portfolios are similar to the two factor model with the last subsample being rejected at all significance levels. For the beta-sorted portfolios, the p-values of the multivariate F test and the average F test increase considerably from those of the two factor model. The p-value of the multivariate F test increases from 6% in the two factor model to 47% in this three factor model and the p-value of the average F test increases from 16% to 78%. This improvement in the performance of tests mainly results from a drop in both the estimates and the significance of pricing errors with the addition of the book-to-market factor. This can be seen if we compare Table 6.26 to that of Panel B of Table 6.37. Except for portfolio 1 and portfolio 6, all other portfolios in the three factor model have low estimates and less significant pricing errors. For the individual assets, the p-value of the average F test, like the value-weighted excess market return case, is lower than the two factor model in the 1991–1995 subsample. This again indicates the book-to-market return adds little explanatory power to the model.

Table 6.36 shows the simulation-based LM zero correlation test for the three factor model. Again, regardless of the excess market return used, the null hypothesis of no correlation between disturbances for the size-sorted portfolios, the beta-sorted portfolios and the individual assets is rejected. The addition of the book-to-market factor does not lower the value of test statistics. They are roughly the same as the two factor model. Thus the addition of the book-to-market factor does not seem to reduce the overall magnitude of the off-diagonal elements of the disturbance covariance matrix.

Table 6.37 and Table 6.38 depict the results of individual regressions of the size-sorted portfolios and the beta-sorted portfolios with the addition of the book-to-market factor. One feature of the two tables is that the addition of book-to-market factor does not help much in pricing portfolios. All estimates of factor loadings

	Size portfolios		Beta portfolios		Individual assets	
	Test stat.	p-value	Test stat.	p-value	Test stat.	p-value
Value-weighted r^e_{mkt}						
1991–1995	247.63	0.00	104.02	0.00	26366.62	0.00
1996–2000	880.86	0.00	587.83	0.00	76671.87	0.00
Equally weighted r^e_{mkt}						
1991–1995	337.63	0.00	272.55	0.00	27963.97	0.00
1996–2000	1051.10	0.00	761.18	0.00	76041.46	0.00

Table 6.36 Exact LM test of zero correlation of residual covariance matrix

with respect to the book-to-market factor are not significantly different from zero. The adjusted R^2 improves only slightly. One possible explanation is data problems. The book-to-market ratio information, which is necessary in the construction of book-to-market factor return, begins to be available in the late 1980s. In addition, the firms that have data on book-to-market ratio tend to be big and well-established firms. Therefore this factor is likely to pick up risk faced by these firms and may be highly correlated with the size factor and thus cause a multicollinearity problem.

Table 6.39 shows the summary of test statistics of the set of individual assets in model 3. The results are in line with that of the size-sorted and beta-sorted portfolios. The addition of the book-to-market factor return does not improve the fit of regression with both types of excess market return: the improvement in mean of adjusted R^2 is less than a percentage point. Moreover, it seems that the number of assets that pick up the book-to-market factor risk is less than that of the size factor. The percentage of estimates of the book-to-market factor loadings being significantly different from zero is a lot lower than the other two factor loadings' estimates. Only about half of the assets have the book-to-market factor estimates significantly different from zero.

Stochastic discount factor-based approach   Table 6.40 shows the results of the addition of the book-to-market factor based on the stochastic discount factor approach. One significant feature is that the pricing of the beta-sorted portfolios improves a lot with the addition of the book-to-market factor in the last subsample. For subsample varying W_T with value-weighted excess market return, the HJ distance shrinks from 0.48 in the second model to 0.15 in the last subsample for the beta-sorted portfolios. The HJ distance of beta-sorted portfolios with equally weighted excess market return shrinks from 0.5246 to 0.1523. Comparing Table 6.43 with Table 6.34, eight of ten beta-sorted portfolios with value-weighted excess market return have smaller pricing errors and nine out of ten beta-sorted portfolios with equally weighted excess market return have smaller pricing errors. As a result, the HJ distance decreases and the pricing of beta-sorted portfolios improves with the book-to-market factor.

The estimates using the stochastic discount factor framework are shown in Table 6.41 and Table 6.42. For the size-sorted portfolios, regardless of the type of excess market return used, the size factor estimate and the book-to-market factor estimate are significant in the last subsample for both versions of W_T. The same applies

Portfolio	1	2	3	4	5	6	7	8	9	10

Panel A: value-weighted excess market return
1991–1995

α	0.28	−0.51	−0.07	−0.34	−0.14	−0.37	−0.51	−0.44	−0.37	0.29
$t(\alpha)$	0.58	−1.67	−0.22	−0.98	−0.48	−1.07	−1.60	−1.04	−0.81	0.52
β_m	0.88	0.75	0.92	0.96	0.97	1.23	1.14	1.19	1.43	1.25
$t(\beta_m)$	5.43	7.38	8.83	8.33	10.07	10.55	10.77	8.44	9.49	6.82
β_s	0.29	0.08	0.06	0.11	0.18	0.16	0.19	0.15	0.40	0.51
$t(\beta_s)$	3.16	1.41	1.08	1.74	3.26	2.32	3.17	1.80	4.56	4.85
β_{bk}	−0.07	0.11	0.11	−0.07	−0.08	0.04	0.11	−0.07	0.13	0.32
$t(\beta_{bk})$	−0.44	1.12	1.09	−0.62	−0.87	0.31	1.09	−0.47	0.86	1.80
adj. R^2	0.42	0.51	0.59	0.56	0.67	0.68	0.71	0.57	0.69	0.61

1996–2000

α	0.61	0.28	0.12	−0.03	−0.33	0.10	−0.90	0.03	−0.79	−0.30
$t(\alpha)$	0.95	0.57	0.23	−0.05	−0.81	0.16	−1.64	0.03	−1.08	−0.34
β_m	0.65	0.67	0.66	0.72	0.71	0.82	0.85	0.85	0.92	1.20
$t(\beta_m)$	6.03	7.99	7.45	7.84	10.23	8.17	9.20	5.95	7.44	8.09
β_s	0.48	0.10	0.18	−0.01	0.19	0.29	0.22	0.42	0.40	1.20
$t(\beta_s)$	5.53	1.47	2.43	−0.10	3.43	3.58	2.95	3.61	3.98	10.08
β_{bk}	−0.16	0.05	−0.04	−0.08	−0.10	−0.02	−0.21	−0.10	−0.21	−0.40
$t(\beta_{bk})$	−1.11	0.44	−0.33	−0.64	−1.07	−0.16	−1.70	−0.53	−1.24	−2.00
adj. R^2	0.58	0.56	0.54	0.50	0.69	0.62	0.63	0.49	0.58	0.78

Panel B: equally weighted excess market return
1991–1995

α	−0.51	−1.00	−0.60	−0.92	−0.65	−1.12	−1.14	−1.10	−1.20	−0.33
$t(\alpha)$	−1.19	−3.07	−1.63	−2.37	−1.77	−2.75	−2.82	−2.19	−2.25	−0.51
β_m	0.91	0.62	0.69	0.74	0.69	0.96	0.83	0.87	1.09	0.85
$t(\beta_m)$	8.12	7.19	7.21	7.32	7.16	8.98	7.88	6.63	7.77	5.03
β_s	−0.21	−0.24	−0.30	−0.28	−0.18	−0.35	−0.24	−0.31	−0.17	0.07
$t(\beta_s)$	−1.98	−3.05	−3.31	−2.91	−1.96	−3.50	−2.42	−2.50	−1.31	0.46
β_{bk}	−0.02	0.14	0.14	−0.04	−0.05	0.08	0.15	−0.03	0.18	0.36
$t(\beta_{bk})$	−0.15	1.39	1.25	−0.30	−0.46	0.62	1.19	−0.17	1.06	1.77
adj. R^2	0.59	0.50	0.49	0.50	0.52	0.61	0.57	0.45	0.61	0.51

1996–2000

α	0.62	0.25	−0.01	−0.20	−0.44	−0.03	−1.02	−0.30	−0.97	−0.53
$t(\alpha)$	0.86	0.44	−0.02	−0.36	−0.92	−0.04	−1.64	−0.37	−1.25	−0.56
β_m	0.38	0.41	0.46	0.51	0.47	0.55	0.56	0.67	0.63	0.82
$t(\beta_m)$	4.38	5.85	6.85	7.62	8.22	6.93	7.49	6.87	6.80	7.28
β_s	0.36	−0.04	0.01	−0.19	0.03	0.10	0.02	0.16	0.17	0.91
$t(\beta_s)$	3.37	−0.47	0.11	−2.38	0.36	1.00	0.23	1.37	1.48	6.59
β_{bk}	−0.12	0.09	−0.01	−0.05	−0.07	0.02	−0.17	−0.07	−0.17	−0.35
$t(\beta_{bk})$	−0.75	0.68	−0.07	−0.38	−0.60	0.13	−1.21	−0.41	−0.94	−1.63
adj. R^2	0.48	0.41	0.50	0.49	0.60	0.55	0.54	0.55	0.54	0.75

Table 6.37 Individual regression results of beta-sorted portfolios returns in model 3

Portfolio	1	2	3	4	5	6	7	8	9	10

Panel A: value-weighted excess market return

1991–1995

	1	2	3	4	5	6	7	8	9	10
α	0.34	−0.06	0.15	−0.56	−0.30	−0.25	−0.47	−0.32	−0.19	0.14
$t(\alpha)$	0.63	−0.15	0.30	−1.29	−0.98	−0.76	−1.84	−1.11	−0.91	1.08
β_m	1.08	0.89	1.20	1.15	0.91	1.00	0.98	1.05	1.07	0.98
$t(\beta_m)$	6.06	6.34	7.39	8.05	9.00	9.35	11.51	11.18	15.18	21.97
β_s	0.98	0.68	0.58	0.36	0.27	0.12	0.02	0.02	−0.04	−0.05
$t(\beta_s)$	9.58	8.45	6.15	4.37	4.67	2.00	0.37	0.33	−0.95	−2.07
β_{bk}	0.18	−0.09	−0.04	−0.01	0.14	−0.06	0.09	0.01	0.02	−0.06
$t(\beta_{bk})$	1.05	−0.63	−0.28	−0.09	1.40	−0.60	1.05	0.09	0.25	−1.38
adj. R^2	0.74	0.69	0.65	0.62	0.68	0.62	0.70	0.68	0.79	0.89

1996–2000

	1	2	3	4	5	6	7	8	9	10
α	3.53	0.14	−0.89	−0.64	−1.29	−0.61	−0.71	−1.25	−0.28	−0.14
$t(\alpha)$	4.53	0.21	−1.54	−1.07	−2.12	−1.00	−1.33	−2.21	−0.56	−0.34
β_m	0.88	0.87	0.85	0.84	0.75	0.75	0.78	0.77	0.79	0.69
$t(\beta_m)$	6.75	7.89	8.75	8.30	7.31	7.37	8.63	8.14	9.37	10.14
β_s	1.52	0.74	0.71	0.40	0.35	0.17	0.02	−0.12	−0.06	−0.17
$t(\beta_s)$	14.34	8.32	9.16	4.92	4.25	2.06	0.32	−1.60	−0.84	−3.15
β_{bk}	−0.18	0.08	−0.14	−0.29	−0.26	−0.14	0.00	−0.02	−0.21	0.01
$t(\beta_{bk})$	−1.02	0.53	−1.04	−2.08	−1.87	−1.02	−0.03	−0.17	−1.82	0.14
adj. R^2	0.85	0.76	0.78	0.64	0.58	0.51	0.56	0.52	0.59	0.64

Panel B: equally weighted excess market return

1991–1995

	1	2	3	4	5	6	7	8	9	10
α	−0.37	−0.65	−0.67	−1.34	−0.86	−0.91	−1.07	−0.91	−0.76	−0.32
$t(\alpha)$	−0.66	−1.47	−1.34	−3.04	−2.54	−2.69	−3.51	−2.53	−2.35	−1.16
β_m	0.89	0.73	1.02	0.97	0.72	0.82	0.76	0.78	0.76	0.65
$t(\beta_m)$	6.02	6.33	7.73	8.39	8.05	9.35	9.59	8.30	9.02	8.94
β_s	0.51	0.29	0.03	−0.16	−0.11	−0.32	−0.38	−0.39	−0.43	−0.39
$t(\beta_s)$	3.71	2.70	0.27	−1.46	−1.27	−3.84	−5.16	−4.42	−5.48	−5.66
β_{bk}	0.23	−0.05	0.00	0.03	0.17	−0.02	0.12	0.04	0.05	−0.03
$t(\beta_{bk})$	1.29	−0.37	0.03	0.25	1.62	−0.23	1.30	0.38	0.50	−0.39
adj. R^2	0.74	0.69	0.66	0.63	0.64	0.62	0.61	0.54	0.57	0.57

1996–2000

	1	2	3	4	5	6	7	8	9	10
α	3.40	−0.02	−0.99	−0.70	−1.46	−0.80	−0.92	−1.40	−0.39	−0.21
$t(\alpha)$	4.07	−0.03	−1.52	−1.00	−2.32	−1.30	−1.70	−2.34	−0.68	−0.43
β_m	0.59	0.59	0.55	0.52	0.52	0.54	0.56	0.53	0.52	0.44
$t(\beta_m)$	5.84	7.03	7.01	6.21	6.95	7.33	8.69	7.40	7.58	7.61
β_s	1.31	0.53	0.52	0.22	0.16	−0.03	−0.18	−0.32	−0.24	−0.33
$t(\beta_s)$	10.67	5.12	5.45	2.16	1.73	−0.32	−2.33	−3.58	−2.88	−4.63
β_{bk}	−0.14	0.12	−0.09	−0.24	−0.23	−0.11	0.03	0.02	−0.17	0.05
$t(\beta_{bk})$	−0.73	0.77	−0.63	−1.51	−1.59	−0.78	0.24	0.11	−1.30	0.46
adj. R^2	0.83	0.73	0.72	0.53	0.55	0.51	0.57	0.47	0.48	0.49

Table 6.38 Individual regression results of size-sorted portfolios returns in model 3

	Mean	Stdc	Max	Min	Median	% of est.
Panel A: value-weighted excess market return						
1991–1995						
adj. R^2	0.16	0.12	0.52	−0.05	0.16	
$t(\alpha)$	0.19	1.10	6.69	−3.48	0.07	9.74
$t(\beta_m)$	10.22	9.22	48.61	−2.04	7.46	84.62
$t(\beta_s)$	0.28	9.10	19.59	−38.00	1.61	73.33
$t(\beta_{bk})$	0.60	3.71	14.58	−12.81	0.68	49.23
1996–2000						
adj. R^2	0.14	0.11	0.52	−0.05	0.13	
$t(\alpha)$	0.04	0.67	2.39	−2.61	0.07	1.71
$t(\beta_m)$	9.42	9.17	70.38	−4.10	6.80	87.33
$t(\beta_s)$	−1.65	9.72	21.33	−44.71	0.28	76.03
$t(\beta_{bk})$	−0.59	3.26	14.64	−12.21	−0.48	45.21
Panel B: equally weighted market return						
1991–1995						
adj. R^2	0.14	0.11	0.44	−0.05	0.13	
$t(\alpha)$	−0.39	1.05	4.33	−4.92	−0.25	7.69
$t(\beta_m)$	10.47	8.91	40.51	−1.94	9.07	84.62
$t(\beta_s)$	−6.02	8.40	6.30	−41.73	−3.60	65.13
$t(\beta_{bk})$	0.90	3.61	14.42	−11.18	0.87	48.72
1996–2000						
adj. R^2	0.13	0.10	0.46	−0.05	0.12	
$t(\alpha)$	0.00	0.65	2.27	−3.08	0.02	1.71
$t(\beta_m)$	11.52	9.68	50.49	−2.69	9.05	90.07
$t(\beta_s)$	−3.99	9.13	15.63	−37.01	−1.84	77.05
$t(\beta_{bk})$	−0.34	3.07	13.91	−8.95	−0.31	43.49

% of est.: percentage of estimates significantly different from zero.
At 5% significance level.
Max: maxima of statistics.
Min: minima of statistics.

Table 6.39 Test statistics summary of individual assets returns in model 3

to the beta-sorted portfolios. One feature of the two tables is that the magnitudes of the book-to-market factor estimates are quite large in magnitude compared to the estimate of excess market return and the estimate of size factor return. It may be a result of the larger values of book-to-market factor return in the late 1990s, as shown in Table 6.5.

6.6 Simulation

The aim of the simulation study is to examine the effect of using different sorting criteria. Two grouping criteria, size of stock and estimated beta, are considered. This simulation study is similar to the Lo and MacKinlay (1990) paper in that the criteria of

	Value-weighted r_m^e				Equally weighted r_m^e			
	Subsample W_T		Whole sample W_T		Subsample W_T		Whole sample W_T	
	HJ dist	p-value*	HJ dist	p-value*	HJ dist	p-value*	HJ dist	p-value*
Size portfolio								
1991–1995	0.27	59.12	0.27	43.11	0.27	56.72	0.27	52.75
1996–2000	0.48	1.57	0.56	1.24	0.48	1.39	0.56	0.68
Beta portfolio								
1991–1995	0.23	84.20	0.20	86.69	0.24	82.09	0.21	90.12
1996–2000	0.15	95.55	0.16	98.25	0.15	95.37	0.16	96.38

*p-value of $T(HJ - dist)^2$.
r_m^e: excess market return.

Table 6.40 Stochastic discount factor-based results of model 3

	b_m	b_s	b_{bk}	$se(b_m)$	$se(b_s)$	$se(b_{bk})$
Panel A: value-weighted excess market return						
Size portfolios						
1991–1995	0.021	0.055	−0.026	0.047	0.038	0.127
1996–2000	0.027	−0.0480	0.1462	0.035	0.019	0.061
Beta-sorted portfolios						
1991–1995	−0.040	0.088	0.006	0.055	0.057	0.121
1996–2000	0.009	−0.0658	0.2314	0.031	0.027	0.087
Panel B: equally weighted excess market return						
Size portfolios						
1991–1995	0.015	0.046	−0.027	0.044	0.053	0.126
1996–2000	0.021	−0.055	0.143	0.023	0.018	0.059
Beta-sorted portfolios						
1991–1995	−0.023	0.096	0.011	0.047	0.078	0.123
1996–2000	0.006	−0.068	0.233	0.023	0.028	0.085

Table 6.41 Parameter estimates of model 3 using stochastic discount
factor approach with W_T created by using subsample return

sorting are generated in-sample, as opposed to the empirical work in this chapter which uses criteria obtained prior to the sampling period. The reason for using in-sample criteria is that we can avoid imposing too many assumptions on the time-series structure of $\hat{\alpha}$. The crucial point which distinguishes this study from Lo and MacKinlay's paper is that we study the effect of sorting on both regression-based and stochastic discount

	b_m	b_s	b_{bk}	$se(b_m)$	$se(b_s)$	$se(b_{bk})$
Panel A: value-weighted excess market return						
Size portfolios						
1991–1995	0.033	0.054	−0.004	0.050	0.040	0.126
1996–2000	0.013	−0.0446	0.1767	0.035	0.022	0.066
Beta portfolios						
1991–1995	−0.041	0.096	−0.002	0.056	0.058	0.118
1996–2000	0.005	−0.0614	0.2310	0.034	0.027	0.091
Panel B: equally weighted excess market return						
Size portfolios						
1991–1995	0.019	0.044	−0.005	0.048	0.056	0.124
1996–2000	0.004	−0.046	0.180	0.024	0.022	0.069
Beta portfolios						
1991–1995	−0.018	0.096	0.008	0.049	0.078	0.122
1996–2000	0.005	−0.063	0.230	0.025	0.029	0.090

Table 6.42 Parameter estimates of model 3 using stochastic discount factor approach with W_T created by using whole-sample return

	1	2	3	4	5	6	7	8	9	10
Panel A: value-weighted excess market return										
Size portfolio										
1991–1995	0.19	−0.30	−0.01	−0.59	−0.21	−0.26	−0.32	−0.23	−0.09	0.17
1996–2000	1.59	−0.47	−0.94	−0.49	−0.90	−0.46	−0.58	−0.84	−0.08	−0.11
Beta portfolio										
1991–1995	0.26	−0.19	0.32	−0.02	0.07	0.05	−0.15	−0.04	−0.16	0.23
1996–2000	0.42	−0.05	0.04	0.14	−0.06	−0.08	−0.11	0.01	−0.15	0.14
Panel B: equally weighted excess market return										
Size portfolio										
1991–1995	0.24	−0.26	0.03	−0.55	−0.18	−0.23	−0.29	−0.19	−0.04	0.22
1996–2000	1.57	−0.48	−0.93	−0.46	−0.93	−0.51	−0.62	−0.85	−0.08	−0.08
Beta portfolio										
1991–1995	0.27	−0.26	0.23	−0.11	−0.02	−0.06	−0.27	−0.17	−0.28	0.12
1996–2000	0.46	−0.02	0.06	0.16	−0.03	−0.05	−0.07	0.01	−0.12	0.17

Table 6.43 Pricing errors of stochastic discount factor framework in model 3

factor-based frameworks. Lo and MacKinlay's paper studied the test's size distortion on the linear factor model in regression framework. More specifically, their study shows the size distortion of the asymptotic χ^2 test and the GRS test. The asymptotic χ^2 test they examined is not very practical: it assumes that the variance of α is the same and uncorrelated across stocks. In addition, their study used only the asymptotic χ^2 test to analyse the test size distortion in beta-sorted portfolios. Lastly, their work did not include any analysis of the stochastic discount factor-based asset pricing test.

The asset pricing tests examined in this study include both regression-based tests and stochastic discount factor-based tests. For the regression based-test, we examine the empirical distribution of the GRS test and the average F test. Although the average F test also imposes the assumption of uncorrelated residuals, it allows heteroscedastic idiosyncratic risk. Thus it relaxes the constraint of the asymptotic χ^2 test examined in Lo and MacKinlay's work. For the stochastic discount-based tests, we examine the empirical distribution of the J_T test instead of the Hansen and Jagannathan test (HJ test) considered here. The reason is that the distribution of the HJ test is sample dependent and thus does not have a unique distribution. The distribution of the J_T test follows χ^2 distribution asymptotically. The J_T test statistic is produced by the following standard two-stage procedure: in the first stage, the weighting matrix of pricing errors is set to an identity matrix, i.e.

$$g_T' I_N g_T \tag{6.24}$$

in which N is the number of portfolios. In the second stage, under the assumption of serially uncorrelated random errors, the optimal weighting matrix is created by the sample average of the outer product of pricing errors, i.e.

$$\widetilde{W}_T = \frac{1}{T} \sum_{t=1}^{T} g_t g_t' \tag{6.25}$$

and the J_T test statistic is the following,

$$g_T' \widetilde{W}_T g_T \tag{6.26}$$

Artificial data of asset returns is generated by $r_{it}^e = \alpha_i + \beta_i r_t^{em} + \epsilon_{it}$. The pricing errors, α_i, are set to zero so that the CAPM holds. The cross-section of β_i follows normal distribution with mean equal to 1, which corresponds to the case of CAPM. Random errors ϵ_{it} are serially uncorrelated and independently distributed so that the cross-sectional covariance matrix of ϵ_{it}, Σ, is an identity matrix I with dimension equal to the number of assets. Ten thousand artificial samples of 100, 500 and 1000 stocks are drawn. Stocks are sorted into portfolios based on two criteria: estimated beta and size of stocks. The estimated beta is obtained by

$$\hat{\beta}_i = \left(r_t^{em'} r_t^{em}\right)^{-1} r_t^{em'} r_t^{ei} \tag{6.27}$$

for each i. Following Lo and MacKinlay (1990), the size of stocks, X_i, is created such that it is spuriously correlated to the estimated pricing errors

$$X_i = \hat{\alpha}_i + \eta_i \tag{6.28}$$

in which

$$\eta_i \sim N(0, \sigma_n) \qquad (6.29)$$

and

$$\sigma_n = \frac{1 - \rho^2}{T \rho^2} \qquad (6.30)$$

The correlation coefficient, ρ, is the correlation between $\hat{\alpha}_i$ and X_i. Note that under null, the estimates of $\hat{\alpha}$ are solely estimation errors.

We examine two cases. In the first case, the sample mean of excess market return is set to zero. It is created by drawing half of the time series of the excess market return from normal distribution and setting the other half to be the negative of the first half. Three values of correlation, ρ, 0.05, 0.1 and 0.2, are considered. The variance of factor loadings, β, is set to be 1. Under this setting, sorting by estimated beta is not correlated with the estimation errors of α. It is because the correlation between $\hat{\alpha}_i$ and $\hat{\beta}_i$ is 0 with

$$cov\left(\hat{\alpha}, \hat{\beta}\right) = -\frac{\bar{r}^{em}}{T \sum_{t=1}^{T} \left(r_t^{em} - \bar{r}^{em}\right)^2} I_N \qquad (6.31)$$

and the two sorting procedures are linearly independent from each other. This case serves as a comparison between sorting based on a characteristic which correlates with estimation errors of pricing errors and one which does not. In the second case, we concentrate only on the beta-sorting procedure. In this setting, $\hat{\alpha}_i$ and $\hat{\beta}$ are correlated through the sample mean of the excess market return. The excess market return, r_t^{em}, follows normal distribution with mean 0.66% and standard deviation 5.74%. The mean and variance correspond to those of monthly excess return from 1926 to 2000 for the US stock market. As we look at the effect of correlation with $\hat{\alpha}$ in the first setting, we focus on the effect of the cross-sectional dispersion of β. More specifically, we study the effect of successively more dispersed β on the test size distortion. We examine three cases in which β is generated from the multivariate normal distribution

$$\beta \sim N\left(1_N, \sigma_\beta^2 I_N\right) \qquad (6.32)$$

and the variance of β, σ_β^2, takes the value 1, 2 and 3 respectively. Though Lo and MacKinlay already pointed out in general that a more dispersed β leads to less distortion, their study only examined the case of asymptotic χ^2 test empirically and they did not examine systematically the effect of a more dispersed β.

Table 6.44, Table 6.45 and Table 6.46 show the results of a 1%, 5% and 10% test of size-sorted portfolios and beta-sorted portfolios in the first setting. We divide the sample of stocks into 10 and 20 portfolios based on the sorting characteristic. Table 6.44 shows the results with the GRS test. One central result is that if the sorting criteria are uncorrelated with the estimation errors of α, the test size is undistorted. Thus the beta-sorted portfolios all have the correct test size. Other findings which conform to the Lo and MacKinlay paper are the following: (1) the distortion in the size of

No. of stocks	No. of portfolios	Size of size-sorted portfolios			Size of beta-sorted portfolios		
		1%	5%	10%	1%	5%	10%
$\rho = 0.05$							
100	10	1.08	4.92	9.9	0.96	4.78	10.07
500	10	2	7.48	14.09	1.14	5.04	9.74
1000	10	3.16	11.24	19.99	1.07	4.76	9.6
100	20	0.94	4.35	8.91	0.82	4.42	8.81
500	20	1.12	5.28	11.35	0.87	4.39	8.9
1000	20	1.85	7.52	14.12	0.71	3.75	8.35
$\rho = 0.1$							
100	10	1.71	6.92	12.96	0.96	4.78	10.07
500	10	7.2	20.44	31.86	1.14	5.04	9.74
1000	10	19.78	41.63	55.22	1.04	4.93	9.67
100	20	0.95	5.1	10.42	0.82	4.42	8.81
500	20	3.47	11.96	20.81	0.87	4.39	8.9
1000	20	8.52	24.22	36.73	0.77	4.33	9.03
$\rho = 0.2$							
100	10	4.9	15.95	25.98	0.96	4.78	10.07
500	10	54.43	77.67	86.74	1.14	5.04	9.74
1000	10	94.04	98.85	99.46	1.04	4.93	9.67
100	20	2.09	8.56	16.13	0.82	4.42	8.81
500	20	25.74	52.05	66.54	0.89	4.21	8.67
1000	20	70.74	89.84	95.24	0.77	4.33	9.03

Table 6.44 GRS statistics in case 1

test increases as the sorting characteristic becomes more correlated with the estimation errors of α, (2) holding the number of portfolios constant, the size distortion increases as the number of stocks in a portfolio increases and (3) the size distortion decreases as more portfolios are constructed for a given number of stocks. The intuition of findings (2) and (3) is that stocks are grouped into portfolios based on the estimation errors and thus the estimation errors do not diversify away as they are grouped into portfolios. The above findings do not mean that using estimated beta is better than using the size of stocks in sorting. Rather the implication is that using a characteristic correlated with estimation errors of α leads to test size distortion. In all the cases we considered, estimated beta is constructed to be uncorrelated with $\hat{\alpha}$ which solely contains estimation errors under the null. As a result, using estimated beta as sorting characteristic does not lead to size distortion.

Table 6.45 shows the results with the average F test. Although the general pattern of results is the same as the GRS test, the test size of the average F test is in general higher than that of the GRS test. This is especially so when the correlation of the sorting characteristic and the estimation errors of α are high. For example, with $\rho = 0.1$, the size of the 1% average F test with 1000 stocks and 20 portfolios is 17.06%, which is double that of the GRS test. Also, the average F test exhibits a more rapid increase in

No. of stocks	No. of portfolios	Size of size-sorted portfolios			Size of beta-sorted portfolios		
		1%	5%	10%	1%	5%	10%
$\rho = 0.05$							
100	10	1.19	5.85	11.33	1.11	5.35	10.81
500	10	2.57	9.02	16.39	1.26	5.46	10.76
1000	10	4.66	13.41	22.77	1.22	5.37	10.77
100	20	1.1	5.67	11.07	1.04	5.15	9.96
500	20	1.69	7.36	13.31	1.23	5.44	11.01
1000	20	2.56	10.49	17.95	0.9	4.77	9.71
$\rho = 0.1$							
100	10	2.16	8.11	14.72	1.11	5.35	10.81
500	10	9.98	25.14	37.12	1.26	5.46	10.76
1000	10	27.79	49.72	62.8	1.22	5.42	10.23
100	20	1.19	6.55	12.26	1.04	5.15	9.96
500	20	6.13	18.01	27.46	1.23	5.44	11.01
1000	20	17.06	37.35	50.54	1.15	5.36	10.39
$\rho = 0.2$							
100	10	7.16	19.1	29.64	1.11	5.35	10.81
500	10	68.22	85.87	91.73	1.26	5.46	10.76
1000	10	98.23	99.61	99.88	1.22	5.42	10.23
100	20	3.65	12.33	20.67	1.04	5.15	9.96
500	20	49.14	72.9	82.5	1.13	4.99	9.85
1000	20	93.74	98.5	99.38	1.15	5.36	10.39

Table 6.45 Average F statistics in case 1

test distortion as we increase the number of stocks within a portfolio. For example, as the number of stocks increases from 100 to 1000 with 20 portfolios, the 1% test size distortion increases by 90% for the average F test whereas that of the GRS test increases by 44%. Table 6.46 shows the results with the J_T test based on the stochastic discount factor framework. Though the general pattern of results are the same as the GRS test, the J_T test performs better than the GRS test in terms of size distortion. The test size is in general smaller, especially when the number of portfolios is large. Even in the case with the highest correlation setting, $\rho = 0.2$, the size distortion is minimal with 100 stocks and 20 portfolios: both the sizes of the 1% test and the 5% test are actually slightly lower than the correct significance level. For the beta-sorted portfolios, all of the test sizes of the J_T test are lower than the correct size of test. For the cases in which stocks are divided into 20 portfolios, the sizes of the 1% test and the 5% test are less than half of the correct size.

Table 6.47, Table 6.48 and Table 6.49 show the results of a 1%, 5% and 10% test of beta-sorted portfolios in the second setting. The aim of the second setting is to examine the effect of more dispersed β on test size given that $\hat{\beta}$ and $\hat{\alpha}$ are correlated. The Lo and MacKinlay study examined only the asymptotic χ^2 test with the beta-sorted portfolio. Also, the effect of the dispersion of beta is not studied systematically

No. of stocks	No. of portfolios	Size of size-sorted portfolios			Size of beta-sorted portfolios		
		1%	5%	10%	1%	5%	10%
$\rho = 0.05$							
100	10	0.47	3.94	9.72	0.54	3.99	9.67
500	10	1.05	6.38	13.97	0.57	4.03	9.42
1000	10	1.85	10.07	19.7	0.56	4.04	9.19
100	20	0.13	2.02	6.47	0.08	2.06	6.53
500	20	0.16	2.32	8.37	0.09	1.99	6.61
1000	20	0.16	3.84	10.9	0.08	1.66	6.09
$\rho = 0.1$							
100	10	0.91	5.77	13.13	0.54	3.99	9.67
500	10	4.57	18.91	32.24	0.57	4.03	9.42
1000	10	15.01	39.85	57.04	0.43	3.86	9.19
100	20	0.08	2.29	7.8	0.08	2.06	6.53
500	20	0.68	6.56	16.68	0.09	1.99	6.61
1000	20	2.33	15.59	32.09	0.1	2.05	6.74
$\rho = 0.2$							
100	10	2.83	14.55	26.4	0.54	3.99	9.67
500	10	47.06	77.49	87.99	0.57	4.03	9.42
1000	10	91.87	98.87	99.54	0.43	3.86	9.19
100	20	0.34	4.52	12.68	0.08	2.06	6.53
500	20	9.27	39.61	62.28	0.11	1.89	6.41
1000	20	44.55	83.2	94.11	0.1	2.05	6.74

Table 6.46 J_T statistics in case 1

in their paper: their study used only $\hat{\beta}$ and $\hat{\alpha}$ estimated from the sampling period 1954 to 1988 to examine the effect of the dispersion of beta. Table 6.47 shows the results of the GRS test. The results in general conform with findings in Lo and MacKinlay (1990). Test size distortion is more severe with a small dispersion of β. For 1000 assets with ten portfolios, the size of the 1% test and the 5% test doubles those of the correct size with $\sigma_\beta^2 = 1$. In contrast, for $\sigma_\beta^2 = 2$ and $\sigma_\beta^2 = 3$, the size of the test is slightly lower than the correct size. Another finding is that for a more dispersed beta, the test size remains generally the same as the number of stocks increases with the number of portfolios held fixed. For example, with $\sigma_\beta^2 = 2$ and ten portfolios, the size of a 10% test remains about 9.5% as the number of stocks in a portfolio increases from 10 to 100. As pointed out by Lo and MacKinlay, with a more dispersed β, the correlation between $\hat{\alpha}$ and $\hat{\beta}$ drops which leads to less test size distortion. It seems that their findings on the asymptotic χ^2 test holds true for the GRS test as well. What happens here is that with a larger dispersion of β, the spurious correlation becomes so minimal that increasing the number of stocks within a portfolio has no effect on the size of test (same as the case of uncorrelated $\hat{\beta}$ and $\hat{\alpha}$ in which increasing the number of stocks does not impose any effect on test size).

No. of stocks	No. of portfolios	Size of beta-sorted portfolios		
		1%	5%	10%
$var(\beta) = 1$				
100	10	1.21	5.19	10.33
500	10	2.15	8	14.39
1000	10	3.49	11.67	19.83
100	20	0.86	4.46	9.03
500	20	1.34	5.82	11.62
1000	20	1.68	7.85	15.05
$var(\beta) = 2$				
100	10	1.05	4.78	9.92
500	10	0.96	4.93	9.7
1000	10	0.99	4.81	9.56
100	20	0.72	4.28	8.86
500	20	0.7	3.88	8.34
1000	20	0.95	4.42	8.95
$var(\beta) = 3$				
100	10	1	4.71	9.98
500	10	0.96	4.92	9.66
1000	10	1.01	4.74	9.67
100	20	0.88	4.58	8.85
500	20	0.75	4.15	8.48
1000	20	0.88	4.24	8.95

Table 6.47 *GRS statistics in case 2*

Table 6.48 shows the results of the average F test in the second setting. As in the first setting, the distortion of test size is more serious than the GRS test. This is especially so when the dispersion of β is small. Also, as in the first setting, the size distortion of the average F test increases more rapidly than that of the GRS test as the number of stocks within a portfolio increases. Table 6.49 shows the results with the J_T statistics. The size distortion of the J_T statistics, as in the first setting, is smaller than that of the GRS test. In fact, even with the smallest dispersion of β considered, the test sizes are all smaller than the correct test size with 20 portfolios. With greater dispersion of β and 20 portfolios, the size of test in all cases is actually lower than half of the correct size.

6.7 Conclusion and implication

In the empirical part of this chapter, we studied three major issues. The first issue is whether using different attributes to sort stocks into portfolios affects asset pricing inference. It is found that portfolios formed from different attributes can lead to contradictory inference in the same model specification. For example, with equally weighted

No. of stocks	No. of portfolios	Size of beta-sorted portfolios		
		1%	5%	10%
$var(\beta) = 1$				
100	10	1.52	6.18	11.51
500	10	2.55	9.13	16.32
1000	10	4.39	13.87	22.71
100	20	1.33	5.72	10.73
500	20	1.94	8.05	14.26
1000	20	2.67	10.62	18.44
$var(\beta) = 2$				
100	10	1.28	5.21	10.49
500	10	1.33	5.76	10.83
1000	10	1.29	5.32	10.42
100	20	0.96	5.08	9.77
500	20	1.05	4.95	9.9
1000	20	1.13	5.17	9.98
$var(\beta) = 3$				
100	10	1.25	5.15	10.58
500	10	1.27	5.65	10.88
1000	10	1.26	5.38	10.34
100	20	1.11	5.2	9.96
500	20	0.99	5.13	9.97
1000	20	1.12	5.24	9.99

Table 6.48 Average F statistics in case 2

excess market return and size factor return as explanatory variables, the beta-sorted portfolios and the size-sorted portfolios give inconsistent results from 1985 to 2000. The second issue is about whether the use of individual assets can solve the problem of grouping. It is found that the disturbances of individual assets are correlated, which violates the central assumption of the average F test. Also, the poor fit of individual assets suggests that the average F test has poor power. The final issue examined is whether different asset pricing tests give the same inference. It is found that the multivariate F test, the average F test and the robust specification test can give different inference for the same specification. It is because the definition of pricing errors and the weighting matrix used are different for the three tests.

The simulation study of this chapter examines how robust are the asset pricing tests to spurious correlation between sorting attribute and estimation error. In both scenarios examined, it is found that the average F test is most prone to the spurious correlation of the three tests we examined. Also, another finding is that the stochastic discount factor-based J_t test is less prone to the spurious correlation.

The findings in this chapter suggest that care should be exercised when interpreting the results from asset pricing tests since results can differ for different portfolio formation. For published results one needs to ask the question: has a certain portfolio

No. of stocks	No. of portfolios	Size of beta-sorted portfolios		
		1%	5%	10%
$var(\beta) = 1$				
100	10	0.6	3.82	9.41
500	10	0.95	6.03	13.43
1000	10	1.66	9.56	19.27
100	20	0.08	1.44	5.27
500	20	0.08	2.15	7.25
1000	20	0.17	2.79	9.49
$var(\beta) = 2$				
100	10	0.44	3.69	9.29
500	10	0.4	3.58	8.93
1000	10	0.49	3.56	8.4
100	20	0.06	1.15	5.11
500	20	0.06	1.2	4.81
1000	20	0.05	1.33	5.5
$var(\beta) = 3$				
100	10	0.41	3.6	9.22
500	10	0.32	3.5	8.93
1000	10	0.5	3.65	8.69
100	20	0.04	1.31	5.15
500	20	0.04	1.17	4.82
1000	20	0.07	1.39	5.04

Table 6.49 J_T statistics in case 2

grouping been chosen to ensure a particular outcome? Also with different tests giving different results, one needs to question the testing procedure chosen or justify its use. A final issue is that since these tests and procedures are usually applied to only 60 monthly observations, are our results on testing merely a function of the small sample size? Irrespective of the answers to these questions, we would advocate more experimentation with portfolio construction and testing procedures.

References

Belsey, D., Kuh, E., and Welsch, R. (1980). Regression Diagnostics: Identifying Influential Data and Sources of Collinearity. New York: John Wiley and Sons.
Berk, Jonathan B. (2000). Sorting Out Sorts. *Journal of Finance*, 55:407–427.
Cochrane, John H. (2001). *Asset Pricing*. Princeton University Press, Princeton, NJ.
Elfakhani, S., Lockwood, L. J., and Zaher, T. S. (1998). Small Firm and Value Effects in the Canadian Stock Market. *Journal of Financial Research*, 21(3):277–291.
Fama, E. F. and French, K. R. (1993). Common risk factors in the returns on stocks and bonds. *Journal of Financial Economics*, 33:3–56.

Fama, E. F. and French, K. R. (1996). Multifactor Explanations of Asset Pricing Anomalies. *Journal of Finance*, 51:55–85.

Gibbons, M., Ross, S. A., and Shanken, J. (1989). A Test of the Efficiency of a Given Portfolio. *Econometrica*, 57:1121–1152.

Griffin, J. M. (2001). Are the Fama and French Factors Global or Country-Specific? *Review of Financial Studies*, 14:215–241.

Hansen, L. P., Heaton, J., and Luttmer, E. G. (1995). Econometric Evaluation of Asset Pricing Models. *Review of Financial Studies*, Vol. 8, Iss. 2 (Summer):237–274.

Hansen, L. P. and Jagannathan, R. (1991). Implications of Security Market Data for Models of Dynamic Economies. *Journal of Political Economy*, Vol. 99, Iss. 2 (April):225–262.

Hansen, L. P. and Jagannathan, R. (1997). Assessing Specification Errors in Stochastic Discount Factor Models. *Journal of Finance*, Vol. 52, Iss. 2 (June):557–590.

Hodrick, R. and Zhang, X. (2001). Evaluating the Specification Errors of the Asset Pricing Models. *Journal of Financial Economics*, 62:327–376.

Hwang, S. and Satchell, S. E. (1997). Improved Testing for the Efficiency of Asset Pricing Theories in Linear Factor Models.

Jagannathan, R. and Wang, Z. (1996). The Conditional CAPM and the Cross-section of Expected Return. *Journal of Finance*, Vol. 51:3–53.

Lo, A. W. and MacKinlay, A. C. (1990). Data-Snooping Biases in Tests of Financial Asset Pricing Models. *Review of Financial Studies*, Vol. 3, Iss. 3:431–467.

7 The small noise arbitrage pricing theory and its welfare implications[*]

Stephen E. Satchell[†]

Abstract

This chapter presents a small-noise version of the Arbitrage Pricing Theory (APT) which allows us to interpret the approximate linearity of the risk premia in terms of factor exposures for a fixed number of assets. The approximation becomes more accurate as the noise of the system decreases, even though the number of assets stays fixed. The Pareto optimality of such noise reduction is proven for a particular economy.

7.1 Introduction

Arbitrage Pricing Theory (APT) stresses the approximate linearity of the risk premia of assets in terms of the factor loadings. The basic assumption is that returns are generated by a linear factor model and the theory shows that the above linear approximation becomes increasingly accurate as N, the number of assets, increases to infinity.

The original paper by Ross (1976) has been generalized in many directions. The linear factor model has been dispensed with by Bansal and Viswanathan (1993). The problem has been put in an equilibrium setting by Connor (1984) and has been given a very general factor structure by Chamberlain and Rothschild (1983) and Reisman (1992). Many other important papers have been put forward but they all stress the approximate linearity of the risk premia for large N. It should be said that there is an interesting sub-question as to when the linear APT restriction holds exactly, see Connor (1993) and Huberman and Kandel (1987) among many others.

The contribution of this chapter is to demonstrate that it is not just large economies that matter for the approximation; it is also the magnitude of idiosyncratic noise. Econometricians of a certain age will not be surprised by this assertion. In the simultaneous equation literature, asymptotic properties were analysed both as large sample calculations or, alternatively, as small sigma (noise) calculations, see Kadane (1971), for example. Our goal is to construct small-noise bounds for the APT. A small-noise APT theorem is presented in section 7.3 together with the conclusion.

To achieve this goal, we define a concept of system-wide risk – and we show in section 7.2, proposition 1, that in an exchange equilibrium, all investors will have

---

[*] This chapter was written when the author was visiting the University of Technology, Sydney. He would like to thank A. D. Hall, J. Knight, S. J. Lin and L. Middleton for their helpful advice and comments.
[†] Trinity College, University of Cambridge, Cambridge, UK.

their expected utility reduced by an increase in noise; we assume constant absolute risk aversion utility functions and normally distributed returns.

Our results have some empirical meaning. In particular, a market with a small number of assets may still be subject to the APT restrictions if most of the risk to assets in that market is factor risk. Likewise, large markets that have substantial idiosyncratic risk may have large deviations from the APT restrictions, a point that is already understood.

7.2

We assume the following linear model,

$$\tilde{r} = \tilde{E} + \tilde{B}\tilde{\delta} + \tilde{\varepsilon} \tag{7.1}$$

where $\tilde{r}$ is a $(N \times 1)$ vector of asset returns, $E(\tilde{r}) = \tilde{E}$, $E(\tilde{\delta}) = E(\tilde{\varepsilon}) = 0$ and $\tilde{\delta}$ is a $(k \times 1)$ vector of factors, $\tilde{B}$ is an $(N \times k)$ matrix of loadings of rank k and $\tilde{\varepsilon}$ has a diagonal $(N \times N)$ covariance matrix, $\tilde{D} = (d_{ii})$. It is further assumed that $\tilde{\delta}$ and $\tilde{\varepsilon}$ are uncorrelated and that the unconditional covariance matrix of $\tilde{r}$ is $\tilde{\Omega}$.

Before we proceed to discuss how to quantify system-wide idiosyncratic risk, we discuss some results in the literature that point to a linkage between the exact APT restriction holding and the absence of idiosyncratic risk. We do this as a reinterpretation of the existing literature so as to show that our 'noise' view of the APT is, perhaps, a simpler way to think about the APT, rather than varying the number of assets.

For this model, the exact APT restriction is defined as $\tilde{E} = \lambda_0 \tilde{i} + \tilde{B}\tilde{\lambda}$ where $\tilde{i}$ is an $(N \times 1)$ vector of ones and λ_0 and $\tilde{\lambda}$ are $(k + 1)$ constants.

First it is well known, see Ingersoll (1987), that if $\tilde{\varepsilon} = 0$, then the exact APT restriction holds. Second, Connor (1984) presents an economy, called an insurable factor economy, where each investor's equilibrium portfolio consists of a linear combination of $(k + 1)$ mutual funds (see Corollary 2.1, p. 22, op. cit.). These mutual funds are simply portfolios that fully replicate the factors and have zero idiosyncratic variance. Connor shows that in such an economy, see Theorems 2 and 3, the exact APT restriction holds for finite N. In this economy, although idiosyncratic risk exists, it is not present in equilibrium. Likewise Huberman and Kandel (1987) present results which show that the exact APT restriction holds if the vector of mutual funds corresponding to the factors intersect the mean-variance frontier of the assets, see Proposition 1. The intuition is the same. Again, the existence of the portfolio of factors/mutual funds on the frontier allows investors to hold an 'optimal' portfolio that contains no idiosyncratic risk. Last, the infinite economy and limiting economy arguments all have the implication that the idiosyncratic risk should be reduced by diversification, i.e. by holding a large enough number of assets. Taken together these results suggest strongly that the arguments for the APT should be restructured in terms of noise/idiosyncratic risk and that an alternative way to think about when the exact APT restriction holds can be rephrased in terms of idiosyncratic noise.

We now turn to issues concerned with the definition of a scalar measure of system noise. In equation (7.1), we have defined $\tilde{D}$ to be diagonal with ith element d_{ii}. A useful system measure of idiosyncratic noise should have the property that as it tends to zero, the d_{ii} should all tend to zero. Accordingly, define

$$d_{ii} = \gamma \sigma_{ii}, i = 1, N \tag{7.2}$$

and set $\sigma_{jj} = 1$, where $j = \arg\max_i (d_{ii})$.

It follows immediately that

$$\lim_{\gamma \to 0} d_{ii} = 0 \quad \forall i.$$

Since we are taking continuous limits here rather than limiting on a sequence as is usual in the APT literature, we need to consider what a continuum of different γ economies might be.

We define a γ continuum of economies as

$$\tilde{r}^\gamma = \tilde{E} + \tilde{B}^\gamma \tilde{\delta}^\gamma + \tilde{\varepsilon}^\gamma \text{ for } \gamma \in R^+$$

where R^+ is the set of non-negative real numbers.

We now consider the concept of small γ arbitrage. Consider a continuum of portfolios $\{x^\gamma\}, x^\gamma \in R^+$. Each portfolio x^γ has typical ith element x_i^γ and is of length N, where N is fixed. We assume the following.

Assumption 2.1

(a) $\sum_{i=1}^{N} x_i^\gamma = 0$
(b) $\sum x_i^\gamma E(r_i) \geq \delta > 0$
(c) $\sum \sum x_i^\gamma x_j^\gamma \, \text{cov}(r_i, r_j) \to 0$ as $\gamma \to 0$.

The above assumptions tell us that (a) x^γ is a hedge fund, (b) the expected return on the portfolio is bounded above zero, and (c) the variance of the portfolio tends to zero as γ tends to zero. We have used $E()$ and $\text{cov}(,)$ to have their usual meanings rather than express the above in terms of (7.1).

It is appropriate to give some intuition as to what a continuum of γ economies might mean. The usual assumptions in APT studies is that the return distributions discussed in Section 7.1 are exogenous. In the case of γ economies, these different distributions could be thought of as arising from various actions by regulators that inhibit idiosyncratic noise or perhaps the introductions of mutual funds that effectively mimic some of the risk factors and whose introduction leads to new exogenous distributions through some external equilibrating process that leaves the noise component less noisy.

It is straightforward to demonstrate that an individual with an increasing concave expected utility function U will, ceteris paribus, prefer less system-wide noise to more.

Let the individual's optimized return be r_p where

$$x_p = e_p + \sum_{j=1}^{k} B_{p,j} f_j + \sqrt{\gamma \sigma_{pp}} \varepsilon_p' \tag{7.3}$$

In the above, ε_p' is standardized idiosyncratic noise; the standard deviation of the noise being $\sqrt{\gamma \sigma_{pp}}$. Equation (7.3) is a consequence of equation (7.1).

Let the value of the expected utility be denoted by $V = V(\gamma)$ where we have written V in terms of the value of the system-wide noise. We denote initial wealth by W_0 which here is set to 1. Thus,

$$V(\gamma) = E(U(1 + r_p))$$

If we compute $\partial V / \partial \gamma$, we see that

$$\frac{\partial V}{\partial \gamma} = E\left(U'(1 + r_p)) \frac{\partial r_p}{\partial \gamma} \right)$$

$$= \frac{1}{2} \gamma^{-1/2} d_{pp} E(U'(1 + r_p) \varepsilon_p')$$

It follows from the concavity of U and the positive dependence of r_p on ε_p' that $\partial V / \partial \gamma$ must be negative. Thus a decrease in γ leads to all investors being better off if their optimal portfolio remains factor equivalent to the previous optimum. That such a shift in γ is actually Pareto improving, however, does not follow from the above result without further argument. In what follows we establish this Pareto improving proposition for a simple exchange economy.

To further appreciate the impact of system-wide noise we now consider a particular, simplified model where all agents have differing-constant absolute risk aversion utility function and $\tilde{r}_i$ in equation (7.1) is equal to $P_{it+1} - P_{it}$, where P_{it} is the price of asset i at time t, is the present set to $t = 0$ where t will take the values 0 or 1. The utility function of investor j, $U_j(W)$, is given by

$$U_j(W) = -\exp(-\beta_j W) \tag{7.4}$$

and individual j is endowed with the vector $\bar{x}_j$ units of the n risky assets and $\bar{M}_j$ bonds. Thus his time zero wealth, W_{0j}, which satisfies

$$W_{0j} = \bar{x}_j' P_0 + \bar{M}_j \tag{7.5}$$

where P_0 is the $(n \times 1)$ vector of time zero prices and the time zero price of a bond is set at one. At time 1, investor j has wealth W_{1j} where

$$W_{1j} = x_j' P_1 + M_j(1 + r_f) \tag{7.6}$$

where P_1 is the vector of time price, x_j is the vector of demands of investor j, M_j is the quantity of bonds demanded, and r_f is, as before, the riskless rate of interest. This model is well known, see, for example, Grossman and Stiglitz (GS) (1980), and it is straightforward to calculate both the formulae for x_j, and the value of expected utility, see Grossman and Stiglitz (GS) (1980), equations (2) and (8). Let θ be the vector of expected prices at time 1, then, denoting $E(P_1) = \theta$,

$$E(U_j(W_{1j})) = \exp\left(-b_j[(1 + r_f)W_{0j}] + \frac{b_j^2}{2}(\theta - (1 + r_f)P)'\Omega^{-1}(\theta(1 + r_f)P) \right)$$

and the demand vector of investor j, x_j is given by

$$x_j = \tilde{\Omega}^{-1}(\theta - (1+r_f)P)/b_j \tag{7.7}$$

In this economy, the aggregate supply vector for risky assets S is given by

$$S = \sum_{j=1}^{M} \bar{x}_j \tag{7.8}$$

and equilibrium will result in the following formula,

$$\tilde{\Omega}S = (\theta - (1+r_f)P^*)d \tag{7.9}$$

where $d = \sum_{j=1}^{M}(1/b_j)$, and P^* is the equilibrium (time zero) price vector for the risky assets.

Thus

$$P^* = \theta/(1+r_f) - \frac{1}{d}\tilde{\Omega}S/(1+r_f) \tag{7.10}$$

Given that $\tilde{\Omega} = \tilde{B}\tilde{B}' + \gamma\tilde{D}$, where $\tilde{B}$ is the matrix of exposures and $\tilde{D}$ is the idiosyncratic covariance matrix, it follows immediately that

$$\frac{\partial P^*}{\partial \gamma} = -\frac{1}{d}\tilde{D}S/(1+r_f) \tag{7.11}$$

We have shown that the equilibrium price of all assets rises (falls) if noise decreases (increases).

We now consider the evaluation of expected utility when $P = P^*$.

Let $c(P) = (\theta - (1+r_f)P)'\tilde{\Omega}^{-1}(\theta - (1+r_f)P)$ then, from (7.10), we see that

$$c(P^*) = \frac{1}{d^2}S'\tilde{\Omega}S \tag{7.12}$$

We also need to compute W_{0i} as a function of P^*.

Now $W_{0i} = \bar{x}_j\,'P^* + \bar{M}_j$ so that $W_{0i}(1+r_f) = \bar{M}_j(1+r_f) + \bar{x}_j\,'(\theta - d\tilde{\Omega}S)$.

Hence, assuming that the interest rate is exogenous,

$$\frac{\partial W_{0i}(1+r_f)}{\partial \gamma} = -d\bar{x}_j'DS$$

It now follows that, letting $V_j(P^*) = E(U_j(W_{ij}))|_{P=P^*}$

$$\frac{\partial E(U_j(W_{ij}))}{\partial \gamma}\bigg|_{P=P^*} = V_j(P^*)\left(b_j d\bar{x}_j'DS + \frac{b_j^2}{2d^2}S'DS\right) \tag{7.13}$$

Since $V_j(P^*)$ is negative we have shown that an increase in noise reduces all investors' expected utility taken at the equilibrium prices $P = P^*$ and assuming that interest rates are fixed. If the interest rate is effected by the change in noise, then we get an extra term so that

$$\left.\frac{\partial E(U_j(W_{ij}))}{\partial \gamma}\right|_{P=P^*} = V_j(P^*)\left(h_j d\bar{x}'_j DS + \frac{h_j^2}{2d^2}S'DS - h_j \bar{M}_j \frac{\partial r_f}{\partial \gamma}\right)$$

Clearly if $\partial r_f/\partial \gamma$ is negative, our result is not changed, the only remaining issue is what happens if $\partial r_f/\partial \gamma$ is positive. We shall come back to this point in the conclusion.

Collecting these arguments we present the results as Proposition 1.

Proposition 7.1 *In a one-period world with exponential one-period utility, normally distributed returns for the vector of risky assets, an exogenous interest rate, and an exchange equilibrium in shares; then:*

1. *An decrease (increase) in system-wide noise as defined in equation (7.3) is Pareto improving (worsening).*
2. *The equilibrium price of equity, P^*, increases (decreases) if system-wide noise decreases (increases).*

Proposition 7.1 is not, in itself, surprising. It is not as general as one might think. In the case where we make similar assumptions to Proposition 7.1 and where the interest rate is endogenous, then an increase in noise can increase the value of bonds so that an individual with a sufficient endowment of bonds will become better off while others may be worse off. Such results can be found in the thesis of L. Middleton (2000), the key point is that we no longer have a Pareto worsening (improving) situation.

7.3

We now prove the following proposition about small γ arbitrage. We omit the tildes on the variables defined in equation (7.1).

Proposition 7.2 *In a γ continuum of economies with fixed N and no small γ arbitrage,*

$$\lim_{\gamma \to 0}\left(e_i^\gamma - \lambda_0^\gamma - \sum_{j=1}^{K} B_{ij}^\gamma \lambda_j^\gamma\right) = 0$$

Proof: The proof is standard and follows Ingersoll (p. 173, op. cit.).

Consider a best linear prediction of e_i^γ, the ith element of E^γ, on a constant and the k exposures B_{ij}^γ, $j = 1, k$. Define the residual v_i as, with the γ superscripts suppressed,

$$v_i = e_i - \lambda_0 - \sum_{j=1}^{K} B_{ij}\lambda_j$$

It follows that $\sum_{i=1}^{N} v_i = 0$, and $\sum v_i B_{ij} = 0$.

We construct our portfolio as $\omega_i = v_i/\|v\|$ where $\|v\|$ is the Euclidean distance of $v = (v_1, v_2, \ldots, v_n)'$. The portfolio $\omega = (\omega_1, \ldots \omega_n)'$ has the following properties:

(i) $\sum \omega_i = 0$.

(ii) $\sum \omega_i e_i = \dfrac{\sum v_i e_i}{\|v\|} = \dfrac{\sum v_i^2}{\|v\|} = \|v\|$

(iii) $\begin{aligned} \text{var}(\sum \omega_i x_i) &= \text{var}(\sum \omega_i e_i + \sum \omega_i \varepsilon_i) \\ &= \gamma \sum \omega_i^2 \sigma_{ii} \\ &= \gamma \sum v_i^2 \sigma_{ii} \Big/ \sum v_i^2 \\ &\leq \gamma \text{ since } d_{ii} \leq 1 \end{aligned}$

It follows that $\lim_{\gamma \to 0} \text{var}(\sum \omega_i x_i) = 0$; this implies that $\lim E(\sum \omega_i x_i) = \lim_{\gamma \to 0} \|v\| = 0$ to avoid small γ arbitrage QED.

It is certainly the case that Proposition 7.2 could be generalized to asset distributions more general than equation (7.1) as in Chamberlain and Rothschild (1983).

In conclusion we have shown that smaller γ economies with no small γ arbitrage lead to broadly the same results as when we increase the number of assets with no asymptotic arbitrage. However, the interpretation here is quite different and, we would argue, more natural. This noise reduction links the APT to the Pareto improving situation of a reduction in system noise which we proved in section 7.2. Broadly this tells us that if it were possible to trade factor portfolios rather than assets then we would all be better off.

Our motivation for presenting the APT in this form allows us to understand how an economy with a small number of assets may be better modelled by the APT than an economy with a large number of assets. We hope to investigate those questions empirically in future research.

References

Bansal, R. and Viswanathan, S. (1993). No Arbitrage and Arbitrage Pricing: A New Approach. *Journal of Finance*, Vol. 48, No. 4:1231–1261.

Chamberlain, G. and Rothschild, M. (1983). Arbitrage, Factor Structure, and Mean-Variance Analysis on Large Markets. *Econometrica*, Vol. 51:1281–1304.

Connor, G. (1984). A Unified Beta Pricing Theory. *Journal of Economic Theory*, Vol. 34:13–31.

Grossman, S. and Stiglitz, J. (1980). On the Impossibility of Informationally Efficient Markets. *American Economic Review*, pages 393–408.

Huberman, G. (1982). A Simple Approach to Arbitrage Pricing Theory. *Journal of Economic Theory*, Vol. 28:183–191.

Huberman, G. and Kandel, S. (1987). Mean-Variance Spanning. *Journal of Finance*, Vol. 42, No. 4 (September):873–888.

Ingersoll, J. E. (1987). *Theory of Financial Decision Making*. Rowman and Littlefield, New Jersey.

Kadane, J. B. (1971). Comparison of K-Class Estimators when Disturbances are Small. *Econometrica*, (September):206–213.

Middleton, L. (2000). The Impact of Changes in System-wide Noise. Mimeo, Judge Institute of Management Studies, Cambridge University.

Reisman, H. (1992). Reference Variables, Factor Structure, Multibeta Representation. *Journal of Finance*, Vol. 47, No. 4:1303–1315.

Ross, S. A. (1976). The Arbitrage Theory of Capital Asset Pricing. *Journal of Economic Theory*, Vol. 13:341–360.

List of symbols

$\tilde{r}$ = vector of returns
$\tilde{E}$ = vector of expected returns
$\tilde{\beta}$ = vector of coefficients of returns
$\tilde{\delta}$ = vector of factors
$\tilde{\varepsilon}$ = vector of errors
$\tilde{\Omega}$ = covariance matrix of $\tilde{r}$
$\tilde{D} = (d_{ii})$ diagonal covariance matrix
$\tilde{i}$ = vector of ones
$\tilde{\lambda}_0$ = APT weight
$\tilde{\lambda}$ = vector APT weights corresponding to factors
N = number of assets
K = number of factors
r = measure of system-wide noise
$\sigma_{ii} = d_{ii}/\tau$
$(\tilde{r}, \tilde{E}, \tilde{\beta}, \tilde{\delta}, \tilde{\varepsilon})$ with superscript γ means a particular economy in a continuum
$x = (x_i)$ is a portfolio, x_i^γ a member of a sequence
δ = positive constant
r_p = optimized portfolio return
$e_p = E(r_p)$
Bp_j = element of $\tilde{B}$
f_j = element of $\tilde{f}$
ε_p' = standardized element of $\tilde{\varepsilon}$
$V = V(\gamma)$ = expected utility
P_{it} = price of asset I at time t
P_0 = time zero price vector
P_1 = time one price vector
$\tilde{x}_j$ = initial endowment of equities of investor j
W_{0j} = initial wealth of investor j
$\overline{M}_j$ = initial endowment of bonds of investor j
r_f = riskless rate of intent
h_j = coefficient of ARA for investor j
$d = \Sigma \dfrac{1}{h_j}$

S = vector of numbers of equities (equation 7.8)
P^* = vector of equilibrium prices
$\theta = e(P_1)$
x_j = vector of equity demands by investor j
M_j = number of bonds demanded by investor j
$c(P)$ is defined in (equation (7.12))
v_i is the best linear prediction residual of e_i^γ on β_{ij}^γ and a constant
$\omega_i = v_i / \|v\|$
$\|v\|$ = Euclidean distance of v

8 Risk attribution in a global country-sector model

Alan Scowcroft and James Sefton

Abstract

As a consequence of market globalization, it is now harder than ever before accurately to attribute portfolio risk to country and sector positions. The increase in industrial concentration with the growth of global stocks has led to a biased sector composition in many smaller markets. This makes it very difficult to separate the impact of domestic market movements from global industry effects. This is particularly so when a few stocks can account for a large proportion of the market capitalization of a single country or region. At the portfolio level this can lead to overestimating the contribution of country factors to portfolio risk.

Here we present a new solution to this problem. Roll (1992) was the first to examine industry composition bias in local market indices; though Heston and Rouwenhorst (1994, 1995) were later to question some of his conclusions. Using the approach of Grinold et al. (1989), he estimated a set of industry-neutral country indices by regressing observed returns on a set of dummy-indicator country and sector variables. However, this approach makes some strong assumptions about the relative sensitivity of the asset returns to these factors. We therefore propose an iterative algorithm. The estimated indices are used then to estimate the asset return sensitivities which, in turn, are used to re-estimate the factor indices. By imposing a set of identifying restrictions on these regressions, we ensure, first, the algorithm converges and, second, the solution has an obvious interpretation.

We estimate our model on current data and compare our results to those obtained using the one-step approach of Roll (1992) and Heston and Rouwenhorst (1994). This suggests that their strong assumptions on asset return sensitivities result in them significantly underestimating the size of the industry composition bias in country indices. We discuss how this affects risk attribution at both the portfolio and stock level. Further we also use our model to make qualitative judgements on how 'global' are the world industry portfolios and how 'local' are the country indices.

Lastly, it is not only active managers who need accurate risk budgets. Passive managers need to ensure that all potential sources of risk are properly neutralized, while hedge funds and structured products often need accurate estimates of factor exposure for hedging purposes. These issues are also discussed.

8.1 Introduction

There are three important trends in equity markets associated with the process of globalization. First, investors are increasingly selecting their stocks from the global market. This is likely to decrease the degree of market segmentation. Second, companies are increasingly conducting their business across domestic markets; increasing the coherence of sector performance across markets. Third, multinational companies are growing as much through foreign acquisitions and investment as through trade, causing both local markets and the global portfolio to become more concentrated. In the first section, we review these trends in detail.

As a consequence of these processes, it is now harder than ever before accurately to attribute portfolio risk to country and sector positions. Further, since an increasing number of markets are now dominated by a small group of stocks or sectors, there is also a significant danger that apparently high levels of correlation are in fact spurious. This is particularly so when a few stocks can account for a large proportion of the market capitalization of a single country or region. At the portfolio level this can lead to overestimating the contribution of country factors to portfolio risk.

In this chapter, we present a new solution to this problem. Roll (1992) was the first to examine industry composition bias in local market indices. Using the approach of Grinold et al. (1989), he estimated a set of industry-neutral country indices and country-neutral sector indices by regressing observed returns on a set of dummy-indicator country and sector variables. This enabled him to ascertain what proportion of the variance of the observed market indices could be explained by the country-neutral industry. He found that the industrial composition could account for a large proportion of the disparate behaviour of different market indices. However, Heston and Rouwenhorst (1994, 1995) argued that Roll had not correctly adjusted for the market factor, and this resulted in him overestimating the size of the bias. Griffin and Karolyi (1998) confirm these findings.

However, these approaches make a strong assumption about the relative sensitivities or betas of the asset returns to these factors. For example, these studies assume that a US banking sector has the same unit sensitivity to global banking factor as the Japanese banking sector; or that a UK energy sector has the same unit sensitivity to changes in the UK market factor as the UK consumer goods sector. Imposing such assumptions is likely to bias results and lead to a misattribution of risk. This chapter proposes a solution. We estimate the asset return sensitivities by regressing the Heston and Rowenhorst country and sector-neutral indices on asset returns. These sensitivities are then used instead of the dummy-indicator variables to re-estimate the set of country and sector neutral indices. However, these regressions are performed subject to a set of constraints or identifying restrictions. It is these restrictions that ensure the regressions have their obvious interpretation, and further that the process can be iterated until convergence. These restrictions effectively relax the Heston and Rouwenhorst assumptions so that they are only satisfied at the global industry or local market level and not at the local sector level. Thus we only require the global banking sector to have unit sensitivity to the country-neutral banking factor, and not each local banking sector. Similarly, we require only the UK market portfolio to have unit sensitivity to the UK industry-neutral country factor, and not each UK sector. Moreover, and it proves to be relatively significant, we can further improve on Heston and Rouwenhorst's treatment of the market factor. Rather than estimate it as a residual constant, we include explicitly the market portfolio as a factor and impose the condition that the estimated country and sector neutral factors are orthogonal to the market factor. The paper that is closest to our study is Marsh and Pfleiderer (1997), though they choose to relax the Heston and Rouwenhorst assumptions in a different manner.

We estimate our model on current data and compare our results to those obtained using the one-step approach of Roll (1992) and Heston and Rouwenhorst (1994). The results suggest that their strong assumptions on asset return sensitivities result in them significantly underestimating the size of the industry composition bias in country indices. We discuss how this affects risk attribution at both the stock and at the portfolio level. At the stock level, we discuss it in terms of the 'Nortel problem'; the problem that because Nortel has at times been a very large proportion of the Canadian market, it appears in a standard risk attribution exercise to be very sensitive to the Canadian market. We show that in our framework, the risk attribution appears more 'plausible' in that the majority of the factor risk is explained by the global sector factors. Similarly, at the portfolio level, we find that on average our estimated country-neutral sector indices explain more of the factor risk than if they had been estimated using the one-step approach.

In a similar vein, we also use our model to make qualitative judgements on how 'global' are the world industry portfolios and how 'local' are the country indices. We consider an industry to be global if a large proportion of the variance of *all* the local industry portfolios can be explained by the industry factor. Similarly, we consider a country to be local if a large proportion of the variance of *all* the local industry portfolios can be explained by the country factor. Because of our treatment of the market factor, we are able to differentiate between high beta industries, such as industrials, and truly global industries such as energy.

Lastly, it is not only active managers who need accurate risk budgets. Passive managers need to ensure that all potential sources of risk are properly neutralized. In particular, hedge funds and structured products often need accurate estimates of factor exposure for hedging purposes. We discuss how our estimated country and sector neutral indices can be used to calculate hedging ratios.

The structure of the chapter is as follows. In the first section, we discuss in detail the recent trends in global equity markets. This section is included by way of background, but we do try to draw out the implications of these trends for risk modelling. Should the reader be more interested in the technical innovation and its consequences, they would be advised to skip this section. The second section discusses developments in risk modelling in the context of the attributing country and sector factor risk. It clearly describes our approach to modelling, but refers the reader to the appendices for technical details. The next two sections describe the results in detail; the first looks at estimates of industry composition bias, while the next examines the effects on risk attribution. The final section concludes and suggests further areas for research.

8.2   Recent trends in the 'globalization' of equity markets

There are three important trends in equity markets, all of them associated with the inexorable process of globalization. First, investors are increasingly selecting their stocks from the global market rather than limiting themselves to those in their own domestic market. Second, in line with the reduction in barriers to trade and capital movements, companies are increasingly conducting their business across domestic markets. Third, these multinational companies are growing as much through foreign acquisitions and investment as through trade, causing the market capitalization of the global portfolio to become more concentrated.

The consensus is that these trends will first decrease the degree of market segmentation, and therefore the benefits to investors of diversifying their portfolio across countries. Second, it will increase the coherence of company performance across sectors and hence the importance of an investor's sector investment strategy. A final consequence, and one less commented on, is that smaller markets, in market capitalization terms, are becoming dominated by a few large multinational firms increasing the industry composition bias of domestic portfolios and indices.

8.2.1 'Home bias'

Despite the benefits of international diversification, the majority of investors hold the greater part of their wealth in domestic assets. Since Grubel (1968), Levy and Sarnat (1970) and Solnik (1974) first highlighted this 'home bias' behaviour, enormous research effort has been devoted to explaining this apparent lack of efficiency on the part of the investor. However, as Lewis (1999) explains in her excellent review paper, a story based on currency or inflation hedging, cannot explain all the empirical facts.

Therefore, researchers have looked to explanations based on market imperfections. Adler and Dumas (1983, p. 964) discuss factors which could lead to market segmentation, such as different tax laws, tariffs on trading or asymmetry in market information. All these factors are likely to increase the importance of country factors in explaining stock return volatility and, as Cooper and Kaplanis (1994, section 6) argue, will imply that these factors are priced.

All recent papers on global pricing models fail to mention this demand side story of stock pricing. It does, however, have important implications for corporate finance. As Bacon and Woodrow (1999) state: 'finance directors at multinational companies have expressed considerable frustration that the country where they choose to list their shares determines the way that they are perceived by investors'. Further, it is the most likely reason that, as Lewis (1999) observes, 'even the stocks of multinationals usually move quite closely with their respective market indices – indeed studies have shown that the betas of these stocks with respect to their own market are usually relatively close to one'.

Yet if investors are becoming more global, in that they hold more foreign equities, then this story will become less important or, in the terms of a global asset pricing model, the explanatory power of country factors is likely to diminish. Unfortunately, as Warnock (2001) details, it is not easy to investigate the international allocation of equity portfolios as there are few data available and, what there is, is relatively unreliable. However, in Figure 8.1, we have reproduced one of his charts on the foreign equity holding of US investors. The degree of home bias is defined as 1 minus share of foreign equities held in US portfolios divided by the share of foreign equity as a percentage of the world market.

The trend is clear, US investors are investing more in foreign equity markets but the change is slow and there still remains a significant 'home bias'. The reduction in the degree of 'home bias' in US portfolios is partly due to US investors trading more

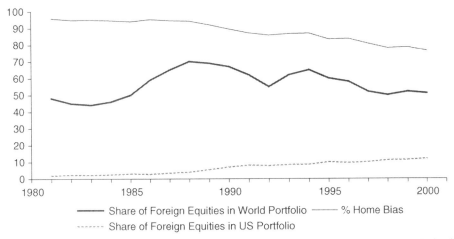

Source: International Finance Corporation, International Federation of Stock Exchanges, and Federal Reserve Board.

Figure 8.1 Home bias of US domestic investors, 1980–2000

		1980	1990	1993	1997
United Kingdom	Pension Funds	10.1	19	19.7	–
	Mutual Funds	–	37.1	36	–
	All Investments	–	18	–	34
Canada	Pension Funds	4.1	5.8	10.3	–
	Mutual Funds	19.9	17.5	17.1	–
	All Investments	–	–	–	36
Japan	Pension Funds	0.5	18	19.7	–
	Mutual Funds	–	7.9	–	–
	All Investments	–	2	–	10
Germany	Pension Funds	–	4.5	4.5	–
	Mutual Funds	–	56.3	45.2	–
	All Investments				

Source: Figures for pension funds and mutual funds are from Lewis (1999). Figures for all equity investments for 1990 are from French and Poterba (1991) and the figures for 1997 are from IMF (2001).

Table 8.1 Home bias of non-US investors: percentage of funds held in foreign equities, 1980–1997

on foreign exchanges but also partly because more firms are listing themselves on US exchanges. As Ahearne et al. (2000) show, non-US firms who list on the US exchanges are far more likely to be held in US portfolios.

Data on other countries are even sparser, but recently the IMF commissioned a survey: the 1997 Co-ordinated Portfolio Investment Survey (CPIS). Table 8.1 compares the result from this survey with data published in French and Poterba (1991)

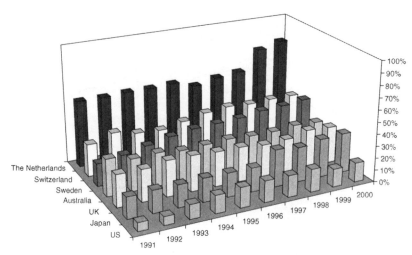

100%
90%
80%
70%
60%
50%
40%
30%
20%
10%
0%

Source: Reprinted by kind permission from Watson Wyatt Global Asset Survey.

Figure 8.2 Home bias of non-US investors: percentage of funds held in foreign equities from
Watson Wyatt Global Asset Survey

and Lewis (1999). The message from these data is broadly the same. Investors are
becoming more open in their investment strategies but the change is slow and relatively
unsensational.

In Figure 8.2 we have plotted a similar statistic from the Watson Wyatt Global Asset
Survey. Their survey contains detailed information on the asset allocation of nearly all
major funds and some smaller ones too; they claim their survey covers over 80% of
the value of all funds under management. Their numbers are in broad agreement with
the IMF numbers for 1997, and show the trend more clearly over the last ten years. In
all the countries charted, except Australia, there has been a significant increase in the
holdings of foreign assets. In the UK and Switzerland, the rise has been only 20% over
the period but in the US, Sweden and Japan the increase has been close to or over 100%.

A further trend, which would also lead to the decline of the importance of country
factors in a global asset pricing model is the increased alignment of the global economies, and therefore the diminishment of any differences between the investors. For
even if investors exhibit 'home bias', the stock returns of companies over the world
will become correlated if the respective aggregate risk faced by these domestic investors
becomes more correlated. In Table 8.2, we have calculated the correlation in real GDP
growth between a selection of countries over a ten-year moving window. The correlation of real GDP growth between the US, the UK, Canada, France and Italy have all
risen over the last 35 years. Japan is the notable exception, where the correlations have
fallen since the mid-1980s. The figures for Germany are less informative as the GDP
series for Germany changes dramatically in 1989 due to German reunification.

The data support the notion that the major economies are slowly becoming more
aligned and therefore that investor preferences are also becoming more aligned.
However, this trend, though pronounced, is again a relatively slow process.

Therefore, to summarize this section: if investors prefer domestic stocks, then this
is likely to result in a priced country factor in any global pricing model. However, the

	1965–1974	1970–1979	1975–1984	1980–1989	1985–1994	1990–1999
US/UK	0.29	0.22	0.20	0.11	0.42	0.55
US/CN	0.38	0.33	0.58	0.67	0.60	0.66
US/JP	0.30	0.45	0.19	0.17	−0.04	−0.24
FR/UK	0.26	0.35	0.13	0.01	0.45	0.66
IT/FR	0.15	0.46	0.34	0.58	0.58	0.43
FR/GE	−0.13	0.57	0.50	0.51	0.12	0.01

Source: OECD National Accounts. Note: Data for Q1–Q4 periods.

Table 8.2 Correlation of real quarterly GDP growth between countries
over selected ten-year periods

data suggest that the importance of these country factors is likely to be diminishing over time as, first, investor 'home bias' diminishes and second as the major economies become more aligned and so do investor preferences. Yet it is important to emphasize that this trend is slow, and the changes, though clearly evident, are not dramatic.

8.2.2 The rise and rise of the multinational corporation

Just as investors are becoming global, so are the companies. In line with the reduction in barriers to trade and capital movements, as a result of the GATT agreements and the emergence of large trading blocs such as the EC, NAFTA and ASEAN, companies are increasingly conducting their business across domestic markets.

A company can enter a new foreign market in two ways. It can sell its product to that market, thereby increasing the levels of trade between the countries. Alternatively, it can create a subsidiary firm in that market, either from new or, more probably, by buying and investing in a going concern there. In contrast, this approach increases the levels of foreign direct investment between the countries. In Figure 8.3, we have plotted the amount of trade as a percentage of the country's GDP for the US and the UK. For the UK, apart from the jump in 1974 following the UK's entry into the EEC, the level of trade in value terms has been relatively constant over the last three decades[1]. In contrast the level of trade into and from the US has increased steadily over this period, but the level still remains relatively low as compared to the UK and most other economies too.

There has therefore been no dramatic change in the levels of economic trade recently, certainly in these economies. Further, in the other main equity market, Japan's level of trade as percentage of GDP has barely risen in the last fifteen years; in real terms exports were about 9.3% in GDP in 1985 and were only 10.8% in 2000.

However, a different story emerges if we look at the levels of foreign direct investment (FDI). As Graham (1995) states, the level of direct investment out of the industrialized countries quadrupled over the period 1985 to 1990 from US$49.5bn to about US$220bn. Figure 8.4 plots the level of direct investment into and out of

---

[1] As the relative price of tradable goods to non-tradable goods has steadily declined over this period, the level of trade to GDP in volume terms has also risen in the UK.

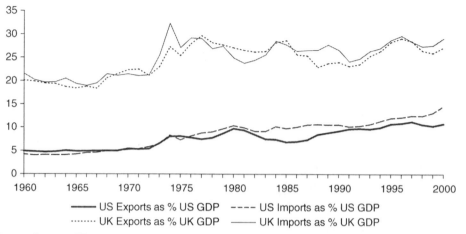

Source: Bureau of Economic Analysis (US) and the Office for National Statistics (UK).

Figure 8.3 Total exports and imports as a % of GDP for the US and UK

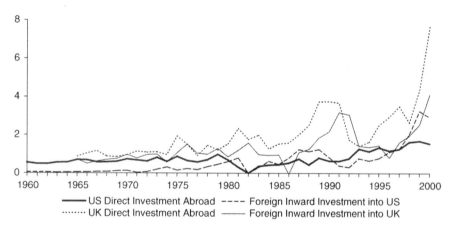

Source: Bureau of Economic Analysis (US) and the Office for National Statistics (UK).

Figure 8.4 Foreign direct investment as a % of GDP into and out of the US and UK

the US and UK as a percentage of GDP over the last 35 years (the history of direct investment in these countries mirrors the story for all the industrialized countries). The chart shows that in addition to the increases in FDI over the late 1980s, after a fall due global slowdown in the early 1990s, the level of direct investment has almost doubled again over the second half of the 1990s.

Has this expansion in foreign direct investment been at the expense of increased trade? Here the bulk of the research is suggestive that the two processes are marginally complementary and not substitutes, see, for example, Bergsten and Graham (1997) and Buigues and Jacquemin (1994). However, as these authors note, increases in the level of direct investment tend to be in line with increases in intra-industry trade rather than across industries, suggesting that much of the trade is in differentiated products.

Further Griffin and Karolyi (1998) also find that a distinction needs to be made between the traded and non-traded goods sectors.

The macroeconomic evidence is therefore that multinationals have increased their influence across markets by investing in new markets rather than solely by increasing their levels of trade. Whether the stocks of these multinational corporations are priced like a portfolio of the smaller local country companies or whether they are priced as a multinational company with an identity that is not simply the sum of its parts, is the central question for any global asset pricing model. As John Cochrane (2001) puts it clearly, would one expect a company formed from the merger of a number of small cap stocks to behave as portfolio of small cap stocks or as a single large cap stock? The evidence is mixed. As we mentioned in the previous section, multinational companies like Vodafone tend to be overly sensitive to the performance of the market in which they are listed. Also Lombard et al. (1999) found that the pricing differentiation between domestic and multinational firms, though apparent among Swiss companies, was very weak among US companies. What is clear is that there is no simple rule or empirical finding that can be followed.

Another direct consequence of the increase in the size and market coverage of these multinationals is that it will increase the level of market concentration. This is the final trend that we shall now investigate in more detail.

8.2.3 Increases in market concentration

The third important global market trend is the ever-increasing degree of market concentration. As the multinationals grew, either through mergers, acquisitions, or direct investment, they account for more and more of the global market capitalization. This trend reduces the effective number of stocks in a market and therefore the ability of an investor to diversify away stock-specific risk.

In order to quantify this trend, we shall define a new market or sector concentration index. However, this index is a simple adaptation of the widely used Herfindahl–Hirschmann Index (HHI). To define this index, let n denote the number of stocks in a market, where each stock i is a proportion w_i of the market. Then we define the concentration index for this market as:

$$\text{Concentration index} = \sqrt{n \sum_{i=1}^{n} \left(w_i - \frac{1}{n} \right)^2}$$

The index is therefore the mean squared distance of the actual market weights from equal market weights. The constant n in the expression is needed to make the index dimensionless or equivalently independent of the number of stocks in the market. To illustrate the use of this index, assume all the stocks in a market are equally weighted, then the concentration index would be 0. Alternatively, assume the market is made up of two groups of stocks; the first group of equally weighted stocks makes up half the market by number of stocks, but constitutes three-quarters of the market by market cap. Then, given that the other group is also made up of equally weighted stocks, the concentration index would be $1/\sqrt{2}$. Finally, if instead the first group of stocks had

Dow Jones Market	Concentration Index		% Mkt Cap of largest 5%		Gini Coefficient	
	January 1992	May 2001	January 1992 (%)	May 2001 (%)	January 1992	May 2001
Canada	1.49	2.02	35.0	44.8	0.63	0.69
UK	1.81	3.22	39.0	59.3	0.66	0.79
Japan	2.08	2.37	40.1	44.9	0.63	0.69
United States	2.46	3.53	46.7	59.4	0.72	0.80
Euro Countries	1.85	2.66	37.8	51.8	0.62	0.78
Europe ex Euro and UK	1.37	4.55	30.7	67.3	0.54	0.88
Pacific ex Japan	2.41	2.68	47.9	51.5	0.72	0.76
Latin America	1.94	1.65	48.4	37.1	0.80	0.67
World	2.41	3.93	44.2	59.7	0.70	0.81

Source: UBS estimates.

Table 8.3 Changes in the level of market concentration by region

made up only a quarter of the market by number but three-quarters by market cap, the index would have been 2.

Table 8.3 records the changes in level of market concentration in the eight main equity regions between January 1992 and May 2001. It also records for comparison the Gini coefficient of market capitalization for all these regions at these dates too. In every region, apart from Latin America, there has been an increase in the level of market concentration and, for all the western industrialized regions this change has been dramatic. To give an idea of the sort of changes in concentration involved, in the US and the UK the largest 5% of stocks have increased their market share of the total market capitalization by 27% and 50% respectively.

In Table 8.4, we investigate whether the increase in market concentration has been due to an increase in concentration in a few sectors or whether there has been a similar increase in all sectors. Table 8.4 records the changes to the concentration index for the ten Dow Jones Industry Groups over the same period. It is immediately apparent that this global trend towards concentration has affected all sectors, utilities excluded, to a more or lesser degree. It is therefore a global phenomenon, rather than a specific sector one.

As we remarked earlier, this trend reduces the ability of an investor to diversify away stock-specific risk by reducing the effective number of stocks in the market. An alternative way of stating the same observation, but in risk modelling terms, is that this increase in market concentration will increase the stock-specific risk content of the market indices.

However, there is another important ramification of this global trend towards higher market concentration, the industrial composition of a given market is likely to become a more important determinant of that market's performance. For if a large multinational was domiciled in a relatively small local market then this large multinational will dominate that market and hence that market's performance. To illustrate with

Dow Jones Market	Concentration Index		% Mkt Cap of largest 5%		Gini Coefficient	
	January 1992	May 2001	January 1992 (%)	May 2001 (%)	January 1992	May 2001
Basic Materials	1.80	2.28	37.3	46.9	0.64	0.73
Consumer Cyclical	2.21	3.50	41.1	57.2	0.68	0.78
Energy	2.45	3.55	53.5	67.1	0.77	0.81
Financial	2.48	3.08	45.7	55.4	0.71	0.80
Healthcare	2.40	3.48	54.8	71.3	0.75	0.84
Industrial	2.21	6.36	37.2	54.9	0.63	0.77
Consumer Non Cyclical	2.48	3.02	45.8	58.2	0.71	0.80
Technology	2.50	4.30	50.1	67.2	0.75	0.85
Telecommunications	1.38	2.75	36.4	60.6	0.65	0.82
Utilities	1.48	1.39	32.5	30.8	0.59	0.61

Source: UBS estimates.

Table 8.4 Changes in the level of concentration by industry group

some rather extreme examples, an investor buying into the Finnish HEX 20 index is taking a disproportionate bet on the Telecommunications sector as Nokia constitutes over 70% of the index; similarly buying the Swiss SMI is taking a large bet on the pharmaceuticals and banking sectors. Lessard (1974) and later Roll (1992) and Heston and Rouwenhorst (1995) all argued that the industrial composition of a market index is important in explaining the returns in that index. Beckers et al. (1992) argued that the low observed correlations between local market indices could be consistent with perfectly integrated markets if the industry composition was significantly different. The recent increases in market concentration are only likely to have made these observations more likely.

To quantify this trend, we shall change our notation slightly. Assume in the world market there are n_S sectors and n_C markets or countries, and that sector i in country j makes up $w_{i,j}$ of the world market capitalization. Then we can denote the industrial composition bias of market j as:

$$\text{Industry bias of market } j = \sqrt{\frac{n_s}{w_{i\Sigma}^2} = \sum_{i=1}^{n_s} \left(w_{ij} - w_{i\Sigma}w_{\Sigma j}\right)^2}$$

$$\text{where} \quad w_{\Sigma j} = \sum_{i=1}^{n_s} w_{ij} \quad \text{and} \quad w_{i\Sigma} = \sum_{j=1}^{n_C} w_{ij}$$

In this expression, market j constitutes a proportion $w_{\Sigma j}$ of the world market capitalization, similarly the proportion of sector i is $w_{i\Sigma}$. The industry bias is defined as the mean squared deviations of the sector proportions in market j by market cap from the world proportions. Therefore, if each sector constitutes the same proportion of the market cap of market j as it does of the world market, then market j is said to have no industry bias.

Table 8.5 records the industry composition bias by market in January 1992 and May 2001. The changes over time have not been so stark. However, there remains a considerable level of industry bias in all markets, save the US.

This measure focuses solely on the breakdown of the local market by market capitalization and therefore investigates only one type of possible bias in a market index. The recent TMT bubble is a perfect example of another type. During this bubble, the performance of one sector dictated the performance of the local market indices. However, this bubble was undoubtedly a global sector phenomenon, and so the local market indices conveyed very little information on the relative performance of the majority of the local market. This example motivates attempts to remove strong global influences from local market indices. We shall refer to this form of bias as 'factor bias' to distinguish it from the industry composition bias discussed earlier.

In the same way that we can examine the industry bias of market, we can investigate the market composition bias of industries. Let us define,

$$\text{Market bias of sector } i = \sqrt{\frac{n_C}{w_{\Sigma j}^2} \sum_{j=1}^{n_C} \left(w_{ij} - w_{i\Sigma}w_{\Sigma j}\right)^2}$$

then Table 8.6 records the market composition bias at the Dow Jones Industry level.

There have been some significant increases in the level of market composition bias over the last nine years, particularly in the communications and auto manufacturing industries. However, overall, the degree of bias has remained significant in well over half of the industries.

8.3 Modelling country and sector risk

In this section we shall discuss the merits and drawbacks of the most commonly used approaches to modelling country and sector risk factors in global risk models. The discussion is deliberately kept discursive rather than technical, but some technical details have been included in the appendices.

The method used to estimate the covariance matrix in the UBS global risk model is based on a Linear Factor Model (LFM) of stock returns. The principal advantage of this approach, over a purely statistical one, is that it naturally allows one to break down or attribute risk from holding a given portfolio.

In a Linear Factor Model, stock returns are assumed to be linearly related to the returns of a given set of factors; specifically, a market index, a set of sector indices, a set of country indices and a set of style indices:

$$r_{it} = \alpha_i + \beta_i^{Mkt} f_t^{Mkt} + \sum_{j \in Sectors} \beta_i^{Sj} f_t^{Sj} + \sum_{k \in Countries} \beta_i^{Ck} f_t^{Ck} + \sum_{l \in Styles} \beta_i^{Fl} f_t^{Fl} + \varepsilon_{it} \qquad (8.1)$$

where r_{it} is the return of stock i at time t, f^{Mkt}, f^{Sj}, f^{Ck} and f^{Fl} are the global market, global sector, local countries and style factor returns respectively, β^{Mkt}, β^{Sj},

	January 1992	May 2001		January 1992	May 2001
Finland	2.55	4.55	Italy	1.82	1.66
Spain	1.94	2.55	Germany	1.28	1.36
Portugal	3.13	2.50	Europe ex Eurobloc and ex UK	1.28	1.17
Mexico	2.43	2.38	UK	0.72	1.12
Ireland	2.45	2.21	Pacific ex Japan	1.22	1.08
Latin America ex Mexico	2.33	2.07	Canada	1.47	1.07
Austria	2.08	2.03	France	0.87	1.00
Belgium	1.92	2.00	Japan	0.91	0.98
Netherlands	2.22	1.88	United States	0.61	0.42

Source: UBS estimates.

Table 8.5 The industry composition bias by market

Dow Jones Industries	January 1992	May 2001		January 1992	May 2001
Water Utilities	3.05	3.34	Aerospace	1.93	0.95
Wireless Communications	0.65	2.27	Food Retailers Wholesalers	0.76	0.92
Auto Manufacturers Parts Makers	0.99	2.11	Tobacco	1.69	0.87
Coal	1.96	2.03	Advertising Media	1.33	0.86
Construction Materials	1.33	1.95	Forest Products Paper	0.63	0.77
Textiles Apparel	1.01	1.77	Home Construction Furnishings	1.16	0.77
Mining Metals	1.22	1.70	Entertainment Leisure	0.73	0.74
Healthcare Providers	2.64	1.61	Oil Gas	1.19	0.73
Gas Utilities	0.97	1.55	Retailers	0.70	0.73
Industrial Transportation	1.28	1.50	Speciality Finance	0.33	0.72
Industrial Equipment	1.54	1.49	Technology Hardware Equipment	0.73	0.69
Medical Products	2.00	1.46	Insurance	0.91	0.65
Technology Software	2.21	1.42	Travel	1.08	0.64
Transportation Equipment	0.68	1.33	Food Beverage Makers	0.70	0.61
Real Estate	2.58	1.26	Pharmaceuticals Biotechnology	1.00	0.58
Industrial Diversified	1.01	1.23	Consumer Services	2.20	0.57
Household Products	2.46	1.16	Containers Packaging	0.73	0.54
Cosmetics	1.15	1.12	Fixed Line Communications	1.31	0.46
Chemicals	0.44	1.05	Electric Utilities	0.42	0.40
Banks	1.29	0.98	General Industrial Services	0.45	0.31

Source: UBS estimates.

Table 8.6 The market composition bias of the 40 Dow Jones Industries

β^{Ck} and β^{Fl} are the corresponding sensitivities of the stock's return to these factors, α_i is the average idiosyncratic stock return and ε_{tt} is the idiosyncratic or stock-specific return which is assumed to be normally distributed with zero mean. The returns r_{it} need not be the returns on individual stocks, but could alternatively be the returns on a group of assets such as returns for a given sector in a local market. Now it is not possible to estimate all the parameters of this LFM, as it is not uniquely defined. For example, we could multiply any of the factor return series f by a constant λ and then divide its corresponding βs by the same constant and the model's description of the returns series r_{it} would be identical. Therefore, it is necessary to make some further assumptions or restrictions so as to estimate the model. There are three alternative approaches:

- *Time Series Modelling (TSM)*: Assumes the factor returns f^{Mkt}, f^{Sj}, f^{Ck} and f^{Fl} are known; the other parameters are estimated. In practice the factor returns are generated as the returns to factor mimicking portfolios.
- *Random Coefficient Modelling (RCM)*: Assumes the factor sensitivities β^{Mkt}, β^{Sj}, β^{Ck} and β^{Fl} are known and estimates the other parameters. In practice, the betas of a particular factor are assumed to be related to an observed characteristic of the stock. For example, one might assume the price to earnings ratio is good proxy for the betas corresponding to the growth style factor or more simply the country of domicile might be used as an indicator of sensitivity to the corresponding country factor.
- *Identifying Restrictions (IR)*: Assume the parameters of the model satisfy a further set of identifying restrictions and estimate the parameters subject to these restrictions. There must be a sufficient number of these restrictions uniquely to identify the model.

We will now discuss the advantages and disadvantages of these approaches. This is not meant to be an exhaustive discussion, but a more focused discussion of the relative merits of the approaches to adapt to and capture the processes of globalization.

Traditionally a time-series modelling approach has used the local market index returns as a proxy for the local market factor, and the sector index returns as a proxy for the sector factor returns. The local market index includes all companies domiciled in that market and thus is likely to consist of few large multinational firms. Because of their size, the performance of these firms, to a great extent, will determine the performance of the market index, even though these firms may have little exposure to local market risk. For example, BP, HSBC, and Vodafone dominate the UK index, yet all have grown recently from a major cross-country merger and conduct an ever-increasing proportion of their business outside the UK.

Diermeier and Solnik (2001) therefore suggest dividing up the local market companies into two: those companies whose foreign sales exceed a certain proportion of their total sales, called multinationals, and those who do not, called domestic firms. MacQueen and Satchell (2001) suggest a similar decomposition but base their identification procedure on a statistical test. Diermeier and Solnik then calculate local market indices by equally weighting the returns of the domestic firms. In this way, they claim, they have constructed local market indices from companies predominantly sensitive only to the local market. MacQueen and Satchell also constructed global sector indices from the multinational companies[2]. The constructed index returns can then be assumed to be good proxies for the country and sector factor returns f^{Sj} and f^{Ck}. The stock returns, stock by stock, are regressed on these factor returns to estimate the sector and country factor sensitivities β^{Sj} and β^{Ck}.

Diermeier and Solnik's solution is ingenious and appealing. These indices are built on the basis of sensible, easy-to-understand rules and their great advantage is that these rules can be institutionalized to build commercially available indices. In fact in October 1999, Bacon and Woodrow, in conjunction with FTSE International, launched a new set of indices constructed using a very similar criterion[3]. They state that these indices would be 'available as a benchmark for UK equities for those investors wishing to adopt the multinationals' structure but retain a broader exposure to the UK'. However, this approach is not without its problems. The first is practical; as Diermeier and Solnik describe in detail, data on foreign sales are often unreliable with different sources quoting wildly different numbers. Often firms simply do not report a geographical breakdown of their sales, and when they do they can be misleading either due to the breakdown of sales between affiliated companies or different national accounting standards. An extreme example of this sort of problem is Boeing, who report only 1% of foreign revenues, because all their foreign sales are done indirectly through a separate domestic holding company. Second, the cut-off between a multinational and a domestic is arbitrary and market dependent. FTSE revised dramatically their first working definition of a multinational index, which was seen as unworkable, and in the end circumnavigated the problem by defining domestic with respect to one of four global regions rather than to a particular country.

On a more theoretical level, there is a number of reasons why foreign sales to total sales may be a poor proxy for stock sensitivities to local market risk. The particular reason, discussed in detail earlier, is the demand side influence of home bias. Further, these sensitivities may be sector or business dependent, with a high proportion of foreign sales implying a strong sensitivity to foreign factors, the auto manufacturing industry being a good example, or only a marginal sensitivity such as in pharmaceutical or insurance industries. Both Diermeier and Solnik (2001) and Cavaglia et al. (2001) test the hypothesis that the foreign sales to total sales ratio is a good proxy for stock sensitivities to various factors. The evidence is mixed. Whereas Diermeier and Solnik find that this ratio has a positive statistical relation with the stock's sensitivity to the global market factor and a negative statistical relation with the sensitivity to the local market factor, Cavaglia et al. find this relationship is more marginal. A final point is that this approach can only hope indirectly to correct for industry composition and factor bias. It is likely that the multinationals are the large firms in the local market, and therefore that their local indices are constructed from smaller cap stocks. It is also likely that these small stocks will be more equally distributed over the sectors and more sensitive to the local market. Therefore, the approach may compensate for

---

[2] Diermeier and Solnik state their reasons in Lombard et al. (1999) for not constructing global sector indices from the multinational companies. The authors in this paper found an asymmetry between US and non-US MNCs in terms of their sensitivity to international factors that would make this approach problematic.

[3] In their case, a company was defined as a multinational if 70% of its sales were outside its home region, and the indices were constructed using a market cap weighting rather than equally weighting the constituents.

some industry composition and factor bias, but it is by no means assured. Despite these qualifications, though, the approach has a great deal to commend it, not least its simplicity. It is clearly suited to benchmark index construction, but its merits for constructing indices for risk attribution still remain to be established.

Solnik and de Freitas (1988), Grinold et al. (1989), Roll (1992), Heston and Rouwenhorst (1994, 1995), Rouwenhorst (1999) and Griffin and Karolyi (1998) have all used a random coefficient modelling approach to examine industry composition bias in local market indices and the relative importance of country and sector factors. They all construct dummy-indicator country and sector variables. A dummy variable for a given country or sector has a value of 1 if the corresponding stock or portfolio belongs to that country or sector and a zero otherwise. Therefore, in the notation of equation (8.1), they assume that the betas β^{Sj} and β^{Ck} are either 0 or 1. The stock returns are regressed on these dummy variables for each period to estimate the sector and country factor returns f^{Sj} and f^{Ck} – the so-called random coefficients. Therefore, this approach consists of T, where T is the number of time periods, cross-sectional regressions. This is in contrast to time-series modelling, time series regressions are undertaken, where N denotes the number of stocks.

This approach is also simple to implement, and further has no data requirements over and above the time series of stock or index return data. The approach will remove some of the industry concentration bias. For if one sector constitutes a greater proportion of a given local market than it does of the global market, then this approach assumes that a greater proportion of the performance of this local market will be explained by the corresponding sector factor. Similarly, if one sector is disproportionately located in one country or market, then again this approach assumes that more of the sector performance will be explained by the corresponding market factor. Therefore, the estimated sector and market factors should give a better reflection of the 'true' performance of the sectors and markets respectively now that any industry or market composition bias has been removed.

A further advantage of this approach is that it will partially adjust for factor bias; when the performance of one sector is so dramatic that the returns in the local markets reflect more the performance of this one sector than the performance of the majority of stocks in these markets. Returning to our earlier example of the TMT bubble, this approach would attempt to explain the bubble observed in all the local market indices with the corresponding Telecommunications and Technology sector factors, leaving the market factors to explain the common performance of all the other sectors in any market.

The main restriction or problem, as Marsh and Pfleiderer (1997) state, is that it makes the 'quite restrictive assumption that all stocks in a country and all stocks in an industry are affected by their respective country and industry factors in precisely the same way'. Further to this we would add that it is also quite restrictive to assume that all stocks in a country or all stocks in an industry are affected by *other* country or industry factors in precisely the same way. As Marsh and Pfleiderer (1997) point out, all these assumptions are likely to cause these studies to underestimate the industry composition bias within local market indices. This could be the reason that all these authors, Roll excluded, using this approach find that industry composition bias can explain little of the variance of market factor returns. Roll, on the other hand, finds that over 40% of the variance of local market returns can be explained by global industry factors, but this figure includes that proportion of the variance that can be explained by the global market factor.

Marsh and Pfleiderer (1997) were the first to suggest using a set of identifying restrictions to relax some of the assumptions of the earlier random coefficient modelling[4]. They suggest relaxing the assumption that each stock has a sensitivity or beta of 1 with respect to its country and industry factor. They do retain, though, the identifying restriction that every stock has a sensitivity or beta of 0 with respect to all other country and industry factors. Having relaxed some assumptions of the random coefficient model, they need to impose some additional identifying restrictions in order to ensure that the linear factor model is uniquely identifiable. They chose to impose the additional identifying restriction that the variance of each of the factor returns series is 1. The linear factor model is then estimated iteratively subject to these restrictions.

The approach of Marsh and Pfleiderer (1997) is the closest in spirit to ours. However, we relax the final assumption that a stock or portfolio of similar assets has no sensitivity or a zero beta with respect to all country or sector factors other than its local country and sector factor. We believe that it is likely that some sectors or markets will be more sensitive to the performance of foreign markets than others and similarly it is likely that some sectors or markets may be sensitive to the performance of other sectors too. A good example is News Corporation, listed on both the Australian and New York Stock Exchanges. With over 90% of its sales being overseas (74% US, 16% UK), and with similar volumes of its stock being traded on both exchanges, one would expect this stock, and hence the media sector in Australia too, to be more sensitive to the US market than other Australian sectors. Our approach allows for this possibility.

In this more general case, the identifying restrictions can no longer be phrased as a constraint on the variance of the factor returns. Constraints of this type cannot distinguish between direct effects and these cross-sensitivities. The constraints must instead be written as a function of the beta's rather than the factor variances. We require that on average the global industry portfolios have a beta of 1 with respect to their respective factors and 0 with respect to other industry factors and country factors. However, we only impose this constraint at the aggregate portfolio level, not at the local sector or stock level. Similarly we require that on average the country portfolios have a beta of 1 with respect to their respective factors and 0 with respect to other country factors and industry factors. We are in effect relaxing the Heston and Rouwenhorst assumptions so that they are satisfied only for the aggregate portfolios and not for the individual constituents.

In addition to these restrictions, we also impose some restrictions of the factor returns. We require the estimated country and sector factor returns to be orthogonal to the known global market factor. This means we can explicitly include the global market returns as a factor. We are able to estimate the sensitivities of our assets to this global market factor too under the restriction that the market cap weighted average of the market betas must equal 1. This treatment of the market factor is different from the approaches of Marsh et al. and Heston et al. As we shall later show, this treatment of the market factor makes a significant difference to the results. We are able to differentiate more clearly between high beta industries, such as industrials, and truly global industries such as energy. Finally, there is one further small difference, the

---

[4] We are grateful to Stefano Cavaglia for drawing this research to our attention.

returns r_{it} in our analysis are the Dow Jones local sector index returns, whereas Marsh and Pfleiderer (1997) use individual stock return data. But, as Griffin and Karolyi (1998) show in their appendix, this does not lead either to a loss of information or to different results.

Earlier we described how the random coefficient approach could partially correct for industry composition and factor bias. Its ability to fully correct for these biases is limited by the assumption that all stocks have a beta equal to one with respect to their sector and local market factors and a beta of zero with respect to all other factors. To illustrate how these assumptions constrain the model, assume a polarized world where half the world's capital markets are fully integrated and the other half are segmented[5]. In the random coefficient model, the global sector factors are forced to try to explain as much of the stock returns of the world's segmented markets as of the world's integrated markets. The result, inevitably, will be that the estimated factor returns will be a compromise between trying to explain as much of the stock returns in the integrated capital markets as possible, without creating too large errors in the segmented markets. If we relax the assumption that every stock has a beta of 1 with respect to its sector factor, then the stocks in the integrated capital markets can have high betas with respect to the sector factors and conversely the stocks in the segmented market can have low betas. The sector factors will then be able to explain as much of the returns in the integrated markets as possible, without creating large errors in the segmented markets.

Similarly, the relaxation of the assumption that all assets have no sensitivity with respect to any sector or local market factors other than their own, enables the model to decouple the factor effects between markets and sectors. In terms of our earlier example of the News Corporation stock in Australia, this stock in all likelihood will have a high beta with respect to the US market factor, implying that the Australian factor will not try to explain the US component of News Corporation returns. Therefore, the Australian factor will be able to concentrate on explaining only all things Australian.

The downside of this extra flexibility is that it is now necessary to estimate more of the parameters of the model. Hence estimating the parameters to a desired level of accuracy will require longer data series than would be required by the other two approaches. This, unfortunately, is a constraint. Often the data series are unavailable for longer timer periods and, even if they were, it is only realistic to assume the structure of the world's capital markets have remained approximately constant over the recent past.

8.4 The estimated country and sector indices

First, we wish to compare our new estimates of the factor returns series, with both the relevant Dow Jones Index return series and with the factor return series estimated using the random coefficient method of Heston and Rouwenhorst (H&R). In the next section, we shall discuss the implications of these new estimates for both individual stock and portfolio risk attribution.

---

[5] This is a world not completely unlike our own, except the proportions are clearly not half-and-half.

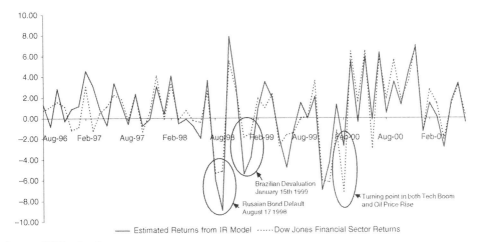

Source: UBS estimates.

Figure 8.5 Comparison of estimated global financial sector factor returns with observed Dow Jones financial sector returns

In Figure 8.5, we have plotted the estimated factor return series of the global financial sector with the observed return of the Dow Jones financial sector. Both return series are the returns relative to the Dow Jones global market index. We can observe from Figure 8.5 that the two series are very closely correlated, but they are different in some key periods. The first of these periods is centred around the Russian Bond Default Crisis in August 1998. On 17 August, the Russian government stopped supporting the rouble, which fell immediately by 35%, suspended foreign debt payments by banks and enterprises and rescheduled all short-term government bonds.

These events had enormous repercussions for the global financial sector, the best known being the collapse of Long-Term Capital Management. The next period occurred a few months later in January 1999, when the Brazilian Government abandoned its pegged exchange rate policy and the real went into freefall. Both of these international events were largely joyless for the large global banks, but did little to affect the performance of local domestic banks. The charted results are in line with these observations, as they also suggest that these events were more deleterious for the sector than the observed sector indices would suggest. The third period in March 2000 is at the turning point of the TMT boom and at the height of the enormous rise in oil prices. Neither of these events are directly associated with the financial sector, yet the financial sector had lent heavily to both the Telecommunications and Technology sectors. Our results suggest that the impact was not as substantial as the observed indices suggest.

In Figure 8.6, we compare our results with those obtained using Heston and Rouwenhorst's random coefficient method on our data set. Their approach picks up the third of these events, but does not pick up the other two.

In Table 8.7 we have reported a set of statistics for all of the ten global sectors indices. The first column reports the correlation coefficient between our new estimated factor returns series and the relevant Dow Jones global sector return series. The second

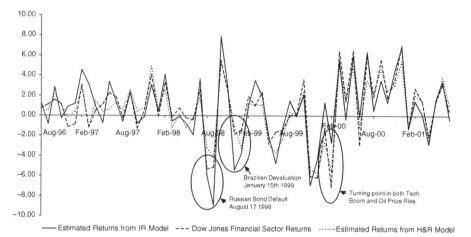

Source: UBS estimates.

Figure 8.6 Comparison of estimated global financial sector factor returns with estimates from the Heston and Rouwenhorst model

	Correlation between estimated factor returns and corresponding Dow Jones Sector returns		Annualized Standard Deviation of return series		
	Our IR Model Factor Returns	H&R Model Factor Returns	Dow Jones Sector Returns	Our IR Model Factor Returns	H&R Factor Returns
Industrial	0.52	0.72	2.23	2.51	1.79
Consumer Cyclical	0.63	0.72	2.30	2.70	2.22
Technology	0.83	0.83	31.36	33.71	28.72
Telecommunications	0.85	0.96	16.01	13.34	14.00
Financial	0.87	0.96	9.32	10.90	7.85
Utilities	0.88	0.88	8.02	6.02	6.59
Consumer Non Cyclical	0.92	0.90	7.58	6.99	7.07
Healthcare	0.94	0.92	13.86	12.60	9.22
Energy	0.95	0.94	21.68	21.42	22.74
Basic Materials	0.96	0.97	14.83	14.44	14.74

Source: UBS estimates.

Table 8.7 Comparison of key statistics of the global sector factor returns

column gives the identical statistic but using the factor returns series estimated in the approach of H&R. The final three columns compare the annualized standard deviation of these three return series. The sectors have been sorted in ascending order of the correlation coefficient in the first column. A low coefficient signifies a greater difference between the estimated and observed series or equivalently a larger adjustment for country bias effects. There is close agreement in the order of the correlation coefficients between the two approaches. Both suggest the result that the country bias is most significant in the cyclical sectors: industrials and consumer cyclicals. It is the cyclical sectors that one would intuitively expect to be the most sensitive to local market factors, and so it is the global sector indices corresponding to these sectors that would be the most 'corrupted' by local market effects. In contrast the Energy and Basic Material sectors exhibit the most coherence, or more precisely the highest correlation coefficients. The goods traded in these sectors are relatively uniform, oil from Texas is similar to oil from the North Sea, and the prices are set globally too. These facts have the implication that the country bias is likely to be minimal in these sectors. The other observation is that the coefficients corresponding to our new approach are in general lower than those corresponding to H&R's approach. This is because our approach is more flexible as it allows for beta sensitivities to differ from either 1 or 0, and is therefore better able to adjust for any biases.

In Table 8.8 we record similar statistics for the estimated local market factor returns. Again the results from our and the H&R approach agree closely, except in the US. The largest adjustment is in those countries with the more open equity markets: Canada, the UK and the US. The Canadian market was dominated for a significant period by the size and volatility of the Nortel technology stock; in January 2000 at its peak value it constituted more than 30% of the market by market cap. Further, in Canada, the sectors, particularly the tradable goods sectors, are very sensitive to the US market. Therefore one might expect there to be a significant industry bias in the Canadian local market index. Similarly the UK is a large open equity markets with a significant industry biases towards Financials, Energy, and Telecommunications. Hence one might also expect to observe the large adjustments for industry bias in the UK. Table 8.11 and Table 8.13, which are discussed in detail later, show where these adjustments have taken place. The country factor in the UK now explains more of the return variance in the Consumer Non-Cyclical, Healthcare and Utility sectors and less

	Correlation between estimated factor returns and corresponding Dow Jones Sector returns		Annualized Standard Deviation of return series		
	Our IR Model Factor Returns	H&R Model Factor Returns	Dow Jones Regional Returns	Our IR Model Factor Returns	H&R Model Factor Returns
Canada	0.68	0.73	12.32	8.48	7.79
United States	0.83	0.67	2.53	5.11	2.29
United Kingdom	0.83	0.86	5.23	5.15	3.29
Europe ex Euro-bloc & UK	0.92	0.82	8.90	7.84	6.75
Euro-Bloc	0.92	0.97	9.94	7.91	9.32
Pacific ex Japan	0.96	0.97	27.41	23.20	21.96
Japan	0.96	0.97	25.28	25.71	21.44
Latin America	0.97	0.97	48.28	41.82	46.99

Source: UBS estimates.

Table 8.8 Comparison of key statistics of the regional market factor returns

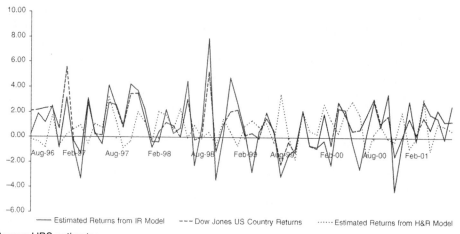

Source: UBS estimates.

Figure 8.7 Comparison of estimated US market factor returns with observed
Dow Jones US market returns

of the return variance in the Industrial sector. Finally now we shall discuss the US,
which is a slightly different case simply because of its size.

In Figure 8.7 we have plotted for comparison our estimated US factor return, with
both the US factor return estimated using H&R's methodology and with the observed
Dow Jones US index return. Our factor return estimates are more volatile than the
observed indices but appear highly correlated except perhaps around the time of the
TMT boom in late 1999 to mid-2000. The returns estimated using H&R's approach
look very different from the observed returns and are difficult to interpret.

Many authors, such as Cavaglia et al. (2000) and Diermeier and Solnik (2001),
have argued that one of the ramifications of the trend towards the globalization of
business is that sector factors will become more important in explaining stock returns.
Figure 8.8 plots the average volatility of the sector and local market factor returns
calculated from our new model over time. The volatility at any date is the unweighted
average of the variance of either all the ten global sectors or eight local market factor
returns over the previous 12 months. A plot using factor returns calculated using
H&R's approach would look very similar. We have also included on the graph the
average volatility of the sector return series ex the technology sector, and the average
volatility of the local market return series ex Latin America as these series are more
representative of the overall trends.

The volatility of the sector factor returns series unequivocally rose over the period
1993–2000. However, so did the volatility of the local market factor returns. The ratio
of sector volatility to local market volatility has also risen over this period from about
0.5 to around 1.5 before falling again to approximately 1. Though the evidence does
support the hypothesis that there has been a rise in the importance of sector factors,
the relationship is clearly not stable. Further this period was marked by two periods
of high uncertainty, the Asian crisis and the TMT bubble, which could be regarded as
abnormal market conditions.

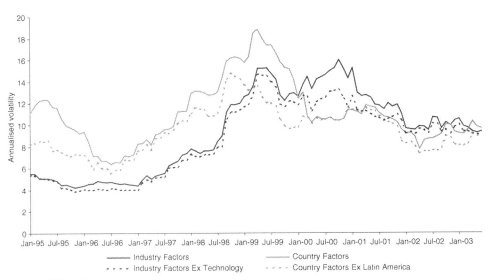

Source: UBS estimates.

Figure 8.8 One-year moving window estimates of average annual variance of global sector factors and local market factors

8.5 Stock and portfolio risk attribution

In this section we shall detail the results from our new country and sector factor model. In the interests of continuity, a detailed description of the new modelling approach and the associated estimation algorithm has all been relegated to the appendices.

Having examined the properties of our new estimated factor returns series, we wish to investigate how these series alter our factor allocation of risk at the stock level. In Table 8.9 we report the results of such an exercise for Nortel, a good example because of its importance to the Canadian market. To allocate the sources of risk from holding this stock, we regress the Nortel price return series on the global market

	Using Published Index Returns		Using Estimated Factor Returns	
	Coefficient	T-Stat	Coefficient	T-Stat
Global Market Beta	2.63	9.13	2.63	9.37
Global Sector Beta (Technology)	0.77	3.15	1.29	5.73
Local Market Beta (Canada)	1.42	3.65	0.85	1.91

Source: UBS estimates.

Table 8.9 Country-sector risk breakdown of Nortel stock returns

returns series, on its global sector return series (the Technology sector), on its local market factor return series (the Canadian market) and on a constant. We record two sets of results: the first uses the published Dow Jones index returns as a proxy for the factor returns, the second uses the new estimated factor return series. In the case of the Dow Jones indices we have removed the global market component from the sector and local market return series, by regressing these series on the global market and using the residual. This condition had already been imposed on our estimated factor return series during the estimation procedure.

The first two columns demonstrate the problem of industry bias within published local market indices. The first column records the beta estimate, the second its statistical significance. Using the Dow Jones indices as proxies for the factor returns suggests that after the global market, the local market is the most important driver of this stock's returns. As we have argued, this result is a direct consequence of industry bias. Nortel is such a major component of the Canadian market that it is unsurprising that it can explain so much of the Nortel return series. However, the causation is in the wrong direction; Nortel moves the Canadian market, it is not the Canadian market or economy moving the Nortel stock performance. In the third and fourth columns we report the results of the same exercise but using our estimated factor return series. The country beta falls in both size and significance, and by contrast the global sector beta rises. This new result suggests the performance of the Nortel stock is primarily related to the performance of its sector, and not its local market.

Table 8.10 performs a similar exercise for the UK stock, Stagecoach, which is a member of Consumer Cyclical sector. We experimented with many stocks in this sector, such as Pilkingtons, Travis Perkins, Smith (David) and Securicor, and all gave very similar results. The results using our new factor return series suggest that risk of holding the Stagecoach stock can be attributed approximately equally to both its sector and market. The same analyses using the published Dow Jones indices suggest that only the local market is significant.

The results reported at the stock level are all suggestive that by correcting for composition bias when estimating the factor returns series, one infers a greater importance to the global sector factors in any risk attribution exercise. Table 8.11 and

	Using Published Index Returns		Using Estimated Factor Returns	
	Coefficient	T-Stat	Coefficient	T-Stat
Global Market Beta	0.87	2.91	0.87	2.98
Global Sector Beta (Consumer Cyclicals)	0.12	0.14	1.24	1.93
Local Market Beta (United Kingdom)	1.18	2.26	1.61	2.96

Source: UBS estimates.

Table 8.10 Country-sector risk breakdown of Stagecoach stock returns

	United States	United Kingdom	Canada	Euro-Bloc	Europe ex Euro-Bloc & ex UK	Pacific ex Japan	Japan	Latin America
				Annual Standard Deviation of Returns				
Energy	18.0	20.7	20.2	17.3	26.8	22.0	29.2	45.8
Basic Materials	21.9	22.3	25.6	20.2	20.6	22.5	22.0	27.9
Industrial	18.1	18.8	24.2	19.7	21.1	21.8	19.9	31.7
Technology	36.5	47.0	58.7	38.9	56.4	36.7	29.1	38.7
Telecommunications	25.1	28.1	25.8	30.9	23.3	27.3	34.8	33.5
Utilities	17.0	12.4	15.9	17.2	19.7	15.1	17.8	37.8
Healthcare	14.3	16.7	31.4	15.9	12.6	19.5	18.2	33.5
Consumer Non Cyclical	13.2	13.0	15.4	14.7	12.7	21.5	20.6	24.6
Consumer Cyclical	18.6	19.4	20.3	22.0	19.5	20.3	17.5	30.6
Financial	19.0	19.1	18.9	23.0	24.5	21.4	26.1	33.7
				% of Variance explained by Global Market Factor (%)				
Energy	38.8	30.0	16.8	39.8	28.0	47.2	7.8	33.5
Basic Materials	50.7	49.3	31.9	52.2	39.7	51.0	29.3	60.4
Industrial	96.1	72.4	77.4	71.2	73.7	62.2	40.7	50.9
Technology	52.8	31.8	20.4	46.4	22.1	52.0	51.6	
Telecommunications	48.3	46.9	51.9	46.1	55.3	61.0	36.5	62.6
Utilities	10.1	9.6	22.6	40.1	14.8	26.1	4.8	37.6
Healthcare	30.3	10.2	44.7	30.1	29.2	49.2	11.4	
Consumer Non Cyclical	59.8	8.6	16.2	43.0	28.0	44.9	18.1	68.9
Consumer Cyclical	87.8	69.0	65.1	72.3	71.5	76.8	50.2	61.1
Financial	58.3	61.1	56.1	72.2	69.6	63.3	20.3	45.8
				% of Variance explained by Global Sector Factors (%)				
Energy	53.3	59.6	59.7	47.5	37.6	26.6	28.6	6.9
Basic Materials	43.8	37.1	37.7	31.5	46.7	27.8	20.9	13.6
Industrial	3.5	12.9	7.8	10.2	14.9	9.7	15.3	10.9
Technology	33.4	36.2	27.8	29.3	19.6	12.9	21.3	
Telecommunications	17.0	40.1	14.9	43.1	20.9	16.6	10.3	4.7
Utilities	52.3	37.0	18.1	15.9	21.3	31.6	29.5	6.5
Healthcare	51.2	42.2	21.8	29.4	27.4	24.5	17.2	
Consumer Non Cyclical	36.1	68.3	40.2	35.7	57.1	27.8	13.5	6.7
Consumer Cyclical	10.1	12.7	15.0	6.8	13.0	7.0	23.2	10.3
Financial	18.7	5.2	8.6	1.4	8.1	3.8	5.6	1.5
				% of Variance explained by Local Market Factors (%)				
Energy	3.6	8.9	17.5	12.6	13.6	18.8	31.2	30.3
Basic Materials	3.5	13.6	21.2	16.4	13.6	19.8	42.8	19.4
Industrial	0.4	14.8	7.6	18.6	11.4	28.1	43.9	22.9
Technology	1.1	5.0	1.4	11.0	3.4	18.7	27.1	
Telecommunications	2.9	8.9	10.7	8.8	21.5	9.5	27.5	19.6
Utilities	7.9	35.9	47.7	40.1	23.4	37.0	29.7	42.6
Healthcare	7.6	14.9	16.1	22.4	28.0	9.1	54.7	
Consumer Non Cyclical	1.0	23.1	30.4	21.3	7.7	20.7	56.9	22.0
Consumer Cyclical	2.1	11.7	14.1	20.9	15.5	16.2	26.6	16.4
Financial	5.5	21.4	26.7	16.6	10.3	26.7	55.1	34.1

Source: UBS estimates.

Table 8.11 Variance breakdown of local market sector returns (July 1998–June 2003) using the method of identifying restrictions

	United States	United Kingdom	Canada	Euro-Bloc	Europe ex Euro-Bloc & ex UK	Pacific ex Japan	Japan	Latin America
				Annual Standard Deviation of Returns				
Energy	18.0	20.7	20.2	17.3	26.8	22.0	29.2	45.8
Basic Materials	21.9	22.3	25.6	20.2	20.6	22.5	22.0	27.9
Industrial	18.1	18.8	24.2	19.7	21.1	21.8	19.9	31.7
Technology	36.5	47.0	58.7	38.9	56.4	36.7	29.1	38.7
Telecommunications	25.1	28.1	25.8	30.9	23.3	27.3	34.8	33.5
Utilities	17.0	12.4	15.9	17.2	19.7	15.1	17.8	37.8
Healthcare	14.3	16.7	31.4	15.9	12.6	19.5	18.2	33.5
Consumer Non Cyclical	13.2	13.0	15.4	14.7	12.7	21.5	20.6	24.6
Consumer Cyclical	18.6	19.4	20.3	22.0	19.5	20.3	17.5	30.6
Financial	19.0	19.1	18.9	23.0	24.5	21.4	26.1	33.7
				% of Variance explained by Global Market Factor (%)				
Energy	40.8	48.8	41.0	56.3	29.1	33.8	24.4	9.9
Basic Materials	43.6	42.1	31.9	51.0	49.1	41.2	36.8	26.9
Industrial	63.8	58.9	35.5	53.5	46.8	43.7	48.8	20.7
Technology	15.7	9.4	6.1	13.8	6.5	15.4	24.5	13.9
Telecommunications	33.0	26.5	31.2	21.9	38.4	28.0	17.2	18.6
Utilities	71.3	45.5	47.0	54.3	54.0	40.5	38.5	14.6
Healthcare	55.9	66.3	21.1	47.2	52.3	54.7	24.9	18.5
Consumer Non Cyclical	63.7	46.1	46.7	45.2	44.2	45.0	40.7	34.4
Consumer Cyclical	60.4	55.1	50.8	42.9	55.0	50.5	42.8	22.2
Financial	57.9	57.1	58.2	39.3	34.7	45.6	30.6	18.3
				% of Variance explained by Global Sector Factors (%)				
Energy	55.7	41.3	43.8	31.2	23.4	40.0	27.5	9.8
Basic Materials	22.0	22.0	17.9	17.6	27.0	27.3	24.1	13.1
Industrial	5.1	5.6	3.6	5.2	5.0	5.3	5.4	2.1
Technology	24.4	15.0	9.7	27.4	11.4	27.9	36.1	25.7
Telecommunications	25.8	19.5	20.7	21.6	31.6	21.7	12.9	14.4
Utilities	24.2	37.7	26.3	21.0	14.6	20.4	16.0	3.6
Healthcare	37.9	24.2	7.3	26.0	29.2	12.8	21.4	4.9
Consumer Non Cyclical	30.3	36.3	25.4	24.2	31.4	12.7	14.5	8.8
Consumer Cyclical	8.4	8.9	9.4	8.0	9.5	9.3	9.0	3.7
Financial	14.5	13.8	11.6	7.9	8.1	7.6	6.8	3.9
				% of Variance explained by Local Market Factors (%)				
Energy	3.5	6.3	15.2	12.5	5.8	26.2	26.8	17.7
Basic Materials	2.3	5.6	10.4	11.7	11.1	30.0	39.2	39.4
Industrial	2.8	7.5	10.9	18.1	10.9	30.6	45.8	33.2
Technology	0.8	1.2	1.8	5.7	1.5	9.5	18.3	24.2
Telecommunications	1.7	3.2	7.7	9.2	8.3	15.1	13.4	27.5
Utilities	4.5	16.8	26.7	24.6	10.6	39.2	45.5	19.2
Healthcare	6.1	9.5	6.5	26.8	18.5	21.6	53.7	22.6
Consumer Non Cyclical	6.0	17.5	27.9	30.6	24.5	26.5	44.7	50.2
Consumer Cyclical	2.9	7.5	17.8	17.5	12.8	33.4	48.2	36.7
Financial	3.4	8.0	15.2	12.0	7.5	18.9	25.1	26.4

Source: UBS estimates.

Table 8.12 Variance breakdown of local market sector returns (July 1998–June 2003) using the Heston and Rouwenhorst approach

Table 8.12 investigate this hypothesis in more detail. The raw data for this exercise are the 80 local market sector index return series; each index is the return on the portfolio of assets that belong to one of the eight country or regions and to one of the ten global sectors. For each of these series we have the beta of that return series to global market factor, ten global sector factors and the eight country factors. Using this information and estimates of the factor return series, we can break down the variance of these index return series into the component that can be attributed to the global market factor, the component that can be attributed to the ten global sector factors, the component that can be attributed to the eight country factors and the residual component, which we shall call the stock-specific risk.

Table 8.11 uses the betas and factor estimates calculated using our approach based on the method of identifying restrictions. Table 8.12 uses the estimates calculated using the approach of Heston and Rouwenhorst.

Table 8.13 uses the Dow Jones global sector indices and the Dow Jones local market indices as the factor returns and estimates the betas by regressing the country/sector index return series on these factor returns. In each table we record the annual standard deviation of each of the country/sector index return series and the percentage of this variance that can be attributed to the three different sets of factors.

There is one further issue. Because the country and sector factor returns are not orthogonal, some of the variance in the index return series will be allocated to the covariance of these factors. We use a rule of thumb to allocate this component; it is allocated to the sector and country factors in proportion to the variance that can be allocated to these factors directly.

These tables enable us to answer the question, for each local sector index how much of the risk from holding this index portfolio can be attributed to the global sector factors and how much can be attributed to the local market factors?

We shall now list what we believe are the principal deductions to all these tables:

- The global sectors, in that more of the risk is attributable to the global sector factors than the country factors, are Energy, Basic Materials, Industrials and Technology and to a slightly lesser extent Consumer Cyclicals.
- There is an important contrast between the Industrial sector and the Energy and Basic Materials sectors, all of which could be classified as global sectors. In the former sector, the returns are driven principally by the market factor whereas in the later two the returns are driven more by their respective global sector factors. This suggests that though Energy and Basic Materials sectors behave as a coherent global sector, the fundamental drivers of these sectors' performance are different to those that drive the global market. One would obviously look to macroeconomic causes such as oil prices, which are likely to affect these sectors disproportionately.
- The defensive sectors, Utilities, Consumer Non-Cyclical and to a slightly lesser extent Healthcare ex US, are the least susceptible to global market risk. However, more surprisingly, we find evidence that there is considerable cohesion across these sectors in that the global sector factor can account for a significant proportion of the risk in these sectors.

	United States	United Kingdom	Canada	Euro-Bloc	Europe ex Euro-Bloc & ex UK	Pacific ex Japan	Japan	Latin America
					Standard			
Energy	18.0	20.7	20.2	17.3	26.8	22.0	29.2	45.8
Basic Materials	21.9	22.3	25.6	20.2	20.6	22.5	22.0	27.9
Industrial	18.1	18.8	24.2	19.7	21.1	21.8	19.9	31.7
Technology	36.5	47.0	58.7	38.9	56.4	36.7	29.1	38.7
Telecommunications	25.1	28.1	25.8	30.9	23.3	27.3	34.8	33.5
Utilities	17.0	12.4	15.9	17.2	19.7	15.1	17.8	37.8
Healthcare	14.3	16.7	31.4	15.9	12.6	19.5	18.2	33.5
Consumer Non Cyclical	13.2	13.0	15.4	14.7	12.7	21.5	20.6	24.6
Consumer Cyclical	18.6	19.4	20.3	22.0	19.5	20.3	17.5	30.6
Financial	19.0	19.1	18.9	23.0	24.5	21.4	26.1	33.7
			% of Variance explained by Global Market Factor (%)					
Energy	32.9	30.3	17.3	41.8	28.3	47.8	8.0	33.5
Basic Materials	49.7	50.7	31.5	56.8	41.3	50.5	29.4	59.6
Industrial	88.2	73.8	77.3	75.0	71.7	61.9	42.9	50.6
Technology	52.8	31.8	20.4	46.4	22.1	52.1	56.6	
Telecommunications	47.1	45.9	51.3	45.7	55.1	60.7	36.6	62.6
Utilities	10.1	9.8	23.3	41.2	48.2	27.0	5.2	37.8
Healthcare	22.7	10.5	45.1	30.5	23.3	50.5	12.1	
Consumer Non Cyclical	48.7	12.3	16.6	46.8	29.1	45.6	18.6	65.0
Consumer Cyclical	81.8	67.7	64.9	72.0	74.7	75.3	48.8	61.1
Financial	55.3	58.3	48.9	66.4	62.5	58.4	21.0	43.8
			% of Variance explained by Global Sector Factors (%)					
Energy	65.6	58.4	66.8	51.8	27.0	23.2	23.0	3.4
Basic Materials	42.8	31.7	38.2	25.3	26.8	18.6	17.9	7.2
Industrial	7.7	6.5	7.4	5.1	10.2	2.3	3.4	8.4
Technology	28.9	20.6	20.6	15.7	12.0	8.9	9.9	
Telecommunications	40.9	38.5	9.2	38.0	22.0	11.2	15.8	4.1
Utilities	70.1	35.9	32.8	19.4	30.2	24.4	24.5	4.8
Healthcare	73.9	41.4	17.6	29.5	29.3	15.1	18.4	
Consumer Non Cyclical	48.2	60.7	21.9	31.3	43.5	18.1	11.8	2.8
Consumer Cyclical	13.9	8.9	6.1	4.9	11.7	4.3	11.9	4.8
Financial	34.3	13.3	26.4	11.1	9.7	8.8	12.8	2.4
			% of Variance explained by Local Market Factors (%)					
Energy	1.5	10.2	13.8	6.3	11.3	20.8	31.5	43.0
Basic Materials	6.8	11.7	21.4	17.9	24.1	28.1	38.8	28.6
Industrial	4.1	19.8	12.3	19.9	18.2	35.7	53.7	28.2
Technology	1.0	4.9	6.8	17.8	6.7	19.8	33.2	
Telecommunications	7.1	9.7	25.3	12.2	16.2	16.1	28.6	30.0
Utilities	4.9	11.9	16.9	30.2	21.6	39.9	19.8	56.8
Healthcare	3.4	11.1	12.5	18.5	47.4	10.2	39.1	
Consumer Non Cyclical	3.2	9.2	19.3	21.9	21.0	25.7	55.4	32.2
Consumer Cyclical	4.3	18.7	24.2	23.1	13.6	20.4	39.3	29.1
Financial	10.4	28.4	24.8	22.5	27.8	32.9	57.0	53.8

Source: UBS estimates.

Table 8.13 Variance breakdown of local market sector returns (July 1998–June 2003) using observed Dow Jones global sector and local market returns as a proxy for factor returns

	United States	United Kingdom	Canada	Euro-Bloc	Europe ex Euro-Bloc & ex UK	Pacific ex Japan	Japan	Latin America
				Standard				
Energy	10.6	11.6	15.4	12.6	17.1	15.4	18.5	29.3
Basic Materials	11.8	11.5	17.4	11.7	12.7	16.2	16.6	21.2
Industrial	10.6	9.2	11.0	10.5	10.4	17.6	15.1	33.4
Technology	19.4	25.3	22.9	15.5	24.7	25.7	18.8	45.3
Telecommunications	10.8	11.9	28.9	15.3	14.4	16.5	22.1	29.0
Utilities	8.7	14.8	8.5	10.2	11.9	17.2	13.1	27.0
Healthcare	12.0	11.6	24.8	11.1	13.8	15.1	13.0	27.2
Consumer Non Cyclical	9.9	10.5	10.8	12.1	9.7	13.5	14.0	21.5
Consumer Cyclical	9.6	10.1	13.0	11.6	12.4	14.9	15.3	34.6
Financial	12.3	11.4	14.1	10.3	11.8	20.6	21.0	28.5
			% of Variance explained by Global Market Factor (%)					
Energy	36.4	44.0	20.3	59.7	7.3	44.0	25.6	27.9
Basic Materials	57.2	38.5	29.6	46.1	39.5	45.6	24.2	17.3
Industrial	77.1	18.4	50.0	46.8	38.8	56.0	42.1	16.6
Technology	37.3	21.6	45.6	38.4	21.8	31.9	59.6	11.7
Telecommunications	35.0	4.9	15.5	34.8	11.0	65.6	31.9	28.6
Utilities	2.6	21.8	25.0	31.3	6.2	46.6	20.8	24.6
Healthcare	44.7	33.2	19.9	20.7	20.0	42.2	55.0	1.5
Consumer Non Cyclical	47.2	27.3	41.4	42.5	22.7	43.5	41.0	25.0
Consumer Cyclical	54.8	33.6	28.9	55.5	34.2	44.8	58.7	20.0
Financial	45.0	34.6	34.2	36.5	27.2	50.7	42.4	20.0
			% of Variance explained by Global Sector Factors (%)					
Energy	58.7	32.0	44.9	23.4	34.8	13.1	8.7	6.0
Basic Materials	28.3	20.7	39.6	19.0	28.8	20.3	16.8	4.0
Industrial	7.4	29.0	8.1	12.1	19.5	5.1	3.0	2.4
Technology	52.8	13.0	12.5	15.8	10.2	13.5	14.7	2.7
Telecommunications	21.0	24.0	16.7	21.1	28.8	8.8	10.0	3.4
Utilities	51.3	18.7	25.0	32.2	33.5	12.1	19.0	12.2
Healthcare	17.6	17.7	13.6	29.7	28.9	7.6	8.9	12.4
Consumer Non Cyclical	28.6	9.8	15.6	23.7	35.2	13.7	3.7	2.3
Consumer Cyclical	18.1	38.3	23.1	8.1	16.2	23.0	8.3	7.9
Financial	16.4	23.0	19.2	30.9	30.8	7.5	4.0	5.9
			% of Variance explained by Local Market Factors (%)					
Energy	2.3	18.6	19.5	15.8	11.7	18.9	48.6	48.6
Basic Materials	6.1	24.9	15.0	30.3	23.4	31.5	51.4	72.7
Industrial	12.5	51.0	39.4	40.8	33.7	37.5	48.1	68.9
Technology	0.8	21.5	16.0	34.6	28.0	11.1	13.7	20.1
Telecommunications	30.8	51.0	31.6	31.2	39.6	15.4	30.9	46.7
Utilities	42.8	28.6	37.6	19.0	35.9	20.5	46.6	48.5
Healthcare	31.2	21.8	8.6	40.5	41.7	35.4	33.0	40.4
Consumer Non Cyclical	18.8	53.7	33.3	28.5	42.0	39.0	47.4	62.3
Consumer Cyclical	25.1	28.1	40.5	34.9	35.7	30.2	29.6	47.7
Financial	37.8	34.8	38.3	26.7	38.6	36.8	37.8	61.9

Source: UBS estimates.

Table 8.14 Variance breakdown of local market sector returns for the earlier 1994–1997 period using the method of identifying restrictions

- In Japan, Latin America and the Pacific countries on average more than 50% of the risk can be attributed to local market factors.
- In the US and the UK across all sectors far less of the risk can be attributed to the local market factors.

The differences between the approaches are more subtle but can be summarized as:

- Our IR approach finds more cohesion across the sectors or equivalently allocates more risk to the sector factors than either of the other two approaches.
- Looking at the open markets of the US, the UK and Canada, our IR approach makes a far stronger distinction between the global sectors – Energy, Basic Materials, Industrials, Technology – and the more local sectors – Utilities, Healthcare, Consumer Non-Cyclicals, Consumer Cyclicals and Financials.

In Table 8.14 we look again at the question of whether sector factors have become more important determinants of risk over time. This table gives a similar breakdown of the variance of the country/sector returns series but for the slightly earlier period of July 1994 to October 1997. The conclusion is dramatic. Over this period the global sector factors, save in the Energy sector, could explain little of the variance in stock returns. This is consistent with the results in Figure 8.8 where it is clear that prior to 1998 average sector factor volatility was far lower than average country factor volatility.

8.6   Conclusions

In the introduction we identified three pronounced trends in the global equity markets:

1. The slow decline in the degree of investor 'home bias'.
2. The dramatic rise in the levels of foreign direct investment as more and more companies increasingly conduct their business across domestic markets.
3. The rise in degree of capital market concentration as the multinationals grow in size. As a direct result of this trend, the industry bias of some domestic markets is becoming more exaggerated.

In discussing these trends, we highlighted two important conclusions. First, these changes to global equity markets are definite but gradual. Therefore, investors should not change global investment strategies radically overnight from a country-based asset allocation approach to a sector-based one. Rather, a more subtle change in emphasis is required. The second conclusion is that these changes are complex and it is unlikely that any single measure will be able to summarize the consequences of these trends on global equity markets.

Therefore, in proposing an approach to modelling these changes, we suggest a new method based on making the minimum of assumptions. This method focuses on estimating both new global sector and local market indices that identify the common component in returns across all markets or all sectors respectively, adjusting for both the relative 'openness' of, and industry composition bias within, markets.

We have argued that these indices can be used to generate risk profiles of stocks and portfolios that are more intuitive in the sense that they more clearly reflect the drivers underlying the return process. We have also shown that these indices can be used to investigate which markets are more 'open' and which sectors are more 'global'. Finally, in the next section, we will discuss how the approach could be used to look at the problems of estimating the cost of capital by sector and country and calculating the optimal hedging ratios with respect to both country and sector factors.

8.7 Further issues and applications

8.7.1 Accounting for currency risk

In the UBS risk model, as well as throughout this publication, currency risk has been treated implicitly as an integral part of country or local market risk. This has been consistently our approach over the years. However, some risk models prefer to separate out currency risk as a separate component of the risk budget, and so this issue deserves some further attention.

If investors hold foreign stocks, then they are explicitly taking on some exchange rate risk due directly to movements in the exchange rate between their domestic currency and the stock's domicile currency. However, even though the investors may hold only their domestic stocks, they are implicitly taking on some exchange rate risk due to the exposure of the underlying companies' profits to exchange rate changes. In theory investors could hedge out the exposure of their portfolios to the former type of explicit exchange rate risk. However, it would be near impossible to calculate, and therefore hedge out, the exposure of their portfolios to the latter type of implicit exchange risk.

The situation is made even more complicated, if one takes into account that some companies hedge their own performance against adverse exchange rate movements and others do not. Therefore, even if one does not take into account the costs of hedging out exchange rate exposure, it is unsurprising that the fund managers do not try to hedge out their exchange rate risk.

We therefore make the following arguments in favour of our approach:

1. That fund managers consider exchange rate risk as an implicit, not explicit, component of stock risk.
2. That fund managers are unlikely ever to hedge out exchange rate risk.
3. Many companies already hedge their performance against exchange rate risk. Therefore hedging the portfolio further could lead to overhedging – an undesirable and costly alternative to not hedging.
4. It is impossible to calculate a portfolio's exchange rate exposure other than by purely statistical means. Dales and Meese (2001) suggest that these statistical approaches highlight many spurious exposures as well as actual ones and the optimal currency hedging ratios are very unstable.
5. That fund managers are usually benchmarked against an unhedged index. Therefore, hedging can be seen as taking an active position against a benchmark.

All the empirical evidence, as well as all the theoretical arguments, suggest that in the medium to long run the expected return to any currency bet is zero. Therefore, the fund manager would be taking an active position for which the expected return is zero in the medium to long term; see the discussion in Binny (2001).

We do recognize that there is no consensus in the industry as to the best approach. However, we do believe that the arguments in favour of our approach are compelling.

8.7.2 Additional applications for this research

The model of country and sector risk developed in this document could be used as the basis for some exciting further work.

- *Calculating optimal hedge ratios.* Recently futures in global sector funds have become more liquid. This is partly driven by the increased demand for sector funds following the increase in global sector volatility, described earlier. Hence it is now a viable investment strategy to hedge out country and sector risk so as to concentrate on stock-specific bets.

Calculating the optimal hedge ratios must take account of the index composition biases. As an example we can use the results in Table 8.9 on the risk breakdown of the Nortel stock. Using the results based on the standard risk analysis on the left of the table, an investor holding this stock would primarily hedge out the country risk. However, our analysis demonstrates the more intuitive result that holders of this stock are primarily exposed to sector risk, and should hedge out this source of risk first.

Further details of this analysis are given in Appendix C, which is an abridged form of an article that appeared in *Risk* magazine in July 2001.

- *Calculating cost of capital numbers for use in valuation models.* The model can be used to calculate average historic cost of capital numbers by sector and country. These are a direction function of the estimated betas, and the average return of the estimated factor returns series. These numbers could be used as the basis or starting point for a more forward-looking measure.
- *Forecasting changes to the cost of risk or the risk premium.* It is well documented that the performance of the FTSE is only weakly correlated with monthly changes to UK GDP. Similar observations have been made in other countries. It is plausible that the estimated UK factor index, which has had some of the composition and concentrations biases removed, will be more correlated with the fundamentals of the UK economy.

References

Aherne, A. W, Griever, W., and Warnock, F. (2000). Information Costs and Home Bias: An Analysis of U.S. Holdings of Foreign Equities. International Finance Discussion Paper No. 691, Federal Reserve Board, Washington.

Adler, M. and Dumas, B. (1983). International Portfolio Choice and Corporate Finance: A Synthesis. *Journal of Finance*, Vol. 38(3):925–984.

Bacon and Woodrow and FTSE International (1999). Multinational and Local Country Indices. October 1999. http://www.baconwoodrow.co.uk/802569750037FE8E/Images/multinationalsindex/$FILE/invest.pdf+1.3MB.pdf

Beckers, S., Grinold, R., Rudd A., and Stefak, D. (1992). The Relative Importance of Common Factors across the European Equity Markets. *Journal of Finance and Banking*, Vol. 16:75–95.

Beckers, S., Connor, G., and Curds, R. (1996). National versus Global Influences on Equity Returns. *Financial Analyst Journal*, March 1996:31–39.

Bergsten, C. F. and Graham, E. (1997). *Global Corporations and National Governments: Re changes needed in the International Economic and Political Order in the Light of the Globalisation of Business.* Institute for International Economics, Washington.

Binny, J. (2001). The Optimal Benchmark for a Currency Overlay. *Journal of Asset Management*, Vol. 2(1):22–34.

Buigues, P. and Jacquemin, A. (1994). Foreign Direct Investment and Exports to the European Community. In Mark Mason and Dennis Encarnation, editors, *Does ownership matter: Japanese Multinationals in Europe*, Oxford University Press.

Bulsing, M., Sefton, J., Jones, A., and Kothari, M. (2000). *Global Style Returns.* Global Equities, UBS Warburg, May 2000.

Cavaglia, S., Brightman, C., and Aked, M. (2000). On the Increasing Importance of Industry Factors: Implications for Global Portfolio Management. *Financial Analyst Journal*, September 2000:41–53.

Cavaglia, S., Cho, D., and Singer, B. (2001). Risks of Rotation Strategies. *Journal of Portfolio Management*, Vol. 27(4):35–44.

Cooper, I. and Kaplanis, E. (1986). Costs of Crossborder Investment and International Equity Market Equilibrium. In Jeremy Edwards, editor, *Recent Advances in Corporate Finance.* Cambridge University Press.

Cochrane, J. (2001). *Asset Pricing.* Princeton University Press.

Cooper, I. and Kaplanis, E. (1994). Home Bias in Equity Portfolios, Inflation Hedging, and International Capital Market Equilibrium. *Journal of Financial Studies*, Vol. 7(1):45–60.

Dales, A. and Meese, R. (2001). Strategic Currency Hedging. *Journal of Asset Management*, Vol. 2(1):9–21.

Diermeier, J. and Solnik, B. (2001). Global Pricing of Equity. *Financial Analyst Journal*, Vol. 57(4):37–47.

French, K. and Poterba, J. (1991). International Diversification and International Equity Markets. *American Economic Review*, Vol. 81(2):222–226.

Graham, E. (1995). Foreign Direct Investment in the World Economy. *Staff Studies for World Economic Outlook*, September 1995, IMF.

Griffen, J. and Karolyi, A. (1998). Another Look at the Role of the Industrial Structure of Markets for International Diversification Strategies. *Journal of Financial Economics*, Vol. 50:351–373.

Grinold, R., Rudd, A., and Stefak, D. (1989). Global Factors: Fact or Fiction. *Journal of Portfolio Management*, Vol. 16(1):79–87.

Grubel, H. (1968). Internationally Diversified Portfolios: Welfare Gains and Capital Flows. *American Economic Review*, Vol. 58:1299–1314.

Heston, S. and Rouwenhorst K. G. (1994). Does Industrial Structure Explain the Benefits of International Diversification. *Journal of Financial Economics*, Vol. 36:3–27.

Heston, S. and Rouwenhorst K. G. (1995). Industry and Country Effects in International Stock Returns. *Journal of Portfolio Management*, Vol. 21(3):53–58.

Lessard, D. (1974). World, National, and Industry Factors in Equity Returns. *Journal of Finance*, Vol. 29(3):379–391.

Levy, H. and Sarnatt, M. (1970). International Diversification of Investment Portfolios. *American Economic Review*, Vol. 60(4):668–675.

Lewis, K. (1999). Trying to Explain Home Bias in Equities and Consumption. *Journal of Economic Literature*, Vol. 37(2):571–608.

Lombard, T., Roulet J., and Solnik, B. (1999). Pricing of Domestic versus Multinational Companies. *Financial Analyst Journal*, Vol. 55(2):35–50.

MacQueen, J. and Satchell, S. (2001). An Inquiry into Globalisation and Size in World Equity Markets. *Mimeo*, Quantec, Thomson Financial.

Marsh, T. and Pfleiderer, P. (1997). The Role of Country and Industry Effects in Explaining Global Stock Returns. *Mimeo*, UC Berkeley, Walter A. Haas School of Business, Berkeley.

Roll, R. (1992). Industrial Structure and the Comparative Behaviour of International Stock Market Indices. *Journal of Finance*, Vol. 47(1):3–42.

Solnik, B. (1974). The International Pricing of Risk: An Empirical Investigation of the World Capital Market Structure. *Journal of Finance*, Vol. 29(2):365–378.

Solnik, B. and de Freitas, A. (1988). International Factors of Stock Price Behaviour. In S. Khoury and S. Ghosh, editors, *Recent Developments in International Banking and Finance*. D.C. Heath, New York, 259–276.

Rouwenhorst, K. G. (1999). European Equity Markets and the EMU. *Financial Analysts Journal*, Vol. 55(2), March 1999:35–50.

Warnock, F. (2001). Home Bias and High Turnover Reconsidered. *International Finance Discussion Papers*, No. 702, Board of Governors of the Federal Reserve System.

Appendix A: A detailed description of the identifying restrictions

In this appendix we detail precisely the identifying restrictions used in our estimation procedure. Our data set constitutes the monthly returns to ten domestic sector indices for eight countries or regions. When tabulated in the form of a matrix, the value-weighted sum of each row equals the global sector return. Analogously, the value-weighted sum of each column equals the return to a country or region. Symbolically we may denote this matrix of local sector returns for M sectors and N countries at time t as:

$$
R_t = \begin{bmatrix} r_{1,1} & r_{1,2} & \cdots & r_{1,N} \\ r_{2,1} & r_{2,2} & \cdots & r_{2,N} \\ \vdots & \vdots & \ddots & \vdots \\ r_{M,1} & r_{M,2} & \cdots & r_{M,N} \end{bmatrix}_t \tag{8.2}
$$

where each element $r_{i,j}$ is the excess returns to sector i in country j in the investor's currency. The excess return is relative to the three-month risk-free government bond rate is the investor's domestic country. In contrast to Marsh and Pfleiderer (1997), we estimate our Linear Factor Model on local index return data rather than on individual stock return data. But, as Roll (1992) and Griffin and Karolyi (1998) show, this does not lead to different results.

In our model there are M country-neutral or 'true' global sector factors and N sector-neutral or 'true' local market factors to estimate. We shall denote the M global sector factor returns as f^{S1}, f^{S2} to f^{SM} and the N country or local market factor returns as f^{C1}, f^{C2} to f^{CN} at time t. When it is necessary to refer to a particular time period, we shall introduce a subscript to denote the period. We also define the matrices β^{S1}, β^{S2} to β^{SM} and β^{C1}, β^{C2} to β^{CN} conformal to the matrix of excess returns R_t, as the matrices of sensitivities to the factors f^{S1}, f^{S2} to f^{SM} and f^{C1}, f^{C2} to f^{CN} respectively. Thus the ij element of the matrix β^{S1} is the sensitivity of the excess return in sector i in country j, to factor f^{S1}. In a similar manner we can define the global market factor f^{Mkt} and the matrix of sensitivities to this factor as β^{Mkt} and the matrix of idiosyncratic average excess returns, α_{ij}, as α. With this notation we can write our Linear Factor Model as:

$$
R_t = \alpha + \beta^{Mkt} f_t^{Mkt} + \sum_{i=1}^{M} \beta^{Si} f_t^{Si} + \sum_{j=1}^{N} \beta^{Cj} f_t^{Cj} + \varepsilon_t \tag{8.3}
$$

or using the notation $vec()$ to denote the column stacking operator, and letting

$$
\beta^S = \left[vec(\beta^{S1}) \cdots vec(\beta^{SM}) \right] \quad f_t^S = \left[f_t^{S1} \cdots f_t^{SM} \right]'
$$
$$
\beta^C = \left[vec(\beta^{C1}) \cdots vec(\beta^{CN}) \right] \quad f_t^C = \left[f_t^{C1} \cdots f_t^{CN} \right]'
$$

we can write

$$R_t = \begin{bmatrix} vec(\boldsymbol{\beta}^{Mkt}) & vec(\boldsymbol{\alpha}) & | & \boldsymbol{\beta}^s & | & \boldsymbol{\beta}^C \end{bmatrix} \begin{bmatrix} f_t^{Mkt} \\ 1 \\ f_t^s \\ f_t^C \end{bmatrix} + vec(\varepsilon_t) \tag{8.4}$$

$$= \boldsymbol{\beta} f_t + \varepsilon_t$$

where the matrix β has been partitioned into four: the market betas, the alphas, the sector and then the country betas. Finally we need to introduce the matrix $\mathbf{W}$ whose elements w_{ij} denote the proportion of global market in sector i in country j. This matrix is also time varying, but we shall assume these proportions are fixed over time so as to linearize the problem. The sums of the rows of this matrix add up to the market cap of each of the global sectors, and the sum of the columns to the market cap of each of the regions or countries. We shall denote the vector of market caps of the global sectors as w^S and of the countries w^C.

We are now in a position to describe our identifying restrictions or constraints. The $M + N$ by NM constraint matrix C is defined as:

$$C = \left[\begin{array}{cccccccccccc} w_{11} & 0 & \cdots & 0 & w_{12} & 0 & \cdots & 0 & \cdots & w_{1N} & 0 & \cdots & 0 \\ 0 & w_{21} & \cdots & 0 & 0 & w_{22} & \cdots & 0 & \cdots & 0 & w_{2N} & \cdots & 0 \\ \vdots & \vdots & \ddots & \vdots & \vdots & \vdots & \ddots & \vdots & \cdots & \vdots & \vdots & \ddots & \vdots \\ 0 & 0 & \cdots & w_{M1} & 0 & 0 & \cdots & w_{M2} & \cdots & 0 & 0 & \cdots & w_{MN} \\ \hline w_{11} & w_{21} & \cdots & w_{M1} & 0 & 0 & \cdots & 0 & \cdots & 0 & 0 & \cdots & 0 \\ 0 & 0 & \cdots & 0 & w_{12} & w_{22} & \cdots & w_{M2} & \cdots & 0 & 0 & \cdots & 0 \\ \vdots & \vdots & \ddots & \vdots & \vdots & \vdots & \ddots & \vdots & \cdots & \vdots & \vdots & \ddots & \vdots \\ 0 & 0 & \cdots & 0 & 0 & 0 & \cdots & 0 & \cdots & w_{1N} & w_{2N} & \cdots & w_{MN} \end{array}\right] = \begin{bmatrix} C_1 \\ C_2 \end{bmatrix}$$

The first M rows of the constraint matrix, C_1, take a value-weighted sum across rows of the individual matrices β^{Si} and β^{Cj} and the next N rows, C_2, take a value-weighted sum across the columns. We experimented with two alternative formulations of the constraints: the first was analytically more straightforward enabling us to derive a global convergence proof, the second, though, is our preferred formulation. The first formulation can be expressed as:

$$\begin{bmatrix} C_1 \\ C_2 \end{bmatrix} [vec(\alpha) \beta^s \beta^C] = \begin{bmatrix} 0 & \text{diag}(w^S) & \mathbf{W} \\ 0 & \mathbf{W}' & \text{diag}(w^C) \end{bmatrix} \tag{8.5a}$$

and the second as:

$$\begin{bmatrix} C_1 \\ C_2 \end{bmatrix} [vec(\alpha) \beta^S \beta^C] = \begin{bmatrix} 0 & \text{diag}(w^S) & \begin{bmatrix} w_{11}\beta_{11}^{C1} & w_{21}\beta_{12}^{C2} & \cdots & w_{1N}\beta_{1M}^{CN} \\ w_{21}\beta_{21}^{C1} & w_{22}\beta_{11}^{C2} & \cdots & w_{2N}\beta_{2N}^{CN} \\ \vdots & \vdots & \ddots & \vdots \\ w_{M1}\beta_{M1}^{C1} & w_{M2}\beta_{11}^{C2} & \cdots & w_{MN}\beta_{MN}^{CN} \end{bmatrix} \\ 0 & \begin{bmatrix} w_{11}\beta_{11}^{S1} & w_{21}\beta_{21}^{S2} & \cdots & w_{M1}\beta_{M1}^{SM} \\ w_{12}\beta_{12}^{S1} & w_{22}\beta_{22}^{S2} & \cdots & w_{M2}\beta_{M2}^{SM} \\ \vdots & \vdots & \ddots & \vdots \\ w_{1N}\beta_{1N}^{S1} & w_{2N}\beta_{2N}^{S2} & \cdots & w_{MN}\beta_{MN}^{SM} \end{bmatrix} & \text{diag}(w^C) \end{bmatrix} \tag{8.5b}$$

In addition to these constraints on the alphas and sector and country betas, we need the single constraint on the global market betas. We require that the market beta of the global portfolio is 1, that is:

$$\sum_{i=1}^{M}\sum_{j=1}^{N} w_{ij}\beta_{ij}^{Mkt} = 1 \tag{8.6}$$

Shortly, we will discuss these constraints on the model betas, but first we shall describe the constraints required on the sector and country factor returns. There are two constraints in each period; the first ensures that the return on the global portfolio equals the market factor return in each period, the second removes a degree of indeterminacy between the sector and country returns. This indeterminacy arises because both the sector and country factors span all the index returns. Therefore one could add any number to *all* the sector factor returns as long as the same number was taken of *all* the country factor returns and leave the achieved fit in equation (8.3) unaffected. These constraints on the factor returns can be written as:

$$\begin{bmatrix} 1 & \overbrace{1 \quad \cdots \quad 1}^{w^s} & \overbrace{-1 \quad -1 \quad \cdots \quad -1}^{w^C} \end{bmatrix} \begin{bmatrix} f_t^s \\ f_t^C \end{bmatrix} = D \begin{bmatrix} f_t^s \\ f_t^C \end{bmatrix} = \begin{bmatrix} 0 \\ 0 \end{bmatrix} \tag{8.7}$$

The last constraints are to ensure the sector and country factors are uniquely determined with respect to the global market factor. We impose this requirement by requiring that all the sector and country factors are orthogonal with respect to the market, that is:

$$\sum_t f_t^{Mkt} f_t^{Si} = 0 \tag{8.8}$$

for all sectors i and:

$$\sum_t f_t^{Mkt} f_t^{Cj} = 0 \tag{8.9}$$

for countries j.

Now a set of values for β and f_t, $t = 1 \ldots T$, is called a feasible point of the model (8.3) if they satisfy all the constraints (8.5)–(8.9), and the union of all feasible points is called the feasible set. A model is called identifiable if every point in the feasible set results in a different representation of the model (8.3). We are now in a position to state the following lemma.

Lemma 1 *Given the constraint (8.6) on the global market betas, either of the constraints (8.5a) or (8.5b) on the country and sector betas and the constraints (8.7), (8.8) and (8.9) on the estimated sector and country factor returns, then the Linear Factor Model Realization in (8.3) subject to these constraints is identifiable.*

The constraints imposed on the Linear Factor Model in equation (8.3) can all be given a straightforward interpretation. Each constraint can be understood in terms of either a global sector portfolio, that is all stocks classified as belonging to a given sector, or a local market portfolio, that is all stocks domiciled in a given region or country. Now, the constraints on the alpha matrix, α, simply state that the idiosyncratic return on these sector or local market portfolios is zero, or alternatively that the risk premium for holding these portfolios is equal to the historical return of the corresponding factor return. These constraints enable us uniquely to break down the historic risk premium of holding a stock in sector i country j into its market premium, its sector premium, its country premium and an idiosyncratic component.

We shall now discuss the constraints $C_1\beta^S = \text{diag}(w^s)$ which are the same in both equations (8.5a) and (8.5b). These constraints dictate that each global sector portfolio has an aggregate beta of 1 with respect to its sector factor and a beta of 0 with respect to all other sector factors. This, therefore, is our relaxation of Heston and Rouwenhorst constraints that every sector in every market has a beta of 1 with respect to its sector factor and a beta of zero with respect to all other factors; we only require a similar condition of the global sector portfolio. It is these constraints that allow us to associate a factor with a corresponding sector.

Earlier we discussed an example where the world's capital markets were divided into two groups: one half was assumed to be fully integrated and the other half to be segmented. Though an extreme take on the present split between Japan, the Far East and the western developed markets, we used this hypothetical example to discuss how a model based on Heston and Rouwenhorst's assumptions would find it difficult to estimate a set of global sector factors. This model, however, would have no such problems; the sectors in the fully integrated half of the world would have large betas with respect to the sector factors whereas the sectors in the other half of the world would have very low betas. The model would then be able to identify the sector factors in the integrated markets without creating large errors in the segmented markets.

The constraints $C_2\beta^C = \text{diag}(w^C)$, which are again identical in equations (8.5a) and (8.5b), are the similar constraints for the local market betas. Therefore each local market portfolio has an aggregate beta of 1 with respect to its country factor and a beta of 0 with respect to all other country factors. Again, these constraints allow us to associate an estimated series of factor returns with a particular country or local market.

The other set of constraints, $C_2\beta^S = W'$ and $C_1\beta^C = W$ in equation (8.5a) or the corresponding more involved ones in (8.5b), require a little more explanation. These constraints disentangle the country and sector effects. The first set constrain the degree to which local market performance can be explained by sector factors, and the second the degree to which the performance of the global sector portfolios can be explained by country factors. The constraints $C_2\beta^S = W'$ state that the sensitivity of a global sector portfolio to a local market factor be in proportion to the percentage of the sector domiciled there. Though this is a reasonable requirement, we prefer the alternative constraints in equation (8.5b) which take the local market betas into account. The corresponding constraints in (8.5b) require that the sensitivity of a global sector portfolio to a local market factor be in proportion to the percentage of the sector domiciled there times its beta to that market factor. An alternative way of stating this is that a global sector portfolio ex all stocks in a given local market must have a zero beta with respect to that given market factor.

A very similar interpretation can be given to the similar constraints of the country betas. We shall state this only for equation (8.5b), the explanation for those in (8.5a) follows identically. These constraints specify that a local market portfolio ex all stocks belonging to a given sector is required to have a zero beta with respect to that given sector factor. It therefore limits the sector explanation of a local market index.

Appendix B: The optimization algorithm

The algorithm estimates the parameters of the Linear Factor Model in equation (8.3) so as to minimize a weighted least-squares error criterion. This quadratic criterion, L, can be written

$$L = \sum_t vec(\varepsilon_t)' diag(vec(\mathbf{W}))vec(\varepsilon_t)$$

$$= \sum_t vec(\varepsilon_t)' V vec(\varepsilon_t) \tag{8.10}$$

The procedure is iterative; given an initial estimate of the model betas, we minimize the criterion L with respect to the factor returns subject to the constraints (8.7), (8.8) and (8.9). Then holding these estimates of the factor returns constant, we minimize the criterion with respect to the model betas subject to either constraint (8.5a) or (8.5b) and (8.6). The procedure can now be repeated starting with these new estimates of the betas until convergence is achieved. Details are in the next section.

Does this optimization problem have a global minimum to which our procedure will then converge? Because the algebraic expression of the constraint (8.5a) is far simpler than for the constraint (8.5b), we have been able to answer this question for this case only.

Lemma 2 *Define θ as the set of all feasible points β and f_t of the Linear Factor Model (8.3) that satisfy constraints (8.5a), (8.6), (8.7), (8.8) and (8.9). Then a point in θ that satisfies the equations*

$$\frac{\partial L}{\partial \theta} = 0 \quad and \quad \frac{\partial^2 L}{\partial \theta^2} > 0 \tag{8.11}$$

is a global minimum of the optimization problem (8.10).

We have been able to show that if we use the constraints (8.5a), (8.6)–(8.9) to identify the model, then our procedure will converge to a unique global minimum. Unfortunately, we have not been able to prove a similar result if the constraints (8.5b) are used instead of (8.5a).

The estimation algorithm

It is first necessary to introduce some further notation. The Linear Factor Model in equation (8.3) is written for one time period only. It is desirable to write this model for all time periods simultaneously by stacking up by row the observations in each period. To this end define the matrices

$$R = [vec(R_1)vec(R_2)\cdots vec(R_T)]$$

$$F = \begin{bmatrix} f^{Mkt} \\ 1 \\ F^a \end{bmatrix} = \begin{bmatrix} f_1^{Mkt} & f_2^{Mkt} & \cdots & f_T^{Mkt} \\ 1 & 1 & \cdots & 1 \\ \hline f_1^S & f_2^S & \cdots & f_T^S \\ f_1^C & f_2^C & \cdots & f_T^C \end{bmatrix}$$

(8.12)

$$\varepsilon = [vec(\varepsilon_1)vec(\varepsilon_2)\cdots vec(\varepsilon_T)]$$

and then the expression for the model in (8.3) can be extended to include all periods $t = 1\ldots T$ to:

$$R = \beta F + \varepsilon \tag{8.13}$$

The constraints (8.7)–(8.9) for all periods can also be simplified to:

$$DF^a = 0 \quad \text{and} \quad F^a\left(f^{Mkt}\right)' = F^a E' = 0 \tag{8.14}$$

The procedure needs to be started with an initial estimate of the beta and alpha parameters. We assume that every $\alpha_{ij,} = 0$ and every element of β^{Mkt} is equal to 1. Given these estimates, we calculate what we shall call the excess index returns relative to the market

$$R^a = R - vec(\alpha)1 - vec\left(\beta^{Mkt}\right)f^{Mkt} \tag{8.15}$$

We initialize our sector and country betas with Heston and Rouwenhorst assumptions that the return in sector i and country j has a beta of one with respect to the corresponding sector and country factors and a beta of zero with respect to all other factors:

$$\left[\beta^S | \beta^C\right] = \begin{bmatrix}
1 & 0 & \cdots & 0 & 1 & 0 & \cdots & 0 \\
0 & 1 & \cdots & 0 & 1 & 0 & \cdots & 0 \\
\vdots & \vdots & \ddots & \vdots & \vdots & \vdots & \ddots & \vdots \\
0 & 0 & \cdots & 1 & 1 & 0 & \cdots & 0 \\
1 & 0 & \cdots & 0 & 0 & 1 & \cdots & 0 \\
0 & 1 & \cdots & 0 & 0 & 1 & \cdots & 0 \\
\vdots & \vdots & \ddots & \vdots & \vdots & \vdots & \ddots & \vdots \\
0 & 0 & \cdots & 1 & 0 & 1 & \cdots & 0 \\
\vdots & \vdots & \ddots & \vdots & \vdots & \vdots & \ddots & \vdots \\
1 & 0 & \cdots & 0 & 0 & 0 & \cdots & 1 \\
0 & 1 & \cdots & 0 & 0 & 0 & \cdots & 1 \\
\vdots & \vdots & \ddots & \vdots & \vdots & \vdots & \ddots & \vdots \\
0 & 0 & \cdots & 1 & 0 & 0 & \cdots & 1
\end{bmatrix} \tag{8.16}$$

We cannot estimate the 'true' factor returns period by period because of the cross-period orthogonality constraints (8.8) and (8.9). Therefore the estimation of all the factor returns must be done in a single step. To this end equation (8.13) can be re-expressed as:

$$vec(R) = (I \otimes \beta)vec(F) + vec(\varepsilon)$$

$$= Y vec(F) + vec(\varepsilon) \qquad (8.17)$$

Now we can rewrite the linear constraints (8.14) as $A^F vec(F) = 0$. Now the solution to the least-squares optimization problem of minimizing (8.10) given β can be expressed[6]:

$$vec(F) = \left(I - A^{F'}\left(A^F(Y'Y)^{-1}A^{F'}\right)^{-1}A^F\right)(Y'Y)^{-1}Y'vec(R) \qquad (8.18)$$

The next step is to use these estimates of the 'true' factor returns to calculate a new estimate of the alpha and beta parameters. Again this problem is a constrained weighted least-squares problem, and so it is possible to write down an analytical solution. Equation (8.13) can be re-expressed as:

$$vec(R) = (F \otimes I)vec(\beta) + vec(\varepsilon)$$

$$= X vec(\beta) + vec(\varepsilon) \qquad (8.19)$$

Now we can rewrite the linear restrictions (8.5) and (8.6) as $A^\beta vec(\beta) = c$. The explicit solution to this regression is[7]:

$$vec(\beta) = (X'X)^{-1}X'vec(R) - (X'X)^{-1}A^{\beta'}\left(A^\beta(X'X)^{-1}A^{\beta'}\right)^{-1}$$

$$\times \left(A^\beta(X'X)^{-1}X'vec(R) - c\right) \qquad (8.20)$$

These steps are now repeated until convergence. The difficulty in solving this problem is therefore not its complexity but its sheer size, making it necessary to design an efficient and robust solution algorithm.

Appendix C: Getting the hedge right[8]

Newly introduced futures contracts on sector indices in Europe may facilitate the process of risk management in European equities. Market makers, traders, and fund managers often have positions that include exposures to risk factors, equity market

---

[6] The matrix $Y'Y$ is singular and so it is necessary to take a pseudo inverse of this matrix rather than inverse.

[7] Again the matrix $X'X$ is singular is so it necessary to take a pseudo inverse of this matrix rather than inverse.

[8] The appendix was originally published in the July 2001 *Risk* magazine as the article 'Stripping Out Specific Risk' by Walter Kemmesies and James Sefton.

risk, for example, that they deem undesirable. Selling the securities may not be an option for strategic or regulatory reasons. One solution is to buy or sell futures on country equity indexes, like the FTSE100, to minimize the exposure of the value of the portfolio to market movements. However, like most solutions to existing problems, the solution introduces new problems. For example, consider a portfolio with a heavy concentration in Swisscom in the middle of 2000. In the absence of other considerations, the portfolio manager might have sold futures contracts on the SMI to reduce the portfolio's exposure to market movements. But, as the Telecommunication sector derated last year and investors fled to more defensive sectors – the SMI being heavily laden with these – both the portfolio and short futures position would have lost money. A short position in the Eurostoxx Telecommunications index would have helped in this case. However, if one wished to hedge both the sector risk and market risk, the problem is to 'get the hedge right' if the local market risk is also heavily dependent on the performance of some sectors and possibly vice versa. The answer lies in determining the true country and sector elements that affect the share price.

To illustrate the concept, consider a portfolio with only one stock and one market index to worry about. The arguments we present here naturally extend themselves to portfolios with larger numbers of shares, but a share portfolio is sufficient to illustrate the issues at hand. The stock we have in mind is large enough that changes in its share price have a non-negligible effect on the index level. To hedge a long stock position, a number of index futures are shorted, based on the hedge ratio in equation (8.21) below:

$$\frac{\Delta S}{\Delta I} = \beta \frac{S}{I} \frac{\text{number of shares}}{\text{index multiplier}} \tag{8.21}$$

where S is the share price, I is the index level, the deltas refer to a change in the share price and index level, and β is the 'beta' of the shares with respect to the index. For portfolios with more than one stock, the hedge ratios can be summed up to give a total number of index contracts to buy or sell to hedge the portfolio. We use Vodafone to illustrate the idea. On our estimates, during the 04/96–02/01 period, Vodafone shares in euros had a beta of 0.91 to the FTSE100 index in euros. The multiplier for the FTSE100 futures is GBP 10 per index point. Given a share price of €3.8 and an index level of 9894.7, the correct hedge ratio for 100 000 Vodafone stocks would be 3.52.

Does this work? The FTSE100 subsequently fell to 9831.0 the next day while Vodafone's share price fell to €3.73. The hedge did not work – net losses were €6537. Even if the position had made a profit overnight, the trader would not be happy because this isn't a hedge – hedged means not making or losing money when a specific exposure changes.

The problem is that an investor holding Vodafone stock is exposed to at least three types of risk: local market risk, sector risk and stock-specific risk. FTSE100, being heavily weighted towards Vodafone, therefore includes a component of Vodafone's sector and stock-specific risk as well as the local market risk; however, we wish to use the FTSE100 futures to hedge only the market risk. Normally in calculating the correct hedge, we estimate a beta by regressing the FTSE100 returns on Vodafone stock returns. However, this beta will be too large as it is a hedge of the component of Vodafone's stock-specific and sector risk in the FTSE100 as well as the local market risk. Hedging with the Eurostoxx Telecom index futures to remove the sector risk still leaves some upward bias as these indices still include some Vodafone stock-specific risk.

To determine a more accurate hedge ratio, one needs a clean measure of the country and sector risks so as to determine their relative effect on the FTSE100 and the Eurostoxx Telecom indexes. One approach to measuring these is to create an index consisting of an amalgam of variables that are closely correlated with country and sector returns. But the FTSE100 and Eurostoxx indexes themselves include country and sector risks, so the estimates remain biased. An alternative approach that we are beginning to use at UBS is to use share returns and index data to 'back out' an estimate of pure country and sector risks. This is explained below:

More efficient hedging

Estimating the beta of Vodafone to the true UK index yields a beta of 0.5, while the beta to the true European Telecom sector is 0.8. The FTSE100 beta to the true UK index is imposed to be 1 and the Eurostoxx Telecom index's beta to the true European Telelcom sector index is also imposed to be 1 (see explanation above). To hedge the Vodafone position with respect to each of these indexes, note that equation (8.21) can be converted into the ratios described in equation (8.22) below:

$$
\frac{\Delta S_{\text{Vodafone}}}{\Delta \text{FTSE}} = \frac{\beta_{\text{Vodafone, True Country Index}}}{\beta_{\text{FTSE, True Country Index}}} \frac{S_{\text{Vodafone}}}{\text{FTSE}} \frac{\text{number of shares}}{\text{index multiplier}}
$$
$$
\frac{\Delta S_{\text{Vodafone}}}{\Delta \text{ETI}} = \frac{\beta_{\text{Vodafone, True Sector Index}}}{\beta_{\text{FTSE, True Sector Index}}} \frac{S_{\text{Vodafone}}}{\text{ETI}} \frac{\text{number of shares}}{\text{index multiplier}}
$$

$$(8.22)$$

These hedge ratios, 1.92 FTSE100 futures and 11.4 Telecom Eurostoxx futures (multiplier is €50 per index point) are quite different to what one would have obtained by estimating betas of Vodafone with respect to each of these indexes in a multiple regression model. More importantly, these hedge ratios can be adapted to determine hedges against a variety of country and/or sector exposures as needed. Nevertheless, correlation risk is not completely eliminated with this approach, but that is not the issue here, but the actual exposures are. Notice also that the true country and sector indexes approach illustrated here can be used to improve the calculation of VAR and other similar measures.

9 Predictability of fund of hedge fund returns using DynaPorte

Greg N. Gregoriou[*] *and Fabrice Rouah*[†]

Abstract

We utilize a linear factor model to regress various funds of hedge fund indices on macroeconomic variables and market factors. Our goal is challenging since FOF returns are non-normal and have an indirect exposure to common factors used for predicting hedge fund returns. We identify a new set of factors that could predict FOF returns.

9.1 Introduction

Over the last two years of high volatility in US stock markets, pension funds, university endowments, and high net worth individuals have turned to funds of hedge funds (FOFs) for downside protection (Schneeweis et al. (2001); Lhabitant (2002)). The majority of these investors do not feel qualified to construct a portfolio of hedge funds on their own. FOFs are popular because they invest in other hedge funds and can spread the risk among many different hedge fund strategies. FOF managers monitor the managers in the basket, relieving their clients of the complicated process of selection, due diligence, and periodic monitoring of individual hedge funds. In addition FOFs reduce downside risk through diversification of hedge fund managers and provide access to a wide variety of hedge fund strategies. They do not compare themselves to traditional performance benchmarks (market indices), because they deliver more consistent returns and lower volatility than many traditional asset classes (da Costa (2001)). However, they often compare themselves to hedge fund indices to offer potential clients a yardstick. Investors have taken notice because the market share of FOFs has increased by 50% between 1996 and 2002 (Acito and Fisher (2002); Clow (2002)).

Experienced FOF managers who have a competitive information advantage will probably create superior and optimal FOFs. At the same time they can attempt to time the market by altering portfolio reallocations, rebalancing the weights of

[*] Greg N. Gregoriou is assistant professor of finance and faculty research coordinator in the School of Business and Economics at the State University of New York (Plattsburgh). E-mail: greg.gregoriou@plattsburgh.edu. Tel: (518) 564-4202.

[†] Fabrice Rouah is the Institut de Finance Mathématique de Montréal Scholar and PhD candidate (Finance) at McGill University, Montreal, Quebec. E-mail: fabrice.rouah@mail.mcgill.ca. We would like to thank Richard E. Oberuc at Burlington Hall Asset Management for providing us with the DynaPorte™ software (www.dynaporte.com).

hedge fund managers due to cash inflows and ongoing active portfolio management (Sharpe (1999); Ineichen (2001, 2002)). FOF managers are notoriously stringent with the hedge funds they hold and will monitor them closely to ensure they do not deviate from their investment strategies. Many hedge funds have been known to alter their main investment strategies during difficult environments.

According to Ineichen (2001), the proportion of talented FOF managers is unfortunately on the decrease. The recent increase in demand for FOF has led to new entrants flooding the market, some with little track record, and existing FOF managers with proven records and satisfied clients are thus becoming sparse. Furthermore, Ineichen (2002) believes the value added of a FOF is due to hedge fund manager selection and monitoring rather than just portfolio construction, whereas Anson (2000, 2001) argues that only portfolio construction plays an important role in creating an optimal FOF. However, each FOF manager has his own recipe for manager selection. An inadequately constructed portfolio of hedge funds with sub-optimal performance is not infrequent.

We use various macroeconomic variables and market indicators to examine the predictability of FOF performance on changing economic conditions. Lagged values of these variables are meant to represent widely available public information. These variables have been previously used in academic studies of hedge fund performance (Kat and Miffre (2002); Amenc et al. (2002); Gupta et al. (2003); Gregoriou et al. (2002); Gregoriou (2002); Kazemi and Schneeweis (2003)).

This chapter is organized as follows. A brief literature review is presented in the next section, followed by sections that describe the methodology and data. The empirical results and concluding remarks appear in the final sections.

9.2 Literature review

The benefits of diversifying traditional investment portfolios (bonds and equities) with FOFs are now firmly documented in the recent academic literature (see, for example, Fung and Hsieh (1999, 2002a); Schneeweis and Spurgin (1998a); deBrouwer (2001); Karavas (2000); Edwards and Caglayan (2001); Gregoriou and Rouah (2002a); Ineichen (2001); Sharpe (1999); Fothergill and Coke (2001). Including FOFs in portfolios can provide a better risk-return trade-off and reduced volatility than bond and equity mutual funds alone (Diz (2001)). Furthermore, the low correlation of FOFs to market indices provides investors with protection in down markets (see especially Schneeweis and Spurgin (1998b); Liang (1999); Gregoriou and Rouah (2000); Fung and Hsieh (1997); Agarwal and Naik (2000)).

In studies of conditional performance of hedge fund classifications, term premium, default spread, and the intra-month volatility index (VIX) are the most prominent variables used (Kazemi and Schneeweis (2003); Amenc et al. (2002); Gupta et al. (2003); Gregoriou (2004)) and represent publicly available information, and their usefulness as predictors of hedge fund returns has been documented – Amenc et al. (2002) find that crude oil was the strongest predictor of hedge fund returns. However, because the Goldman Sachs Commodity Index is heavily weighted towards oil, their results would have been different if another commodity index was used.

9.3   Methodology and data

We apply a regression model on six fund of hedge fund indices, using 50 macroeconomic variables. We find eight macroeconomic variables from the DynaPorte software
to be significant: (1) Commodity Prices London Gold Fix-Spot Price, (2) S&P 500
Dividend Yields, (3) US Industrial Manufacturing Capacity, (4) US Retail Sales, (5)
US Money Supply M3 Seasonally Adjusted, (6) US Exports of Goods, (7) US Export
of Services, and (8) Interest Rates on US T-Bills, 90-Day Monthly. All data correspond
to monthly observations.

We fit models for three FOF indices from the Center for International and Securities
Derivatives Market (CISDM), and for three FOF indices from Hedge Fund Research
(HFR), using the time period from January 1993 to December 2002, a period that
includes both up and down markets, and extreme market events. The model is the
following:

$$R_t = a + \sum_{j=1}^{J} b_j f_{j,t-j} + \varepsilon_t$$

where:

R_t = value of FOF index
a = alpha
b_j = regression coefficient (beta)
$f_{j,t-j}$ = value of lagged macroeconomic explanatory variable (factor)
ε_t = error term.

For simplicity, the software yields the average of the estimated b_j. We use the average
of one to four lags, corresponding to $J = 4$ for each macroeconomic variable in the
model. See Oberuc (2003) for details.

9.4   Empirical results

Exhibit 9.1 presents correlation coefficients between the six FOF indices. As expected,
these are high, ranging from 0.77 to 0.98, with many at 0.90 or higher. The correlation

Fund of funds index	Coefficient of correlation					
CISDM MEDIAN	1					
CISDM NICHE	0.87	1				
CISDM DIVERSIFIED	0.97	0.82	1			
HFR	0.77	0.77	0.87	1		
HFR OFFSHORE	0.90	0.90	0.94	0.88	1	
HFR ONSHORE	0.94	0.79	0.98	0.89	0.94	1

Exhibit 9.1 Correlation matrix of FOF indices, 1993–2002

Macroeconomic variable	Coefficient of correlation							
Commodity Prices London Gold Fix-Spot Price	1							
S&P 500 Dividend Yield	0.89	1						
Manufacturing Industrial Capacity	−0.86	−0.92	1					
Retail Sales	−0.88	−0.89	0.99	1				
Money Supply M3 Seasonally Adjusted	−0.79	−0.81	0.97	0.98	1			
Exports of Goods	−0.83	−0.92	0.96	0.94	0.91	1		
Exports of Services	−0.86	−0.94	0.98	0.96	0.93	0.98	1	
Interest Rate on T-Bills, 90-day monthly	0.09	−0.08	−0.18	−0.19	−0.37	−0.13	−0.10	1

Exhibit 9.2 Correlation matrix of macroeconomic variables, 1993–2002

coefficients of the explanatory variables are much more varied (Exhibit 9.2), ranging from −0.92 to 0.99. The interest rate of T-bills 90-day appears to have the weakest correlation with the other variables (last row of Exhibit 9.2).

Exhibit 9.3 presents the average regression coefficients and corresponding p-values in parentheses of all six models, along with estimated alphas and model R-squared. All selected variables are significant ($p < 0.05$), and most of the models involve only two or three. We find the 90-day T-bill interest rate to be a significant predictor for all three CISDM indices. Moreover, the coefficient and p-value for this predictor are very similar. On the other hand, we find no common predictor for the three HFR indices. We also find exports, in terms of both goods and services, to be significant variables for predicting three of the six indices, again with similar values of estimated coefficients and comparable p-values.

9.5 Discussion

Only a few macroeconomic variables are useful in predicting FOF returns, as evidenced by our models, which are sparse and whose values of R-squared are modest. We find a negative relation between the CISDM indices and the 90-day T-bill interest rates, possibly reflecting outflows from FOFs during times of increased returns on government bonds. We also find a relation between FOF returns and manufacturing capacity, exports of goods and services, and retail sales. Given the high correlation of these variables (see Exhibit 9.2) it is possible that they embody a common factor, reflecting economic health and affecting FOF returns. For example, retail sales are primarily used to measure the sales revenue of goods sold by retail businesses. Moreover, when

Macroeconomic variable (1 to 4 lags used)	Fund of funds indices					
	CISDM MEDIAN	CISDM NICHE	CISDM DIVERSIFIED	HFR	HFR OFFSHORE	HFR ONSHORE
Commodity Prices London					−2.01 (0.0485)	
Gold Fix-Spot Price		−2.25 (0.0280)				
S&P500 Dividend Yield					2.20 (0.0310)	
Manufacturing Industrial Capacity				2.01 (0.0398)		
Retail Sales				−2.26 (0.0269)		
Money Supply M3 Seasonally Adjusted				−2.18 (0.0328)		
Exports of Goods	2.05 (0.0440)	2.20 (0.0316)	2.15 (0.0354)			2.06 (0.0433)
Exports of Services	2.08 (0.0411)					
Interest Rate on T-Bills, 90-day Monthly	−2.43 (0.0176)	−2.36 (0.0213)	−2.30 (0.0243)			
Alpha	40.72	181.14	11.52	−688.95	−136.31	5.70
R-Squared	0.16	0.27	0.24	0.20	0.28	0.20

Exhibit 9.3 Average lagged regression coefficients, p-values, alpha, and model R-squared, for FOF indices, 1993–2002

both short-term interest rates and industrial capacity are high, fixed-income funds will generally perform poorly.

Dividend yields on the S&P 500 index and the money supply (M3) are found to affect two HFR FOF indices. The fact that many FOFs are exposed to a variety of equity indices could explain this dependence. Our finding of a negative relationship between one HFR FOF index and M3 lends credence to what practitioners often observe: FOFs tend to perform well when the money supply shrinks. The market environment became more complex during the second half of 2000 when interest rates rose despite the fact that the growth of M3 was somewhat slowing down. Lastly, we find the gold spot price to be negatively related to FOF indices (CISDM Niche and HFR Offshore). This relation between FOF returns and gold prices is similar to findings by Fung and Hsieh (1997).

The model for HFR Offshore Index has the highest value of the adjusted R-squared (0.28), and is the best predictor of FOF returns, whereas the CISDM is the worst (R-squared of 0.16). It is very difficult to predict FOF returns because of the combination of various hedge fund strategies at work.

The alphas represent the value of the investment return when all of the factor values are zero. They are not alphas in the sense of a CAPM alpha. But some of the factors are never really near zero. If we centered the data so that the factors had zero means, then the alpha would have a different meaning. In the end, there is no easy interpretation to these alphas since the factors frequently never take values near their zero points. They are just the constant term in the equation.

9.6 Conclusion

Using FOF managers whose approach is to buy and hold hedge funds can lead to poor performance due to rapidly changing market conditions. Indeed, our evidence suggests that FOF exposure to market risk, and resulting performance, varies in response to macroeconomic variables. The models, however, suffer from low values of R-squared. One possible explanation is that, although the time span used is long (ten years) only monthly data are available and it is likely that monthly data are simply not able to capture the frequent intra-month trading and rebalancing of FOF managers. Another explanation is that FOF returns are non-normal.

References

Acito, C. J. and Fisher, F. P. (2002). Fund of Hedge Funds: Rethinking Resource Requirements. *Journal of Alternative Investments*, Vol. 4, No. 4: 25–35.

Agarwal, V. and Naik, N. Y. (2000). Multi-Period Performance Persistence Analysis of Hedge Funds. *Journal of Financial and Quantitative Analysis*, Vol. 35, No. 3:327–342.

Amenc, N., Bied, S.E., and Martellini, L. (2002). Evidence in Predictability in Hedge Fund Returns and Multi-Style Multi-Class Tactical Style Allocation Decisions. *Financial Analysts Journal*, Forthcoming.

Anson, M. (2000). Selecting a Hedge Fund Manager. *Journal of Alternative Investments*, Vol. 3, No. 3:45–52.

Anson, M. (2001). Should Hedge Funds Be Institutionalized? *Journal of Portfolio Management*, Vol. 10, No. 3:69–74.

Clow, R. (2002). Pensions Maintain Flows into Alternative Assets. *Financial Times of London*, 30 April, London, UK.

da Costa, A. (2001). *Fund of Funds and Absolute Returns*. Vector Asset Management Inc. London, United Kingdom.

deBrouwer, G. (2001). *Hedge Funds in Emerging Markets*. Cambridge University Press, Cambridge, United Kingdom.

Diz, F. (2001). Are Investors Over-Invested in Equities? *Derivatives Quarterly*, Vol. 7, No. 3:59–62.

Edwards, F. and Caglayan, M. O. (2001). Hedge Fund Performance and Manager Skill. *Journal of Futures Markets*, Vol. 21, No. 11:1003–1028.

Ferson, W. and Warther, V. A. (1996). Evaluating Fund Performance in a Dynamic Market. *Financial Analysts Journal*, Vol. 52, No. 6:20–28.

Fothergill, M. and Coke, C. (2001). Funds of Hedge Funds: An Introduction to Multi-manager Funds. *Journal of Alternative Investments*, Vol. 4, No. 2:7–16.

Fung, W. and Hsieh, D. A. (1997). Empirical Characteristics of Dynamic Trading Strategies: The Case of Hedge Funds. *Review of Financial Studies*, Vol. 10, No. 2:275–302.

Fung, W. and Hsieh, D. A. (1999). A Primer on Hedge Funds. *Journal of Empirical Finance*, Vol. 6, No. 3:309–331.

Fung, W. and Hsieh, D. A. (2002a). Benchmarks of Hedge Fund Performance: Information Content and Measurement Biases. *Financial Analyst Journal*, Vol. 58, No. 1:22–34.

Fung, W. and Hsieh, D. A. (2002b). Asset-Based Style Factors for Hedge Funds. *Financial Analysts Journal*, Vol. 58, No. 5:16–28.

Gregoriou, G. N., Rouah, F., and Sedzro, K. (2002). On the Market Timing of Hedge Fund Managers. *Journal of Wealth Management*, Vol. 5, No. 1:26–38.

Gregoriou, G. N. (2004). Three Essays on Hedge Fund. Doctoral Dissertation, University of Quebec at Montreal.

Gregoriou, G. N. (2000). Funds of Funds: When More Definite Means Less. *Canadian Business Economics Journal*, Vol. 8, No. 2:82–85.

Gregoriou, G. N. and Rouah, F. (2002a). The Role of Hedge Funds in Pension Fund Portfolios: Buying Protection in Down Markets. *Journal of Pensions Management*, Vol. 7, No. 3:237–245.

Gregoriou, G. N. and Rouah, F. (2002b). Large versus Small Hedge Funds: Does Size Affect Performance? *Journal of Alternative Investments*, Vol. 5, No. 3:75–77.

Gupta, B., Cerrahoglu, B., and Daglioglu, A. (2003). Hedge Fund Strategy Performance: Using Conditional Approaches. Working Paper, University of Massachusetts, CISDM.

Ineichen, A. (2001). The Alpha in Funds of Hedge Funds. *Journal of Wealth Management*, Vol. 5, No. 1:8–25.

Ineichen, A. (2002). Funds of Hedge Funds: Industry Overview. *Journal of Wealth Management*, Vol. 4, No. 4:47–62.

Karavas, V. (2000). Alternative Investments in the Institutional Portfolio. *Journal of Alternative Investments*, Vol. 3, No. 3:11–26.

Kat, H. and Miffre, J. (2002). Performance Evaluation and Conditioning Information: The Case of Hedge Funds. Working Paper, University of Reading, ISMA Centre.

Kazemi, H. and Schneeweis, T. (2003). Conditional Performance of Hedge Funds. Working Paper, University of Massachusetts, CISDM, 2003.

Lhabitant, S. (2002). Assessing Market Risk for Hedge Funds and Hedge Fund Portfolios. *The Journal of Risk Finance*, Vol. 2, No. 4:16–32.

Liang, B. (1999). On the Performance of Hedge Funds. *Financial Analysts Journal*, Vol. 55, No. 4:72–85.

Oberuc, R. E. (2003). *Dynamic Portfolio Theory and Management*. McGraw-Hill, New York.

Schneeweis, T., Kazemi, H., and Martin, G. (2001). Understanding Hedge Fund Performance: Research Results and Rules of Thumb of the Institutional Investors. Working Paper, University of Massachusetts, CISDM.

Schneeweis, T. and Spurgin, R. (1998a). Alternative Investments in Institutional Portfolios. Working Paper, University of Massachusetts, CISDM.

Schneeweis, T. and Spurgin, R. (1998b). Multifactor Analysis of Hedge Funds, Managed Futures and Mutual Fund Return and Risk Characteristics. *Journal of Alternative Investments*, Vol. 1, No. 2:1–24.

Sharpe, M. (1999). Constructing the Optimal Hedge Fund of Funds. *The Journal of Wealth Management*, Vol. 2, No. 1:35–44.

10 Estimating a combined linear factor model

Alvin L. Stroyny[*]

Abstract

Most linear factor models used in portfolio risk management employ one of three basic estimation procedures: least squares regression on time-series data, (weighted) least squares regression on fundamental accounting variables, or factor analysis. These are often referred to as *economic*, *fundamental*, and *statistical* factor models. A variety of arguments have been offered as to why one approach or another is purportedly 'better' than the others. We feel that each approach has merit for particular applications and that there may be advantages to building a model that combines all methods. We present an algorithm for estimating a *combined* linear model that incorporates the basic features of all three approaches in a single simultaneous estimation procedure. Under a set of appropriate assumptions, the resulting parameter values are maximum likelihood estimates. The simultaneous estimation procedure allows for some extensions of the linear model as well.

10.1   Introduction

Linear factor models are widely used for modeling portfolio risk. Three popular approaches most frequently used in modeling security returns are:

(a) time-series regression with known factors, and estimated betas (assumed constant across observations),
(b) cross-sectional regressions using known fundamental/technical variables as proxies for betas which may vary from period to period, and estimated factor values, and
(c) factor analysis where factor values and betas are both missing and must be estimated (again beta is typically assumed to be constant across observations).

One of the first multi-factor models of security returns in the financial literature is that of King (1966), using multiple industry-based return indices. Security 'betas' were estimated using ordinary least squares (OLS) regression of each security return series on specified industry portfolios. BIRR is a consulting firm that constructs a variety of proprietary economic data series used to estimate a linear factor model for security returns[1]. While the methodology used to create each of the factor series can

[*] Chairman, EM Applications Limited, St Martin's House, 16 St Martin's LeGrand, London EC1A 4EN, +44 (020) 73978395, astroyny@emapplications.com
[1] BIRR is a commercial portfolio risk consulting firm operated by E. Burmeister, J. Ingersoll, R. Roll, and S. Ross. The company's website is www.birr.com

be quite technically advanced, the estimation of the security *betas* utilizes the same basic linear (times-series) regression methodology as in King (1966). This approach is often referred to as economic factor models. Professional investment managers may feel that choosing data series that they are comfortable with is an advantage of this model, since they may feel that they have the ability to predict changes in the direction and/or volatility of the series.

Rosenberg (1974) proposed a multi-factor model that included market and industry components. This approach has been extended by BARRA to develop a 'fundamental' factor model that is widely used by investment managers[2]. Again, the proprietary statistical methodology used to create the 'fundamental' firm characteristic variables can be quite complex. Once these variables are created, the statistical estimation of the factors is done using weighted least squares regression. One of the main advantages often cited for the fundamental factor model approach is that by utilizing frequently updated accounting data, this approach can predict changes in a company's risk profile before methods that rely solely on historical return data.

Roll and Ross (1980) used factor analysis to estimate a common factor structure for equity returns. Their use of Joreskorg's algorithm along with computational limitations of the time prevented them analyzing large numbers of securities in a single estimation. Factor analysis models of security returns gained widespread use in the mid 1980s as computing power became cheaper and new estimation techniques were developed that made it feasible to apply factor analysis to a data set containing a large number of securities. Connor and Korajczyk (1986) utilized a principal factor analysis algorithm capable of working with very large data sets. EM Applications is one of several consulting firms that offer a variety of factor models that combine both economic data series as well as statistical factors in various global markets[3]. One of the main advantages that is often cited for factor analysis is that it is completely data driven and thus not subject to human-specified available data biases.

Connor (1995) examined the explanatory power of the three forms of factor models. He finds that the fundamental approach performs slightly better than the other two according to his criteria. While the various arguments both for and against each of the three basic forms of factor models make it difficult to choose a single 'best' approach to building a factor model, almost everyone would agree that each of the three methods has useful features not found in the other two. This would seem to raise the question, 'Why not use the best parts of all three methods?'. The objective of this chapter is to present an algorithm for obtaining maximum likelihood estimates of a linear factor model that incorporates *all three* of the basic forms.

10.2 A combined linear factor model

We use the following convention for notation; row and column vectors are denoted as lower case boldface letters, matrices are denoted as upper case boldface letters, while scalars and matrix/vector elements are denoted as non-bold lower case letters. The *i*

---

[2] BARRA is a commercial portfolio risk consulting firm founded by Barr Rosenberg. The company's website is www.barra.com

[3] EM Applications is a UK-based consulting firm. The company's website is www.emapplications.com

subscript is used to refer to the observation (time) domain and the j subscript to refer to the variable (stock) domain. There will be some instances of three-dimensional matrices, in which case we will use an upper case bold letter with a subscript to designate a two-dimensional 'slice' of the full three-dimensional matrix.

The usual form of the economic and statistical factor models can be represented in matrix form as

$$Y = ZB + E \tag{10.1}$$

where Y is the $(n \times p)$ matrix of n return observations on p securities, Z is the $(n \times q)$ matrix of n observations on q factor variables, B is the $(q \times p)$ matrix of q factor sensitivities (betas) on p securities, and E is the $(n \times p)$ matrix of n residuals on p securities. One of the features of the usual form of the above models is that the factor sensitivities matrix, B, is typically assumed constant across the i observations[4]. This assumption allows for compact notation as above.

In the case of fundamental factor models, the factor sensitivity matrix takes on a third dimension associated with each i-observation. Thus the full three-dimensional data set is expressed as a series of two-dimensional slices, B_i, $i = 1, \ldots, n$. It is this large volume of fundamental data that makes the information potential of this type of model appealing. Note that almost any observable feature of a security prior to period i can be used as an input 'fundamental' data characteristic matrix, B_i. In particular, past characteristics of security returns, $g(y_{i-1}, y_{i-2}, \ldots)$, can be input at time i as deterministic variables. Thus an infinite class of 'technical' variables can be constructed from past price series alone. This form of model has been popularized by BARRA using both (industry-normalized) fundamental accounting data as well as technical price/volume type variables. Due to the three-dimensional form of the factor sensitivities, the model is specified in the following notation:

$$y_i = z_i B_i + e_i \quad (i = 1, 2, \ldots, n) \tag{10.2}$$

where y_i refers to the $(1 \times p)$ row vector of ith return observation on p securities, z_i is the $(1 \times q)$ row vector of the ith observation on q factor variables, B_i is now the $(q \times p)$ matrix of the now ith realization of the now observation dependent factor sensitivity matrix, and e_i is the $(1 \times p)$ row vector of the ith observation residuals.

Denoting the three forms described above by the subscripts, a, b, c, we can express a combined linear factor model that incorporates all three basic forms:

$$y_i = z_{ai} B_a + z_{bi} B_{bi} + z_{ci} B_c + e_i \quad (i = 1, 2, \ldots, n) \tag{10.3}$$

where y_i is the $(1 \times p)$ row vector of ith period returns on p securities, z_{ai} is the $(1 \times q_a)$ row vector of observed (regression-type) factors, B_a is the $(q_a \times p)$ matrix of the estimated regression slope coefficients (assumed constant across all observations),

---

[4] While B is typically assumed to be constant, this is not a strict requirement of these models and a variety of time-dependent forms can be utilized.

z_{bi} is the $(1 \times q_b)$ row vector of estimated factors for period i, $\mathbf{B}_{bi}$ is the $(q_b \times p)$ matrix of ith period firm characteristics (e.g. BARRA-type fundamental/technical variables), z_{ci} is the $(1 \times q_c)$ row vector of estimated statistical factors for period i, $\mathbf{B}_c$ is the $(q_c \times p)$ matrix of estimated factor loadings (again assumed constant across i) and e_i is the $(1 \times p)$ row vector of ith period residuals, where $i = 1, 2, \ldots, n$. We do not address any of the asset pricing issues associated with estimates of the mean returns on securities[5]. As such, the standard estimates of the intercepts in both the n and p dimensions can be incorporated in the model by including a unit column vector in $\mathbf{Z}_a$ and a unit row vector in $\mathbf{B}_{bi}$ or by constraining one row of $\mathbf{B}_c$ to equal a unit row vector.

10.3 An extended model

An extension to the above model is to allow for a firm-specific parameter, $\mathbf{A}_j$, $(q_b \times q_b)$, assumed constant across observations (time), controlling the intensity of the response to $\mathbf{Z}_{bi}$. The model now becomes:

$$y_{ij} = z_{ai}\mathbf{b}_{aj} + z_{bi}\mathbf{A}_j\mathbf{b}_{bij} + z_{ci}\mathbf{b}_{cj} + e_{ij} \quad (i = 1, 2, \ldots, n) \quad (j = 1, 2, \ldots, p) \quad (10.4)$$

Equation (10.3) can be viewed as a special case of (10.4) where $\mathbf{A}_j \equiv \mathbf{I}, (j = 1, 2, \ldots, p)$. This second form of the model allows for a *separable* response function combining a time-specific, firm-constant market variable, z_{bi}, and a time-constant, firm-specific intensity variable, $\mathbf{A}_j$. Also note that $\mathbf{A}_j$ is the jth slice of another three-dimensional matrix. As a result, the notation must now be specified at the individual y_{ij} element level.

There are several advantages to this extended form of the linear model. Since the $\mathbf{b}_{bij}$ are constructed variables, there is the potential for scaling errors (e.g. D/E ratios for banks not being comparable to those for technology stocks). By estimating $\mathbf{A}_j$, the model would statistically adjust the response where industry or other *a priori* scaling schemes do not fully account for these differences[6]. A variety of restrictions can be imposed on the form of $\mathbf{A}_j$ such as requiring a single value for all securities within a specified group (e.g. industry). There is now an indeterminacy in the model due to the multiplicative form of the $\mathbf{Z}_b$ and $\mathbf{A}_j$. To avoid this problem, we need to add an additional uniqueness constraint, such as requiring that the average parameter value across all firms of the diagonal elements of $\mathbf{A}_j$ be equal to one:

$$p^{-1} \sum_{j=1}^{p} a_{jkk} = 1 \quad (k = 1, \ldots, q_b) \tag{10.5}$$

---

[5] Additional Arbitrage Pricing Theory (Ross (1976))-type pricing restrictions could of course be imposed on the estimation procedure.

[6] Fundamental data are typically 'normalized' to the industry average in an attempt to adjust for these differences. The advantage of this form of model is that it allows for within-industry scaling as well.

10.4 Model estimation

There are several methods that can be used to obtain parameter estimates for the models described above. Even if we restrict ourselves to obtaining maximum likelihood estimates, there still are several forms of algorithms that can be employed. While methods that calculate the Hessian matrix typically converge in the fewest iterations, the computational burden per iteration grows with the square of the number of parameters in the model making the method impractical in many applications where more than 10 000 financial securities may be involved. This is one of the problems Roll and Ross (1980) encountered when they tried to estimate a statistical factor model using Joreskog's algorithm[7].

Dempster et al. (1977) introduced the concept of the Expectation-Maximization (EM) algorithm for finding maximum likelihood parameter estimates in problems involving missing data. They point out one of the more intriguing aspects of the theory is the application of EM to problems involving *conceptually* missing data, mentioning factor analysis as one example. In these cases, the corresponding EM algorithms lead to simple iterative procedures since the corresponding *complete*-data mle problems have one-step solutions via OLS regression. Rubin and Thayer (1982) develop the EM algorithm for the case of traditional factor analysis, under the assumption that the missing factors are jointly normal with the disturbances.

While their algorithm produced the same mle parameter estimates (to a rotation), it proved to be considerably slower than Joreskog's method for the particular problem. Rubin and Thayer also inadvertently impose an artificial constraint in their algorithm that prevented it from obtaining the steepest ascent path[8]. Stroyny (1991) showed that when this constraint is removed, the convergence rate for the EM factor analysis algorithm actually improves as the number of variables, p, increases. Simulation evidence showed that at between 200 and 300 variables, the EM algorithm converged quicker than Joreskog's method in terms of total CPU time even though it required more iterations.

In applying EM to missing data problems, the E-step involves taking the expectation of the *sufficient statistics* of the corresponding complete-data problem (*not* simply the expected value of the missing data, though for some problems these are one and the same), conditioned on the observed data and current estimates of the parameters. Evaluating the expectation operator in the E-step requires a specific prior for the distributional form of the factors. The general theory of EM, however, can be applied to any distributional prior.

Before we can proceed with estimating the model, several assumptions must be made regarding the forms of statistical processes involved. We will assume that the disturbances, e_{ij}, are identically distributed normal random variables with variance, $var(e_{ij}) = \sigma_j^2$, $i = 1,\ldots,n$, and are independent both between different securities,

---

[7] While current CPU power and greater memory size allow for larger problems, Joreskog's algorithm also contains an additional term, not part of the likelihood function, that prevents estimation when the number of variables, p, exceeds the number of observations, n. This result has led many to erroneously conclude that maximum likelihood factor analysis is not possible in this case.

[8] Liu et al. (1998) develop the PX-EM algorithm which addresses the type of problem encountered by Rubin and Thayer.

$cov(e_{ij}, e_{ik}) = 0, j \neq k$, and through time, $cov(e_{ij}, e_{hj}) = 0, h \neq i$. As is typically done, we will treat the unknown factor sensitivities. $\mathbf{B}_a$ and $\mathbf{B}_c$ as well as $\mathbf{A}_j, j = 1, \ldots, p$, as parameters to be estimated. The observed factors, $\mathbf{Z}_a$, and observed fundamental variables, $\mathbf{B}_i (i = 1, \ldots, n)$, are treated as given non-stochastic variables.

The main difference among the various statistical methods for estimating factor models with latent factors has to do with the assumptions regarding the distributional form of the factor variables, $\mathbf{Z}_b$ and $\mathbf{Z}_c$, in the above model. The latent factors can be treated as either stochastic or non-stochastic variables. Both approaches have advantages and disadvantages. If the unknown factors are treated as stochastic variables, a distributional form must be specified. Again, each specific form of distribution will have advantages and drawbacks. One popular form of stochastic factor model is to treat the factors as normally distributed random variables as in the traditional factor analysis method of Joreskog and as assumed in the EM algorithm for factor analysis of Rubin and Thayer (1982). Stroyny and Rowe (2002) utilized the EM algorithm to examine differences in factor analysis algorithms under a variety of prior distributional forms for the 'missing' factor scores. They extended the normal prior EM algorithm of Rubin and Thayer (1982) to the case of a vague prior on the (stochastic) factor scores. Stroyny and Rowe (2002) also showed that the EM algorithm can be applied to the case of non-stochastic factors by assuming a degenerate or point prior, in which case the EM algorithm is equivalent to the least squares method of factor analysis of Lawley (1942).

The main advantage of a non-stochastic factor model (or equivalently a degenerate prior) is that the estimated residuals, $\mathbf{E}$, are directly observable. This is not the case with stochastic factors as the total error term now includes the unknown variability in the factor score (multiplied by the factor loading), as well as the disturbance term. One of the main limitations of non-stochastic factor models is that they are often unstable, with tendencies to estimate zero residual variances[9]. Another limitation is a degree of freedom required for each observation on each factor score, or a total of $(n \times (q_b + q_c))$.

The main advantage of assuming a normal prior for the factor scores is a reduction in the number of parameters to be estimated. The reduced number of parameters contributes to the stability of the estimation procedure, reducing the tendency of zero residual variance estimates (e.g. Heywood cases). Stroyny and Rowe (2002) show that as the number of variables, p, increases, the parameter estimates under the normal, vague, and degenerate priors converge. They also find that stability issues associated with initial parameter estimates and the tendency for estimating zero residual variances for the non-stochastic factor models tend to diminish as well as p increase[10].

We develop an estimation algorithm under the assumption of non-stochastic factors that allows us to use a relatively simple conditional maximization (CM) algorithm[11]. The CM algorithm alternates between calculating values of the first set of parameters that maximize the likelihood given the second set of parameters, and maximizing the

---

[9] See Anderson and Rubin (1956).

[10] The least squares method of factor analysis (LSMFA) was introduced by Lawley (1942). While the approach was intuitively simple, the method proved to be unstable resulting in estimates of zero residual variances. While less frequent, this also occurs in stochastic factor models as well.

[11] The conditional maximization algorithm is also referred to as the alternating variable method.

likelihood over the values of the second set of parameters given the first. The process is repeated until convergence is obtained.

The key to the CM algorithm for the linear factor models outlined above is that the maximization problem for each group of parameters in the model is in the form of a *linear regression*. As such, we can directly write the (conditional) maximizing parameter estimates using the usual form of the sufficient statistics for either OLS or WLS regression. Under the assumption of non-stochastic factors, the resulting algorithm is also consistent with the general theory of EM under the assumption of a degenerate prior for the factors. In effect, the E-step of the EM algorithm becomes redundant since the expected values of the sufficient statistics given the observed data and current values of the parameters are equivalent to the sufficient statistics evaluated at the expected value of the parameters.

10.5   Conditional maximization

For the first form of the combined linear model, the parameters can be separated into two groups, z_{bi}, z_{ci} and B_a, B_c. The CM algorithm alternatingly maximizes the conditional log likelihood function for one set of parameters given the current values of the other group. The CM equation for the estimates of the first group of parameters, z_{bi}, z_{ci}, is given by the WLS regression as:

$$z_{bci} = (y_i - z_{ai}B_a)\Sigma^{-1}B_{bci}^T \left(B_{bci}\Sigma^{-1}B_{bci}^T\right)^{-1} \quad (i = 1, 2, \ldots, n) \tag{10.6}$$

where

$$B_{bci} \equiv \begin{bmatrix} B_{bi} \\ B_c \end{bmatrix} \qquad ((q_b + q_c) \times p),$$

$$z_{bci} \equiv [z_{bi} \ z_{ci}] \qquad (1 \times (q_b + q_c)),$$

$$e_i = y_i - z_{ai}B_a - z_{bi}B_i - z_{ci}B_c \quad (1 \times p), \text{ and}$$

$$\Sigma = n^{-1}diag(E^T E) \qquad (p \times p)$$

The additional parameters, B_a and B_c, are simply treated as constants based on their latest estimated values. In similar fashion, the second group of parameter estimates, B_a, B_c, is given by the OLS (matrix) regression equations as:

$$B_{ac} = \left(Z_{ac}^T Z_{ac}\right)^{-1} Z_{ac}^T \left(Y - \begin{bmatrix} z_{b1}B_{b1} \\ z_{b2}B_{b2} \\ \ldots \\ z_{bn}B_{bn} \end{bmatrix}\right) \tag{10.7}$$

where

$$B_{ac} \equiv \begin{bmatrix} B_a \\ B_c \end{bmatrix} \quad ((q_a + q_c) \times p), \text{ and}$$

$$Z_{ac} \equiv [z_a \ z_c] \quad (n \times (q_a + q_c))$$

The parameter estimates from equation (10.6), Z_b and Z_c, are now treated as constants and evaluated at their latest estimated values. The CM algorithm thus iterates between equations (10.6) and (10.7) until convergence is obtained.

The CM algorithm can be started with either equation (10.6) or (10.7) and appropriate starting values for the group of parameters in the second equation. A variety of approaches can be taken regarding the initial parameter values. If we begin the algorithm say with equation (10.6) estimating z_{bi}, z_{ci}, then we need to have initial estimates of B_a, B_c, and Σ. Initial estimates for B_a can be easily obtained by OLS regression of Y on Z_a. Initial estimates for the residual variance parameter, $\Sigma = diag(\sigma_1^2, \ldots, \sigma_p^2)$, are used on a relative basis to weight the individual observations and thus the scale of the initial estimates is irrelevant. Several alternative initial values for Σ are I (e.g. equal weighting), $n^{-1}diag(Y^T Y)$ (e.g. proportional to total variance), or $n^{-1}diag(E^T E)$ where $E = Y - Z_a B_a$ from the OLS regression for the initial estimates of B_a.

We have found that in many instances, a pseudorandom number generator can be used to generate the initial estimates of B_c. The initial convergence rate of the CM algorithm is extremely rapid in this case such that only a few additional iterations are saved by using improved estimates of B_c. If convergence problems do occur, then the factor loading estimates corresponding to the first q_c eigenvalues from either principal components or factor analysis of either $cov(Y)$, or $cov(E)$, the residuals from the OLS regression of B_a, could be utilized as improved estimates. Under the assumption of independent, identically distributed normal errors, e_{ij}, the CM algorithm as defined in equations (10.6) and (10.7), results in least squares estimates of the model parameters which, under the assumption of non-stochastic factors, will also be the maximum likelihood estimates.

10.6   Heterogeneous errors

One of the major problems associated with security return data is the presence of outliers. These are often associated with economic events specific to an individual company, such as earnings announcements, corporate actions, verdicts in lawsuits, etc. As such, the assumption of identically distributed errors is typically violated. We can relax the assumption in the above model to allow for heterogeneous error variances across observations (time periods), analogous to the standard weighted least squares (WLS) regression model by assuming that the $(n \times 1)$ variance-scaling vector, $\boldsymbol{\theta}_j = (\theta_{1j}, \ldots, \theta_{nj})$, is known a priori, and θ_{ij} is defined such that:

$$\sum_{i=1}^{n} \theta_{ij} = n \quad (j = 1, \ldots, p) \tag{10.8}$$

The residual variance for the ith observation of the jth security is now given as:

$$\sigma_{ij}^2 = v_j \theta_{ij} \tag{10.9}$$

where v_j is the variance scale constant for security j defined as:

$$v_j = n^{-1} \left(\mathbf{e}_j^T \mathbf{\Theta}_j \mathbf{e}_j \right) \Big/ \left(\mathbf{1}_n^T \mathbf{\Theta} \mathbf{1}_n \right) \tag{10.10}$$

where $\mathbf{1}_n$ is an $(n \times 1)$ unit column vector, and the $(n \times n)$ weighting matrix for security j, $\mathbf{\Theta}_j$, is given as:

$$\mathbf{\Theta}_j = diag \left(\theta_{1j}^{-1}, \theta_{2j}^{-1}, \dots, \theta_{nj}^{-1} \right) \quad (n \times n) \tag{10.11}$$

As a result, the residual covariance matrix, $\mathbf{\Sigma}_i$, will now also be time dependent and is defined as:

$$\mathbf{\Sigma}_i = diag \left(\sigma_{i1}^2, \sigma_{i2}^2, \dots, \sigma_{ip}^2 \right) \quad (p \times p) \quad (i = 1, \dots, n) \tag{10.12}$$

The CM equation for $\mathbf{z}_{bi}$ and $\mathbf{z}_{ci}$ now accounts for the heterogeneity in the disturbances (through time) and is given as:

$$\mathbf{z}_{bci} = (\mathbf{y}_i - \mathbf{z}_{ai}\mathbf{B}_a)\mathbf{\Sigma}_i^{-1}\mathbf{B}_{bci}^T \left(\mathbf{B}_{bci}\mathbf{\Sigma}_i^{-1}\mathbf{B}_{bci}^T \right)^{-1} \quad (i = 1, 2, \dots, n) \tag{10.13}$$

Similarly, the estimates of $\mathbf{B}_a$ and $\mathbf{B}_c$ must account for the specific heterogeneous pattern of each different security, j. The OLS regression estimates of $\mathbf{B}_a$ and $\mathbf{B}_c$ in equation (10.7) are accordingly modified to a corresponding WLS form as:

$$\mathbf{b}_{acj} = \left(\mathbf{Z}_{ac}^T \mathbf{\Theta}_j \mathbf{Z}_{ac} \right)^{-1} \mathbf{Z}_{ac}^T \mathbf{\Theta}_j \left(\mathbf{y}_j - \begin{bmatrix} \mathbf{z}_{b1}\mathbf{b}_{b1j} \\ \mathbf{z}_{b2}\mathbf{b}_{b2j} \\ \dots \\ \mathbf{z}_{bn}\mathbf{b}_{bnj} \end{bmatrix} \right) \quad (j = 1, \dots, p) \tag{10.14}$$

where $\mathbf{b}_{acj}$ is the jth column of $\mathbf{B}_{ac}$ as defined in equation (10.7). The CM algorithm now iterates through equations (10.9) to (10.14) until convergence is obtained. The model can be extended to allow for simultaneous estimates of the weighting matrix under a variety of assumptions regarding the specific form of the heterogeneity. We limit our analysis to the case where the weights are given exogenously.

10.7 Estimating the extended model

If we now relax the restriction that $\mathbf{A}_j \equiv \mathbf{I}, \forall j$, the model estimation becomes slightly more complex. The model parameters will now include a third group for the CM of $\mathbf{A}_j$. The estimation equations for $\mathbf{z}_{bci}$ and $\mathbf{b}_{acj}$ are a straightforward extension of the previous section equations since $\mathbf{A}_j$ is treated as a constant, although the resulting matrix notation becomes slightly more involved. The CM estimates for the factor scores, $\mathbf{z}_{bci}$, are again of the form of a WLS regression as:

$$\mathbf{z}_{bci} = (\mathbf{y}_i - \mathbf{z}_{ai}\mathbf{B}_a)\mathbf{\Sigma}_i^{-1}\mathbf{G}_{bci}^T \left(\mathbf{G}_{bci}\mathbf{\Sigma}_i^{-1}\mathbf{G}_{bci}^T \right)^{-1} \quad (i = 1, 2, \dots, n) \tag{10.15}$$

where

$$\mathbf{G}_{bci} = \begin{bmatrix} \mathbf{G}_{bi} \\ \mathbf{B}_c \end{bmatrix} \qquad ((q_b + q_c) \times p), \text{ and}$$

$$\mathbf{G}_{bi} \equiv [\mathbf{A}_1 \mathbf{b}_{bi1} \ \mathbf{A}_2 \mathbf{b}_{bi2} \dots \mathbf{A}_p \mathbf{b}_{bip}] \quad (q_b \times p)$$

Likewise, the estimate for $\mathbf{b}_{acj}$ is essentially the same as it was for the previous model in equation (10.11) except that $\mathbf{A}_j$ now appears as an additional constant:

$$\mathbf{b}_{acj} = \left(\mathbf{Z}_{ac}^T \boldsymbol{\Theta}_j \mathbf{Z}_{ac} \right)^{-1} \mathbf{Z}_{ac}^T \boldsymbol{\Theta}_j \left(\mathbf{y}_j - \begin{bmatrix} z_{b1} \mathbf{A}_j \mathbf{b}_{b1j} \\ z_{b2} \mathbf{A}_j \mathbf{b}_{b2j} \\ \dots \\ z_{bn} \mathbf{A}_j \mathbf{b}_{bnj} \end{bmatrix} \right) \qquad (j = 1, \dots, p) \qquad (10.16)$$

As mentioned earlier, an intercept term for the fundamental factor model can be incorporated by having a unit row vector in either $\mathbf{B}_{bi}$ or $\mathbf{B}_c$. When using the extended form of the model with $\mathbf{A}_j$, it will be notationally more convenient to constrain a row of $\mathbf{B}_c$ to equal a unit row vector due to the interaction of $\mathbf{A}_j$ with $\mathbf{B}_{bi}$[12]. In this case the estimates of $\mathbf{b}_{acj}$ are given by:

$$\mathbf{b}_{acj}^* = \left(\mathbf{Z}_{ac}^{*T} \boldsymbol{\Theta}_j \mathbf{Z}_{ac}^* \right)^{-1} \mathbf{Z}_{ac}^{*T} \boldsymbol{\Theta}_j \left(\mathbf{y}_j - \begin{bmatrix} z_{b1} \mathbf{A}_j \mathbf{b}_{b1j} \\ z_{b2} \mathbf{A}_j \mathbf{b}_{b2j} \\ \dots \\ z_{bn} \mathbf{A}_j \mathbf{b}_{bnj} \end{bmatrix} - z_{c1} \right) \qquad (j = 1, \dots, p)$$

$$(10.17)$$

where z_{c1} is the $(n \times 1)$ column vector corresponding to the first row of $\mathbf{b}_{cj}$ which is constrained to equal a unit row vector for all securities, $\mathbf{b}_{acj}^*$ is the $((q_a + q_c - 1) \times 1)$ vector of estimated factor sensitivities corresponding to $\mathbf{Z}_a$ and the 2nd through q_b columns of $\mathbf{Z}_c$ (e.g. the columns corresponding to the unconstrained rows of $\mathbf{b}_{cj}$), and $\mathbf{Z}_{ac}^*$ is the $(n \times (q_a + q_c - 1))$ matrix formed from $\mathbf{Z}_a$ and $\mathbf{Z}_c^*$, where $\mathbf{Z}_c^*$ represents the 'unconstrained' factors and is constructed from the 2nd through q_c columns of $\mathbf{Z}_c$, corresponding to the unconstrained factor loadings, $\mathbf{B}_c^*$.

The estimation of $\mathbf{A}_j$ requires some additional algebraic manipulation to simplify the form of the model. We assume that $\mathbf{B}_{bi}$ does *not* contain a unit row vector for an intercept term[13]. Let $vec()$ denote the operation creating an $(mk \times 1)$ column vector

---

[12] If the first row of $\mathbf{B}_{bi}$ in the extended model is set equal to a unit row vector for estimating an intercept, then an additional constraint should be placed on the first row and column of $\mathbf{A}_j$ such that $a_{1,1} = 1$ and $a_{1,k} = a_{k,1} = 0$ for $k = 2, \dots, q_b$. Without this restriction, the form of term $z_{bi} a_{j,1,1}$ is equivalent to a regular factor analysis term in $z_{ci} \mathbf{b}_{cj}$. While the model can estimate $\mathbf{A}_j$ in this case, the algorithm will tend to converge more slowly as the two forms of the 'statistical' factors are estimated in opposing steps.

[13] If an intercept is estimated, we assume it is in the form of a constraint on $\mathbf{B}_c$ containing a unit row vector as discussed above.

by stacking the columns of the $(m \times k)$ argument matrix, and $\otimes$ denote the Kronecker product operator. The elements of the $(q_b \times q_b)$ matrix A_j can now be expressed as a $(q_b^2 \times 1)$ column vector:

$$vec(\mathbf{A}_j) \equiv [a_{11j}\, a_{21j} \ldots a_{qbqbj}]^T \quad \left(q_b^2 \times 1\right) \tag{10.18}$$

Define $\mathbf{h}_{ij}$ as the $(1 \times q_b^2)$ row vector formed by the Kronecker product of $\mathbf{b}_{bij}^T$ and $\mathbf{z}_{bi}$ and $\mathbf{H}_j$ as the $(n \times q_b^2)$ matrix formed by stacking the n rows of $\mathbf{h}_{ij}, i = 1, \ldots, n$, as:

$$\mathbf{h}_{ij} \equiv \mathbf{b}_{bji}^T \otimes \mathbf{z}_{bi} \quad \left(1 \times q_b^2\right), \text{ and}$$

$$\mathbf{H}_j = \begin{bmatrix} \mathbf{h}_{1j} \\ \mathbf{h}_{2j} \\ \ldots \\ \mathbf{h}_{nj} \end{bmatrix} \quad \left(n \times q_b^2\right) \tag{10.19}$$

With the above definitions, we can now express the term:

$$\mathbf{z}_{bi}\mathbf{A}_j\mathbf{b}_{bij} = \mathbf{h}_{ij}vec(\mathbf{A}_j) \quad (1 \times 1) \tag{10.20}$$

and model (10.2) in the form:

$$\mathbf{y}_j = \mathbf{Z}_a\mathbf{b}_{bj} + \mathbf{H}_j vec(\mathbf{A}_j) + \mathbf{Z}_c\mathbf{b}_{cj} + \mathbf{e}_j \tag{10.21}$$

With this definition, the second part of the M-step conditional maximization process can be expressed as a (WLS) linear regression to estimate $\mathbf{A}_j$:

$$vec(\mathbf{A}_j) = \left(\mathbf{y}_j - \mathbf{Z}_a\mathbf{b}_{aj} - \mathbf{Z}_c\mathbf{b}_{cj}\right)^T \mathbf{\Theta}_j\mathbf{H}_j \left(\mathbf{H}_j^T\mathbf{\Theta}_j\mathbf{H}_j\right)^{-1} \tag{10.22}$$

10.8 Discussion

The construction of the economic factors, $\mathbf{Z}_a$, may be done such that they are either directly comparable to certain economic data series, and thus typically somewhat collinear, or constructed to be standardized orthogonal variates, arranged in some meaningful ordering of importance. For example, a simple three factor model comprised of a market index and two industry/sector indexes would begin with a market proxy such as the S&P 500, and then use an 'energy' index that has been designed to be orthogonal to the market index as factor 2, and finally use a 'financial' index that is orthogonal to both the market and the 'energy' series. The predicted values and estimated residual variances would of course be unchanged if the order of index construction was reversed. We assume that any issues regarding the make-up of the economic factors are addressed prior to model estimation and thus treat $cov(\mathbf{Z}_a)$ as given. Similarly, the form of $cov(\mathbf{Z}_b)$ will be determined by the methods used to construct the 'fundamental' data, $\mathbf{B}_{bi}, i = 1, \ldots, n$, and thus we also treat $cov(\mathbf{Z}_b)$ as given[14]. As a result, the covariance structure between the economic and fundamental factors, $cov(Z_{ab})$, is treated as given.

The 'statistical' factor analysis portion model, $Z_c B_c$, ($Z_c^* B_c^*$ if the first row of B_c is constrained to a unit vector), results in the usual rotational indeterminacy problems. These are compounded due to the presence of the Z_a and Z_b factors as well. A 'pure' rotation of the factors does not impact the value of the likelihood function but simply moves the parameter values to a point of equal 'altitude' on the ridge of the likelihood surface[15]. The choice of any rotational transformations is of course subject to individual interpretation. The statistical factors, Z_c, can be rotated to an orthogonal form (i.e. linearly independent of one another). In addition, the unconstrained factors, Z_c^*, can be scaled to have unit variance as well such that $cov(Z_c^*) = I$[16]. Additional constraints are required to produce a unique rotation of the factor scores[17].

Since the economic and statistical factors are multiplied by static (i.e. through time) factor loading matrices, B_a, B_c, the statistical factors can also be rotated to be orthogonal to Z_a without impacting the value of the likelihood function. Note that due to the time variation in the fundamental variable matrix, b_{bi}, it is not possible to simply orthogonalize the statistical factors, Z_c, to the fundamental factors, Z_b, without impacting the value of the likelihood function. This is due to the fact that the factor loading matrix for each variable, B_j, $(n \times q_b)$, has a different time variation 'pattern' for each variable[18]. While it is thus possible to define a unique rotation for the entire factor space, there are nonetheless an infinite number of these and thus the choice of a specific rotation and its interpretation is left to the user.

10.9   Some simulation evidence

As mentioned earlier, non-stochastic factor models have a tendency to produce estimates of zero residual variance when the number of variables, p, is small. The above models have a non-stochastic factor component and thus will also have this characteristic. A simulation data set is constructed with $n = 100, p = 50, q_a = 2, q_b = 2, q_c = 3$. The first column of Z_a is set to a unit column vector and the first row of B_c to a unit row vector. We assume a homoskedastic residual variance process (e.g. $\theta_{ij} = 1 \forall i,j$).

In the first set of simulation trials, the residual variance is scaled such that the average multiple correlation coefficient across all variables is 0.85, a high value relative to what

---

[14] It is our understanding that BARRA also performs a post-estimation process to address collinearity issues and reduce the dimensionality of the estimated fundamental factors, Z_b.

[15] The estimates of the residual variance, s, are also invariant to 'pure' rotational transformations.

[16] The unit variance of Z_c^* is of course achieved by scaling the corresponding B_c^*. Since the factor loadings for the constrained factors are defined as a unit vector, the variance of the constrained factors cannot be rescaled.

[17] A variety of methods can be used to obtain a unique rotation such as ordering by decreasing eigenvalues of the (weighted) predicted factor covariance matrix.

[18] One way to view this problem is to note that any rotation of the fundamental and statistical factors effectively transfers part of the time variation of the fundamental factors to the statistical factors and vice versa. The variation from the statistical factors is now compounded by the variation in B_j and the previous interaction effect between Z_b and B_j is now lost as the transferred variation is now multiplied by a constant B_{cj}.

might be expected using historical security returns. The initial parameter estimates of $\mathbf{B}_a$ are based on an OLS regression of $\mathbf{Y}$ on $\mathbf{Z}_a$. To test the robustness of the algorithm to the initial parameter estimates, the same simulated data set is used to estimate the model for a variety of random initial parameter estimates for the residual standard deviation, σ_j, and the unconstrained statistical factor loadings, $\mathbf{B}_c^*$. The initial values of σ_j are drawn from a uniform $(1,6)$ distribution and $\mathbf{B}_c^*$ from an $N(0,1)$ distribution. For small data sets, $p = 50$, the algorithm consistently converged to a zero estimated value of σ_j for at least one security. All else being equal, increasing the number of variables to $p = 200$ resulted in consistent convergence in 20 iterations on average to the same value of the log likelihood for all 200 trials. A unique rotation is applied as described above to the factors such that the estimated covariance structure of all the factors is identical for all trials[19].

A second simulation data set is then constructed with the residual variance scaled such that the average multiple correlation coefficient across all variables is 0.27, which is more in line with what might be expected with, say, historical weekly return data. The average number of iterations required for convergence increases to approximately 60. With $p = 200$, all trials converged to non-zero estimates of σ_j and identical values of the log likelihood and factor covariance structures. While the simulation results are of course subject to the particular simulation construction, it would seem reasonable to expect similar results with actual data for a model with a similar average multiple correlation coefficient. One caveat to note, however, is that the simulated data had homogeneous errors by design. The presence of heteroskedasticity in actual return data may present more of a problem.

We also examine the performance of the algorithm using historical daily return data on 500 stocks for 499 days. An equally weighted return index is created as the single 'economic' data series in addition to a unit vector in $\mathbf{Z}_a$. The previous day's return for each stock is used as the single 'fundamental/technical' data item, $\mathbf{B}_{bi}$. Three statistical factors, one with $\mathbf{B}_c$ constrained and two unconstrained, are also estimated. The initial estimates of the parameters are constructed as in the above simulations.

In four of the ten trials, the algorithm converged to a value of the likelihood function of 237 263.1765710403 and to a value of 237 219.4498132423 in the remaining six trials, indicating the presence of at least two local maxima of the likelihood surface. We estimated the model again using the variance estimate from the residuals of the $\mathbf{B}_a$ regressions for the initial value of the residual variance. The initial values of the unconstrained factor loadings, $\mathbf{B}_c^*$, are estimated by regressing $\mathbf{Y}$ on the first two principal components obtained from the residual covariance matrix from same $\mathbf{B}_a$ regressions. With these initial parameter values, the algorithm converges to the larger of the two values of the log likelihood function given above.

10.10 Model extensions

The assumption of non-stochastic factors results in the estimates of $\mathbf{Z}_b$ and $\mathbf{Z}_c$ being treated as parameters and thus using $n(q_b + q_c)$ degrees of freedom. The model could

---

[19] The rotation of the unconstrained statistical factors is based on the eigenvalues of the predicted factor covariance matrix, $\mathbf{B}_c^{*T} \mathbf{Z}_c^{*T} \mathbf{Z}_c^* \mathbf{B}_c^*$.

be extended to allow for a normal prior on the factors which would involve only the $q_b + q_c$ estimated means of the factor series and the estimated factor covariance parameter, R. This reduction in the size of the parameter space should reduce the tendency to estimate zero variances in small data sets as well as less of a tendency to create factors that over fit the data. The CM algorithm above would now become an ECM algorithm as described in Meng and Rubin (1993).

One of the prominent characteristics of security return data is that often some of the returns are missing, particularly when using daily data. Many approaches to estimating factor models use ad hoc procedures for dealing with missing data points. The EM algorithm can be easily adapted to account for (partially) missing returns in Y as well under certain assumptions regarding the missing data process[20].

As mentioned earlier, a characteristic of security return data is the presence of occasional 'outliers'. The above algorithms account for heteroskedastic errors when the variance scaling parameter, v_{ij}, is known *a priori*. The above algorithms can be extended simultaneously to estimate the variance scaling process under a variety of assumptions. Obviously it is not possible to estimate each v_{ij} as a parameter since the model would be underidentified. In the case of the standard time-series regression model, the assumption that the disturbances arise from, say, a two-component mixture-normal model results in an iteratively reweighted least squares (IRLS) EM algorithm of Dempster et al. (1980). A similar approach can be taken to extend the above models as well.

10.11   Conclusion

We present a combined linear factor model that incorporates all three basic factor model types, economic, fundamental, and statistical, in a single simultaneous estimation procedure. The algorithm is consistent with the general theory of EM estimation of Dempster et al. (1977) under the assumption of non-stochastic factors, but can be extended to several forms of stochastic factor models as well. Under the assumption of non-stochastic factors, the algorithm simplifies to conditional maximization algorithm. Several extensions of the model are presented, allowing for heteroskedastic errors and a separable response function for the fundamental data types. Under appropriate assumptions, the parameter estimates are maximum likelihood estimates. Simulation results show that the iterations of the algorithm result in monotonic increasing values of the log likelihood function. We find an example of at least two local maxima in the case of historical return data. While improving the initial parameter estimates results in convergence to the larger of the two values of the log likelihood function, we cannot be certain that we have in fact obtained the global maximum of the log likelihood function. We note several areas for extentions of the model.

While the above algorithm provides a theoretical framework for estimating a combined linear model, the major elements of estimating such a model will be in the construction of sound economic and fundamental data series. We would also expect

---

[20] For example, the factor estimation procedures used by EM Applications Ltd are consistent with maximum likelihood estimation under the assumption that the data are missing at random as defined by Rubin (1976).

that the inclusion of both data types will result in a significant degree of multicol-linearity in the resulting factors. Additional work would need to be done to reduce the size of the data sets to avoid issues of overfitting the data set. The estimation of the statistical factors can be controlled to avoid collinearity issues with the economic and fundamental leaving only the issue of how many additional factors to estimate. Additional research will be required to determine if the performance of the combined model exceeds each of the individual model approaches.

References

Anderson, T. W. and Rubin, H. (1956). Statistical Inference in Factor Analysis. *Berkeley Symposium* (5):111–150.

Connor, G. (1995). Three Types of Factor Models: A Comparison of their Explanatory Power. *Financial Analysts Journal*, 51 (May/June):42–46.

Connor, G. and Korajczyk, R. A. (1986). Performance Measurement with the Arbitrage Pricing Theory: A New Framework for Analysis. *Journal of Financial Economics*, 15 (March):373–394.

Dempster, A. P., Laird, N. M., and Rubin, D. B. (1977). Maximum Likelihood from Incomplete Data via the E-M Algorithm. *Journal of the Royal Statistical Society Series B*, Vol. 39:1–38.

Dempster, A. P., Laird, N. M., and Rubin, D. B. (1980). Iteratively Re Weighted Least Squares for Linear Regression when Errors are Normal/Independent Distributed. *Multivariate Analysis – V*, North-Holland Publishing.

Jöreskog, K. G. (1969). A General Approach to Confirmatory Maximum Likelihood Factor Analysis. *Psychometrika*, Vol. 34:183–202.

King, B. F. (1966). Market and Industry Factors in Stock Price Behavior. *Journal of Business*, 39, No. 1 (January):139–190.

Lawley, D. N. and Maxwell, A. E. (1971). *Factor Analysis as a Statistical Method*, Second edition. London, Butterworth.

Lawley, D. N. (1942). Further Estimation in Factor Analysis. *Proceedings of the Royal Society of Edinburgh, Series A*, Vol. 61:176–185.

Liu, C., Rubin, B. D., and Wu, Y. (1998). Parameter Expansion to Accelerate EM the PX-EM algorithm. *Biometrika*, 85:755–770.

Meng, X.-L. and Rubin, D. B. (1993). Maximum Likelihood Estimation via the ECM Algorithm: A General Framework. *Biometrika*, Vol. 80.

Roll, R. W. and Ross, S. A. (1980). An Empirical Investigation of the Arbitrage Pricing Theory. *Journal of Finance*, Vol. 35:1073–1103.

Rosenberg, B. (1974). Extra-Market Components of Covariance in Security Returns. *Journal of Financial and Quantitative Analysis*, 9 (March):263–274.

Ross, S. A. (1976). The Arbitrage Theory of Capital Asset Pricing. *Journal of Economic Theory*, 13 (December):341–360.

Rubin, D. B. (1976). Inference and Missing Data. *Biometrika*, 63:581–592.

Rubin, D. B. and Thayer, D. T. (1982). *EM* Algorithms for ML Factor Analysis. *Psychometrika*, Vol. 47:69–76.

Rubin, D. B. and Thayer, D. T. (1983). More on *EM* for ML Factor Analysis. *Psychometrika*, Vol. 48:253–257.

Stroyny, A. L. (1991). Heteroskedasticity and the Estimation of Systematic Risk. Ph.D. Dissertation, The University of Wisconsin, Madison.

Stroyny, A. L. and Rowe, D. (2002). A Re-examination of Some Popular Latent Factor Estimation Methods. Presented at the 15th Annual Investment Seminar, Cambridge, UK.

11 Attributing investment risk with a factor analytic model

*Dr T. Wilding**

Abstract

A factor analytic model has many advantages when used as a model of equity returns. However, the attribution of the raw risk statistics to familiar stock and market phenomena is not a natural by-product of the factor analytic risk model estimation process. In this chapter, we address this issue and describe several methods that can be used to translate data from factor analysis-based risk models into traditional fundamental information that can assist with portfolio management and trading. First, we develop tests to determine whether selected real world attributes indicate anything significant about risk. After we have established a useful set of attributes, we develop further methods to characterize the risk of a portfolio. Finally, we apply these methods to a variety of fundamental attributes, sectors, countries, and macroeconomic time series, in order to analyse a sample UK portfolio.

11.1 Introduction

Factor analysis based models (Stroyny (1991)) are increasingly used as models of equity returns due to their many advantages. However, results from such models can be difficult to interpret. Although factor analytic models can establish the proportion of risk due to common effects as opposed to stock-specific effects, and can rank stocks according to their marginal contribution to risk, factor analytic models are not naturally suited to characterizing the systematic bets being taken. As the factors are derived from returns data alone they do not, *a priori*, have any familiar characteristics associated with them.

Consequently, in this chapter, our goal is to produce a projection of the statistical factors on to familiar stock characteristic data so that we can answer questions such as 'What happens if we increase the portfolio's average market capitalization by buying larger stocks?' We can then project any real world attribute on to the statistical factor loadings and switch between 'real-world' and statistical factors. After a brief introduction to the advantages of factor analytic models in comparison with other approaches to investment risk model construction, this chapter discusses several issues – what sort of attributes we could consider when analysing a portfolio, whether there is a relationship between these real-world attributes and the statistical factors, and how we can make the projection. We will discuss three types of attributes – valuation attributes,

* Head of Research & Development, EM Applications Limited, St Martin's House, 16 St Martin's Le Grand, London EC1A 4EN, +44 (020) 73978395, tim.wilding@emapplications.com

categories, and sensitivity to macroeconomic time series. We will end by discussing how to use these results to analyse a real portfolio. This approach separates risk modelling from risk attribution, and that gives us the benefit of attributing risk without compromising the specification of the model used to measure risk.

11.2 The case for factor analytic models

Linear factor models assume that a multi-factor return-generating processing is responsible for securities' returns:

$$R_t = \mu + Bf_t + \varepsilon_t$$

$$E(\varepsilon) = 0$$

$$E(\varepsilon\varepsilon') = \Psi\,(diagonal)$$

In other words, the returns are a function of a security's exposure to k underlying factors and a stock-specific component. The returns (also known as factor scores) for the underlying factors are given in f, while the stock-specific returns are given by ε. Each security has a set of loadings against these factors and these are contained in the $n \times k$ matrix of factor loadings B, where n is the number of securities. Each security also has an associated average return μ. The multi-factor model is a common model for security returns, and the model is used as the starting point for the derivation of the Arbitrage Pricing Theory (Ross (1976)).

11.2.1 Types of linear factor model

In practice, there are several types of factor models that can be estimated when constructing an equity market risk model based on the Arbitrage Pricing Theory. These models vary in the assumptions they make and the techniques used for estimation. For example, fundamental models (e.g. Beckers et al. (1992)) assume that company attributes such as size and dividend yield explain the common return among securities and provide a measure of the sensitivity (B) of the securities to pervasive factors. Macroeconomic models (e.g. Chen et al. (1986)) assume that observable economic time series such as inflation can be used as measures of the pervasive factors (f) in security returns. It has often been the case that both of these models have been contrasted with 'statistical' models. We do not think 'statistical' is a helpful label since all models, including fundamental and macroeconomic models, are statistical in nature and there are significant differences between non-stochastic factor analytic models such as principal components-based models (e.g. Connor and Korajczyk (1988)) and stochastic factor analytic models. In this volume, Stroyny discusses some of the differences between stochastic and non-stochastic factor models. Non-stochastic factor models are often used to model returns without assumptions about the loadings or factors, but such techniques have no guarantees of convergence, and can produce less stable results (Krzanowski, 2000). On the other hand, stochastic factor analysis using the EM algorithm to generate a maximum likelihood solution (e.g. Stroyny (1991)) can be used to estimate factor analytic models that make minimal assumptions about either the factor loadings or scores, and are robust.

11.2.2 Estimation issues

11.2.2.1 Data

Estimation of any one of the preceding models will require the analyst to address various problems including availability of data, data quality, selection of estimation technique and model misspecification. For example, data availability and quality can be a particular problem for both macroeconomic and fundamental models. Macroeconomic time series may not be available as frequently as returns data and this may limit the selection of factors for a macroeconomic model. Similarly, good fundamental data may not be available in a form that is suitable for estimating. Typically, the fundamental attributes used are accounting data such as the price/book ratio. Accounting standards may not be comparable internationally and this will hinder the construction of an international fundamental model. One-half of a fundamental ratio is also typically updated infrequently (the other half often being the price). Factor analytic models require only stock returns data, and returns data are widely available and of good quality. As a consequence, factor analytic models are able to extract the risk factors that explain the most covariance between stock returns over the model construction period.

11.2.2.2 Misspecification

Another significant issue is model misspecification. This can take a number of forms: inclusion of insignificant factors, exclusion of significant factors, and non-linearity. Macroeconomic models require us to identify the major sources of pervasive shocks affecting security returns. If we do not identify or are unable to find frequent time-series data that represents the source of the shocks, we are likely to build a model that will be misleading when analysing security returns. Macroeconomic models further assume that securities respond linearly to macroeconomic shocks.

11.2.2.3 Linearity

Fundamental models also require us to identify attributes that are a linear measure of the sensitivity of a particular set of securities to pervasive factors. It may be very hard to find attributes that model some portion of the risk. For example, fundamental models often use binary variables to model a country effect. These binary variables indicate whether a security is a member of one country or another. However, in the case of multinational companies such as HSBC, this simple model may be wrong. It is unclear whether HSBC is American, British, or Chinese and it is almost certain that a more complicated, and potentially arbitrary, model of country membership would be required. For example, one could assign country membership on the basis of revenue, profit, staff, etc., but any choice would be subject to criticism. Even if one finds suitable attributes to model an exposure to a particular factor, the exposure may be a non-linear function of the attribute. Again, factor analytic models are robust to this scenario.

11.2.2.4   Responsiveness to change

The degree to which the chosen factors are a function of data availability and human selection may make macroeconomic and fundamental models slow to react. As new factors arise, a user would have to both identify and source suitable data for the new factor in order to add the factor to a fundamental or macroeconomic model. Many equity returns models underreported risk during 2000 as the technology stocks in the US started crashing and this may have been exacerbated by issues such as the need to identify any new factor and source any new data. Even though it may lag the appearance of a new factor, a factor analytic model will include the factor as the stock returns data become available.

11.2.2.5   Convergence

Selection of the estimation technique can also be a problem – principal components-based statistical models are not very robust estimation procedures. Grinold and Kahn (1999) characterize statistical risk factors as 'prone to discovering spurious correlations'. We argue that many of these problems are artefacts of the estimation procedure. Non-stochastic models such as principal components-based estimation procedures are usually ad hoc and give no mathematical guarantee of convergence and this, in turn, makes it difficult to compare different models estimated with different time periods. These models increase the number of parameters to be estimated significantly and this may contribute to the lack of stability of the estimated model. Often, the estimation procedures are unstable or are prone to situations such as Heywood cases, in which the model assigns an estimated residual variance of zero to a subset of securities (e.g. Krzanowski (2000)), and this would cause various problems with portfolio construction.

11.2.2.6   Summary

Factor analytic models make minimal assumptions about the factor loadings when building models and require only returns data for construction. The easy availability of good quality, high frequency data makes it simple to build weekly models or even daily models without compromising the amount of data required to reduce estimation error to an acceptable level. We favour factor analytic models because we believe that such a model is most robust to many of the typical problems encountered in constructing a model. It is worth noting that Roll and Ross (1980) originally modelled equity returns with a factor analytic model when they were testing the Arbitrage Pricing Theory.

11.3   Attributing investment risk with a factor analytic model

In this chapter, we use a variety of factor analytic models developed for different regions and countries. We estimate models with 20 factors using 200 weeks of equity returns and the EM Maximum Likelihood Factor Analysis (MLFA) algorithm (www.emapplications.com, Stroyny (1991)). The factor model for a particular country then allows us to examine portfolio risk when the holdings are changed in a particular security.

However, the factor loadings have two features that make interpretation of the factor model's results difficult. First, the loadings are unique (only) up to a rotation by a full-rank orthonormal matrix. We can rotate the factor loadings without altering any observable characteristic of the model. Second, the loadings are statistical attributes and may not obviously have a linear relationship with any real-world attribute. Clearly, we need to combine stock-level attribute data with the factor analytic model so that we can more readily interpret the results of the risk model. The approaches shown in this chapter mean that the inability to identify factors is no longer a significant problem for factor analytic models.

11.3.1   *Which attributes* can *we consider?*

Since we are trying to answer practical questions, we should focus on the attributes and time series that portfolio managers typically look at when determining how risky their portfolio is. We can separate these into three types:

- Valuation attributes – attributes of a security that can take on continuous values:
  - Size, yield, earnings surprise, momentum, growth/value, PEG, EBITDA, PriceToCashFlow, other fundamental ratios, technical indicators, debt ratios, etc.
- Category attributes – attributes of a security that may take on discrete values depending on whether a security is assigned to a particular sector:
  - Sector, country, etc.
- Sensitivity to macroeconomic time series – sensitivity of a security to time series of data that can be used as an indicator of economy-wide shocks:
  - Oil price, inflation, industry index returns, gold, credit spreads, commodities, etc.

This list is by no means comprehensive – it could be extended to encompass any metric that a fund manager might use to manage a portfolio.

For a universe of securities, a selection of attributes would give us an $n \times q$ matrix $A(a_1 \ldots a_i \ldots a_n)$ containing a row of measurable attributes for each security (for instance, column 1 contains the six-month price change and column 2 the earnings price ratio for each security). These are the 'real-world' attributes that fund managers may use to judge whether they are comfortable with the risk exposures in their portfolio.

The rest of this chapter discusses the following for each of the attribute types:

- Which attributes we should consider – determining whether a selected attribute is a significant indicator of risk.
- Attributing risk – how to use a particular attribute to determine the riskiness of your portfolio.
- Comparing risks – how to bring together and compare results from all of the attribute types when examining a particular portfolio.

For each type of attribute, we use selected examples to perform significance tests and show how to use these in constructing a risk report.

If an attribute does have an effect on the risk of a security, then we would expect the attribute to show up in the factor model as a combination of factor loadings that would correlate with the real-world attribute. We can use this to test whether attributes are significant indicators of risk. These tests vary for each of the attributes. Once we have determined whether a particular attribute is significant in determining risk, we need to determine how our exposure to the risk factors changes with the value of the attribute, and then use that to determine how the risk of a particular portfolio varies with exposure to the attributes.

We use various techniques to calculate the expected value of the factor loadings (b_j) given a certain value of the attribute $(a_i) - E(b_j|a_i)$. Given $E(b_j|a_i)$ we can use the derivatives $\partial E(b_j|a_i)/\partial a_i$ to calculate the effect of changing our average exposure to an attribute on our exposure to the underlying factors. This derivative allows us to determine what happens if we change our exposure to a particular attribute and, hence, to examine the effect of trades on a portfolio. We can calculate marginal contributions to determine the effect of changing the attributes. In other words, since we now have estimates of how the risk profile of a particular security changes with the attribute, we can predict how changes in the attribute will alter the risk of a portfolio. Since we know that some attributes may not make a significant difference to the risk profile, we also examine what effect this has on the statistics that we can generate for a portfolio.

11.4 Valuation attributes

Valuation attributes are attributes of a particular security that may take on continuous values. Quite often these attributes are based upon accounting data, for example the price-to-earnings ratio. In this chapter, we will test and use the following attributes:

- Price change – the most recent three-month price change for each security.
- Earnings/price – the most recent earnings-to-price ratio for each stock (we chose the reciprocal to prevent problems with stocks that have low or negative earnings).
- Log size – the logarithm of the market capitalization in US dollars.
- Yield – the most recent yield.
- Liquidity – the logarithm of the average daily dollar volume of the stock traded over the past six months.

11.4.1 *Which attributes* **should** *we consider?*

Before we estimate a relationship between security attributes and the factors generated by a factor analytic model, the first question is 'do any of these attributes have significant effect on risk?' Research has indicated that several of the valuation attributes have a significant impact on equity returns (e.g. Fama and French (1993, 1995)), and we show that some attributes also have a significant effect on equity risk. However, while some attributes have an impact on risk, not all of the attributes have a significant independent effect on risk.

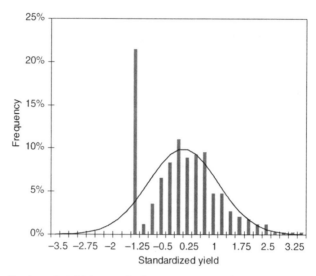

Figure 11.1 Distribution of yield for stocks from a universe of UK securities at the end of June 2003. The yield was standardized before constructing the distribution. The bars show the frequency, while the curve shows a normal distribution with the same average and standard deviation

Before we examine whether the valuation attributes really are an indicator of the factor risk, we will look at the distribution of values for each attribute. For example, Figure 11.1 shows the distribution of yield in the UK.

The distribution of attributes highlights interesting features that may cause problems if we were to use the attributes to create a fundamental risk model. Figure 11.1 shows a large grouping of zero-yield securities, and that the distribution is non-normal and asymmetric. If we use yield as a measure of exposure to a particular risk factor, it is counterintuitive to expect that zero-yield securities all have the same exposure to a yield factor as it would mean that there would be no discrimination between the group of securities that have zero yield. This will be illustrated later when we compare the attribute data with the factor loadings. An additional problem is that many of these valuation attributes are correlated and this may cause problems with the estimation of risk. For example, LogSize is often highly correlated with liquidity.

As previously mentioned, we can arbitrarily rotate the loadings from the factor analytic model by any full rank orthonormal k-by-k matrix to generate a factor model that would have the same observable characteristics. Since the factor loadings are generated purely from returns data and have no physical basis, we cannot say whether any particular rotation is correct. Therefore, we cannot simply examine the regression statistics for each loading individually to say whether a particular attribute is significant. Hence, we need to examine whether the attributes are independent of all factor loadings before we decide whether the attributes are useful for modelling variability in stock returns. The technique of canonical correlations (see appendix) allows us to test for the independence of two subsets of variables. Canonical correlation analysis finds the linear combinations of two subsets of variables that are most closely correlated. For the valuation attributes, we use canonical correlation analysis to determine whether the attributes correspond to the statistical loadings. We perform two types of canonical correlation analysis for each model.

First, we use canonical correlation analysis to compare the factor loadings with each attribute independently. In this case, canonical correlation analysis searches for the linear combination of factor loadings that is most highly correlated with the attribute, and can be used to indicate whether a particular attribute tells us anything about the risk profile of a stock. For instance, if the size attribute is negatively correlated with factor loadings then a larger stock will have a lower risk than a smaller stock.

We show two examples – the correlations for the UK attributes (Table 11.1) and the European attributes (Table 11.2). Both tables show that each of the five attributes is significantly correlated with the factor loadings from the relevant model. The correlation coefficients generated by the European model are lower than those generated by the UK model with the exception of price change, suggesting that the attributes are not as important a determinant of risk in the European model as they are in the UK model. There may be several reasons for this, but we propose that the correlations are not as high because European accounting standards are not comparable and investors from different countries value the accounting attributes differently. If one examines the

	Canonical correlation	Wilks lambda	Rao's F	Numerator degrees of freedom	Denominator degrees of freedom	Probability of F (%)	Significant at 5% level
LogSize	0.83	0.31	34.16	20	309	0.00	Yes
Yield	0.52	0.73	5.72	20	309	0.00	Yes
EarningsPrice	0.64	0.59	10.63	20	309	0.00	Yes
PriceChange	0.60	0.64	8.81	20	309	0.00	Yes
Liquidity	0.81	0.34	30.08	20	309	0.00	Yes

Table 11.1 Significance of canonical correlations for the UK model at the end of June 2003. All of the attributes are correlated with the UK factor loadings

	Canonical correlation	Wilks lambda	Rao's F	Numerator degrees of freedom	Denominator degrees of freedom	Probability of F (%)	Significant at 5% level
LogSize	0.65	0.58	17.25	20	479	0.00	Yes
Yield	0.47	0.78	6.76	20	479	0.00	Yes
EarningsPrice	0.51	0.74	8.46	20	479	0.00	Yes
PriceChange	0.75	0.43	31.59	20	479	0.00	Yes
Liquidity	0.65	0.58	17.63	20	479	0.00	Yes

Table 11.2 Significance of the attributes for the European model at the end of June 2003. All the attributes are correlated with the European loadings. However, the correlations are lower than the single country correlations

correlations of attributes such as LogSize within other individual European countries, one finds that the correlation coefficients are as high as the UK numbers and generally higher than the correlations for the European regional model. For example, the canonical correlation for LogSize in the French model is a high 0.87, while the canonical correlation for LogSize in the Europe model is 0.65. This lower correlation for the European model would again suggest that someone attempting to build international fundamental factor models may face some difficult choices about how to model any size effect. Should they just use size as the factor or should they choose relative size within country?

Second, we use canonical correlation analysis to compare the factor loadings with all of the attributes together. In this case canonical correlation analysis searches for the linear combination of attributes that generates the highest correlation coefficient with a linear combination of factor loadings. This second analysis shows whether each of the attributes indicates something different about the risk profile, or whether two attributes are really giving us the same information. For instance, since size and liquidity are usually highly correlated, we might expect that these attributes are telling us about the same dimension of risk for a particular stock, that is, the 'bigness' or otherwise of a particular stock. In this case, although we may find that the attributes are individually significantly correlated with the factor loadings, less than five canonical variates are correlated with the factor loadings. This implies that there are only four independent attributes.

For both of these analyses, we examine the test statistic developed in Wilks (1935) to determine whether two subsets of variables are independent – Wilks' lambda. The value of Rao's F corresponding to these tests, the numerator and denominator degrees of freedom of F, and the significance level of F are computed as in Rao (1973). In many cases we do find a statistically significant correlation between the factor loadings and the attribute. However, it is important to distinguish between statistically significant and practically significant. Even when we do find that all of the attributes generate significant information about the factor profile, the lowest correlation coefficient generated by the canonical correlation analysis with all of the attributes is sometimes very low (for example, 0.12 for EarningsPrice in the USA model). Although numbers as low as these are statistically significant correlations in larger markets, they are not practically significant or useful if we wish to determine how our risk changes with different values for the attribute. Low figures almost certainly show that the attribute has very little practical effect on the factor profile indeed and is not much use in determining the risk of a portfolio when compared with the statistical factors.

For the purpose of analysis, we have assumed that the relationship between the factor loadings and the valuation attributes is linear, although recent research suggests this may not be the case. Connor (2000) investigated using piecewise linear functions of attributes such as size as estimates of a security's risk exposure. Although it would be possible to extend this technique to cover non-linear relationships between the factor loadings and the attribute, we use the simpler model for this analysis.

In order to determine whether non-linear relationships between the attributes and the factors may be important, we examined graphs of the relationship between a valuation attribute and the linear combination of the factor loadings that is most highly correlated with it. Figure 11.2 was constructed for the UK model and shows the relationship between the loading on the compound factor and the Yield valuation

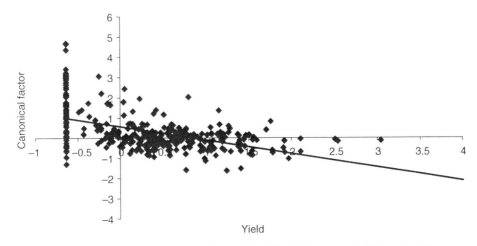

Figure 11.2 Relationship between standardized yield and the canonical factor loading most correlated with it for the UK model at the end of June 2003. Note the large grouping of zero-yield securities to the left of the chart

	Canonical correlation	Wilks lambda	Rao's F	Numerator degrees of freedom	Denominator degrees of freedom	Probability of F (%)	Significant at 5% level
Canon 1	0.86	0.08	9.83	100	1492.61	0.00	Yes
Canon 2	0.70	0.33	5.18	76	1207.74	0.00	Yes
Canon 3	0.46	0.64	2.73	54	915.56	0.00	Yes
Canon 4	0.36	0.82	1.94	34	616.00	0.13	Yes
Canon 5	0.26	0.93	1.34	16	309.00	16.93	No

Coefficients	Canon 1	Canon 2	Canon 3	Canon 4	Canon 5
LogSize	0.887	−1.549	0.095	3.575	−1.174
Yield	0.244	0.018	0.445	−0.363	−0.867
EarningsPrice	0.173	−0.313	0.586	−0.366	0.894
PriceChange	−0.063	0.555	0.637	0.587	0.264
Liquidity	−0.074	1.985	−0.553	−3.236	1.205

Table 11.3 Showing the canonical correlations for the UK model. Here we show the correlations for the linear combination of attributes that most closely corresponds to the factor loadings. The linear combinations are in the bottom half of the table, while the correlation coefficients are in the top half. There are only four significant canonical attributes even though each of the attributes was independently correlated with risk (Table 11.1)

	Canonical correlation	Wilks lambda	Rao's F	Numerator degrees of freedom	Denominator degrees of freedom	Probability of F (%)	Significant a 5% level
Canon 1	0.78	0.12	12.42	100	2321.96	0.00	Yes
Canon 2	0.66	0.32	8.40	76	1877.38	0.00	Yes
Canon 3	0.54	0.56	5.67	54	1422.09	0.00	Yes
Canon 4	0.42	0.80	3.41	34	956.00	0.00	Yes
Canon 5	0.18	0.97	1.06	16	479.00	39.25	No

Coefficients	Canon 1	Canon 2	Canon 3	Canon 4	Canon 5
LogSize	0.007	0.689	−0.234	−1.184	0.192
Yield	−0.013	0.183	0.594	−0.218	−0.827
EarningsPrice	−0.181	0.111	0.609	0.078	0.845
PriceChange	0.837	−0.292	0.351	−0.380	0.190
Liquidity	0.308	0.319	0.051	1.366	−0.014

Table 11.4 Showing the canonical correlations for the European model. The top table shows the correlation between each of the canonical variables. The lower table shows the linear combinations used to construct the canonical variables. As in the UK model, we find that only four of the attributes are significant for determining the factors. We also find that the canonical correlations are lower for the European model than for the UK model

attribute. Figure 11.2 illustrates some of the issues a model builder would face trying to use Yield as a factor. The left of the chart shows a large grouping of zero-yield securities that have significantly different exposures to risk, while for the rest of the securities there is an apparently linear relationship between yield and risk. This would suggest that using yield in a fundamental model would not provide a complete picture of the risk.

11.4.2 Attributing risk with valuation attributes

In order to determine the expected value of the factor loadings given a valuation attribute, we assume the following linear model for security factor loadings:

$$E(b_j|a_i) = c_{ij}a_i + u_{ij}$$

where c_{ij} is the rate of change of the loading with the attribute, a_i is the value of the attribute, and $u_{ij}j$ is a constant term. In other words the factor loadings for security i against factor j are a linear function of the attribute for that security. The coefficients of this model allow us to use the valuation attributes almost as if they were exposures to underlying risk factors. We can make a direct comparison between our factor analytic model and models such as that of Beckers et al. (1992) in which the attributes are assumed to be the exposure to an underlying risk. Obviously, this simple model of how our factor loadings vary with exposure to the attribute could be extended and we could look at the factor loadings as a function of all of the attributes. However, that can cause significant problems with the interpretation of the results explained later.

We estimate the coefficients c_{ij} using a universe restricted to the securities which have a sufficiently liquid returns history. We standardize the attribute by subtracting the average and dividing the result by the standard deviation of this restricted universe. Standardizing the attribute ensures a common scale across each of the different attributes, so we can more readily compare earnings price with the log size, for example. Finally, we use robust regression techniques on this restricted universe of securities to estimate the coefficients of the relationship between the valuation attribute and the factor loading. We perform a cross-sectional regression for each factor loading in which we assume each factor loading is the dependent variable and the valuation attribute is the independent variable.

We can now use this linear model to determine what we would expect our risk to be at various levels of the attribute. The linear model also allows us to examine the marginal effect of changing our exposure to an attribute for a particular portfolio. For the valuation attribute, we are interested in how the tracking error changes with the value of the attribute. Therefore, we can simply replace the $\partial b_j / \partial a_i$ by the values c_{ij} calculated previously to give us the following formula:

Marginal contribution to tracking error due to an increase in exposure to attribute

$$i = \frac{\partial \sigma}{\partial a_i} = \frac{1}{\sigma} \sum b_j c_{ij}$$

We can now answer 'What happens to my tracking error if I increase my exposure to the log-size attribute?'

Since we have seen that some attributes do not influence the risk of a particular security, these sorts of attributes may generate spurious results. If we think that the risk profile does not alter with changes in a particular attribute, we will find that the estimated c_{ij} are not significantly different from zero. In other words, a change in this attribute does not contribute much to a change in the risk profile. If this were the case, then we would intuitively expect that changing our exposure to this attribute should not change our risk significantly. If we examine the formula for calculating the risk exposure, we see that in this situation it will generate a marginal value of zero for the effect of changing our exposure to the attribute. Hence, if we see a zero marginal contribution for a particular attribute, then either the attribute is not a significant source of risk, or the portfolio is not underexposed or overexposed to that attribute.

11.5 Category attributes

Category attributes are attributes of a particular security that may take on discrete values depending on whether a security is assigned to a particular sector. For instance, a security may be assigned to one of several sectors or one of several countries. In this

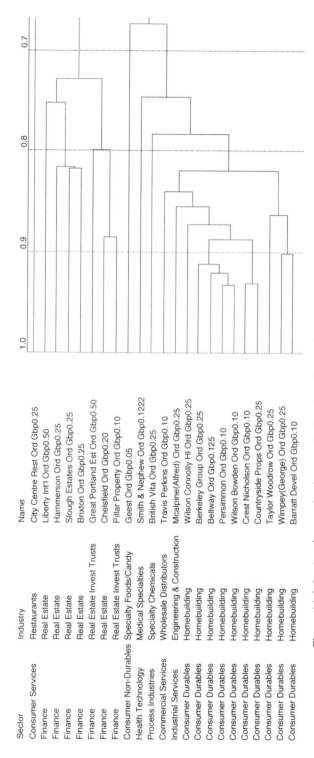

Sector	Industry	Name
Consumer Services	Restaurants	City Centre Rest Ord Gbp0.25
Finance	Real Estate	Liberty Int'l Ord Gbp0.50
Finance	Real Estate	Hammerson Ord Gbp0.25
Finance	Real Estate	Slough Estates Ord Gbp0.25
Finance	Real Estate	Brixton Ord Gbp0.25
Finance	Real Estate Invest Trusts	Great Portland Est Ord Gbp0.50
Finance	Real Estate	Chelsfield Ord Gbp0.20
Finance	Real Estate Invest Trusts	Pillar Property Ord Gbp0.10
Consumer Non-Durables	Specialty Foods/Candy	Geest Ord Gbp0.05
Health Technology	Medical Specialties	Smith & Nephew Ord Gbp0.1222
Process Industries	Specialty Chemicals	British Vita Ord Gbp0.25
Commercial Services	Wholesale Distributors	Travis Perkins Ord Gbp0.10
Industrial Services	Engineering & Construction	Mcalpine(Alfred) Ord Gbp0.25
Consumer Durables	Homebuilding	Wilson Connolly Hl Ord Gbp0.25
Consumer Durables	Homebuilding	Berkeley Group Ord Gbp0.25
Consumer Durables	Homebuilding	Bellway Ord Gbp0.125
Consumer Durables	Homebuilding	Persimmon Ord Gbp0.10
Consumer Durables	Homebuilding	Wilson Bowden Ord Gbp0.10
Consumer Durables	Homebuilding	Crest Nicholson Ord Gbp0.10
Consumer Durables	Homebuilding	Countryside Props Ord Gbp0.25
Consumer Durables	Homebuilding	Taylor Woodrow Ord Gbp0.25
Consumer Durables	Homebuilding	Wimpey(George) Ord Gbp0.25
Consumer Durables	Homebuilding	Barratt Devel Ord Gbp0.10

Figure 11.3 Section from a dendrogram built using the UK factor model as of the end of June 2003. The dendrogram shows that stocks are mainly clustered by sector and industry

chapter, we will test and use two types of categories:

- Sectors – we use standardized sectors.
- Countries.

11.5.1 *Which categories* should *we consider?*

For the category attributes, we use various tests to determine whether the sectors or countries tell us about risk. For example, we can look at dendrograms constructed from the factor loadings to see whether sectors and countries are clustered together on the dendrogram (Figure. 11.3). See the appendix for details on the construction of dendrograms.

We further examined the category attributes to see whether the loadings for a particular category were significantly different from another category (for example, for countries we asked the question 'Are the loadings of British securities different from American securities?'). We use a multivariate analysis of variance (Krzanowski (2000)) to test whether different sectors have different factor loadings. We again use Wilks lambda as a test statistic (Wilks (1935)), and convert the value to an approximate F value to test whether the differences between categories are significant. Table 11.5 shows that there are significant differences between the factor loadings for the UK sectors in the UK model, while Table 11.6 shows that there are significant differences between the European countries in the European model, confirming our initial intuitions that sectors and countries are good indicators of risk.

	Degrees of freedom	Wilks lambda	Approx F	Numerator degrees of freedom	Denominator degrees of freedom	PR($>F$)
Sectors	17	0.069	4.07	340	6071	<1E-10
Residuals	482					

Table 11.5 Significance test for sectors in the UK model. Sector provides a highly significant differentiator of risk for different securities in the UK model

	Degrees of freedom	Wilks lambda	Approx F	Numerator degrees of freedom	Denominator degrees of freedom	PR($>F$)
Countries	19	0.002	20.68	380	13 341	<1E-10
Residuals	980					

Table 11.6 Significance test for countries in the European model. Country provides a highly significant differentiator of risk for different securities in the European model

11.5.2 Attributing risk with categories

To determine the expected value of the factor loadings given a category, we assume that each different category has a different set of expected factor loadings associated with it. For instance, British securities are typically exposed to a different set of factors than American securities and would have a different factor profile. We need to estimate

$$E(b_j|d) = c_{dj}$$

where d is a particular value that the category can take.

In this case, our exposure to risk is a linear function of the weight of the portfolio in a particular category allowing us to interpret our risk as a function of the weight of the portfolio in an industry or a country. We estimate the valuation risk coefficients using the weighted average of the factor loadings for each security in each category in a restricted universe of 10 000 securities. We weight the average by the market capitalization of the security in US dollars. This has considerable intuitive appeal, because it gives us the factor loadings of a cap-weighted portfolio of securities within a particular category. For instance, if we were looking at countries, we would construct the cap-weighted portfolio of securities in the UK and calculate the factor loadings of that portfolio. Questions about changing the risk exposure of a portfolio correspond to asking what would happen to risk if we bought or sold a cap-weighted basket of securities from a particular sector.

For the category attribute, we are interested in how the tracking error changes with the holdings we have in any particular category. Therefore, we can simply replace the $\partial b_j/\partial a_i$ by the values c_{dj} calculated for the sector and country loadings to give us the following formula:

Marginal contribution to tracking error due to an increase in holdings in category

$$d = \frac{\partial \sigma}{\partial x_d} = \frac{1}{\sigma} \sum b_j c_{dj}$$

where x_d is the active weight in category value d. Since the c_{dj} are the loadings of a cap-weighted portfolio in category d, we are calculating the effect of adding this cap-weighted portfolio to our portfolio at the margin. We can now answer 'What happens to my tracking error if I increase my holdings in the telecommunications sector?'

If we think that a particular category does not have a significant difference in risk profile, we will find that the weighted average of the factor loadings for a security in that sector will not be significantly different from a size-weighted average of the factor loadings. In most cases, a size-weighted average of the factor loadings should be representative of the market. Hence, we can say that the marginal contribution of a category to the portfolio will be the same as the marginal contribution of a cap-weighted basket of stocks. This is a sensible result to generate if the factor loadings are not significantly different from that of the market.

11.6   Sensitivities to macroeconomic time series

Macroeconomic series are time series of data that can be used as an indicator of economy-wide shocks. We will test and use the following time series in the UK model:

■ The UK FTSE Oil and Gas index.
■ The UK FTSE Real Estate index.

11.6.1   *Which time series* should *we consider?*

It is possible to judge the significance of macroeconomic time series by looking at how much of the time-series returns are explained by the factor loadings – the R-squared. The R-squared can be calculated by regressing the security returns on the factor scores for a particular model. For example, if we choose to look at the UK FTSE Real Estate index and the UK FTSE Oil and Gas index (Table 11.7), we can regress their returns against the factor scores for the UK, Europe, and world models. The significance of the R-squared depends on the number of time periods used for the regression and can be judged using traditional significance tests for regression statistics.

For the macroeconomic series, we can use the factor model to calculate how sensitive equities are to the selected macroeconomic series. We can calculate a beta between any equity in the model and the macroeconomic factor, and this beta tells us the expected returns of our security conditional on the value of the macroeconomic factor. We can use these derived betas to manage a portfolio's sensitivity to a particular microeconomic factor.

11.6.2   *Attributing risk with macroeconomic time series*

Estimating risk coefficients is a simple extension of the test for significance. The risk coefficients are simply the factor loadings for the index against each of the factors calculated by regression. These loadings can be used to work out the correlation of every stock with the macroeconomic time series and the sensitivity of stocks' returns to the macroeconomic time series. Although this approach appears to produce results

Name	UK (%)	Europe (%)	World (%)
UK FTSE Real Estate	77.1	66.9	59.2
UK FTSE Oil & Gas	71.9	65.1	61.8

Table 11.7 R-squareds for two indices used as macroeconomic time series in the UK, Europe, and world model illustrating that both indices are fairly good representations of factors in the UK.

The R-squared indicates how much of the index returns are explained by the factor models and allows one to assess whether the indices are a good representation of particular factors. Since we used 200 time periods, the R-squareds are highly significant

that are very similar to a model constructed from macroeconomic time series, it must be remembered that this is a separate process from constructing the risk model and thus removes several possible sources of bias that might appear if we were using a macroeconomic series as a model of risk.

Here, we are interested in how the tracking error changes with the sensitivity of the portfolio to the time series. We use a beta as the measure of sensitivity of the portfolio to the macroeconomic time series. The marginal calculation is then simply:

Marginal contribution to tracking error due to an increase in the exposure to the macroeconomic time series $\dfrac{\partial \sigma}{\partial \beta_d} = \dfrac{1}{\sigma} \sum b_j c_{dj}$

where β_d is the sensitivity to the macroeconomic time series. The c_{dj} are the loadings of the macroeconomic time series d. The marginal contribution calculates the effect of adding this time series to our portfolio at the margin. We now have the answer to 'What happens to my tracking error if I increase my exposure to the oil price?'

11.7   Reporting risk – relative marginals

We have shown how to calculate marginal contributions – the effect of changing attribute values on risk. Unfortunately, calculating marginal contributions to risk for the various attributes does not make it easy to compare the risks of the category attributes with those of the valuation attributes or the sensitivities to macroeconomic time series, because it is not possible to make a direct comparison between a small percentage change in a sector with the change in an attribute. In order to compare risks, we switch to the concept of the relative marginal (Grinold and Kahn (1999)):

Relative Marginal Contribution to Active Risk = $RMCAR = \dfrac{x}{\sigma}\dfrac{\partial \sigma}{\partial x}$ = Percentage Change in Tracking Error for Each Small Percentage Change in Exposure to the Attribute x

This relative marginal contribution is often more useful than the actual marginal contribution, since it allows us to compare marginals between continuous attributes and discrete attributes. For example, it is difficult to compare a marginal contribution for a yield factor with a marginal contribution for a sector weight. Users of marginal calculations must ask how equivalent a 0.001 change in yield is to a 0.1% (absolute) change in the sector weight. Although both of these changes can be interpreted as adding marginal amounts of specially constructed portfolios, those portfolios are obscure and do not necessarily shed light on the investment process. Instead, the relative marginal allows a 'simple' direct comparison; if I make a 1% change in the exposure to the yield factor it corresponds to a 1% (relative) change in the sector weight, allowing the user to rank the importance of the valuation factors, the sector factors, and the macroeconomic time series. The relative marginal can also be interpreted as an estimate of the amount the tracking error would be reduced by if the bet on a particular attribute were removed completely.

For a particular attribute, we can see that the size of a relative marginal is determined by the riskiness of the position and the correlation of the attribute with the risks already in the portfolio:

$$RMCAR = \frac{c_x b}{bb + \Psi} = \rho x \frac{\sigma_x}{\sigma}$$

where:

b is the active portfolio's exposure to a particular factor
Ψ is the residual risk of the portfolio
c_x is the rate of change of the factor loadings with exposure to attribute x (see earlier sections for a discussion of the calculation)
ρ is the correlation of the attribute factor loadings with the active risk of the portfolio.

The above approach shows us how to calculate a relative marginal, but what does it mean if the Technology Services sector is 39% of the portfolio risk? Let us assume the active weight of the Technology Services sector is 10%, and the tracking error is 8%. If we make a small change in the Technology Services weight to 10.1% by purchasing a cap-weighted portfolio of the securities in the Technology Services sector funded with cash, then the percentage change in the tracking error will be $(0.1\%/10\%) \times 39\% = 0.39\%$. In other words, the change in tracking error would be 0.39% of 8% = 0.05%, and the final tracking error would be 8.05%.

If we had used these attributes to build a fundamental model, we could calculate relative marginals for each of the attributes from the model parameters and determine the sum of the relative marginals. It is a standard result that the sum of the relative marginals across all attributes would be 100% for such a fundamental model. This feature of a fundamental model is apparently quite attractive since it allows users of fundamental models to discuss 'the percentage of risk attributable to a particular attribute'. However, it should be stressed that the interpretation of those relative marginals becomes complex. When we consider one of the attributes in such a fundamental model, we must consider the purchase of that attribute in isolation. It can be difficult to conceptualize what it means to purchase one attribute in isolation when considering all of the possible attributes that make up the model. For example, when considering the effect of LogSize on a portfolio, we would have to consider the effect of increasing LogSize while keeping all other model attributes such as sector weightings constant, and this does not result in an obvious investable portfolio.

The interpretation of relative marginals for fundamental models shows that the set of relative marginals can be interpreted as risk decomposition because we can sum this number across various attributes and arrive at the proportion of risk due to each of the attributes in the situation where the attributes span the factor space. Practically, it is unlikely that the attributes represent all of the factors, and may overrepresent one underlying factor, or underrepresent another factor. We bundle this into another term that represents the exposure to the remainder of the statistical factors. In most cases, this will be negative. When creating a report, we would typically select the top exposures from each type – top attributes, top sectors, etc. By selecting the top exposures, we are focusing on the sectors that do a good job of representing the active risk and ignoring those that underrepresent the factor risk and we end up with a negative number.

In fact, the fundamental risk attribution corresponds to a more complex model for attributing the risks of a portfolio. In the previous section, we have used results from single regressions performed with the loadings against a single attribute. However, we could have used multiple regression to determine how the loadings change with changes in all of the attributes at once rather than separately. In other words, instead of determining $E(b_j|a_i)$, we determine $E(b_j|a)$ and account for changes in all of the attributes at once. If multiple regression were used to determine the risk attribution, it would diminish problems with overrepresentation of the statistical factors. Fund managers would be able to use the results from the multiple regression to see how much of the statistical risk they have explained with their selection of attributes, and, in turn, highlight where their selection of attributes has performed poorly as a guide to the risk in the manager's portfolio.

However, using multiple regression introduces two problems. First, it would make interpretation of risk attributions difficult. Using single regression allows the fund manager to think about the effect of changing an attribute on their portfolio. When a fund manager actually does attempt to change an attribute, the fund manager is likely to change other attributes, but the results from the multiple regression force the manager to consider the effect of changing only one attribute while holding all other attributes constant. In a real example, the manager has to consider with multiple regression what happens if he increases his exposure to a particular sector in his portfolio, but does not alter his exposure to any other sectors, countries or attributes. This requires the manager to consider the purchase of a specially constructed sector portfolio with no exposures to the other attributes under consideration. It seems unlikely that this is what a fund manager has in mind when they consider the effect of changing sector exposure on the risk of their portfolio. Second, managers are typically uncertain which attributes to consider. For example, suppose the manager has two selections of attributes under consideration, and both selections contain the LogSize attribute. A report on the relative marginal contribution based on multiple regression could return very different results for the LogSize attribute depending on the selection of attributes, particularly if that selection of attributes contains variables that are closely correlated with LogSize such as liquidity.

11.7.1 Case study: Analysis of a UK portfolio

Now we have all of the details of the calculations, we can look at an analysis of a typical UK portfolio. The portfolio is a cap-weighted basket of the top 50 UK securities. We are comparing the portfolio to a benchmark consisting of a cap-weighted basket of the top 500 UK securities. Figure 11.4 shows the results of the portfolio analysis for the selected sectors, attributes, and time series. The results show that the largest bet of the portfolio is on LogSize (the natural logarithm of the market cap), which was expected because the portfolio has a high bias towards the larger, more liquid securities. Figure 11.4 also shows a bet on liquidity. If the portfolio manager chooses to cut his size risk, it is likely that he will also cut his liquidity risk. For sectors, the

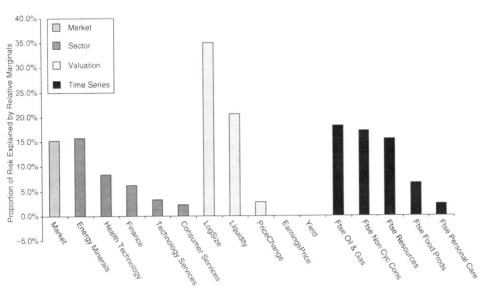

Figure 11.4 Chart of the relative marginals for a UK cap-weighted portfolio

portfolio has an overexposure to the oil and gas industries. The portfolio shows this in both the sector and the time series portion of the chart. In the time series portion we see that the FTSE Oil and Gas index has the largest relative marginal. Meanwhile, in the sector portion we see that the Energy Minerals sector is the largest contributor to the overall risk. This bet on the oil industry also shows up in the high exposure to the FTSE Oil and Gas index.

In order to check the stability of this risk decomposition we examined the portfolio's risk in a factor model constructed as of the end of the 1st Quarter 2003 as well. We found the results to be little different from the chart shown in Figure 11.4. Although this is not a totally rigorous test, it does suggest that the results are stable and can be used to gain real insight into a portfolio.

11.8 Conclusion

This chapter has shown several useful methods for analysing portfolio risk using factor analytic models. These methods can provide valuable insight into portfolio risks and allow managers to decide what trades to make without sacrificing the robustness of a factor analytic model. In effect, it allows risk managers to separate their processes into two steps – risk measurement and risk attribution. As we have shown, this gives significant advantages. Risk managers can avoid the problem statistical models are perceived to have in determining sources of risk in their portfolio. Users of the model can also be flexible in choosing how to attribute risk, and can test the significance of the selected attributes. Finally, the requirement for risk attribution no longer causes problems for the risk measurement by forcing unnecessary specifications on the risk model.

References

Beckers, S., Grinold, R., Rudd, A. and Stefek, D. (1992). *Journal of Banking and Finance*, Vol. 16, No. 1:75–96.

Chen, N. F., Roll, R. and Ross, S. A. (1986). *Journal of Business*, Vol. 59, No. 3: 383–404.

Connor, G. and Korajczyk, R. A. (1988). *Journal of Financial Economics*, Vol. 21, No. 2:255–289.

Connor, G. (2000). Semiparametric Estimation of a Characteristic-Based Factor Model of Stock Returns. LSE Working Paper (http://fmg.lse.ac.uk/publications).

Fama, E. and French, K. (1993). *Journal of Financial Economics*, Vol. 33:3–56.

Fama, E. and French, K. (1995). *Journal of Finance*, Vol. 50:131–155.

Grinold, R. and Kahn, R. (1999). *Active Portfolio Management*. McGraw-Hill.

Krzanowski, W. J. (2000). *Principles of Multivariate Analysis*. Oxford University Press.

Lehman, B. and Modest, D. A. (1988). *Journal of Financial Economics*, Vol. 21, No. 2:213–254.

Rao, C. R. (1973). *Linear Statistical Inference and its Applications*. John Wiley and Sons, Inc.

Roll, R. and Ross, S. A. (1980). *Journal of Finance*, Vol. 35, No. 5:1073–1103.

Ross, S. A. (1976). *Journal of Economic Theory*, Vol. 13:341–360.

Stroyny, A. (1991). Heteroskedasticity and the Estimation of Systematic Risk, Ph.D. Dissertation, University of Wisconsin-Milwaukee.

Wilks, S. S. (1935). *Econometrica*, Vol. 3:309–326.

Appendix

Constructing dendrograms

You will find discussions on how to construct dendrograms in a standard statistical textbook such as Krzanowski (2000). For our example, the dendrogram is constructed using the complete linkage method and the pairs score as the measure of similarity. The pairs score is a correlation coefficient constructed from the factor model ignoring stock-specific variance. If the factor loadings of a particular security are thought of as locating a security in a 20-dimensional space, then the pairs score can be thought of as the cosine of the angle between the two sets of loadings. Dendrograms were constructed as follows:

Step 1 – We first construct a dissimilarity matrix. The dissimilarity is the reciprocal of the pairs score – the correlation due to the factor scores alone. Set k, the number of clusters, to 1.

Step 2 – The distance/dissimilarity matrix is searched to find the two closest clusters, and those clusters are merged to form a new cluster, numbered $n + k$. The cluster numbers of the two clusters joined at this stage are saved, and the distance measure between the two clusters is stored. The 'Complete Linkage' method sets the distance between the new cluster and any existing cluster to be the maximum distance between either of the new cluster members and the existing cluster member.

Step 3 – Set $k = k + 1$. If $k < n$, go to Step 2.

It is often observed that the complete linkage method leads to 'spherical clusters' of high affinity (as opposed to single link which leads to long clusters often containing quite dissimilar members). We chose the complete-linkage method to avoid clusters with very dissimilar members.

Canonical correlations

The method of canonical correlations and full details of all of the tests used in the text can be found in a standard statistical textbook such as Krzanowski (2000). Canonical correlation is used when variables can be separated into two groups. The technique develops a measure of the association between the two groups of variables. Canonical correlation analysis finds the linear combination of variables from the first group that has the highest correlation with a linear combination of the variables from the second group. In our case, we find the linear combination of factor loadings that is most correlated with the linear combination of valuation attributes. The linear combination of a particular group of variables is known as a canonical variable. After finding this first linear combination or canonical variable, canonical correlation analysis then proceeds to extract the next most highly correlated linear combinations of the two sets of variables while keeping the new canonical variables orthogonal to the original canonical variables. In other words, we find linear transforms of the two sets of original variables such that the correlation matrix is as follows:

$$
\begin{pmatrix}
1 & 0 & 0 & \cdots & R_1 & 0 & 0 \\
0 & 1 & 0 & \cdots & 0 & R_2 & 0 \\
0 & 0 & 1 & \cdots & 0 & 0 & \ddots \\
\vdots & \vdots & \vdots & \ddots & & & \\
R_1 & 0 & 0 & & 1 & 0 & 0 \\
0 & R_2 & 0 & & 0 & 1 & 0 \\
0 & 0 & \ddots & & 0 & 0 & \ddots
\end{pmatrix}
$$

We standardize the valuation attributes before performing the canonical correlation analysis. Standardizing allows us to interpret the results more easily since all attributes should now be on the same scale. In particular, standardizing allows us to determine how important a particular variable is in determining the canonical variable by looking at absolute magnitude of its coefficient. For our purposes, we have performed canonical correlations in two ways – on an attribute-by-attribute basis, and using all attributes together.

12 Making covariance-based portfolio risk models sensitive to the rate at which markets reflect new information

Dan diBartolomeo and Sandy Warrick, CFA[†]

Abstract

Multiple factor models of security covariance have been widely adopted by investment practitioners as a means to forecast the volatility of portfolios. In that such models arise from the tradition of Markowitz's Modern Portfolio Theory, they have generally been based on a single period assumption, where future risk levels are presumed not to vary over time. In reality, risk levels do vary substantially and modifications of the underlying assumptions of multiple factor covariance models must change to reflect this fact. This chapter reviews the way new information is absorbed by financial markets and contributes a model of how such information can be reflected more efficiently in estimates of future covariance, through the inclusion of implied volatility information. We conclude with an empirical example regarding market conditions before and after the events of September 11, 2001. Not only does this example illustrate the value of including implied volatility as a component to covariance forecasts, but also suggests that some market participants may have acted in anticipation of the tragedies.

12.1 Introduction

Multiple factor models of security covariance have been widely adopted by investment practitioners as a means to forecast the volatility of portfolios. In that such models arise from the tradition of Markowitz's Modern Portfolio Theory (1952), they have generally been based on a single period assumption, where future risk levels are presumed not to vary over time. In reality, risk levels do vary substantially and modifications of the underlying assumptions of multiple factor covariance models must change to reflect this fact. This chapter reviews the way new information is absorbed by financial markets, and how such information can be reflected more efficiently in estimates of future covariance through the inclusion of implied volatility information.

To the extent that levels of risk within an investment market do vary over time, such changes are due to the arrival of new information. Such new information being absorbed by market participants can be categorized into two types: 'news'

[*] Northfield Information Services, Inc.
[†] Northeastern University.

that is wholly unanticipated, and 'announcements' that are anticipated with respect to time but not with respect to content. Conditional heteroskedasticity models (ARCH, GARCH, etc.), as pioneered by Engle and Bollerslev (1986) are often used to model changes in volatility levels. However, we argue that to capture properly the dynamics of announcement data in covariance models, methods incorporating data on implied volatility are necessary, and that use of implied volatility data is also the preferred approach to reflecting properly wholly unanticipated news in such models.

One practitioner model of equity security covariance incorporating implied volatility information has been commercially available for a few years. The model has been used by numerous hedge funds since 1999. We present the estimation process for this model as an example of how such incorporation is possible, and to highlight some of the related difficulties.

Finally, we will turn to an empirical example. We will illustrate how quickly the model was able to adapt to the changes in the apparent risk levels of various US stock market sectors connected with the tragic events of September 11, 2001. A surprising aspect of this example is the emergence of data suggesting that some market participants may have acted in anticipation of these tragedies.

We conclude that both a growing body of finance literature and the practitioner experience support the usage of implied volatility information in the estimation of future portfolio risk levels.

12.2   Review

The most widely known common factor model of security covariance is the single index model. The Capital Asset Pricing Model developed by William Sharpe (1964) is a special case of the single index model. In the usual implementation of the single index model, the common factor is the excess return over the risk-free rate on a portfolio consisting of the entire equity market. Typically, time-series regression analysis is used to estimate the relationship between the returns on a particular stock and the market return factor. The resultant measure of systematic (pervasive) risk is called β (beta).

The CAPM is a special case of the index model, where we make the additional assumption that higher long-term returns may be expected from stocks with higher levels of β (more systematic risk). It should be noted that while there has been much controversy in recent years in the effectiveness of the CAPM (see Grinold (1993)) as a predictor of expected returns, little if any of the criticism of the CAPM has been directed to the use of β as a measure of risk for well-diversified portfolios. Many studies such as Petingill et al. (1995) have confirmed the effectiveness of β as a means of risk prediction.

Models with multiple common factors are currently the most popular mechanisms for predicting equity risk. The use of multiple factor models arises from the belief that, while a single factor may describe a large portion of the common aspects of security returns, many other factors may influence some important subset of the universe of equities without having any influence on all securities. As an example, it might seem obvious that the variances and correlation of returns of two gold mining stocks would be influenced by the changes in the price of gold, as well as changes in broad economic conditions that are presumed to affect returns of equity securities in general.

Three types of multiple factor covariance models are currently popular. The first is an exogenous factor model, where the common factors are typically macroeconomic state variables such as interest rates, levels of production, inflation, and energy costs. In essence, each stock is presumed to have several βs, each with respect to a particular aspect of the economy. If two securities (or portfolios) produce similar returns in response to shifts in the prescribed economic variables, they are presumed to be similar. While the changes in the economic variables may be readily observed, the sensitivity of individual stocks to those changes must be statistically inferred. The β values are usually estimated using time-series regression analysis, as in the case of the single index model. As in all factor models, security return variations not explainable through the common factor structure are presumed to be security specific and pair-wise uncorrelated.

Proponents of specified macroeconomic factor models point out that such models typically exhibit stable behavior because they are tied to the real economy through genuinely pervasive factors, as discussed in Chen et al. (1986). They also provide the opportunity for portfolio managers to gain a new level of insight into top-down economic effects on their portfolios and allow them to forecast likely performance under different scenario forecasts. The primary criticism of models with exogenously specified factors is that they cannot readily capture risks that are not part of the economic state. For example, such a model would not capture the product liability risks of tobacco companies.

The second (and most widely used) type of covariance model uses observable security characteristics as proxies for factors of commonality. Such proxy factors might include stock fundamentals, such as the price/earnings ratio, dividend yield, market capitalization, balance sheet leverage, and industry participation. Repeated cross-sectional regression analyses are usually used to estimate the returns to the factors in such models. A time series of the vector of the regression coefficients is then used to form a covariance matrix of the factor returns. Prominent related literature includes papers by Hamada (1972) and Rosenberg (1974).

The strength of 'fundamental' common factor models is that they use security characteristics that are very familiar to portfolio managers. Such models usually also have higher in-sample explanatory power than exogenously defined models. Another advantage of such models is that, since factor exposures can be immediately observed, changes in a company's fundamental make-up, such as a merger, will be immediately incorporated into the model. Similarly, new issues can be analyzed almost immediately. The primary criticism of endogenous common factor models is that there are often so many overlapping effects that it is nearly impossible to correctly sort them all out, making such models less effective at predicting future conditions than they are at explaining the past. Nevertheless, the success of these models at predicting and controlling (optimizing) future portfolio risk has resulted in the popularity of these models with practitioners.

The final type of model in use today is the so-called blind factor model. In such models, the factors are not specified as being any measurable real world phenomena, but rather both the factors and the βs to those factors are inferred from the security behaviors themselves. In essence, we find those common factors that the security returns suggest must be present, even if we cannot identify the nature of the factors. Such models are estimated from the security returns using techniques such as principal components regression (see Ball and Torous (1998)) or maximum likelihood factor analysis. The resultant sets of spanning factors are usually orthogonal. The primary benefit of such models is that, since the nature of the common factors is derived inferentially, the structure of the common factors can evolve over time to fit new conditions. Unfortunately critics argue this is also the primary detraction. Without any tie to the real world, such models may be unduly influenced by transitory noise in the data, resulting in unstable results.

All of the models described maintain the usual Markowitz assumption of a single future period. No provision is made for forecast levels of portfolio volatility to vary through time. Security returns are presumed to be independently and identically distributed random walks with no serial correlation, despite extensive empirical evidence to the contrary such as the research of Lo and MacKinlay (1988). Of course, not only do we observe persistent departures from the classical random walk, we also observe significant changes in volatility levels through time, as new information is incorporated into the beliefs of market participants.

For our purposes, we will separate the mechanism of new information arrival into two segments. The first is news, which we define as being new information that is wholly unanticipated by market participants. The second mechanism is announcements, information arrivals that are anticipated with respect to time but not within respect to content. Falling in this second category would be scheduled announcements from government commercial and economic agencies and publicized upcoming announcements such as periodic earnings releases by companies. The differing rate at which market participants are able to assimilate new information contained in news and announcements has been the subject of substantial research. Most closely related to our topic is the work of Ederington and Lee (1996), who studied the impact of information releases on changes in levels of market uncertainty. Similarly, Abraham and Taylor (1993) studied the pricing of currency options (a direct corollary to expected volatility) in the context of the two mechanisms of information arrival.

Early literature on the issue of partially anticipated events in stock markets comes from Malatesta and Thompson (1985). Kwag et al. (2000) recently studied upcoming dividend announcements in the context of partially anticipated information.

Some researchers have studied the application of conditional heterskedasticity models (i.e. ARCH, GARCH) to changes in risk levels of financial markets. Among these are Chong et al. (1999) who apply GARCH procedures to forecasting stock market volatility and Choudhry (1997) who used GARCH procedures to examine data for markets during the periods surrounding the Second World War.

Numerous studies have considered the usage of option implied volatility as a mechanism for predicting future volatility levels. Bartunek et al. (1995) compare GARCH and implied volatility methods. Among the latest works in this area are Ederington and Guan (1998) and Shu et al. (2001). Both of these papers attempt to correct for biases in previous studies of the effectiveness of implied volatility as a predictor of future volatility for stock market indices. Both conclude that implied volatility is a very efficient predictor and that historical volatility adds little predictive power to models that already utilize option implied volatility. Ederington and Guan (2000) find that models that average multiple strikes to compute implied volatility can be improved by correcting for the permanent biases that result in the well-known 'volatility smile'.

A recent working paper by Malz (2000) deals with how changes in implied volatility may be signaling changes in anticipated levels of skewness or kurtosis in return distributions, as well as expected changes in variances. This paper provides very vivid examples of how small changes in higher moments can be reflected as large changes in implied volatility. Related work includes that of Corrado and Su (1997) who examine the forward return distribution implied by individual stock option prices. Jiltsov (1999) studies the implied state densities arising from option prices. He finds that the implied distributions are relatively stable in shape, suggesting that new information arrives gradually into the market and is absorbed in a smooth fashion.

12.3   Discussion

Despite the literature on whether GARCH and implied volatility models are efficient estimators of the future volatility of markets, we found no existing research on how to incorporate such work into models used to estimate portfolio risk over a large range of securities. GARCH processes have been used to some extent in multiple factor models of security covariance. In particular, the BARRA company has used GARCH processes to improve their estimates of factor variances and asset-specific variances in their E2 and E3 models that are widely used by practitioners. The general aspects of the implementation are discussed in Sheik (1994) and Kahn (1994).

   In diBartolomeo (2000a) a controversy regarding using a GARCH approach is discussed. Most importantly, a GARCH process is clearly inconsistent with the assumptions of a pure random walk that underlie traditional portfolio theory. It is essentially universal in the investment industry to quote security and portfolio volatility information in annual units (e.g. 30% per year). However, in order to have enough data to practically estimate models, periodicities of sample observations of daily to monthly are always utilized. Once we discard the random walk assumption, we can no longer assume that variances are a simple function of time, and the standard procedure of rescaling daily, weekly or monthly standard deviations into annual units by multiplying by the square root of time is no longer valid. While we could try to annualize the higher frequency risk estimates by the explicit time-series process embodied in the GARCH model, we cannot simultaneously assume a GARCH process for estimating the risk forecast and assume a random walk process for rescaling that estimate to annual units.

   A critical problem with GARCH approaches are market microstructure effects having to do with differences in the rates at which markets adjust to unanticipated news as compared to partially anticipated announcements. GARCH processes are designed to model the impact of a shock on the system that is already close to an equilibrium condition. While the impact of unanticipated news may sometimes fit this description, it is clearly not consistent with trading before surrounding announcements.

   Market actions around announcement dates often bear specific patterns of liquidity that confound the GARCH process. For example, take the case of an individual stock with an upcoming earnings announcement. Anecdotal evidence from option market makers such as Hull Trading indicate that intra-day volatility for individual stocks on earnings announcement days can be as much as nine times as great as non-announcement days. The days before the announcement are apt to be quiet as traders await the news, reducing both trading volume and volatility. As the quiet period continues, a GARCH process will adjust the conditional volatility estimate downward relative to the long-term mean. Unfortunately, volatility will then spike upward dramatically as the actual announcement is made and traders respond. In that the announcement was anticipated, all market participants had time to think through their intended actions, to be promptly implemented once the content of the announcement was revealed. Accordingly, the market adjustment to announcement information is very rapid. Since our process has now badly underestimated volatility on the announcement date, the GARCH process will upwardly adjust the volatility estimate for future days. Again our estimate will prove wrong, as volatility reduces to normal once the post-announcement flurry of activity is now over. For a good discussion of the issue of liquidity-driven effects around events, see Taleb (1997) and Shanken (1987).

An implied volatility approach offers the hope of getting correct adjustments to volatility forecasts with respect to announcements. Option traders anticipate announcements alongside other market participants involved in the underlying security. As such, option implied volatilities ought correctly to account for the dynamics of volume and short-term volatility variations around announcement dates, as has generally been reported in the cited literature. Option traders also respond very rapidly to true news in an intelligent rather than mechanical fashion, particularly when that news has wide-ranging implications, again offering an apparent advantage over GARCH approaches.

12.4   The model

Our chosen approach is to condition our estimates of risk in our multiple-factor security covariance model with information derived from changes in the relationship between implied volatility and historic sample volatility. The implied volatility information is used to condition both the factor variances and asset-specific variances within the multi-factor model.

Linear factor risk models express the expected covariance matrix of security returns in the form of a factor covariance matrix to which each security is exposed and a security-specific portion. Such models are estimated over historical sample periods. The usual mathematical formulation is:

$$V_p = \sum_{i=1}^{n} \sum_{j=1}^{n} e_{p,i} e_{p,j} \sigma_{f(i)} \sigma_{f(j)} \rho_{i,j} + \sum_{k=1}^{m} w_k^2 \sigma_{s(k)}^2 \qquad (12.1)$$

$$e_{pi} = \sum_{k=1}^{m} w_k \beta_{k,j} \qquad (12.2)$$

where:

V_p = variance of portfolio return
n = number of factors in the risk model

m = number of securities in the portfolio
$e_{p,i}$ = exposure of the portfolio to factor i
$\sigma_{f(i)}$ = standard deviation returns attributed to factor i
$\rho_{i,j}$ = correlation between returns to factor i and factor j
w_k = weight of security k in the portfolio
$\sigma_{s(k)}$ = standard deviation of security specific returns for security k
$\beta_{k,i}$ = beta of security k to factor i

For a portfolio of just one security k, this expression simplifies to

$$V_k = \sum_{i=1}^{n} \sum_{j=1}^{n} \beta_{k,i} \beta_{k,j} \sigma_{f(i)} \sigma_{f(j)} \rho_{i,j} + \sigma_{s(k)}^2 \tag{12.3}$$

If we have implied volatility information on a given security k, we can separately estimate the value of V_k as the square of the implied volatility. However, implied volatility is often considered an upward biased estimator of expected volatility for markets that do not have extremely high levels of liquidity. This arises because option traders do not use exact delta hedging because:

1. The Black–Scholes (1973) assumption of costless hedging does not hold even weakly for many securities.
2. Return distributions often vary from geometric Brownian motion.

To avoid the bias problem, we choose to condition our model by assuming that changes in implied volatility levels are useful estimators of the changes in expected volatility levels, rather than using the implied volatilities themselves. This also reduces the importance of any other persistent biases in our process to estimate implied volatility values. Accordingly, we introduce V_k^* as our conditional estimate of the future volatility of security k, as normally V_k times an adjustment factor M_k.

$$V_k^* = V_k \times M_k \tag{12.4}$$

Adding time subscripts to allow us to evaluate our situation at a particular moment, we obtain

$$M_{k,t} = \frac{I_{k,t}/V_{k,t}}{\left(\dfrac{\sum_{s=t-z}^{t-1} I_{k,s}/V_{k,s}}{z-1} \right)} \tag{12.5}$$

where:

$I_{k,t}$ = implied volatility of security k at time t
$V_{k,t}$ = the volatility of security k obtained from the multi-factor risk model before adjustment at time t
z = the number of past periods over which we choose to observe the relation between implied and multiple factor estimates of volatility.

Equation (12.5) should be intuitive. The numerator is the ratio of the current implied volatility to the current value of expected volatility obtained from our multiple factor risk model. The denominator is merely z period moving average of that ratio. Our logic is that changes in the ratio of the two volatility estimates are likely to occur, as new information is reflected in financial markets. In that the option implied values adjust more rapidly than the factor risk model that is estimated over a historic sample period, changes in the ratio will be an efficient estimator of changes in future risk levels. Implied volatilities are based on closing bid prices of the average of multiple strikes with the expiration date closest to 45 days. Closing bid prices at or below intrinsic values are removed from the sample (treated as if the stock did not have traded options).

One can easily envision a hypothetical scenario wherein a major event occurs to a single company. Imagine Bill Gates coming out of his home and being run over by an autobus. As soon as the information comes over the news wires, option prices on Microsoft stock are apt quickly to reflect the uncertainty arising from this event. In this contrived example, we would expect the increase in uncertainty to be concentrated in Microsoft alone, although one could make an argument for some sort of contagion effect that would impact Microsoft suppliers and customers.

In the real world, we sometimes live through sudden, yet pervasive events such as the tragedies of September 11, 2001. While we could observe the impact on overall market uncertainty through implied information on index options, we can readily incorporate concurrent changes in the implied volatility of numerous individual securities into our factor covariance matrix. Our approach is to construct our factor model using a variation of principal components analysis, such that our factor covariance matrix is itself diagonal. This simplifies equation (12.3) to:

$$V_k = \sum_{i=1}^{n} \sum_{j=1}^{n} \beta_{k,i} \beta_{k,j} \sigma_{f(i)} \sigma_{f(j)} \rho_{i,j} + \sigma_{s(k)}^2 \tag{12.6}$$

$$V_k^* = M_k \times \left(\sum_{i=1}^{n} \beta_{k,i}^2 \sigma_{f(i)}^2 + \sigma_{s(k)}^2 \right) \tag{12.7}$$

Rearranging we obtain:

$$V_k^* / M_k - \sigma_{s(k)}^2 = \sum_{i=1}^{n} \beta_{k,i}^2 \sigma_{f(i)}^2 \tag{12.8}$$

If we have expressions like equation (12.8) for many securities, we can set them up as a set of simultaneous equations and solve for the maximum likelihood values of $\sigma_{f(i)}$ (the factor variances), subject to the condition all values of $\sigma_{f(i)}$ are non-negative. Once we have obtained conditional estimates for the factor variances we can substitute these values back into equation (12.8) for each security and obtain a new value for the asset-specific risk $\sigma_{s(k)}$. Using this two-step procedure it is possible that the final resulting estimate of $\sigma_{s(k)}$ is improperly negative. To avoid this possibility we arbitrarily define a limit at which the value of $\sigma_{s(k,t)}$ can decline from prior values. It should be noted that given this ability to condition both factor variances and specific variances, stocks within the model universe, on which no options are traded, are still subject to adjustments in the factor variances.

$$\sigma_{s(k,t)} = max[\sigma_{s(k,t)}, \sigma_{s(k,t-1)} \times p]$$
$$0 < p < 1 \tag{12.9}$$

We believe this treatment for $\sigma_{s(k,t)}$ is appropriate. While it is easy to envision many circumstances that would cause the rapid increase in the expected volatility of a stock, it is harder to conceive of economic events that would create a dramatic decline in expected volatility from one time period to the next.

The described model has actually been implemented for US equity securities and has been utilized for portfolio trading purposes by numerous hedge funds. The principal components-based multiple factor model is estimated from a covariance matrix of stock returns representing 250 trading days of returns (corrected for serial correlation and heteroskedasticity) of each stock. The model is freshly estimated at the close of each trading day with a 20 trading day moving average used to estimate the typical bias in implied volatility relative to historic values and the maximum allowable daily decline of asset-specific variance set to 25% ($p = 0.75$).

12.5   A few examples

The ability of this model to adapt to unusual market conditions surrounding the behavior of Internet stocks has already been examined in diBartolomeo (2000b). This study found that after extensive adjustments specific to the Internet stock phenomenon, an endogenous factor model produced risk estimates of portfolios that were consistent with this model operating in its typical fashion.

The tragedies of September 11, 2001 provides an example of how rapidly this model can adapt to violent changes in market conditions. As an example we created a capitalization-weighted (as of September 10) portfolio of the 42 airline stocks within the coverage universe. The risk level of the portfolio was evaluated on September 10, on September 17 when trading resumed, and on November 30. The expected volatility of the portfolio was 26%, 54% and 35% respectively.

With the suspension of trading at September 11, there was no way for a model based solely on backward looking information to have made a substantial adjustment in the estimated risk level by the time that trading resumed. The more than doubling of the risk level of an all airline portfolio was anecdotally consistent with qualitative views of financial institutions that have the model in use.

Given that only a handful of the airline stocks in the portfolio have options traded on them, we wanted also to check an equal-weighted portfolio, where the smaller non-optionable stocks would predominate. For the purposes of comparison, we constructed similar equal-weighted portfolios for three other industries: property and casualty insurance, food production and manufacturing. We estimated risk levels for the four industry portfolios as of August 31, and again at September 30. Our expectation was that the airline and insurance portfolios should show a marked increase in risk, while the foods and manufacturing portfolios should not. These results are presented in Table 12.1 and are exactly as anticipated.

Industry	August 31, 2001	September 30, 2001	% Change
Airlines	23.77	29.69	+24.9
Property and casualty	13.04	16.87	+29.4
Food production	20.88	19.38	(7.2)
Manufacturing	11.56	11.31	(2.2)

Table 12.2 Portfolio risk levels at August 31, 2001 and September 30, 2001

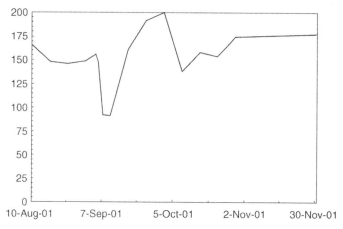

Figure 12.1 Asset-specific volatility – Southwest Airlines – August through November 2001

Once we had established that our initial results did not appear to be driven by random noise, we undertook a more detailed examination of the model output for the capitalization-weighted airline portfolio in the days surrounding September 11. The 54% total risk estimate (standard deviation) as of September 17 equates to 2916 units of variance. Of this total, 2755 units arose from factor risks and 161 units were the aggregate asset-specific risk of the portfolio. As of September 10, the total volatility figure was 26% standard deviation, or 676 variance units. Of that total 588 arose from common factor risks and 98 units arose from aggregate asset-specific risk. While the vast increase in common factor risk was immediately understandable, the increase of more than 60% in the asset-specific portion of the portfolio risk from 98 units to 161 units was less intuitive. As of November 30, the values were 35% volatility, 1223 units of variance, of which 1145 arose from common factors and 177 arose from asset-specific risks.

To further investigate the shift in the perceived level of asset-specific risk, we calculated the portfolio asset-specific risk for various dates from August 10 to November 30. This information is portrayed in Figure 12.1. What is striking about these data is the precipitous decline of approximately 60% in portfolio asset-specific risk for the two trading days immediately preceding September 11. This is extremely counterintuitive.

Even if information about the terrorist attacks had somehow leaked into financial markets, we would have expected an increase, rather than a decrease in risk expectations.

As shown in Figure 12.1, the drop in estimated asset-specific risk of the portfolios could be traced to a dramatic decline in the implied volatility of options on Southwest Airlines (LUV) for the two trading days prior to September 11. For all trading days in 2001 prior to September 7, the implied volatility for Southwest had a mean value of 45% with a daily standard deviation of 13%. For September 7, the implied volatility value was 22%, followed by 15% on September 10. For all trading days from September 17 to November 30, the mean implied volatility was 54% with a standard deviation of 18%. Of more than 400 stocks analyzed for implied volatility as of September 10, Southwest options ranked in the bottom 1% (seemingly inconsistent with the normally volatile operations of an airline). As of September 17, Southwest's rank implied volatility was in the ninth (91st from the bottom) percentile of the universe of stocks with options.

One could draw an inference that the market in LUV options had been subject to transactions, such as call writing that drove down the implied volatility of the options. Examination of volume and open interest data in LUV options did not reveal levels of trading volume on the dates in question that were statistically significantly different from the average of the prior month. We also reviewed news wire reports on LUV for the period prior to September 11 and did not find any fundamental information relating to Southwest Airlines that would provide an immediate explanation of the apparent collapse of implied volatility.

12.6 Conclusions

An increasing body of literature supports the use of implied volatility in forecasting financial market risks and their changes in the level of such risk. Analytical methods utilizing implied volatility seem appropriately to capture the dynamics of information release around announcement dates, while time-series methods do not.

We have presented a method to incorporate volatility data in a multi-factor security covariance model. Such a model has proven to be of practical value to hedge fund managers and other financial market participants.

The model reacted rapidly and sensibly to the changing financial market circumstances surrounding the September 11, 2001 terrorist attacks. Furthermore, the model provides evidence of a potential anomaly in option pricing that could be construed as weak evidence of irregular market trading in anticipation of the tragedies.

References

Abraham, A. and Taylor, W. M. (1993). Pricing Currency Options with Scheduled and Unscheduled Announcement Effects on Volatility. *Managerial and Decision Economics*, Vol. 14(4):311–326.

Bartunek, K. S., Chowdhury, M., and Mac, F. (1995). Implied Volatility vs. GARCH: A Comparison of Forecasts. *Managerial Finance*, Vol. 21(10):59–73.

Ball, C. and Torous, W. (1998). Stochastic Covariance Estimation: A Principal Components Approach. Vanderbilt Working Paper, 1998.

Black, F. and Scholes, M. (1973). The Pricing of Options and Corporate Liabilities. *Journal of Political Economy*, Vol. 81(3):637–654.

Chen, N.-F., Roll, R., and Ross, S. A. (1986). Economic Forces and the Stock Market. *Journal of Business*, Vol. 59(3):383–404.

Chong, C. W., Ahmad, M. I., and Abdullah, M. Y. (1999). Performance of GARCH Models in Forecasting Stock Market Volatility. *Journal of Forecasting*, Vol. 18(5, Sep.):333–343.

Choudhry, T. (1997). Stock Return Volatility and World War II: Evidence from Garch and Garch-X Models. *International Journal of Finance and Economics*, Vol. 2 (1, Jan.):17–28.

Corrado, C. J. and Su, T. (1997). Implied Volatility Skews and Stock Return Skewness and Kurtosis Implied by Stock Option Prices. *European Journal of Finance*, Vol. 3(1, Mar.):73–85.

diBartolomeo, D. (2000a). Recent Time Variation in the Level of US Equity Security Risk. Northfield Working Paper, http://www.northinfo.com/papers/pdf/20000322_risk_horizon.pdf

diBartolomeo, D. (2000b). Spotting the Next Really Big Thing. *Indexes: The Journal of Index Issues in Investment*, Winter.

Ederington, L. and Guan, W. (1998). Is Implied Volatility an Informationally Efficient and Effective Predictor Future Volatility? University of Oklahoma Working Paper, January.

Ederington, L. and Guan, W. (2000). Measuring Implied Volatility: Is an Average Better? University of Oklahoma Working Paper, August.

Ederington, L. H. and Lee, J. H. (1996). The Creation and Resolution of Market Uncertainty: The Impact of Information Releases on Implied Volatility. *Journal of Financial and Quantitative Analysis*, Vol. 31(4, Dec.):513–539.

Engle, R. F. and Bollerslev, T. (1986). Modeling the Persistence of Conditional Variances. *Econometric Reviews*, Vol. 5(1): 1–50.

Grinold, R. C. (1993). Is Beta Dead Again? *Financial Analyst Journal*, Vol. 49(4): 28–34.

Hamada, R. S. (1972). The Effect of the Firm's Capital Structure on the Systematic Risk of Common Stocks. *Journal of Finance*, Vol. 27(2):435–452.

Jiltsov, A. (1999). Implied State Price Densities: Predictive Power, Stability and Information Content. London Business School Working Paper, September.

Kahn, R. (1994). The E3 Project. *BARRA Newsletter*, Summer.

Kwag, A., Shrieves, R., and Wansley, J. (2000). Partially Anticipated Events: An Application to Dividend Announcements. University of Tennessee Working Paper, March.

Lo, A. W. and MacKinlay, A. C. (1988). Stock Market Prices do not Follow Random Walks: Evidence from a Simple Specification Test. *Review of Financial Studies*, Vol. 1(1):41–66.

Malatesta, P. H. and Thompson, R. (1985). Partially Anticipated Events: A Model of Stock Price Reactions with an Application to Corporate Acquisitions. *Journal of Financial Economics*, Vol. 14(2):237–250.

Malz, A. (2000). Do Implied Volatilities Provide Early Warning of Market Stress? *Riskmetrics* Working paper, February.

Markowitz, H. (1952). Portfolio Selection. *Journal of Finance.*

Pettengill, G. N., Sundaram, S., and Mathur, I. (1995). The Conditional Relation Between Beta and Returns. *Journal of Financial and Quantitative Analysis,* Vol. 30(1):101–116.

Rosenberg, B. (1974). Extra-Market Components of Covariance in Security Returns. *Journal of Financial and Quantitative Analysis,* Vol. 9(2):263–273.

Shanken, J. (1987). Nonsynchronous Data and the Covariance-Factor Structure of Returns. *Journal of Finance,* Vol. 42(2):221–231.

Sharpe, W. (1964). Capital Asset Prices: A Theory of Market Equilibrium under Conditions of Risk. *Journal of Finance.*

Sheik, A. (1994). Barra's New Risk Forecasts. *BARRA Newsletter,* Winter.

Shu, Y., Vasconellos, G., and Kish, R. (2001). The Information Content of Implied Volatility: An International Investigation of Index Options. Lehigh University Working Paper, April.

Taleb, N. (1997). *Dynamic Hedging,* Chapter 4. Wiley.

13 Decomposing factor exposure for equity portfolios

David Tien, Paul Pfleiderer, Robert Maxim and Terry Marsh[*]

Abstract

This study addresses the problem of accurately forecasting and attributing risk in equity portfolios. We develop a hybrid methodology which takes advantage of the superior forecasting power of implicit factor models while also attributing portfolio risk to economic factors and firm-specific characteristics. We then compare the relative accuracy of risk attribution using our hybrid approach versus an explicit cross-sectional factor model. We present simulation results which suggest, given realistic parameter values, that the estimation efficiency gained by using the hybrid approach yields substantial improvements over explicit models.

13.1 Introduction

It is well known that the tendency of stock prices to move together is the primary source of return risk for equity portfolios containing more than just a few stocks. Factor models are used to describe and predict these price co-movements across stocks. The factor models can, roughly, be categorized as either implicit or structural; implicit models infer the common factors driving stock returns by looking at the factors' 'footprints' in observed returns, while the structural models specify the factors *a priori* in terms of observable characteristics of stocks or macroeconomic variables.

It seems generally agreed that the implicit models afford superior prediction of stock return risk, e.g. King et al. (1994) who show that changes in stock price volatilities can generally be better explained in terms of cross-sections of stock price changes than as a function of economic variables. Nevertheless, users of implicit risk models often want to decompose an equity portfolio's projected risk exposures with respect to economic variables or corporate characteristics. We begin, in section 13.2, by presenting such a decomposition procedure whereby conditional implicit factor exposures are projected onto a given set of cross-sectional characteristics of stocks that include industry classification, book-to-price, earnings-to-price, dividend yield, log market capitalization, and prior 12-month price momentum. Our procedure is similar in approach to that of

[*] Respectively, Santa Clara University and Quantal International Inc.; Stanford University and Quantal International Inc.; Quantal International Inc.; and UC Berkeley and Quantal International Inc.

hybrid models for default risk, for example Duffie and Singleton (1999) hazard-rate models for debt default that are mapped into the Merton (1974) structural model for default risk.

In section 13.3, we turn to an example in which industry classification is postulated to be an explicit cross-sectional characteristic that is associated with stocks' risk exposures. For illustration, we assume that there are only two industries, and that the *unlevered* returns on stocks in each of these two industries have the same true industry exposure. Although evidence[1], indeed casual observation, suggests that it is quite unrealistic to assume that the asset exposures of all firms in an industry are identical, this assumption (or something like it) is implicitly made by extant cross-sectional models which use zero-one dummy variables for industry. If, in our example, the unlevered companies in the same industry have identical exposures, their levered return exposures cannot be identical save in the unlikely case where their leverage ratios are identical. Our objective is to compare the estimation performance of the implicit factor model *cum* decomposition outlined in section 13.2 with that of a 'straight' cross-sectional model approach in which the levered returns are regressed cross-sectionally on a zero-one industry dummy. We find that the implicit factor model quite readily detects the differences in leverage-induced exposures, while the estimates of 'true' exposure in the cross-sectional approach are thrown off by the misspecification that the levered returns on stocks in the same industry have the same exposure. We also show that the specification error inherent in the explicit model is not corrected by adding leverage as an additional characteristic in the cross-sectional model.

Finally, we compare our procedure for decomposing conditional factor exposures in terms of cross-sectional characteristics of stocks with a recently proposed two-step approach, sometimes also called a 'hybrid' model. In this two-step approach, 'factors' that are specified to be explicit characteristics of stocks are 'taken out' as a risk exposure in a first step, and then an implicit model is fitted to the 'residual' co-movement in equity returns in a second step – all else equal, any significant residual co-movement indicates that there is a misspecification in the first-step explicit model. We show that specification errors such as the intra-industry differences among levered equity exposures are not corrected in this two-step procedure, in contrast to our hybrid model.

We include expected return as well as risk exposure parameters in our analysis since, in an arbitrage pricing theory framework, apparent 'alphas' may indicate misspecification in the risk model (e.g. MacKinlay and Pastor (2000)). Moreover, it is extremely important in practice to know how risk model misspecification affects expected return estimates, since the latter become the benchmark for measuring manager performance. Or, from the opposite point of view, if a manager wants to 'bet on' certain characteristics of stocks that, for example, look cheap, it is very important to know how much added risk is associated with that characteristic.

Like our hybrid implicit factor *cum* decomposition model, the two-step explicit-implicit 'hybrid' model can provide more accurate estimates of total risk exposure and expected return than the explicit cross-sectional risk model. However, the decomposition of that risk with respect to the cross-sectional characteristics can be misleading.

---

[1] For example, Tufano (1997) looks at stocks in the gold mining industry, commonly considered one of the more homogeneous industry groups, and finds that their exposures in fact vary considerably and also vary across time.

Indeed, there is something of an internal contradiction in the two-step procedure, viz. if the specification for the explicit cross-sectional characteristics in the first step is well specified, then there is no need for a second implicit-factor step. On the other hand, if the first explicit-factor step is misspecified so that indeed the second step is internally consistent, the cross-sectional attribution of risk to characteristics in the first step is potentially flawed and thus the first step attribution is not useful. A recent paper by Asgharian and Hansson (2003) suggests that our results may be quite general, i.e. they find that orthogonal implicit factors better capture risk than a two-step procedure where pre-specified market or industry indexes are fit in a first step, and then implicit factors are fit to the residuals.

13.2   Risk decomposition: cross-sectional characteristics

In this section we show how common factor exposures in a conditional factor model estimated using implicit techniques can be projected onto a set of cross-sectional characteristics of stocks. There are two goals to the exercise:

(a) decomposition of a portfolio's forecasted risk in terms of cross-sectional characteristics of stocks such as industry classification, P/E and/or P/B as measures of value-growth, (log of) market capitalization as a size measure, and momentum; and
(b) use of the estimated parameters for the conditional factor model to compute risk parameters in the cross-sectional 'space', such as the variance-covariance matrix of returns associated with the cross-sectional characteristics.

We show how the variance-covariance matrix of returns associated with the cross-sectional characteristics can be computed from the conditional factor exposures at a point in time, rather than from a time series of coefficients from successive cross-sectional regressions.

Let B_t be the $N \times k$ matrix of time-t conditional risk exposures for N stocks to k factors in the conditional factor model (or, more generally, any model with a set of k factors). Under this formulation the return vector of the N stocks, $\widetilde{R}_t$, is given by

$$
\begin{array}{ccccccc}
\widetilde{R}_t & = & E_t(\widetilde{R}_t) & + & B_t & \widetilde{F}_t & + & \widetilde{\varepsilon}_t \\
N \times 1 & & N \times 1 & & N \times k & k \times 1 & & N \times 1
\end{array}
\tag{13.1}
$$

In this specification we assume without loss of generality that the factors themselves are uncorrelated and have unit variance. This means that the variance-covariance matrix of $\widetilde{R}_t$ is $B_t B_t' + var(\widetilde{\varepsilon}_t)$. Now let H be an $N \times j$ matrix with N rows of stocks and j columns of explicit cross-sectional characteristics for the stocks, e.g. industry classification with a dummy variable equal to unity if a stock is in a given industry, and zero otherwise. Other columns of H might contain characteristics such as P/B and P/E as value/growth measures, dividend yield, log market capitalization, and prior 12-month price momentum. We assume that H has full column rank and in particular $H'H$ is invertible.

To decompose the factor exposures B_t with respect to the cross-sectional characteristics H, we formally project these factor exposures onto the space of the explicit characteristics. Consider the regression of B_t on H:

$$B_t = HQ_t + \Lambda \qquad (13.2)$$

where the $(j \times k)$ matrix Q is a mapping from the explicit factor exposures H to the factor exposures B_t. The 'residuals' (Λ) in (13.2) are risk components picked up by the conditional factor exposures B_t that cannot be accounted for by the pre-specified list of characteristics in H. Then we have

$$Q_t = (H'H)^{-1}H'B_t \qquad (13.3)$$

and

$$\widehat{B}_t = H(H'H)^{-1}H'B_t \qquad (13.4)$$

where $\widehat{B}_t$ is a (linear) projection of B_t onto the space spanned by the characteristics H. Note that if H spans exactly the same space as B_t (possibly with a rotation but without noise), then the H characteristics 'explain' 100% of the B_t and $\widehat{B}_t = B_t$. Also note that if there are characteristics in H that are not related to the conditional systematic risk, B_t, then these spurious characteristics 'drop out', i.e. they do not distort the estimated mapping.

Now we can solve for the variance-covariance matrix G of the returns associated with the cross-sectional coefficients that is implied by the projection of those characteristics on the conditional factor exposures B_t. That is, we can solve for G where:

$$
\begin{aligned}
HGH' &= \widehat{B}_t\widehat{B}'_t \\
&= H(H'H)^{-1}H'B_tB'_tH(H'H)^{-1}H'
\end{aligned}
\qquad (13.5)
$$

We obtain:

$$G = (H'H)^{-1}H'B_tB'_tH(H'H)^{-1} \qquad (13.6)$$

We now illustrate the projection (13.4) for some actual 'real-world' portfolios where the cross-sectional characteristics are those often used in industry risk models, specifically: 59 dummy variables for (GIC) industrial classification, plus book-to-price, earnings-to-price, dividend yield, log market capitalization, and prior 12-month price momentum.

We will use (2.4) to decompose a portfolio's forecasted factor risk with respect to the cross-sectional characteristics. As is well known, there is no unambiguous way to decompose a portfolio's volatility in terms of various risk attributes if those attributes are not uncorrelated. We use the following procedure to decompose the portfolio volatility across the factors implied by the cross-sectional characteristics. To begin we identify the cross-sectional characteristic that taken on its own explains the largest portion of the portfolio's systematic risk. Call this characteristic 'a' and let the associated column in H be h_a. We then take all the other characteristics and make them orthogonal relative to characteristic 'a'. This means that column i of H becomes $h_i - h_a(h'_a h_a)^{-1} h'_a h_i$. We then identify the characteristic among the remaining characteristics (orthogonalized relative to 'a') that explains the greatest portion of the risk that is unexplained by characteristic 'a'. We call this characteristic 'b'. We then take all of the remaining characteristics and orthogonalize them relative to both characteristic 'a' and characteristic 'b' and determine which among these remaining characteristics explains the greatest portion of the portfolio risk unaccounted for by both 'a' and 'b'. We proceed in this fashion until all the characteristics have been used. Note that after this procedure is completed there may still be some systematic risk left unexplained. This will occur if the conditional factor exposures are not completely spanned by the cross-sectional characteristics.

We did a cross-sectional decomposition of the sort described above for a set of domestic portfolios using the conditional factor exposure matrix B_t estimated as of 30 July 2003. Summary results are presented in Table 13.1 for the following:

(a) a market cap-weighted portfolio of the largest 5000 exchange-listed US stocks;
(b) an equally weighted portfolio of these 5000 stocks;
(c) a 'small cap-tilted' portfolio where the portfolio weights are inversely proportional to the 5000 stocks' market caps.

As can be seen, the cross-sectional characteristics explain roughly half of the conditional factor exposure for these three portfolios on 30 July – slightly less than

	Largest 5000 listed stocks			Largest 300 stocks	Smallest 300 stocks
	Mkt cap weights	Equal weights	Small cap weights	Equally weighted	Equally weighted
% of factor exposure explained	48	54	53	47	52
Breakdown: (fundamental first)					
Expl. by fundamentals	39	44	43	38	42
Expl. by sector	9	10	10	9	10
(Sector first)					
Expl. by sector	45	51	50	44	49
Expl. by fundamentals	3	3	3	3	3

Attribution of the decomposition given by the projection:

$$\widehat{B}_t \quad H(H'H)^1 H' B_t$$

where: H is the $n \times m$ matrix with m fundamental characteristics and industrial classifications for the n stocks, where $n = 5000$ or 300, and B_t is the $n \times k$ matrix of Quantal conditional factor exposures on 31 July 2003.

Table 13.1 Cross-sectional attribution of conditional factor exposures estimated by Quantal for a selection of portfolios of US stocks on 30 July 2003

50% when stocks are market cap weighted and slightly more than 50% when stocks are equally or 'small cap' weighted. As just discussed, the decomposition of the portfolio risk exposure is not unique since the fundamental characteristics (e.g. size and E/P) are cross-sectionally correlated with industry classification and with each other. If we first attribute the risk cross-sectionally to fundamentals, and then to orthogonalized industry classifications, roughly 40 percentage points are associated with fundamentals, and 10 percentage points with industry classification.

Although not shown in the table, the most important of the fundamental characteristics in the conditional risk exposure projection is size, i.e. log market cap. This result may not hold in all time periods but we do find that it holds for the projection on 30 July 2003. The result does support the researchers who argue that so-called size effect anomalies in historically observed average returns are due to a higher market risk for small firms. The measures E/P, B/P, and D/P are cross-sectionally correlated with each other and with size (they are all 'inverse of price' characteristics). Once the log of market cap is 'taken out' as a characteristic, only the residual factor exposure remains to be attributed to characteristics such as E/P, B/P, and D/P, and thus the risk attributed to them is less than it would be if size had not been 'taken out' first.

If the factor exposures are first associated with industry classification rather than fundamentals, the fundamentals explain only about 3% of the 30 July 2003 factor risk for the 5000 stocks that is not explained by industry classification.

The last two columns in Table 13.1 provide a straightforward robustness check on the results for the 5000 stocks. They show the decomposition of the factor exposure for (a) an equally weighted portfolio of the largest 300 US stocks; and (b) a portfolio of the smallest 300 US stocks. As can be seen, the decomposition remains roughly the same when applied to these 300-stock portfolios.

To further analyze how conditional risk breaks down in terms of the cross-sectional characteristics of stocks, we formed 59 portfolios of stocks where each portfolio contains only stocks within a single GIC industry classification, equally weighted. We examine the breakdown of conditional systematic risk exposures for these portfolios. Again, the decomposition will not be unique because industry classification and fundamentals are cross-sectionally correlated. To analyze the relation between an industry portfolio's risk exposures on 30 July and its respective industrial classification as a cross-sectional explanatory characteristic, we first 'took out' cross-sectional size (log market capitalization) before projecting conditional factor exposure onto industry classification.

Figure 13.1(a) presents results for the portfolio of Energy Equipment stocks, and Figure 13.1(b) the results for the portfolio of Oil and Gas Industry stocks. As can be seen, the energy equipment classification explains about 8% of the total conditional risk that can be attributed to all industry classifications. Interestingly, about 13% of the energy industry's conditional risk exposure appears to be explained by the semiconductor industrial classification, i.e. since industrial classification is a dummy, the systematic risk of a portfolio of energy stocks might appear to have more to do with semiconductors than with energy! Further (not shown), the Semiconductor, Communications, Software, and Biotech classification appear to explain much of the risk of a number of other industry portfolios as well.

As noted earlier, the cross-sectional analysis was performed as of 30 July 2003. During the preceding months, stocks in the Semiconductor, Communications, Internet Software, and to a lesser extent Biotech and Banks classifications were widely cited as

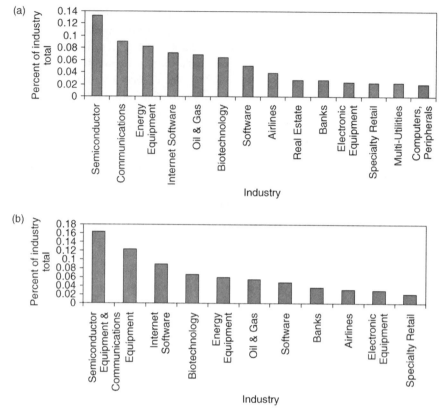

Figure 13.1 (a) Decomposition of energy equipment portfolio risk exposure by industry.
(b) Decomposition of Oil and Gas portfolio risk exposure by industry

'driving the market'[2]. Thus, one might hypothesize that the Figure 13.1 results suggest that these 'technology stocks' are in fact proxying for 'the market' in the 30 July environment, and thus that (loosely) a market-wide risk impact is being confounded with an industry effect.

If some of the dimensions of market exposure are being confounded with industry in the Figure 13.1 results, a traditional solution in cross-sectional risk models is to include a historical, say five-year, beta as an additional cross-sectional characteristic in explaining the conditional risk exposures. However, including historical beta leaves the results substantially unchanged. It is perhaps not surprising that unconditional historical beta appears to be a poor proxy for factor exposure given the evidence that it is a reasonably poor predictor of cross-sectional expected returns. To control for 'the market' in a different way, we tried to mimic a market-neutral (and dollar-neutral) energy equipment industry portfolio that is long energy stocks and short NASDAQ 100 stocks where the latter is a one-dimensional proxy for the market. The apparent association between the factor exposures of this long-short energy equipment stock

---

[2] In Semiconductors: INTC, KLAC, AMAT, NVLS, QCOM, QLGC; in Communication: CISCO, JNPR, RBAK, and NT; in Internet Software: EBAY, YHOO, AMZN; in Banks: C, JPM, BAC, COF, GS, MDW.

portfolio and the technology stock dummy variable is considerably reduced, though not eliminated. Again, this result itself should not be too surprising when the multiple factor exposures are not perfectly captured by the single NASDAQ 100 index. Also, 'interest rate factors' *qua* time-series variables, which are potentially important on 30 July, are not taken into account in the cross-sectional decomposition framework.

The results in Figure 13.1(a) do, however, suggest that industry classification is somewhat informative about the conditional risk exposures of stocks in the respective industry, even though market exposures are confounded with the industry dummies. The Energy Equipment Industry classification is the industry characteristic with the highest explanatory power outside of the groups of stocks that were 'driving the market' in the second quarter of 2003. The results in Figure 13.1(a) are roughly the same as those for the portfolio of Oil and Gas Industry stocks, given in Figure 13.1(b). Both Energy Equipment and Oil and Gas are arguably more homogeneous than most industry groupings, and thus the relative importance of the own-industry classification in explaining factor exposures does not extend across all industry classes. For example, the most important industrial classification in the decomposition of factor exposure for a portfolio of Construction Materials stocks (equally weighted) is not the respective Construction Materials industry dummy variable, but the Real Estate classification dummy variable – it seems completely plausible that real estate would explain the market exposure of construction materials stocks.

Taken together, we think these results point to the zero-one industry classification scheme as a relatively poor instrument for conditional factor exposure. Marsh et al. (1997) show that a classification of stocks into nine market sectors explains roughly the same amount of *ex post* stock return volatility as do much finer gradations in industry classification, e.g. into 29 industries within the nine sectors, a result that is also consistent with industrial classification as being a 'very noisy' indicator of equity risk.

In the next section, we examine a best case in which there is no noise in industrial classification as an instrument for unlevered equity risk. That is the noise consists of differences in leverage across firms in an industry where it is assumed *a priori* that, leverage aside, all firms in an industry have exactly the same all-equity (or asset) factor exposure.

13.3 Decomposition and misspecification in the cross-sectional model: a simple example

13.3.1 *Industry classification projected onto factor exposures*

In this section, we consider a very simple example of risk decomposition in a cross-sectional model that is misspecified. We consider a case in which all stocks in one of two industries would have the same factor exposure if none of the firms were levered, i.e. their 'asset' or unlevered factor exposures are identical. We make this quite extreme assumption not because it is likely to be realistic, but rather to show that even in this best of possible cases for the cross-sectional model, differences in leverage among the otherwise identical exposure firms is a problem. We show that the implicit model of estimating the factor exposures quite readily detects these differences in exposures – it is the cross-sectional decomposition that is thrown off by the misspecification. Finally, we show that adding leverage as a cross-sectional characteristic in addition to the dummy variables for industrial classification *will not* compensate for the incorrect assumption in the cross-sectional model that within-industry exposures are homogeneous.

To study the effect of varying levels of financial leverage across firms, we simulate a stylized market where asset returns are solely driven by orthogonal industry factors and all firms belong to one of two industries. In this setting a firm's asset return would have an exposure of one to its own industry factor and zero to the other industry factor. Mathematically, the true data generating process for a firm's asset returns is:

$$\tilde{r}_{it}^a = \begin{cases} \tilde{f}_{1t} + \tilde{\varepsilon}_{it}, & \text{if the firm is in industry 1} \\ \tilde{f}_{2t} + \tilde{\varepsilon}_{it}, & \text{if the firm is in industry 2} \end{cases} \tag{13.7}$$

where r_{it}^a is the asset return on firm i at time t, $\tilde{f}_{jt}$ is the return on the industry factor (for industry $j = 1$, or 2) in period t (industry factor returns are assumed to be uncorrelated and assumed be normally distributed), and $\tilde{\varepsilon}_{it}$ is the idiosyncratic return.

Despite the fact that asset returns on all firms have the same exposure to the industry factor, differing levels of financial leverage will cause *equity* returns to have varying industry factor exposures. We have

$$\beta_A = \frac{E}{V}\beta_E + \frac{D}{V}\beta_D$$

$$\beta_E = \frac{V}{E}\beta_A - \frac{D}{E}\beta_D \tag{13.8}$$

where E is the equity market capitalization of the firm, D is the market value of the firm's debt, V is the total value of the firm, and $\beta_D(\beta_E)$ is the firm's debt (equity) beta. If the firm's debt has a beta close to zero, i.e. $\beta_D \approx 0$, then $\beta_E \approx (V/E)\beta_A$. Thus, if we assume, as above, that $\beta_A = 1$, the exposure of a firm's *equity* returns is approximately V/E, not 1.

13.3.2 Incorporating expected return information

Standard approaches to asset pricing would suggest that the conditional exposures B_t will be priced if they are sources of risk to investors, e.g. if the factors reflect the systematic impact across stock returns of shifts over time in perceived investment opportunities (e.g. Merton (1973)). There is also evidence that when stocks are ranked on the basis of cross-sectional characteristics such as relative market capitalization, dividend yield, and value-growth measures (price-earnings or price-book), their average returns have historically differed from those predicted by at least simple unconditional CAPM predictions. One might, then, infer that the cross-sectional characteristics can be linked directly with compensated risk in the factor exposures, and indeed some researchers have taken these historical 'left-hand-side' return anomalies to the 'right-hand side' of asset pricing models by simply labeling the cross-sectional characteristics as 'factors'.

We now include expected returns in addition to factor exposures as parameters to be estimated in the presence of the misspecification in the cross-sectional model due to intra-industry leverage differences. MacKinlay and Pastor (2000) take a similar approach in examining a situation where stock returns have an exact factor structure but a factor is omitted. In an exact factor model, and with the original no-arbitrage reasoning from Ross (1976), an 'alpha' would appear in average returns reflecting the unobserved exposure to the factor that is not correctly included in the model. In our example, the misspecification involves the effect of leverage on intra-industry risk exposures.

We show that, when the standard error of noise in expected returns is comparable to that in practice, incorporating the restrictions on expected returns implied by the factor model is of little help in overcoming the cross-sectional misspecification. Thus, the distortion in the link running from the cross-sectional characteristics, here industry classification and leverage, through equity factor exposures and subsequent expected returns causes a severe problem in measuring alphas, in assessing portfolio manager performance, and in enabling managers to understand where their active 'bets' are incurring risk.

Having generated simulated stock returns using the model outlined above, we compare the performance of our hybrid (implicit *cum* decomposition) model, an explicit model, and a two-step explicit/implicit 'hybrid' model in estimating expected returns on individual stocks. The implicit factor approach essentially allows the data to guide the creation and selection of factors. In this approach, the modeler analyzes the variance-covariance matrix of stock returns using the principal components decomposition, selecting some subset of eigenvectors from the decomposition to serve as implicit factors. Individual stock returns can then be regressed onto these constructed implicit factors (which are orthogonal by construction) to get the implicit factor exposures. The implicit factor exposures are then mapped onto a given set of cross-sectional characteristics as in (13.4).

The explicit cross-sectional approach takes a subset of observed firm characteristics and treats these as exposures to fundamental factors believed to be driving stock returns. The explicit approach takes a long time series of characteristics and runs cross-sectional regressions each time period of returns onto the characteristics (factor exposures in the model) to estimate fundamental factor returns.

In the so-called two-step hybrid risk model, a cross-sectional explicit exposure is estimated first, then the return residuals after adjusting for those first step exposures are analyzed using implicit factor methods. Mathematically, the model below summarizes the gist of the hybrid approach:

$$r_{it} = \beta_{i1}f_{1t} + \beta_{i2}f_{2t} + \varepsilon_{it}$$

$$\varepsilon_{it} = \gamma_{i1}g_{1t} + \gamma_{i2}g_{2t} + \eta_{it} \tag{13.9}$$

where β_{ij} represent observable firm characteristics used to estimate the factor returns, f_{jt}, in the cross-section. The residual, ε_{it}, is then decomposed into (in this example) two implicit factors, g_1 and g_2, with exposures γ_i. Note that this process effectively orthogonalizes the residuals from the explicit model estimated in the first step. As MacKinlay and Pastor (2000) show, the second step in the hybrid procedure can also potentially improve the estimation of expected returns, and thus of portfolio managers' true alphas, by fully exploiting information contained in the covariance among returns on stocks in estimating expected returns.

Table 13.2 outlines the performance of the three approaches along various metrics. In estimating expected returns for industry as a whole, none of the modeling approaches suffers from biased estimates of expected returns – intuitively, the biases in factor exposures and expected returns for individual stocks aggregate away at the industry level. The models diverge somewhat when looking at the efficiency of expected return estimation. The two-step model is roughly on a par with that for the hybrid implicit-*cum*-decomposition approach – like the implicit-decomposition model, the two-step approach benefits from the flexibility of specification that allows it to approximate the nonlinear relation between leverage and industry betas. In contrast, the explicit model seriously lags the competition, since it is a 'prisoner' of its misspecification.

Expected return estimation

	Annualized bias (%)	Mean squared error (%)
Hybrid method	−0.04	1.99
Explicit method	0.02	4.53
Two-step method	0.03	2.01

Industry factor risk estimation

	Annualized bias			Mean squared error		
	Industry 1 (%)	Industry 2 (%)	Leverage (%)	Industry 1 (%)	Industry 2 (%)	Leverage (%)
Hybrid method	4.08	4.08	13.08	0.44	0.45	0.95
Explicit method	4.18	4.20	14.05	0.44	0.45	0.74
Two-step method	4.18	4.20	14.05	0.44	0.45	0.74

Systematic risk, stock level

	Annualized bias (%)	Mean squared error (%)
Hybrid method	2.82	3.71
Explicit method	12.86	16.57
Two-step method	12.86	16.57

Simulated industry returns were generated iid from a normal distribution with mean return of 10% annually and 20% annualized volatility. Firm leverage was drawn from a uniform distribution on [0,1). Results are based on 1000 trials.

Table 13.2

Though the hybrid and two-step models perform similarly in the sense of estimation accuracy, they do differ dramatically in their ability to correctly attribute risk
exposures across stocks. The two-step model assumes that the modeled explicit characteristics capture all observable factors driving returns. Since the portion of risk
captured by the implicit step is orthogonal to the explicit factors by construction,
there is no way for the second implicit factor step to make up for the first-step specification error in equally attributing risk (assumed to be equal exposures) to the industry
classification. In essence, the two-step procedure faces a Catch-22: if the first-step
explicit factor exposure step is correct, there is no need for the second implicit factor
step; if the explicit factor exposure is misspecified so that there is a need for the implicit
factor step, then the implicit factor step will not repair the misspecification in the first
step. The fully implicit-*cum*-decomposition approach, however, does not suffer from
this weakness. This advantage is apparent when looking at how the models perform
when estimating systematic risk at the stock level. The implicit-*cum*-decomposition
approach clearly dominates the other estimation strategies. This is not surprising since
the explicit and two-step methods are restricted in the sense that all firms are assumed
to be equally exposed to their respective industry.

Lastly, we examine the ability of the three models to estimate the association between
systematic factor risk exposure and the respective zero-one industry classification. This
association is estimated 'directly' in both the explicit and two-step approaches, while
we use equation (13.6) to estimate the association in the implicit-*cum*-decomposition
approach. Here, we see that the models perform quite closely with the hybrid implicit-
cum-decomposition approach just beating the explicit and hybrid models.

13.4   Summary and discussion

We have analyzed the decomposition of conditional factor exposures for equities with
respect to cross-sectional characteristics of the stocks at a point in time. We found that
the decomposition in terms of commonly used characteristics explains roughly one-half
of the factor exposure captured by the conditional implicit model. We also showed that
the decomposition is critically dependent upon the ordering of the cross-sectionally correlated characteristics. We compared the estimates in our decomposition with that of a
'plain vanilla' explicit cross-sectional risk model, and with a so-called two-step hybrid
model which combines the plain vanilla cross-sectional model with a second-step
implicit model, when there is plausible misspecification in the industry dummy of the
cross-sectional model due to intra-industry leverage differences. We find that both of
the cross-sectional and two-step hybrid models are 'thrown off' by the misspecification.

It might appear at first glance that the two-step model would be more robust to
misspecification problems. Alas, the problem lies with the two-step model's schizo-
phrenia, at least with respect to a wide range of the misspecification problems against
which it is intended as protection. The objective of the two-step model's first step –
a cross-sectional regression of returns against predetermined characteristics – is the
decomposition of risk with respect to these observable characteristics. If the cross-
sectional step is correctly specified, there is no need for the second-step implicit
procedure. If, however, the cross-sectional step does contain specification error, one
might hope that the second step will correct for this, thus better capturing the 'total

risk' of a stock or portfolio. But the misspecification in the first step throws off the decomposition with respect to the cross-sectional characteristics, so that it is not obvious what is gained at that step. Decomposition of our (implicit) conditional factor exposures with respect to the cross-sectional characteristics is not thrown off by misspecification in the characteristics, as is the two-step model, while at the same time we suffer no relative loss of prediction in the factor exposures.

Of course, a correct model connecting factor exposures to cross-sectional characteristics could be quite useful, just as are correctly specified structural models and rosetta stones in general. For example, suppose that one knew that 'truth' is that market-to-book is the one and only linear risk factor. Then clearly we know immediately that a manager whose projected returns do literally 'line up' with respect to market-to-book has no portfolio problem – by construction, there is no alpha. If, on the other hand, the manager's projected returns depend on other characteristics as well as market-to-book, it would be very useful to be guaranteed that market-to-book is the only source of systematic risk, since in this case the manager is in a position to form a portfolio that 'zeros out' exposure to that one 'factor' (this is feasible if the alpha characteristics are not perfectly co-linear in market-to-book), and asymptotically the portfolio will have a positive alpha and be risk free.

Unfortunately, we believe that the more realistic situation is one where the portfolio manager has alphas that he or she might know are related to market-to-book (e.g. the manager has discovered a downward bias in earnings expectations for high-tech, high market-to-book stocks), but he or she doesn't know the degree to which these apparent alphas are real, i.e. he/she doesn't know if the market-to-book completely captures the factor risk inherent in this alpha strategy. For concreteness, suppose that a second tech/Internet/'bubble' factor has emerged, and the earnings-expectation-biased/high-tech stocks have an exposure to this second factor and thus a market exposure beyond market-to-book – indeed, even if market-to-book were known with certainty to be related to risk exposure, high-tech stocks which tend to have high market-to-book would look *less* risky along the market-to-book *cum* risk dimension. The argument in this chapter is that in situations like this, using an implicit model with up-to-date conditional exposures can accurately detect the hidden risk and produce better decompositions of that conditional risk with respect to characteristics like market-to-book when high-tech industry is an 'omitted' factor. The manager can then intelligently decide how good a deal the stock is – he or she does not do this using a risk model that is defined along the same dimensions on which alphas are being constructed!

References

Asgharian, H. and Hansson, B. (2003). Investment Strategies using Orthogonal Portfolios. Working Paper, July, Department of Economics, Lund University.

Chen, C.-J. and Panjer, H. (2002). Unifying Discrete Structural Credit Risk Models and Reduced Form Models. Working Paper, 15 July, University of Waterloo.

Duffie, D. and Singleton, K. J. (1999). Modelling Term Structures of Defaultable Bonds. *Review of Financial Studies*, 12:687–720.

King, M., Sentana, E., and Wadhwani, S. (1994). Volatility and Links between National Stock Markets. *Econometrica*, 62(4), July:901–933.

MacKinlay, A. C. and Pastor, L. (2000). Asset Pricing Models: Implications for Expected Returns and Portfolio Selection. *Review of Financial Studies*, 13(4):883–916.

Marsh, T., Pfleiderer, P., and Tien, D. (1997). The Role of Country and Industry Effects in Explaining Global Stock Returns. Working Paper, September 16.

Merton, R. C. (1973). An Intertemporal Capital Asset Pricing Model. *Econometrica*, 41(5), September:867–887.

Merton, R. C. (1974). On the Pricing of Corporate Debt: The Risk Structure of Interest Rates. *Journal of Finance*, 29:449–470.

Ross, S. A. (1976). The Arbitrage Theory of Capital Asset Pricing. *Journal of Economic Theory*, 13:341–360.

Tufano, P. (1997). The Determinants of Stock Price Exposure: Financial Engineering and the Gold Mining Industry. Working Paper 97-040, Harvard Business School.

Index

Lightning Source UK Ltd.
Milton Keynes UK
20 April 2010

153041UK00002B/80/P